CIN**É**FRANCO
2 | 0 | 0 | 5

Thank you sponsors
for your invaluable support.

Thank you audience
for making the 8th annual celebration
a great success.

See you in 2006!

www.cinefranco.com

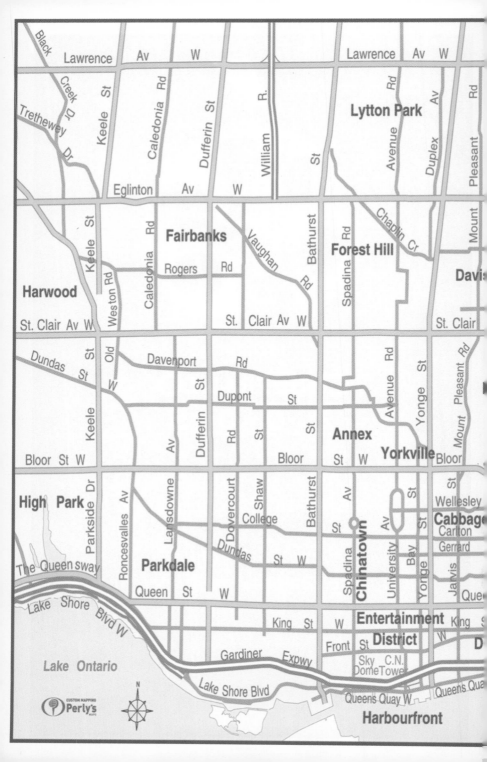

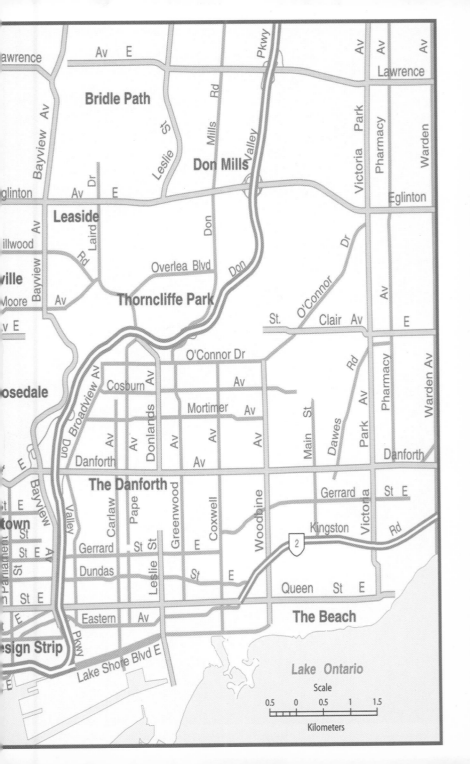

We'd like to make a difference

We've been so fortunate to have so many people give of themselves to help us achieve our dreams that, in return, we want to support a couple of organisations that are particularly close to our hearts: Second Harvest and the Daily Bread Food Bank. Franco Toronto Media & Publishing will donate a percentage of pre-tax profits from our retail sales to food and nutrition programs that assist low-income members of the community. We've also offered ad space in our guide as a way to highlight the extraordinary work of these organisations. We thank you, our faithful readers, for making this support possible.

The Franco Toronto team

franco **toronto**

the french side of toronto

The essential guide to French food
and culture in Toronto

2006 edition

franco **toronto**

FRANCO TORONTO MEDIA & PUBLISHING

Published by: Franco Toronto Media & Publishing
Ordering: contact@franco–toronto.ca
Advertising inquires: ads@franco–toronto.ca

Special Sales: Bulk purchases are available to corporations, organisations,
                         mail-order catalogues, institutions and charities at special
                         discounts.

Printed and bound in Canada by: AGMV Marquis
Maps of Toronto provided by: Perly's Maps, www.perlys.com

Visit our Web site at **www.franco–toronto.ca**

contents

A Culinary Adventure

FRENCH FOOD SHOPPING

DINING OUT

FRENCH COOKING

A Cultural Adventure

INFORMATION & ENTERTAINMENT

OTHER RESOURCES

Here's what readers had to say about *The French Side of Toronto:*

"*Congratulations on the 2004 edition of* The French Side of Toronto / Vivre en français à Toronto *which I recently acquired (at Pusateri's), and which I have enjoyed immensely. I particularly appreciate the well-researched anecdotes you have added about French food and culture and their special connections to Toronto.*"

—ANDREW OATES, TORONTO

'The French Side of Toronto *was a challenge no one had yet dared to undertake. The Franco Toronto team has revealed to us all how rich the French culture is in Toronto. From the downtown core to the outskirts, we are everywhere, yet it's hard to find us as there is no real quartier français! Bravo Franco Toronto! You let the world know we are a rich, colourful, and vibrant community.*"

— VÉRONIQUE PEREZ, OWNER/MANAGER, CRÊPES À GOGO, TORONTO

"*As a French food lover,* The French Side of Toronto *is my new bible! Fabulous work!*"

— NATASHA JONES, WHITBY

"*This is a unique and useful guide which everyone visiting or living in Toronto should have.*"

— KARIN GENTON-L'EPÉE, PRAGUE

"*One can really appreciate the multiculturalism of Toronto through this guide. It is a treasure for those who love anything French!*"

— SANDRA SKAIRJEH, MISSISSAUGA

"*… The book offers a wealth of information on French stuff.*"

— SAMANTHA GRICE, *NATIONAL POST*, "A FEW FRENCH FACTS" ARTICLE, PUBLISHED JULY 3, 2004

"*… The newly released paperback guide … not only directs you to French eateries from patisseries to bistros, it provides taste-tested suggestions on what to order …*"

— JENNIFER BAIN, *TORONTO STAR*, "MANGEZ FRANÇAIS" ARTICLE, PUBLISHED JULY 24, 2004

'The French Side of Toronto *is filled with everything you need to know …*"

— ANTOINE TEDESCO, SCENEANDHEARD.CA, "VIVE LA DIFFERENCE!" ARTICLE, PUBLISHED VOLUME 4, ISSUE 7

acknowledgments

The following individuals have been instrumental in the pursuit of this dream. Thank you all for your support and guidance:

Dominic Canazzi, Alexandre Colliex, Jacques Hétu, Rony Israel, Marcelle Lean, Réjean Nadeau, RDÉE Centre Sud Ontario, la Société d'histoire de Toronto and Darren Weeks.

We would also like to express our gratitude to all the merchants who have valiantly sold our past editions.

The French Side of Toronto team

Head Writer & Editor-in-Chief: Krizia de Verdier

Translator: Krizia de Verdier

English Writer & Editor: Fionna Boyle

Line Editor: Mary Nersessian

French Editor: Aude Lemoine

French Writers: Aude Lemoine, Sophie Hautcoeur

Cultural Editor for the Web site: Thomas Chanzy

Creative Director: Debi De Santis

Research: Krizia de Verdier, Fionna Boyle, Dominic Canazzi, Thomas Chanzy, Derek Lowe, Nicholas Palmer, Franck Nanguy, Prashant Ramesh and Hilda Toh

Fact Checker: Mary Nersessian

Advertising Layout: Ksenia Onosov

Web site: Helios Lab Design

Publishing Consultant: Dan Mozersky

Contact: contact@franco-toronto.ca

Advertising: ads@franco-toronto.ca

Publisher: Franco Toronto Media & Publishing

Visit our Web site at **www.franco-toronto.ca**

This third edition is but a continuation of a grand phenomenon: the celebration of French food and culture in Toronto.

The thriving French cultural scene in Toronto is expanding by leaps and bounds and this new edition is a testament to this joyous growth. We're thrilled to share all the new French *pâtisseries* and restaurants that are burgeoning across our city with you (to be completely honest, we could hardly keep up with the expansion!). Francophones and francophiles may not have their own distinct neighbourhood within Toronto, but their undeniable contribution and presence can be felt from every corner of the Greater Toronto Area.

Once again, we came across many products that were thought to be impossible to find in Toronto – until recently. Many merchants import, with much gusto, products from France and Quebec that capture the essence of French cuisine and culture. The invitation is open to all: eat French, and as often as you can!

This proliferation of new products has forced us once again to ingest many calories in the process of sampling the food mentioned in this guide, but such is the sacrifice we are willing to make for our readers year after year. We hope this guide enables you to find the French products you love with ease. After all, to fully appreciate the wealth of France and French-speaking countries and regions, one must dive wholeheartedly into the food, the wine and the culture.

The core philosophy of *The French Side of Toronto* is to give you easy access to some of the finest French addresses in Toronto. Some listings seem as if they have been transported straight from France; others have more of a Quebec influence and the rest are sparkling gems that will satisfy the most ardent francophile living in Toronto. All appear in this guide for one purpose: to celebrate authentic French gastronomic and cultural experiences in our city.

Enjoy and *au plaisir!*

Krizia de Verdier
Head Writer & Editor–in–Chief

finding the right words

So many food terms, so little time! In an attempt to keep *The French Side of Toronto* as authentic as possible, we've kept many of the French names for products and dishes. To brush up on your French culinary language, visit our Web site at **www.franco-toronto.ca** and order your FREE e-book of English translations: *Glossary of French Food Terms.*

What's the difference between a francophone and a francophile?

The most commonly asked question we encounter is: "What is the difference between a francophone and a francophile?" The simplest explanation is this:

• A **francophone** is a person of French descent, or a person who originates from any French-speaking country or region (such as Calgary, New Brunswick, New Orleans, Northern Ontario or Quebec).

• A **francophile** is a person who is not of French descent, but who has a passion for all things French.

breads, pâtisseries and french sweets

One might think a North American francophile living outside Quebec would have a difficult time locating many of the French delights easily found in Paris, Belgium, Switzerland or Montreal. After all, once you've tasted exquisite breads, croissants, sweets and chocolates you can never go back to the mundane! (Asking a self-professed francophile to live without French or Quebecois cheese is like asking him or her to stop breathing.)

Luckily, francophiles living in Toronto never have to compromise when it comes to French food, nor do they have to take a trip abroad to enjoy French culinary pleasures. There is an extensive range of products at our disposal from Franco-European countries, as well as *la belle province*. This first section might well be the one you use the most – happy shopping!

breads, pâtisseries & french sweets

ACE BAKERY

1 Hafis Road (South of Lawrence Avenue West, East of Keele Street) ☎ 416 241-3600 (office); 416 241-8433 (Ace Bakery Fresh Bread Store and Café)

Monday-Friday 10-4; Saturday 10-3; closed Sunday (Ace Café)

Subway: LAWRENCE WEST + bus

www.ace-bakery.com

GOOD BREAD Without a doubt, Ace makes one of Toronto's best baguettes – crusty on the outside and chewy on the inside. The popularity of the Ace baguette is such that it is the baguette of choice on Air France's flights from Toronto to Paris. No wonder Ace Bakery has been a thriving business since 1993. While nothing beats buying fresh from the oven at the bakery, you can also find Ace products in more than 700 stores, restaurants and hotels in Canada and the U.S. (Ontario, Quebec,

Michigan and New York). Ace also specialises in a variety of sumptuous breads that should not be missed, including whole wheat and multi-grain sandwich breads, a fig-and-nut round loaf, cranberry and rosemary focaccias and a terrific organic sunflower-seed bread. During the Christmas and Easter holidays, Ace offers a selection of breads that are almost too cute to eat: a fig-and-nut, multi-grain or whole wheat large flower and a whole wheat or multi-grain bear.

ALL THE BEST FINE FOODS

1099 Yonge Street (North of Roxborough Street) ☎ 416 928-3330

Monday–Wednesday 8:30–6:30, Thursday–Friday 8:30–7, Saturday 8:30–6, Sunday 10–5

Subway: SUMMERHILL

www.allthebestfinefoods.com

Did you know?

The baguette is perhaps the second-strongest visual symbol of France (the Eiffel Tower being the first). A day without a baguette is simply inconceivable for the true francophile, so it's fortunate there is no shortage of these delicious baked goods here in Toronto. The French baguette evolved from the need to create a product to satisfy the demands of French consumers on the eve of the First World War. At the beginning of the last century, French consumers could only buy two types of breads – *la miche ronde* (a round bread) and *le pain long* (a fairly long bread). Very much like today's baguette, *le pain long* had a crusty exterior, but unlike our current baguette, it had a very dense and coarse texture inside. Most consumers liked the outer crust, but were not so keen on the rest of the baguette. Bread-makers of the time saw this dissatisfaction as a challenge to come up with a better product. Many failed attempts finally led to the creation of the baguette we know and love – crusty on the outside, while moist and soft on the inside. If you want to know more about the origins of bread, consider a visit to the following museums devoted to the craft of bread-making on your next trip to Europe: le Musée des Arts et Traditions Populaires (France), le Musée de la boulangerie (Switzerland) and La Maison du Blé et du Pain à Echallens (Switzerland).

FRENCH DELIGHTS All the Best Fine Foods sells *pains au chocolat* (chocolate croissants), butter croissants, *croissants aux amandes* (almond croissants) and a few other selections from premier French pastry shops in the city.

GOOD BREAD The in-house artisan baker makes many types of country-style breads. The *pain au levain* (sourdough bread) and rustic baguettes are only a couple of the tasty selections you'll find. You'll be able to buy bagels from St. Urbain Bagel Bakery here, as well.

ARZ BAKERY

1909 Lawrence Avenue East (between Warden Avenue and Pharmacy Avenue) ☎ 416 755-5084

Monday-Saturday 8-9:30; Sunday 8-7; statutory holidays 8-5

Subway: LAWRENCE + bus

FRENCH DELIGHTS Armenian brothers Jack and Armand Boyadjian run Arz Bakery – Jack is the owner, whilst Armand is the pastry chef. The experience and education of its staff is a good indication of the quality of the pastries – French-trained Armand heads a kitchen full of pastry chefs who have also been through rigorous French training, including a graduate of the prestigious Lenôtre culinary school. At Arz, you'll discover large counters filled with scrumptious French pastries and Lebanese-style baklavas. The baklava counter in particular promises a sweet treat. Visually, the presentation of these light caramel-coloured desserts sprinkled with ground pistachio nuts and laid out on large metallic wheels is stupendous. Take your selections home to

end a good dinner, or take a break at the café adjacent to the store and enjoy them on the spot.

FRENCH SWEETS Arz Bakery also has a large selection of French and Lebanese cookies. Those on the lookout for the popular European sugar-coated almond candy known as *dragées* need look no further – Arz Bakery sells varieties from France and Spain.

BALZAC'S COFFEE HOUSE

Please refer to our directory on page 132 to find all locations for this merchant.

www.balzaccoffee.com

FRENCH DELIGHTS Located in the artistic Distillery District, Balzac's Coffee House is not a *pâtisserie* but a coffee shop. Luckily for patrons, the owners rely on Clafouti and Daniel et Daniel to satisfy the pastry needs of their clientele. Clafouti's popular selections include butter croissants, sandwiches, apple turnovers, *pains au chocolat* and *amandines*. From Daniel et Daniel, you can savour croissants, *amandines, pains au chocolat, croissants au fromage* (cheese croissants) and fruit danishes. Although Daniel et Daniel pastries are only available on Mondays, this is surely a reason to look forward to the beginning of the week!

BONJOUR BRIOCHE

812 Queen Street East (East of Broadview Avenue) ☎ 416 406-1250

Closed Monday, Tuesday–Friday 8–5, Saturday 8–4, Sunday 8–3

Subway: QUEEN + streetcar

FRENCH DELIGHTS You need only to open

the doors at Bonjour Brioche to be greeted with the warm, delicious scent of sugar and butter. Croissants and brioches of every conceivable variation await you. The almond croissants and sugar brioches are undoubtedly delicious, but without a doubt, the star is the *brioche royale,* filled with *crème pâtissière* (custard) and lemon. This is also the perfect *pâtisserie* for fans of the lemon tart, though the pear and almond variety is also mouth-watering. You'll also want to try their decadent and superb flourless chocolate cake.

GOOD BREAD If you are on a low- or no-carbohydrate diet, this may not be the best place for you. Few can resist the seduction of Bonjour Brioche's wonderful baguettes – they simply melt in your mouth, and when combined with a little butter and jam, you can almost hear the angels sing. This is the ideal version for those who like their baguette soft inside and out. Bonjour Brioche also sells a nice selection of multi-grain and whole wheat breads. Another specialty is their olive and rosemary loaf – simply *magnifique!* – which, unfortunately, is only available on weekends. New on the menu is the focaccia, equally as tempting and memorable as Bonjour Brioche's other breads.

FRENCH SWEETS Bonjour Brioche sells a variety of delicious homemade cookies individually or in small packs, including shortbreads, *macarons* (lightweight shell, filled with different flavours), *tuiles* (thin cookies) and a few other French-inspired varieties.

CASA AÇOREANA

235 Augusta Avenue (inside Kensington Market) ☎ 416 593-9717

Monday–Saturday 8–6:30, closed Sunday

Subway: SPADINA + streetcar; QUEEN'S PARK + streetcar

FRENCH SWEETS At Casa Açoreana, they offer a wide variety of French treats to suit palates of all ages – including the hard-to-find sugar-coated almond candy known as *dragées.*

CLAFOUTI

915 Queen Street West (East of Strachan Avenue, across from Trinity Bellwoods Park) ☎ 416 603-1935

Closed Monday; Tuesday–Saturday 8–6, Sunday 9–5

Subway: OSGOODE + streetcar

FRENCH DELIGHTS When it comes to croissants, Clafouti reigns supreme – after being open less than six months, Clafouti received the "best croissant in

Did you know?

A *clafouti* is traditionally defined as a rustic dessert made with black cherries and dough similar to the kind used to make crêpes. *L'Académie française* compares the *clafouti* to a fruit flan. But Boris Dosne, co-owner and pastry chef at Clafouti, believes traditions were meant to be broken, which is why he offers us his own variations – fig and grappa, lychee and caramel, wild berry and raspberry and pomegranate are just some of the combinations he uses to stir things up in Toronto.

T.O." distinction from *NOW* magazine in 2003. While pastry chef Boris Dosne is a genius at work creating Clafouti's sweet concoctions, his brother and co-owner Olivier Jansen-Reynaud is the one greeting customers. Dosne's croissants are both tasty and unique – flavours including fig and brown sugar, cannot be found in any other *pâtisserie* in town. If Clafouti runs out of these two favourites, we recommend the *pain au chocolat* or *pain au raisins* (raisin danish), both of which are mouth-watering. Apricot, cherry and *crème pâtissière* (custard) brioches are also some of the other tempting treats Dosne whips up in his kitchen. Clafouti's dessert selections are delicious and original. Choose from coconut and apple, *clafouti* and their signature offering, Dominus (chocolate mousse cake topped with caramelized apples). A rare treat in Toronto: during the first two weeks of January, Dosne makes *galettes des rois* – flaky little pastries filled with frangipane and traditionally eaten in France on January 6 to celebrate *l'Épiphanie* (visit www.franco-toronto.ca's glossary for more details). If you are lucky enough to live or work in the Queen and Bathurst area, Clafouti will undoubtedly become a favourite. Come early to avoid disappointment.

GOOD BREAD Clafouti's French charm shines through in its fine details, like the wooden wine boxes used to present their homemade breads, including olive, rosemary focaccia, spinach focaccia and muesli. Clafouti is also a hot spot for St. Urbain's Montreal-style bagels in the Queen West area.

FRENCH SWEETS Cookie connoisseurs won't be disappointed – bergamot; Grand Marnier; and vanilla and hazelnut are amongst some of the more exotic varieties found at Clafouti, as well as more traditional French favourites such as *madeleines, quatre-quarts* (pound cake), and *langues de chat*. You'll also find Bonne Maman cookies in three flavours.

DANIEL ET DANIEL – FOOD SHOP

248 Carlton Street (corner of Parliament Street) ☎ 416 968-9275

Closed Sunday; Monday–Saturday 7:30–6

Subway: **CASTLE FRANK** + bus; **COLLEGE** + streetcar

www.danieletdaniel.ca

FRENCH DELIGHTS In addition to its reputation as one of Toronto's finest caterers, Daniel et Daniel's Cabbagetown headquarters offers French temptations such as *croissant aux amandes, pain au chocolat* and *croissant au fromage*. Their selection of classic tarts and decadent cakes are not only outstanding but ideally priced for dinner parties. Speaking of dinner parties, you'll be sure to impress guests with Daniel et Daniel's signature *crème brûlée*, sold in little ceramic containers that make it easy to achieve a perfectly burnt sugary crust at home. Given Daniel et Daniel's stellar reputation and legion of devoted fans, you might find it prudent to order your treats in advance in order to avoid disappointment.

breads, pâtisseries & french sweets

DINAH'S CUPBOARD

50 Cumberland Street ☎ 416 921-8112

Monday–Friday 8–7, Saturday 9–6;
closed Sunday (open Sundays in
December)

Subway: YONGE or BAY

FRENCH DELIGHTS This charming little
store is hidden on Cumberland Street,
just behind the Holt Renfrew Centre,
and features brioches and croissants
from Patachou.

FLEURDELYS PATISSERIE

2046 Yonge Street (South of Eglinton
Avenue) ☎ 416 545-0509

Closed Monday; Tuesday-Saturday 8-6;
Sunday 9-4

Subway: DAVISVILLE or EGLINTON

www.fleurdelyspatisserie.com

FRENCH DELIGHTS Pastry chef Miro
Musil bakes an impressive selection of
cakes using some of the finest ingredients from Belgium and France –
Belgian dark chocolate and nut mousse,
kir royale mousse (*cassis*/blackcurrant
and champagne) and Grand Marnier
cheesecake are only a few of the many
fabulous combinations. In fact, you'll
find as many as 30 different varieties of
cakes at Fleurdelys. If you have a particular weakness for chocolate, you
might want to try Europa, a best-sell-
ing triple-chocolate mousse served on a
chocolate brownie that is sure to cause
"death by chocolate." The vanilla and
chocolate *baba au rhum* (rum cakes) are
another sought-after specialty, prepared
in-house and preserved in small jars
filled with rum! These are perfect
desserts for home entertainment.
Simply place them in martini glasses,

scatter a few berries on top and *voilà*,
you've got a dessert that is so chic and
so French! You'll also find an assortment of pastries at Fleurdelys. If you're
planning a trip to Aix en Provence, be
sure to stop by their second location.

FRENCH SWEETS Fleurdelys offers six or
so different varieties of homemade
cookies. The *sablé marbré* (marbled
shortbread) was our favourite, and happens to be another bestseller. You'll also
find fruit meringues and caramel treats
that are sure to please.

FRANGIPANE PÂTISSERIE

215 Madison Avenue (a few steps away
from Dupont subway station)
☎ 416 926-0303

Monday-Thursday 8-6:30; Friday 8-7;
Saturday 9-6:30; Sunday 10-4

Subway: DUPONT

FRENCH DELIGHTS Annex residents are
waking up to entrancing smells cour-
tesy of Frangipane Pâtisserie! Claudia
Egger and Mary Skey are the two pastry divas behind this new addition to
Toronto's French culinary scene.
Baking is in Egger's DNA (both her
Swiss grandmother and her mother
were accomplished bakers), and the
passion and pride on which she built
her career can surely be tasted in her
pastries. Tarts are definitely a signature
item here. You'll find classics such as
tarte aux poires, tarte aux pommes, a wild
berry tart and *tarte au citron.* You'll also
find uncommon combinations such as
coconut and pineapple, and
caramelized walnut and frangipane
tarts. For the more courageous among
us, the dark chocolate tart is an

breads, pâtisseries & french sweets

"Entre la baguette et le camembert, au panthéon des gloires supposées du patrimoine gastronomique français se trouve le croissant." –Le Monde, 2003.

Translated, this passage from the French newspaper *Le Monde* says: "in between the baguette and camembert cheese, at the top of the list of food honouring French heritage, one can find the glorious croissant." Well said! There is no doubt the French have perfected the croissant (which, translated, means "crescent"); however, it might be surprising to discover the origins of the croissant are not, in fact, French! We can trace the origins of this rich, buttery pastry back to the time when the Turks were at war with Austria. By 1683, the Turks were planning to take over Vienna. In the middle of the night, a few local bakers heard the Turks tunnelling under their kitchens and quickly spread the alarm. Because of their bravery, Vienna was saved from the hands of the enemy. To reward the vigilant bakers, King Jean III Sobieski of Poland awarded them the privilege of creating a commemorative pastry, shaped like the crescent on the Turkish flag. This how the *Hörnchen* came to life ("little horn" in German).

Another story attributes the invention of the croissant to a man by the name of Kolschitski. This Austrian coffee shop owner lived in Vienna during the war between the Austrians and the Turks, and showed immense courage in protecting his country. He was given a large amount of coffee beans taken from the enemy as a reward, and came up with the idea of serving a crescent-shaped pastry with each cup of coffee.

It was only in 1770 when Marie-Antoinette, wife of King Louis XVI, introduced the croissant to French royalty. During a trip to Austria she was seduced by the charms of this pastry and brought some back with her to France. But it took until 1920 for bakers to perfect the recipe and give the croissant the distinctive buttery, flaky taste so well associated with France. Like any lover of good bread, lovers of good croissants will often travel far to find the best variety. The best Montreal-style croissants were, until recently, treated with the same reverence as their siblings, the Montreal-style bagel – smuggled back into Toronto by expats and savoured as a special treat!

absolute must-try. All tarts come in three convenient sizes (perhaps too convenient!). Most cakes are custom orders; however, you're sure to find a few key specialties behind the glass cases. Forgo the too-common flourless chocolate variety and try Frangipane's Swiss specialty, a flourless hazelnut version. The *Reine de Saba* (Queen of Sheba) is yet another cake that will sur-prise you, made from ground almonds and chocolate, covered in ganache and decorated with toasted slivers of almonds ... wow! If you're indulging in a sugary fix for one, consider the mini fruit mousses. You'll also find an assortment of croissants from Toronto's famed *pâtisserie* Patachou.

breads, pâtisseries & french sweets

FRENCH SWEETS Frangipane sells a great selection of cookies. Lemon shortbread, Florentine, walnut pecan and chocolate espresso are just some of the tempting selections.

Fred's Bread

45 Brisbane Road, Units 13–14
☎ 416 736-3733
Note: Bakery not open to the public

GOOD BREAD Andrea Damon-Gibson and husband Steve Gibson are the artists behind Fred's Bread, and have been making artisan-inspired breads since 1995. Of all the bakers listed in this guide, Fred's has an assortment of flavours that would make carbohydrate junkies out of the most sensible of us, including: sourdough, raisin, walnut, green and black olive, cheese, herb and onion, ancient grain and wild honey, three types of focaccia (potato, rosemary and tomato), an extra-crunchy baguette, a brioche-like bread and a sweet black bread (a heavenly mixture of chocolate, espresso, molasses and honey). Fred's breads are available across Toronto at The Big Carrot, All the Best Fine Foods, Pusateri's, Holt Renfrew, Max's Market, Le Gourmand, York's Deli and IGA in the Beach.

Harbord Bakery

115 Harbord Street (West of Spadina Avenue) ☎ 416 922-5767
Monday-Thursday 8-7; Friday-Saturday 8-6; Sunday 8-4
Subway: SPADINA + streetcar

A Jewish bakery that serves succulent butter croissants? In Toronto, everything is possible! Not only is Harbord Bakery one of Toronto's oldest Jewish bakeries, it also happens to bake a great French butter croissant. We've been told by the owners that their well-guarded recipe rivals any croissant from the long list of fabulous French *pâtisseries* in the city. They're quite right – Harbord Bakery's butter croissants are perfectly flaky and never greasy, not to mention it costs only a loonie (including tax) to take one of these delicious golden crescents home! Their chocolate croissants are also well worth a try.

Holt Renfrew – Epicure and Gourmet shops

50 Bloor Street West (corner of Bay Street)
☎ 416 922-2333
Monday–Wednesday 10–6, Thursday–Friday 10–8, Saturday 10–6, Sunday 12–6
Subway: YONGE or BAY

FRENCH DELIGHTS Holt Renfrew has a well-deserved reputation for serving only the best products, so it is no surprise this famous Canadian retailer has joined forces with Patachou to offer an array of croissants.

GOOD BREAD Every day, eager Parisian *gourmands* flock to *rue du Cherche-Midi* to buy a sourdough loaf from the late celebrity baker Lionel Poîlane's famous bakery. Luckily, Toronto francophiles need not cross the Atlantic to buy their pain Poîlane – we can enjoy this designer bread right here at home, as Holt Renfrew flies the bread in twice a week. You can purchase the *boule* (round loaf) or quarter-*boule* at the Gourmet shop, located on the store's concourse level. If you've never tasted

Did you know?

Lionel Poîlane's breads are sold in more than 600 locations and available in more than 300 restaurants in the City of Lights. In addition, pain Poîlane is exported daily to points all around the globe, including Tokyo, New York and Chicago. Even though the king of Parisian bread-making passed away a few years ago, the tradition of Poîlane's breads has not changed. Each *boule* is still made with natural fermentation, stone-ground flour and sea salt, shaped by hand and cooked in a wood oven. This artisanal method of making the bread guarantees that no two loaves will ever be identical. In fact, this built-in imperfection is what makes these breads so perfect.

Poîlane bread before, don't let the price deter you. Although France's most famous bread does not come cheap, those who have already had the pleasure of sampling it before can tell you it's worth every penny.

FRENCH SWEETS Holt Renfrew imports many higher-end sweets from France (complete with a higher-end price tag). That said, an occasional indulgence is well worth the splurge – particularly during Christmas, Valentine's Day and Easter, when the imported items are especially dazzling.

LA CIGOGNE

1626 Bayview Avenue (South of Eglinton Avenue) ☎ 416 487-1234

Monday–Friday 7:30–7, Saturday 8–7, Sunday 8–5

Subway: EGLINTON + bus

FRENCH DELIGHTS Residents of Bayview Avenue are incredibly blessed. New owner and pastry chef Thierry Schmitt is from Alsace, and brings with him some of the region's favourite dishes, including the house specialty *tarte flambée d'Alsace*. If it sounds like a mouthful, it is – this Alsatian-style, thin crust

pie is stuffed with bacon, chopped onions and cream cheese, then baked in a stone oven. It's a weekends-only feature, which is almost a blessing as it would prove to be too tempting to have such a dish available seven days a week! Once you've tried the house specialty, try sampling La Cigogne's numerous pastries, including *pain perdu* (French toast), crème brûlée, danishes, croissants, almond croissants, chocolate croissants and apple turnovers. During Christmas and Easter, chef Schmitt prepares a special holiday menu featuring a variety of delectable desserts that will leave your guests wanting more. An annual favourite is the hard-to-find (in Toronto) *galette des rois,* consisting of puff dough filled with almond cream, traditionally served on January 6.

GOOD BREAD La Cigogne is known for its signature baguettes and sourdough bread.

FRENCH SWEETS The following French treats will tempt you at La Cigogne – *madeleines, petits sablés* and *langues de chat.*

Le Comptoir de Célestin

623 Mount Pleasant Road (corner of Manor Road) ☎ 416 544-1733

Closed Monday-Tuesday; Wednesday-Saturday 7:30-7, Sunday 8:30-5

Subway: EGLINTON + bus

www.celestin.ca

FRENCH DELIGHTS Adjacent to Célestin restaurant, this little *pâtisserie* is owned by brothers Martial and Pascal Ribreau, innovators who brought the French concept of restaurant and *comptoir* (upscale food counter) to Toronto. Le Comptoir de Célestin offers an array of classic French pastries such as *pains au chocolat, pains au raisin,* apple turnovers and brioches. Pastry chef Martial Ribreau also introduces Torontonians to other French selections such as *la viennoise* (a brioche-like baguette), *la viennoise chocolat* and *bostock* brioche. When it comes to desserts, Le Comptoir de Célestin's list is long and very French. Tried-and-true classics include *tarte tatin, tarte citron* (lemon tart), and an assortment of pastries that were, until now, found only in France, such as *gland* and *religieuse.* However, Le Comptoir de Célestin's *pièce de résistance* is surely its *millefeuille* – so exqui-

site, it is only available by special order.

GOOD BREAD Bursting with complex flavours, Le Comptoir de Célestin's seven-grain bread is the best artisanal bread in Toronto. Other varieties include rye and honey, sourdough, and both regular and whole wheat baguettes. A rare find is the traditional French *viennoise* – shaped like a baguette, but very close to a brioche in taste. Le Comptoir de Célestin's *viennoise* comes in plain or chocolate. If you thought a croissant was the only way to start your weekend, now you know better!

FRENCH SWEETS The delectable pastries at Le Comptoir de Célestin more than make up for the small selection of sweets and treats. You will, however, find a dozen or so flavours of French *macarons.*

• •

You can now buy a great selection of croissants, breads and desserts from Le Comptoir de Célestin at Cheese Boutique.

• •

Le Gourmand

152 Spadina Avenue (corner of Queen Street) ☎ 416 504-4494

Monday–Friday 7–8, Saturday 9–6, Sunday 9–4

Subway: OSGOODE + streetcar; SPADINA + streetcar

FRENCH DELIGHTS Although Le Gourmand may not have a resident pastry chef, a selection of croissants from Rahier compensates nicely. The owners of Le Gourmand also offer a refined selection of superb desserts from Dessert Trends. When it comes to the perfect accompaniment to your

Did you know?

It might be common knowledge in France, but few North Americans are aware of the many names to refer to the infamous baguette – *baguépi, banette, flûte Gana* and *rétrodor* are only a few of the variations that will come in handy on your next trip to France!

croissant or pastry, we strongly suggest you try Le Gourmand's exceptional coffee or espresso.

LE PETIT GOURMET

1064 Yonge Street ☎ 416 966-3811

Monday–Friday 7:30–7, Saturday 7:30–6, closed Sunday

Subway: ROSEDALE

FRENCH DELIGHTS Rosedale residents are not shy in buying half a dozen croissants at a time from Le Petit Gourmet (it's no wonder they are usually sold out by 11 a.m.!). Croissants, almond and chocolate croissants, raisin and cinnamon danishes, and apple and fruit turnovers are just some of the baked goods prepared by owner Christian Boniteau over the past 20 years. Other luscious offerings include 15 varieties of cakes and tarts including a *gâteau basque,* which you might recognise from the menu at L'Escargot Bistro. The chocolate, pear and cream tart is especially fantastic, but be sure to leave room for the ganache cake and the *tarte tatin.*

MA MAISON

4243 Dundas Street West (East of Royal York Road) ☎ 416 236-2234

Closed Monday; Tuesday-Wednesday 8-6; Thursday-Friday 8-7; Saturday 8-6; Sunday 8-4

Subway: ROYAL YORK + bus

www.UR2Busy2Cook.com

FRENCH DELIGHTS If our homes smelled as good as Ma Maison, chances are we would never set foot outside. We were delighted by the extensive selection of French delicacies prepared at this charming *pâtisserie.* Clients of

Tournayre will recognize a friendly face when they walk through the door – Michel Longuet, who used to work at the now-defunct French pastry shop at the Beach, is now co-owner of this soon-to-be Toronto favourite. Longuet has joined forces with pastry chef Patrick Alléguède to offer west-end residents an abundance of French fare. "To choose or not to choose", that is the question at Ma Maison. That said, the *pain perdu* is an absolute must. You'll also notice many delicious *tartes* and cakes. The flavours vary from one day to another, but the apple *tarte* and prune and custard *tarte* we tried received high marks.

GOOD BREAD The rustic selection of artisanal breads is another reason to visit Ma Maison. A classic baguette is *de rigueur,* of course, but you'll also find many irresistible flavours such as seven grain, sourdough, focaccia and raisin and nut. We cannot stress enough how pleased we are that chef Alléguède loves carbs as much as we do!

FRENCH SWEETS It's pointless to try to resist the temptation of the bags of homemade cookies strategically placed on top of the counters. You'll find an enticing selection of six varieties, including *madeleines, langues de chat* and shortbread.

MONTREAL BREAD COMPANY (MBCo)

Please refer to our directory on page 132 to find all locations for this merchant.

FRENCH DELIGHTS Montreal Bread Company has been stirring things up in

breads, pâtisseries & french sweets

a city accustomed to French-style croissants and pastries. From butter croissants to chocolate *torsade*, MBCo offers a surefire way to start your day on a tasty note. Desserts are equally tempting. To satisfy your sugar fix, try their Death by Chocolate cake (the name says it all) or the lime pie *brûlée* – both knockouts.

PAIN PERDU

736 St Clair Avenue West (West of Christie Street) ☎ 416 656-7246

Closed Monday; Tuesday–Friday 8-7, Saturday 8–5, Sunday 8–4

Subway: ST CLAIR WEST + streecar

www.painperdu.com

FRENCH DELIGHTS This *pâtisserie* is named after the house specialty – *pain perdu*, or French toast. Owners Yannick and Christophe Folgoas prepare theirs in the French tradition by using day-old baguettes and an old family recipe. Pain Perdu offers a wide variety of tempting delights to both start and end your daily meals. Breakfast treats include a selection of croissants, *pain aux raisins* and *brioche sucré* (brioche with a sugary top), whilst traditional desserts range from *religieuse* and *béret basque* to *millefeuille*. Pain Perdu's signature desserts include a delicious *tarte au citron* (lemon custard) and the best *gâteau basque* in Toronto, which can only be fully appreciated when tasted. Those watching their waistlines will be pleased to know most desserts come in small, medium and large sizes, so you can decide how decadent you want to be. Best of all, Pain Perdu might be one of the only *pâtisseries* in the city that

doesn't run out of goods before 11 a.m. The reason is simple – Pain Perdu provides a continuous supply of fresh pastries and desserts throughout the day!

GOOD BREAD Good baguettes and mouth-watering sourdough bread have been hallmarks of Pain Perdu ever since it opened its doors in May 2003.

FRENCH SWEETS It simply never ends at Pain Perdu! The delicate little French cookies are as equally tempting as the desserts. Among the sweets offered you'll find chocolate-covered candied orange treats, shortbread, thin almond sheets and flaky sugar-coated *palmiers*, all strategically placed in baskets that are hard to ignore. You'll also find nougat, chocolate candies, and blackcurrant and raspberry fruit paste.

Did you know?

Mercatto and Magnolia are two merchants who have a serious love affair with French goodies. Mercatto's and Magnolia's croissants are from Clafouti, and like those found at the *pâtisserie* on Queen Street, they tend to disappear fast. Fortunately, the croissants are available five days a week at Mercatto and all week long (including weekends) at Magnolia.

- Magnolia Fine Foods
  548 College Street
  ☎ (416) 920-9927

- Mercatto
  15 Toronto Street
  ☎ (416) 366-4567

  330 Bay Street
  ☎ (416) 306-046

PATACHOU

Please refer to our directory on page 132 to find all locations for this merchant.

FRENCH DELIGHTS Patachou has offered Rosedale and Summerhill residents bite after bite of pure pleasure since 1978. Their fabulous selection of pastries, desserts and cakes includes croissants, brioches, almond and chocolate croissants and raisin danishes. When it comes to desserts, the *gâteau basque* and *tarte au citron* are must-haves. You'll also be delighted to discover a number of specialty holiday items for Christmas, New Year, Easter and *l'Épiphanie* that will certainly impress your guests, including the house specialty – *petits fours glacés*. These miniature flavoured cakes are impossible to resist (you can easily eat four or five without realising it!). To enjoy Patachou's holiday desserts, you need only place an order. Patachou is also the place to find the proper pastry shells to make *bouchées à la reine* (pastries filled with chicken or shrimp in a *béchamel* sauce). If you prefer to linger and savour your selections inside the *pâtisserie*, there is a small area at the back where you can sit and eat. A word of warning, however, most desserts are gone by early afternoon on weekends, so don't sleep in too late on Saturday!

FRENCH SWEETS Patachou sells three flavours of macarons, as well as many flavours of homemade cookies.

PÂTISSERIE D'OR

301 Robinson Street, Oakville (South of Lakeshore Road) ☎ 905 815-8999

Closed Monday-Tuesday; Wednesday-Friday 8-5:30; Saturday 8-6; Sunday 8-6

FRENCH DELIGHTS If you are looking for the best French pastries prepared by a master pastry chef, you must stop by this Oakville shop. Owners Jean-Luc Soulabaille and his wife Monica are both former employees at Toronto's Four Seasons Hotel who decided to open their own *pâtisserie* in August 2000. One taste and you immediately know Soulabaille has classical French training – his pastries are so delicate, only a master pastry chef could create them. Pâtisserie d'Or features butter, almond and chocolate croissants and raisin danishes (made with a croissant dough and not a brioche dough) by the basketful. Fruit-filled danishes are prepared using seasonal fresh fruits only – you will taste the difference from the very first bite – while all chocolate desserts are made with Switzerland's Lindt chocolate. Indeed, ingredients really do make the difference at Pâtisserie d'Or. When it comes to desserts, the list is long and classically French. In fact, you'll find specialties here that are found in few other regional *pâtisseries*, including *saint-honoré* (layers of sweet puff dough filled with pastry and whipped cream, covered with caramel), *millefeuille* and Black Forest cake. Be sure to consult our French Frozen Goods listing to see all the amazing goodies Soulabaille keeps in his take-out freezers!

breads, pâtisseries & french sweets

GOOD BREAD Pâtisserie d'Or's baguette is classic yet simply delicious, and a favourite of Oakville residents.

FRENCH SWEETS Whether it's *macarons*, vanilla cigarettes, shortbread or perfectly-prepared *madeleines*, you're bound to succumb to trying the variety of tasty cookies prepared by Soulabaille.

. . . .

A delicious and ingenious solution!

Large slabs of cake that serve 20 to 30 people often turn out to be a big disappointment. They may do the job of serving many guests, but they often lack the delicate taste of smaller, more refined cakes. Pastry chef Jean-Luc Soulabaille of Pâtisserie d'Or offers a superior solution by creating large-scale cakes that are moist, refined and delicate, adding a rhapsody of chocolate swirls for a finishing touch.

. . . .

PÂTISSERIE DAUDET

4335 Bloor Street West, Markland Wood Plaza (on the corner of Mill Road)
☎ 416 626-6310

Closed Sunday-Monday; Tuesday-Saturday 8-6

FRENCH DELIGHTS Europe's loss is Toronto's gain! Master pastry chef Bruno Respecte-Daudet and his charming wife Pascale emigrated to our city from France, where Respecte-Daudet received his *maître pâtissier* designation (France's highest distinction for pastry-making). Since it opened in December 2004, the family's Etobicoke *pâtisserie* has showcased his extraordinary talent – just one look at the perfect little pastries, and your mouth will

water in anticipation. Almond croissants, fruit danishes, apple turnovers and chocolate brioches are just some of the temptations you'll find (and if you're worried about over-indulging, don't – Respecte-Daudet's selection of miniature chocolate and plain croissants will cut your guilt in half). *Pain au lait* (brioche) is celestial, flavoured with a delicate *fleur d'oranger*. Desserts vary on a daily basis, but staples include rum cakes, mini *croquembouches*, *éclairs* and *marquise au chocolat*. *Tartes* are available in many scrumptious flavours, and priced far below others in the city. Respecte-Daudet also has an unparalleled mastery of *pièces montées* (layer cakes) and theme cakes, which are great for kids. (Due to the detail and preparation involved, cakes are order-only.) For something truly spectacular, consider a traditional French *croquembouche* (small, filled puff pastries joined together by caramel to form a tapering tower), some of which take on an architectural presence with their sophisticated construction.

GOOD BREAD A hearty selection of homemade breads are available, including baguettes, whole wheat, multigrain, flax seed, sourdough and rye.

FRENCH SWEETS It's impossible not to notice the cookies at Pâtisserie Daudet! Temptation comes in the form of almond *croquets, tuiles, macarons*, meringues and shortbread.

PÂTISSERIE LE PAPILLON

This merchant will reopen in 2005

9425 Leslie Street, Unit 9, Richmond Hill
☎ 905 918-0080

Monday-Thursday 12-8; Friday-Sunday 12-10

www.finecakes.ca

FRENCH DELIGHTS You are always greeted with warmth and kindness when you stop by this lovely *pâtisserie*, owned by Wilfred and Elizabeth Chang. A graduate of George Brown College and Le Cordon Bleu Paris school in Ottawa, Elizabeth Chang discovered her passion for French pastry by accident when she enrolled in an evening class at George Brown College. The undisputed star at Pâtisserie Le Papillon is the mini mousse cake, which is sure to leave a lasting impression on your guests. Available in over 20 flavours, these beautiful, airy little cakes are dangerously tempting – you can easily sample three or four in one sitting! For damage control, you may want to try some of the desserts prepared in less sinful sizes, such as *saint-honoré, opéra, profiteroles* and *tartes aux amandes* (almond tarts).

FRENCH SWEETS Chang bakes 10 different varieties of cookies. Bestsellers include lemon, coffee, walnut, black-currant and almond, but we recommend trying them all!

PÂTISSERIE SAINT HONORÉ

2945 Bloor Street West (corner of Grenview Boulevard, East of Royal York Road) Note: no telephone is available

Closed Monday Tuesday–Thursday 8–7, Friday 8–9, Saturday 8–7, closed Sunday

Subway: **ROYAL YORK**

FRENCH DELIGHTS Jean-Jacques Carlier's *pâtisserie* features a scrumptious array of almond, chocolate and plain croissants, fruit danishes and raisin brioches. Savoury (but equally appealing) croissant flavours include cheese and ham, as well as feta and spinach. Pâtisserie Saint Honoré also produces an impressive variety of cakes and tarts.

GOOD BREAD The staple French *pâtisserie* in Kingsway Village, Pâtisserie Saint Honoré makes a tasty baguette that can be enjoyed with or without garnish.

PUSATERI'S FINE FOODS

Please refer to our directory on page 132 to find all locations for this merchant.

www.pusateris.com

FRENCH DELIGHTS Pusateri's has a well-deserved reputation for both excellence and exclusivity. This is evident in the way they pamper their upscale clientele with selections of pastries, tarts and cakes from four renowned local French *pâtisseries* – Clafouti, Le Comptoir de Célestin, Patachou and Rahier.

RAHIER

1586 Bayview Avenue (South of Eglinton Avenue) ☎ 416 482-0917

You heard it here first!

Pastry chef Elizabeth Chang from Pâtisserie Le Papillon revealed that many *au courant* brides are opting for tiers of mini mousse cakes instead of a traditional wedding cake on their big day. Not only do mini mousse cakes create a stunning visual effect, they offer guests a choice of different flavours in a more manageable size.

breads, pâtisseries & french sweets

Closed Monday–Tuesday,
Wednesday–Friday 8–5, Saturday 8–4,
Sunday 8–3

Subway: EGLINTON + bus

FRENCH DELIGHTS Some have dubbed Rahier the Rolls-Royce of Toronto's *pâtisseries*. In fact, many of the newer French pastry shops attribute their existence to Rahier's success. Rahier has tickled our taste buds and tempted our tummies with its delectable and fragrant confections since 1996. This is a great place for croissants, cakes, pastries, fresh fruit tarts and plenty of other French sweet delicacies, all made on the premises. The pistachio danish and the almond croissant are especially recommended. During the holiday season, Rahier offers an impressive collection of specialty items your guests will be sure to love, including a classic Christmas log *(la bûche de Noël)* that is unparalleled by other *pâtisseries* in the city.

GOOD BREAD Rahier makes a traditional French baguette.

FRENCH SWEETS Rahier has the most plentiful selection of homemade French cookies in the city, available individually or in packs.

St. Urbain Bagel Bakery

Please refer to our directory on page 132 to find all locations for this merchant.

GOOD BREAD St. Urbain Bagel Bakery is an excellent source for Montreal-style bagels in Toronto. St. Urbain has three stores in the Greater Toronto Area, but you can also purchase their bagels at the following locations: All the Best

Fine Foods, Clafouti, Cheese Boutique and My Market Bakery (Kensington Market).

SENSES

Please refer to our directory on page 132 to find all locations for this merchant.

www.senses.ca

FRENCH DELIGHTS The location may have changed (formerly at 15 Bloor Street West), but the quality has remained intact. Senses has it all under one roof: catering services, a fine-dining restaurant and a take-out pastry store. While not a proper French *pâtisserie* per se, most of Senses's desserts are infused with a French influence, and when it comes to French pastries, you can be assured you'll find the best of the best here – the assortments of croissants, fruit and chocolate tarts, fruit mousses and chocolate cakes is mind-boggling. You'll also find many unique local creations that should not be missed, such as a sublime chestnut cake. Everything looks so good that choosing is a near-impossible task – we recommend at least two goodies each visit!

The Bagel House

Please refer to our directory on page 132 to find all locations for this merchant.

GOOD BREAD Montreal expatriates Jessie Sahdra and Sat Chouhan have been crafting their bagel-making expertise in some of the most popular bagel shops in Quebec since 1985 – and it shows. There are only a handful of places in Toronto that make authentic Montreal-style bagels, with their distinctive tex-

Did you know?

While it is true the bagel doesn't have French roots, you'd be hard-pressed to find a Quebecker who hasn't embraced this dense, round-holed bread as much as the croissant. Originally derived from the culinary history of Russian and European Jews, the history of the bagel in Canada can be traced to 1919, when a Jewish immigrant by the name of Isadore Shlafman opened his first bagel shop in Montreal on St. Laurent Street. A second shop followed in 1949 on Fairmount Street, a region that would become known as the bagel district. There are bagels, and then there are Montreal-style bagels. Their distinctive taste and texture is achieved by a process of hand-rolling, boiling and baking in a wood-burning oven. Montreal-style bagels are exactly what real bagels are meant to be – slightly chewy, a little sweet and perfectly sprinkled with sesame or poppy seeds. For many years, the only hope Montreal expats in Toronto had of satisfying their bagel cravings was to stock up with each trip to *la belle province,* then deep-freeze this manna from heaven, to be savoured on special occasions only. *Mais, enfin!* There is a small but steady supply of Montreal-style bagel shops right here in the city for your convenience and continuous enjoyment.

Where to find Montreal-style bagels

1. All the Best Fine Foods
2. Cheese Boutique
3. Clafouti
4. My Market Bakery (Kensington Market)
5. Pusateri's Fine Foods
6. St. Urbain Bagel Bakery
7. The Bagel House

ture, taste and preparation, and The Bagel House is one of them. Sahdra's and Chouhan's mastery of this art is evident with every bagel they produce. The bagels at The Bagel House come in 12 or so flavours, although purists will likely stick to the sesame or poppy varieties! Bagels from The Bagel House have scooped up big honours in Toronto – *Toronto Star, Montreal Gazette* and *Toronto Life* have all voted these bagels the best in the city. The expatriate Montrealers on our team wholeheartedly agree!

WHOLE FOODS MARKET

87 Avenue Road (North of Bloor Street)
☎ 416 944-0500
Monday–Friday 9–10, Saturday–Sunday 9–9
Subway: BAY or MUSEUM
www.wholefoodsmarket.com

FRENCH DELIGHTS Whole Foods Market offers a respectable variety of pastries from Patachou. Although the selection might be a fraction of what you'll find at the Rosedale *pâtisserie,* the convenience makes up for the limited assortment.

breads, pâtisseries & french sweets

Glossary of French Sweets

Sweets may be the one common global food item amongst all cultural groups, and the French are no exception. Fortunately, there's no shortage of shops in Toronto that sell goodies from France to satisfy all varieties of sweet tooths. If you haven't already done so, make a point of trying one (or all!) of the French sweets listed below – sheer decadence with every bite! Sweets are listed by their French brand names.

BONBON ANIS DE L'ABBAYE DE FLAVIGNY: flavoured candy drops made with anise

BONBON BARNIER: flavoured lollipops

BONBON LA VIE DE LA VOSGIENNE: small flavoured candy drops

PASTILLES VICHY: candy that is not overly sweet, made with water from Vichy Falls

CACHOU LA JAUNIE: liquorice drops

CARAMBAR: caramel sticks

GÂTEAU BROSSARD: small, flavoured butter cakes sold in boxes

LANGUES DE CHAT: Translated as "cat's tongues", this delicate oval-shaped vanilla-flavoured cookie is an ideal accompaniment to ice cream, but is equally delicious by itself.

MADELEINES GAILLARD: small coffee-like cakes flavoured with orange blossom water

MACARON: light shells, filled with different flavours

QUATRE-QUARTS: pound cake _à la française_

SIROP WILLIAM/WILLIAM SYRUP: fruit-flavoured syrups that can be added to drinks or desserts

NOUGATS AUX AMANDES CHABERT ET GUILLOT: almond nougat

RÉGLISSES HARIBO: liquorice

PÂTE DE FRUITS DE PROVENCE: fruit paste

SUCETTES PIERROT GOURMAND: lollipops

Where to find these French sweets

1. All the Best Fine Foods
2. Arz Bakery
3. Brandt Meat Packers Ltd.
4. Cheese Boutique
5. Clafouti
6. Daniel et Daniel
7. Dinah's Cupboard
8. La Cigogne
9. Le Comptoir de Célestin
10. Le Gourmand
11. Max's Market
12. Mercatto
13. Pâtisserie d'Or
14. Rahier
15. Scheffler's Delicatessen

GOOD BREAD Like everything else in the store, Whole Foods Market has a remarkable selection of breads that are baked on premise. Varieties include country-style, raisin and pecan, multigrain, olive and, of course, the famous baguette. You'll also find more unconventional choices, such as a roasted garlic loaf.

ZANE PÂTISSERIE & BOULANGERIE

1852 Queen Street East (West of Woodbine Avenue) ☎ 416 690-2813

Monday closed; Tuesday–Sunday 7:30–5:30

Subway: QUEEN + streetcar

FRENCH DELIGHTS The *grande dame* of French *pâtisseries* in the Beach, Zane Pâtisserie & Boulangerie is owned by Mo Zane, who also doubles as the pastry chef. Zane felt obliged to extend his apologies for being covered in flour and sugar when we first met, but we found this a charming testament to his dedication to his craft. Where to begin? Classic French pastries can be found here in abundance. For starters, there are plain, almond and chocolate croissants, as well as lemon, apricot, blueberry and hazelnut danishes. For a different taste, consider the custard-filled twists and squares. A dozen cakes and close to a dozen tarts are also all very tempting, as is the *quatre-quarts* (pound cake) – with three flavours to choose from (lemon, vanilla/chocolate and hazelnut/chocolate), it is quite a popular item and tends to sell out on Saturday mornings within a few hours. If you're looking for bite-sized treats,

Zane prepares a wonderful assortment of *petits fours frais* (mini pastries), including fruit, chocolate and raspberry tarts, *tarte au citron*, *éclairs* and *choux* (cream-filled puff pastries). And as if all that weren't enough, you'll also find *financiers* (similar to *madeleines*) – little almond and hazelnut butter cakes that will seduce you.

GOOD BREAD All breads are made on the premises, *naturellement!* You'll be hard-pressed to choose between the great baguette, the fabulous nut loaf and the tasty multi-grain, not to mention the delicious rosemary, black olive and sun-dried tomato varieties. The sun-dried tomato loaf in particular is simply sinful, and can easily be eaten on its own or as a perfect accompaniment to soups and salads.

FRENCH SWEETS Residents of the Beach can satisfy their sugar cravings with more than 15 different varieties of cookies, all baked by Zane himself.

chocolatiers

White? Dark? Milk? Bittersweet? Flavoured? The possibilities
are endless. People the world over have a love affair with
chocolate, and the French are no exception. Of course, it is only
fitting for a country that celebrates both passion and food so
intensely to take that love affair to another level.

In fact, the French are so serious about chocolate, they've
created an exclusive club of connoisseurs who meet regularly to
taste and critique the newest creations. When it comes to
chocolate, le Club des Croqueurs du Chocolat (The Chocolate
Lovers Club) is comprised of the *crème de la crème* of France's
chocolatiers.

However, the French are not the only nation to master the art
and technique of fine chocolate-making; Swiss and Belgian
chocolate is of an equal calibre of refined quality and taste. In
this section, we shine the spotlight on all three!

chocolatiers

Arz Bakery

1909 Lawrence Avenue East (between Warden Avenue and Pharmacy Avenue)
☎ 416 755-5084

Monday-Saturday 8-9:30; Sunday 8-7, statutory holidays 8-5

Subway: LAWRENCE + bus

Chocoholics won't be able to tear their eyes away from Arz's long counter of truffles and pralines, imported directly from France.

Belgian Chocolate Shop

2455 Queen Street East (West of Victoria Park Avenue) ☎ 416 691-1424

Closed Monday; Tuesday–Friday 11–7, Saturday–Sunday 11–5

Subway: QUEEN + streetcar

www.belgianchocolateshop.ca

Just in case the name didn't give it away, owners Eric Smets and Patricia Cohrs proudly display two clocks behind the counter to hint at their heritage – one is set to local time; the other, Brussels. Since 1984, the duo has been making truffles, pralines and ganaches in the true artisanal tradition, right on the premises, using only the best quality ingredients and no preservatives. Unlike imported sweets, the chocolate confections in this shop never see a warehouse or airline container so they are guaranteed to be the freshest they can be. Classic and exotic flavours include crunchy almond nougat, poached pear in vodka, bergamot, lemon cream, caramel, Grand Marnier and champagne … tempted yet?

Cheese Boutique

45 Ripley Avenue (South of South Kingsway and North of The Queensway)
☎ 416 762-6292

Monday–Friday 8–9, Saturday 8–8, Sunday 10–6

Subway: RUNNYMEDE + bus

www.cheeseboutique.com

Chocolate at a cheese shop? *Mais oui!* In fact, there is so much chocolate from France, Belgium and Switzerland here, "Chocolate Boutique" may be a better name for this store! On the mezzanine level, you'll find everything from hot chocolate powder from *Poulain* to fondue chocolate from Lindt to chocolate butter from Côte d'Or to refrigerated Michel Cluizel truffles. In addition, Cheese Boutique carries an array of gift boxes for an elegant finishing touch to your gift-giving.

• •

A first in Toronto!

Leave it to one of Toronto's pre-eminent cheesemongers to reinvent the wheel – literally! Only Cheese Boutique sells decadent Swiss chocolate by the wheel. Choose from marble, white, mild or half-and-half. Each will add an exquisite final touch to your homemade desserts. Ingenious!

• •

Chocolate Addict

185 Baldwin Street (inside Kensington Market) ☎ 416 979-5809

Monday–Friday 10-6:30; Saturday 10-7; Sunday 10-6

Subway: SPADINA + streetcar; QUEEN'S PARK + streetcar

www.911chocolate.com

Chocolate Addict is a great little find

A lesson in chocolate

If all you know about chocolate is that it tastes good, it's time to learn a thing or two. And who better than to explain some of the most common terms associated with chocolate-making than one of Toronto's top chocolatiers? Patricia Cohrs, from the Belgian Chocolate Shop in the Beach, explains how some of the most delicious chocolate treats are made.

Truffle: First, the centre of the truffle is created. After it hardens, the truffle is dipped in liquid chocolate and usually rolled in powdered chocolate. Powdered chocolate is the traditional way of covering truffles; however, you'll also find many truffles covered with shredded coconut or slivers of almond.

Ganache: Ganache is usually made from two-thirds chocolate and one-third boiling *crème fraîche* (fresh cream).

Praline: A praline describes any chocolate where the centre is made of roasted or caramelized hazelnuts that have been ground into a smooth paste and folded into chocolate.

inside Kensington Market. Truffle fans will find more than 20 flavours to choose from, all handmade with the finest Belgian chocolate. For the purist, there is an impressive assortment of nut, fruit and liqueur-filled truffles, while those with more exotic tastes might be tempted by the lavender, basil or Sambuca varieties.

CHOCOLATES & CREAMS

207 Queen's Quay West (Queen's Quay Terminal) ☎ 416 368-6767

Monday–Sunday 10–6 (in the winter), Monday–Friday 10–8, Saturday–Sunday 10–6 (in the summer)

Subway: UNION + streetcar

www.chocolatesandcreams.com

Chocolates & Creams is the exclusive Canadian importer of Belgium's hand-made Manon chocolates. Prepared in the artisanal fashion by Christian

Vanderkerken, Manon chocolates are well-known in Europe for their meticulous selection of quality ingredients and the many awards of excellence they've won since 1985. Chocolates & Creams carries one of Manon's most sumptuous pralines – *le bouchon* (cap), part of the collection *Des créations de Christian Vanderkerken*. Each *bouchon* requires three days of preparation, and may involve up to 10 different fillings. Once finished, bouchons are hand-dipped in chocolate, then covered with 24-carat gold. Now *that's* rich chocolate!

CHOCOLATES BY BERNARD CALLEBAUT

Please refer to our directory on page 132 to find all locations for this merchant.

www.bernardc.ca

Bernard Callebaut chocolates are made with a perfect balance of modern flair and old world Belgian tradition, passed down from one generation to the next. Headquartered in Calgary, Callebaut's creations are inspired by different cultures and religions. This originality, coupled with ingredients of only the best quality, makes Callebaut chocolates truly stand out from the rest. Available in mostly traditional flavours, their distinctive, rich taste can be attributed to a reduction in the amount of sugar used during preparation, in favour of an increase in the amount of cocoa. Naturally, Callebaut chocolates are also prepared without preservatives – but when chocolate tastes this good, it doesn't last very long to begin with! Be sure to try the chocolate banana popsicles – whole bananas dipped in

Callebaut chocolate, then frozen on sticks. Sinfully good!

CLAFOUTI

915 Queen Street West (East of Strachan Avenue, across from Trinity Bellwoods Park) ☎ 416 603-1935

Closed Monday; Tuesday–Saturday 8–6, Sunday 9–5

Subway: OSGOODE + streetcar

Clafouti has a good selection of well-known Franco-European brands of chocolates, as well as powdered chocolate (you can even order a hot cup of *Poulain* cocoa to go!).

DANIEL ET DANIEL FOOD SHOP

248 Carlton Street (corner of Parliament Street) ☎ 416 968-9275

Monday–Saturday 7:30–6, closed Sunday

Subway: CASTLE FRANK + bus; COLLEGE + streetcar

www.danieletdaniel.ca

Although Daniel et Daniel only carries a limited range of truffles, they are well worth a try. Choose from traditional favourites including hazelnut, white chocolate, nut and coconut, as well as champagne truffles from France.

EVE'S TEMPTATIONS

93 Front Street East (basement of St. Lawrence Market) ☎ 416 366-7437

Closed Sunday-Monday; Tuesday-Thursday 8-6; Friday 8-7; Saturday 5-5

Subway: UNION

Eve's Temptations carries an impressive selection of approximately 20 varieties of truffles from The Chocolate Messenger, Bayview Avenue's favourite chocolatier.

Le GOURMAND

"passionate about quality"

Le GOURMAND
152 Spadina ave. #416.504.4494
www.legourmand.com

915 Queen Street West
Toronto, Ontario
Tel: (416) 603-1935
Fax: (416) 603-3040

Our efforts are deliciously rewarding. Clafouti
is part of a long history in which the creative
processes of making food and art are intertwined.

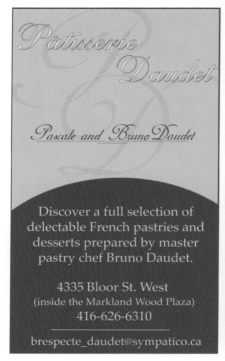

ARZ
FINE FOODS

1909 Lawrence Ave. E.
Scarborough, Ontario
Phone:416-755-5084
www.arzbakery.com

FINE FOODS
Delicatessen
Mediterranean Gourmet

BAKERY
French Cakes
Mediterranean
Pastries

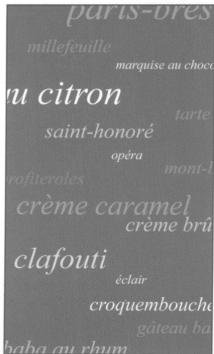

FRANGIPANE PÂTISSERIE

215 Madison Avenue (a few steps away from Dupont subway station)
☎ 416 926-0303

Monday-Thursday 8-6:30; Friday 8-7; Saturday 9-6:30; Sunday 10-4

Subway: DUPONT

Claudia Egger uses Lindt and Callebaut chocolates to prepare her wonderful selection of pralines. Just like her tarts and cakes, these exquisite chocolates are prepared in-house. There are many flavours to choose from, but we suggest *le fondant* – Italians may call it *gianduia*, but we call a morsel of hazelnut paste covered with milk chocolate "yummy"!

HOLT RENFREW – EPICURE AND GOURMET SHOPS

50 Bloor Street West (corner of Bay Street)
☎ 416 922-2333

Monday–Wednesday 10–6, Thursday–Friday 10–8, Saturday 10–6, Sunday 12–6

Subway: YONGE or BAY

With their tantalizing display of *Neuhaus* and *Joseph Schmidt* chocolates, Holt Renfrew has mastered the art of silent seduction. You won't be able to resist these smooth, silky chocolates, available in a variety of classic and exotic flavours to tempt your palate (the orange and macerated cherry in Armagnac is simply divine!). Both Belgium's *Neuhaus* and America's *Joseph Schmidt* use Belgian chocolate in their creations, for a taste unlike any other. During the holidays, Holt Renfrew pulls out all the stops with numerous imported festive chocolates from

France and Belgium. It's not easy to overshadow *Neuhaus* and *Joseph Schmidt* chocolates, but the chocolate-covered almonds from *Fauchon* are certainly worth your attention. You'll also find *Neuhaus* chocolate in bar sizes – a sinful pleasure at a simple price!

J.S. BONBONS

Please refer to our directory on page 132 to find all locations for this merchant.
www.jsbonbons.com

A visit to J. S. Bonbons is an assault on the senses. As you walk in the door, you are met by the sweet and intoxicating smell of chocolate. Then, feast your eyes on the antique-looking counter, which displays a multitude of preservative-free creations, including truffles (more than 30 flavours!) that can be packaged in beautiful chocolate bowls and an assortment of sugar-coated, chocolate-dipped fruit. Finally, let your taste buds succumb to the amazing variety of herbal, floral and tea-infused flavours, such as tarragon and black pepper, coriander and lime, lavender, chai tea, bergamot and rosemary. Although some of these combinations may sound a bit unusual, the end results are truly unique, impressive and, most of all, delicious.

LA CIGOGNE

1626 Bayview Avenue (South of Eglinton Avenue) ☎ 416 487-1234

Monday–Friday 7:30–7, Saturday 8–7, Sunday 8–5

Subway: EGLINTON + bus

On special occasions such as Christmas, Valentine's Day, Mother's

chocolatiers

Day and Easter, pastry chef Thierry Schmitt creates a delicious selection of 10 or so truffles, made with French chocolate, that should not be missed.

LA MAISON DU CHOCOLAT

☎ 1 800 988-5632
Monday–Saturday 10–7, Sunday 12–6

If you've had the privilege of indulging in chocolates from La Maison du Chocolat's shops in Paris or New York, you already know they taste simply sublime. To our detriment, La Maison du Chocolat does not have a Toronto location; however, their irresistible chocolates can be ordered by phone from the New York boutique and shipped directly to your home via air mail. However, at $100 (CDN) for a box of 77 pieces, this is an indulgence best saved for the most special of occasions!

LE GOURMAND

152 Spadina Avenue (South of Queen Street) ☎ 416 504-4494

Monday-Friday 7-8; Saturday 9-6; Sunday 9-4

Subway: OSGOODE + streetcar;
SPADINA + streetcar

Though Le Gourmand is a small bistro/merchant located on the fringes of Toronto's Fashion District, inside, you'll find an impressive selection of

Did you know?

Appointed by King Louis XIV, the first chocolatier in Paris was one of Queen Anne's officers, who opened his doors in 1659 on *la rue de l'Arbre* in *le 1er arrondissement*.

chocolates from France. You can even order a cup of *Poulain*'s decadent hot chocolate – *fantastique!*

LEONIDAS

Please refer to our directory on page 132 to find all locations for this merchant.

The must-try at Leonidas is the *crème fraîche* (fresh cream) praline. It's almost too perfect to eat. The plain dark chocolate and cream is also exquisite, but the other varieties, in an assortment of milk, dark and white chocolate flavours, are equally dazzling. Needless to say, Leonidas does not use preservatives in the preparation of their chocolates. As a result, the *crème fraîche* pralines have a shelf life of only eight days, but it is highly unlikely anyone buying them will wait this long to eat them!

PAIN PERDU

736 St Clair Avenue West (West of Christie Street) ☎ 416 656-7246

Closed Monday; Tuesday–Friday 8–7, Saturday 8–5, Sunday 8–4

Subway: ST CLAIR WEST + streetcar
www.painperdu.com

Truffles, truffles and more truffles! How does pastry chef Christophe Folgoas create an assortment of superb truffles in mouth-watering flavours, such as white chocolate, bittersweet chocolate and rum and bittersweet chocolate and raspberry? Why, a gold medal winner for his accomplishments in pastry- and chocolate-making can only produce heavenly chocolate treats!

PÂTISSERIE D'OR

301 Robinson Street, Oakville (South of Lakeshore Road) ☎ 905 815-8999

Closed Monday–Tuesday; Wednesday–Friday 8–5:30, Saturday–Sunday 8–6

This gourmet pastry shop carries a few well-chosen Swiss chocolates, delicately and artistically displayed in a glass case at the back. Flavours are mostly traditional, yet never bland – orange, pistachio, violet, pecan, nut, coconut and white chocolate flavours are all highly recommended!

PÂTISSERIE DAUDET

4335 Bloor Street West, Markland Wood Plaza (on the corner of Mill Road) ☎ 416 626-6310

Closed Sunday-Monday; Tuesday–Saturday 8–6

Chef Bruno Respecte-Daudet is not only a *maître pâtissier* (master pastry chef), he is also a *maître chocolatier* (master chocolate maker)! Respecte-Daudet uses French *Valhrona* chocolate to create his chocolatey confections. While his truffles are available any day of the week, his store really comes alive during holidays such as Valentine and Easter, when Respecte-Daudet truly unleashes his creative talents and turns ordinary chocolate into decadent treats.

PÂTISSERIE LE PAPILLON

This merchant will reopen in 2005

9425 Leslie Street, Unit 9, Richmond Hill ☎ 905 918-0080

Monday–Thursday 12–8, Friday–Sunday 12–10

www.finecakes.ca

Simple pleasures!

Although chocolate is a pleasure that should be enjoyed as often as possible (daily!), some of the more exclusive Franco-European varieties tend to be priced out of range for regular indulgences. For everyday treats that will satisfy both your craving and your pocketbook, any of the following brands are sure to delight: *Alprose, Côte D'or, Dolfin, Jacques de Belgique, Galler de Belgique, Lindt, Marquise d'Angélis, Maxim's, Mazet, Michel Cluizel, Petite Périgord Gold, Pierre Ledent, Poulain, Révillon, Sarments, Suchard, Swiss Delic* and *Valrhona.*

WHERE TO FIND THESE FRANCO-EUROPEAN CHOCOLATES

1. Arz Bakery
2. Brandt Meat Packers Ltd.
3. Cheese Boutique
4. Chocolates & Creams
5. Daniel et Daniel
6. Domino Foods Ltd.
7. La Cigogne
8. Le Comptoir de Célestin
9. Le Gourmand
10. Leonidas
11. Loblaws
12. Max's Market
13. Mercatto
14. Pâtisserie d'Or
15. Pusateri's Fine Foods
16. Rahier
17. Scheffler's Delicatessen
18. Simone Marie Belgian Chocolate
19. Sobeys
20. Sun Valley Fine Foods

chocolatiers

Exclusive to Pâtisserie Le Papillon is the truffle tart – a unique creation from pastry chef Elizabeth Chang. French or Belgian chocolate is infused with traditional and exotic flavours to create a perfect little truffle, which is then placed in a miniature tart shell. *Voilà!*

PUSATERI'S FINE FOODS

Please refer to our directory on page 132 to find all locations for this merchant.

www.pusateris.com

Tucked away in a little corner of this luxury grocery store you'll find a glass counter full of pralines from *Neuhaus*, Belgium's premier house of chocolate.

SENSES

Please refer to our directory on page 132 to find all locations for this merchant.

www.senses.ca

Senses sells a variety of outstanding and unforgettable creations from Vancouver-based chocolatier Thomas Hass. Hass uses only Belgian chocolate in his truffles and pralines. For the most part, flavours are classic but they do include unique combinations such as champagne and espresso, white chocolate and rum and blackberry and honey.

SIMONE MARIE BELGIAN CHOCOLATE

126 Cumberland Street (corner of Bellair Street) ☎ 416 968-7777

Monday–Saturday 10:30–6:30, closed Sunday

Subway: BAY (Cumberland exit)

www.simonemarie.net

Simone Marie opened her Yorkville

chocolate shop in 1993. Since then, it has become one of the city's most treasured spots for imported Belgian truffles and sweets. Unusual flavours include cinnamon, black chocolate orange and orange peel, dark chocolate and violet cream, lemon cream and orange cream. There's also a nice selection of liquor-filled truffles, including champagne, Cointreau and Amaretto. Be sure to enquire about the flavour of the month, which is always something especially exotic.

SWISS-MASTER CHOCOLATIER

2538 Bayview Avenue (corner of York Mills Road, North of The Bridle Path/Post Road) ☎ 416 444-8802

Monday–Saturday 10–6, closed Sunday

Subway: YORK MILLS + bus

www.swissmaster.com

Imported directly from the Swiss Alps, Swiss-Master chocolates are truly exquisite. One of their signature pieces is the pastel chocolate. Available only during the summer months, these delicate white chocolate and fruit truffles come in orange, strawberry, lime, lemon and passion fruit flavours and simply must be tasted to be believed. Other truffle flavours are more traditional, yet no less satisfying. Be sure to try the rum and raisin, and the Grand Marnier, which comes in two varieties – *crème fraîche* and liqueur. Swiss-Master makes gift-giving simple. Those who traditionally say it with flowers can now say it with chocolate instead – Swiss-Master has a line of sweet treats that literally say "I love you", "For you" and "Thank you". During the holidays, the shop is transformed into a small storybook castle filled with tonnes of chocolate specialties created exclusively for the occasion.

TEUSCHER CHOCOLATES

55 Bloor Street West (corner of Bay Street, inside the Manulife Centre)
☎ 416 964-8200

Monday–Wednesday 10–6,
Thursday–Friday 10–7:30, Saturday 10–6,
closed Sunday

Subway: YONGE or BAY

You know you're on to something good when *Bon Appétit* magazine declares Teuscher "the most meltingly marvellous of all chocolate creations." What a statement! For more than 65 years, Teuscher has developed a well-deserved reputation for excellence and quality based on their guarantee of freshness and commitment to using only the most refined ingredients. Teuscher's Zurich headquarters produces more than 100 different flavours (!) of chocolate, which are flown weekly to all parts of the world, including Toronto. With so many flavours to choose from it's hard to pick a favourite, however the orange, apricot, white chocolate, lemon, nougat and caramel are exceptional.

THE CHOCOLATE MESSENGER

1645 Bayview Avenue (South of Eglinton Avenue) ☎ 416 488-1414

Closed Sunday–Monday; Tuesday–Friday 10–6, Saturday 10–5

Subway: EGLINTON + bus

www.chocolatemessenger.com

This Swiss chocolatier uses *Lindt*

chocolate to create a marvellous assortment of preservative-free pralines and truffles – more than 20 different flavours of each. Fresh cream truffles are the specialty of the house. Be sure to try the port, green tea, peach and vodka and orange and vodka ... heavenly! During Valentine's Day, Christmas and Easter, this little shop is filled with boxes of truffles and chocolates treats. During the Christmas holidays, you can also find candied fruits and *marrons glacés* (sugar-coated chestnuts).

TRUFFLE TREASURES

15751 Island Road, Port Perry
☎ 905 982-0506

Monday-Sunday 10-5:30

www.truffletreasures.com

There can be little doubt chocolatier Lara Vaarré is passionate about her craft. After apprenticing with a veteran chocolatier who had 70 years of experience, she perfected her craft at the renowned Lenôtre culinary school in Paris. The care and dedication Vaarré puts into her truffles are evident from the very first bite. With more than 30 flavours ranging from the traditional to the original, there is a Truffle to be Treasured by every palate, including the

chocolatiers

ultimate in decadence – Veuve Clicquot champagne and strawberry. If travelling to Port Perry is a bit out of your way, fear not. You can also find Truffle Treasures at many Fortinos grocery stores throughout Toronto, or you can stop by the Truffle Treasures booth at many of the food and wine shows in the Greater Toronto Area.

WHOLE FOODS MARKET

87 Avenue Road (North of Bloor Street)
☎ 416 944-0500

Monday–Friday 9–10, Saturday 9–9, Sunday 9–8

Subway: BAY or MUSEUM

www.wholefoodsmarket.com

Whole Foods Market carries a small selection of Callebaut and *Valhrona* chocolates.

Too much chocolate?

It seems that will never be the case for American chocoholics! These hard-core chocolate lovers have created a magazine devoted to their passion. Not only is chocolate front and centre in *The Magazine for Gourmet Chocolate Lovers,* it also forms the composition of the magazine – the pages are scented with chocolate! Now that's a subscription we'll be sure to renew on time.

Source: Salon du chocolat's Web site

cheese shops
& crème fraîche

Though France is as well-known for its creamy camembert as its crispy baguettes and good wine, it is not the only country that produces a wide variety of outstanding cheeses. Belgium, Switzerland and the province of Quebec also export hundreds of kinds of cheese all over the world, from soft bries and *chèvres* to ripe roqueforts and okas. Let your taste buds be your guide as you enter the delicious world of cheese!

cheese shops & crème fraîche

France's *Appellation d'Origine Contrôlée*/Appellation of Controlled Origin (AOC) designation guarantees a product has been produced within a specified region following established methods of production. Although the French AOC system can't guarantee quality, it can control most of the elements that go into making the product. The AOC designation applies to wines, eaux-de-vie, dairy and farm products, and is administered by the Institut National des Appellations d'Origine (INAO). The French initiated the AOC system as a means of safeguarding the more quality-conscious winemakers, vineyards and certain areas in France from unethical producers who were taking advantage of better-known names. In the case of cheese, the AOC has established precise definitions for source milk, regions, methods of production and length of maturity. Some of the more well-known AOC cheeses include cantal, fourme d'ambert and roquefort (made exclusively with sheep's milk). These cheeses have been made in the same tradition for centuries. To illustrate the strict controls and stringent approval needed to produce an AOC cheese, consider this: there are more than 2,000 different types of brie cheeses, but only two have earned the AOC distinction.

ALEX FARM PRODUCTS

Please refer to our directory on page 132 to find all locations for this merchant.

☎ 1 877 488-7778 (main number)

www.alexcheese.com

France produces close to 400 different varieties of cheese, and you would easily think Alex Farm Products imports them all. All the classics are covered, including brie, morbier, *Belle des Champs,* raclette, chèvre and camembert. Rarer selections like etorki, pouligny-saint-pierre, coulommiers, pont l'évêque, époisses de Bourgogne, saint-andré, fourme d'ambert, saint agur, rondin du Poitou, brique du Jussac and grain d'orge from Normandy are also available. Alex Farm Products even sells a small selection of AOC (see above) cheese – cantal lagioule, chaumes, abondance, chaource and vacherin Mont-d'Or de Badoz. The

selection from Switzerland is more limited, but you'll be sure to find raclette, gruyère and three varieties each of emmenthal and appenzeller.

ALL THE BEST FINE FOODS

1099 Yonge Street (North of Roxborough Street) ☎ 416 928-3330

Monday–Wednesday 8:30–6:30, Thursday–Friday 8:30–7, Saturday 8:30–6, Sunday 10–5

Subway: SUMMERHILL

www.allthebestfinefoods.com

This Rosedale shop has an interesting selection of cheese from France, Switzerland and Quebec that covers everything from well-known classics to hard-to-find varieties. From France, you'll find a huge assortment of popular choices (époisses, comté, morbier, camembert Jort, livarot, mothais, selles-sur-cher, pouligny-saint-pierre and many varieties of brie) to specialized artisanal varieties (chèvre chabichou of Poitou, fourgerus, colombier, Riblaire, champenois and édel de cléron). You'll also find saint-basile, saint-félicien, Lechevalier Mailloux, le pied-de-vent and ange cornu from Quebec, as well as several unpasteurized varieties.

ARZ BAKERY

1909 Lawrence Avenue East (between Warden Avenue and Pharmacy Avenue)
☎ 416 755-5084

Monday-Saturday 8-9:30; Sunday 8-7, statutory holidays 8-5

Subway: LAWRENCE + bus

This empire of Middle Eastern cuisine imports a nice selection of cheese from France, Quebec and Switzerland. Interestingly, you'll also find a good selection of feta cheese from Macedonia, Greece and Bulgaria.

CHEESE BOUTIQUE

45 Ripley Avenue (South of South Kingsway and North of The Queensway)
☎ 416 762-6292

Monday–Friday 8–9, Saturday 8–8, Sunday 10–6

Subway: RUNNYMEDE + bus

www.cheeseboutique.com

As you would expect, Cheese Boutique has an impressive and vast range of cheese from around the world, including 10 or so varieties from Switzerland, 30 from Quebec and more than 100 from France. It's also one of the only shops in Toronto to age imported cheese on the premises, including the hard-to-find French explorateur. Most cheesemongers only import this cheese

for a short time during Christmastime – you will be hard-pressed to find it during the remainder of the year. However, not only will you find explorateur at Cheese Boutique year-round, you can choose between non-aged and aged-on-premises varieties – *magnifique!* Another item of note at Cheese Boutique is the many kinds of artisanal cheeses imported from Quebec.

CHEESE MAGIC

182 Baldwin Street (inside Kensington Market) ☎ 416 593-9531

Monday–Saturday 8:30–7, Sunday 9–6

Subway: SPADINA + streetcar;
QUEEN'S PARK + streetcar

The smallest of the cheesemongers inside Kensington Market, Cheese Magic carries a nice selection of Swiss appenzeller, gruyère, emmenthal and raclette, French roquefort, morbier, bleu d'Auvergne, port-salut and raclette and Quebecois oka, saint-benoît bleu bénédictin, brie and chèvre.

CHRIS' CHEESEMONGERS

93 Front Street East (St. Lawrence Market)
☎ 416 368-5273

Closed Sunday–Monday; Tuesday–Thursday 8–6, Friday 8–7, Saturday 5–5

Subway: UNION

Chris' Cheesemongers is an affiliate of Alex Farm Products, but while the

Did you know?

France produces over 160,000 tonnes of camembert every year – now, that's a lot of cheese!

cheese shops & crème fraîche

latter focuses on French cheese, Chris' Cheesemongers spotlights cheese from Quebec. In fact, the list of *fromages* found here from *la belle province* is simply mind-boggling – more than 60 varieties! To whet your appetite, here's a sampling of what Chris' Cheesemongers has to offer: chèvre noir (black chèvre), grand cru de Chaput, herb double-brie, double-brie au poivre, pied-de-vent and jeune cœur from *Îles-de-la-Madeleine*, capra, freddo, mi-careme from *Île aux Grues* (very similar to camembert from Normandy) and cendré de Warwick (the Quebecois version of morbier). There is also a respectable selection of cheese from France, including chaumes, saint-paulin, brie triple crème, port-salut, bresse bleu, camembert from Normandy, pont l'évêque, boursault, rouy and vacherin Mont-d'Or.

DINAH'S CUPBOARD

50 Cumberland Street ☎ 416 921-8112
Monday–Friday 8–7, Saturday 9–6, closed Sunday (open Sundays in December)
Subway: YONGE or BAY

Although the selection of cheese at Dinah's Cupboard is fairly small, it includes about a half a dozen or so of some of the most popular varieties from France.

GLOBAL CHEESE

76 Kensington Avenue ☎ 416 593-9251
Monday–Friday 8:30–7, Saturday 8–6, Sunday 9–5
Subway: SPADINA + streetcar;
QUEEN'S PARK + streetcar

Vive le fromage! French cheese is well represented at Global Cheese – there are about 25 different types available, including staples like morbier, saint-agur, truffier, fourme d'ambert, champagne, chèvre, saint-andré, saint-paulin, pont l'évêque, bleu d'Auvergne and roquefort. Global Cheese also has a nice selection of cheese from Quebec including herb, pepper and regular varieties of brie, camembert and oka, while gruyère and emmenthal represent the shop's Swiss selection. The best part about shopping at Global Cheese – other than the very reasonable prices – is the free samples you can nibble on before you make your purchase!

LOBLAWS

Various locations across the
Greater Toronto Area.

If you are pressed for time and cannot
pop by your favourite cheese shop, you
can always pick up the basic varieties of
French cheese at Loblaws. While not at
par with most of the other cheesemongers listed here, Loblaws's selection
of cheese from France and Quebec is
still quite respectable. You'll find brie,
camembert, *Boursin, Caprice des Dieux,*
emmenthal, coulommiers, comté, bleu
d'Auvergne, oka, blue cheese and
chèvre. Loblaws also imports raclette
and gruyère from Switzerland.

MAX'S MARKET

2299 Bloor Street West (West of
Runnymede Road) ☎ 416 766-6362

Monday–Wednesday 9–7, Thursday
9–7:30, Friday 9–8, Saturday 9–7,
Sunday 9–6

Subway: RUNNYMEDE

Max's Market stocks a decent variety of
cheese from France, Quebec and
Switzerland including morbier, raclette,
appenzeller, bleu d'Auvergne, fourme
d'ambert, saint-agur, roquefort, chèvre
Riblaire, oka and gruyère.

MENDEL'S CREAMERY
N' APPETIZER

72 Kensington Avenue (inside Kensington
Market) ☎ 416 597-1784

Monday–Friday 8:30–7, Saturday 8–6,
closed Sunday

Subway: SPADINA + streetcar;
QUEEN'S PARK + streetcar

Though Mendel's Creamery n'
Appetizer is small in size, the amount

of French, Swiss and Quebecois cheese
they import is huge! You'll find about
80 kinds from France, 10 from Quebec
and half a dozen from Switzerland.
Must-try French cheeses include morbier, roquefort, saint-paulin, saint-
andré, chèvre from Corsica and brie
bleu (a cross between brie and blue
cheese). When it comes to Quebec, the
oka, camblu (a cross between a camembert and blue cheese) and brie are noteworthy, while Swiss selections include
gruyère, raclette, emmenthal, appenzeller and vacherin Mont-d'Or.

OLYMPIC CHEESE MART

Please refer to our directory on page 132
to find all locations for this merchant.

Talk about selection – more than 400
kinds of cheese under one roof! You're
guaranteed to discover something new
with every visit. Olympic Cheese Mart
has more than 100 types of French
cheese alone. Among the more popular
choices, you'll find camembert, brie *en
brioche,* saint-morgon, saint-andré,

Where to buy AOC cheese year-round

1. Alex Farm Products
2. All the Best Fine Foods
3. Cheese Boutique
4. Chris' Cheesemongers
5. Global Cheese
6. Mendel's Creamery n' Appetizer (Christmastime only)
7. Olympic Cheese Mart
8. Pusateri's Fine Foods
9. Scheffler's Delicatessen
10. Whole Foods Market

cheese shops & crème fraîche

raclette and chèvre. Lesser-known varieties include pepper camembert, gourmelin, époisses, roquefort, comté, beaufort and *p'tit reblo*. There's also an impressive selection of rare cheese from Quebec – mouton noir, saint-ambroise (a cheese made with beer), frère jacques, moine, le douanier, mamirolle, Sir Laurier d'Arthabaska, cantonnier and cheeses from the Plessisville and Saint-Benoît regions. If your tastes lean more towards cheese from Switzerland, you'll find varieties of gruyère, emmenthal, raclette, vacherin fribourgeois, vacherin Mont-d'Or, maréchal, mont vully, weinkäse, tête de moine and three types of appenzeller. Olympic Cheese Mart also imports many cheeses made with raw milk.

PUSATERI'S FINE FOODS

Please refer to our directory on page 132 to find all locations for this merchant.
www.pusateris.com

Pusateri's imports some of the best Franco-European and Quebecois cheese in Toronto. From France you'll find roquefort, époisses, bleu d'Auvergne, saint-agur, etorki, tomme de Savoie, morbier, saint-albray, chaumes and welsche, a rare aged cheese from Alsace. There's also chimay from Belgium and rebloch'art from Quebec.

Did you know?

Cantal is one of the oldest French cheeses, predating both roquefort (dating back to the eleventh century) and livarot (dating back to the thirteenth century).

QUALITY CHEESE

111 Jevlan Drive, Vaughan (corner of Highway 7 and Weston Road)
☎ 905 265-9991
Monday–Friday 8:30–6, Saturday 8:30–5, closed Sunday

This family-owned shop is renowned for its prize-winning cheese, including a rich and creamy French brie.

SCHEFFLER'S DELICATESSEN

93 Front Street East (St. Lawrence Market)
☎ 416 364-2806
Closed Sunday–Monday;
Tuesday–Thursday 8–6, Friday 8–7, Saturday 5–5
Subway: UNION

The St. Lawrence Market has a number of excellent cheesemongers, and Scheffler's Delicatessen is no exception. Imported from France you'll find saint-agur, camembert, saint-andré, l'ermite, chèvre and saint-paulin, as well as cheese made with sheep's milk. There's also Swiss gruyère and emmenthal, and camembert, brie, chèvre, oka, frère jacques and bleu bénédictin from Quebec.

SOBEYS

81 St Clair Avenue East (East of Yonge Street) ☎ 416 413-0594
24 hours a day, 7 days a week
Subway: ST CLAIR

Sobeys' new Yonge and St. Clair location satisfies the needs of neighbourhood francophiles with a variety of French products, including cheese. French selections include saint-aubin, morbier, *p'tit reblo*, saint-paulin, emmenthal, brie, camembert and rustique from Normandy; while closer to home, there is Quebec oka and *chèvre*.

SUN VALLEY FINE FOODS

583 Danforth Avenue (West of Pape Avenue) ☎ 416 469-5227

Monday-Friday 8:30-9; Saturday 8-8; Sunday 8:30-8

Subway: PAPE

Because of its location in the heart of Toronto's Greektown, Sun Valley Fine Foods has developed a reputation for good quality feta. But you probably didn't know it's also also developing a reputation as a purveyor of good quality Franco-European cheese. Although the selection is not extensive, there is gruyère and emmenthal from Switzerland, and about 15 varieties from France, including morbier, tomme de montagne, fourme d'ambert, saint-nectaire, roquefort and bleu d'Auvergne.

THE CHEESE DAIRY

454 Bloor Street West (West of Howland Avenue) ☎ 416 533-3007

Monday-Friday 9-7; Saturday 9-6; Sunday 11-5

Subway: BATHURST

www.thecheesedairy.com

Recommended to us by the owner of Michelle's Brasserie, The Cheese Dairy offers an impressive selection of French and Quebecois cheese. Among the many varieties from France, you'll find saint albray, tome de Pyrénées, tome de Savoie and chaume. From Quebec, The Cheese Dairy offers saint-benoît, victor et bertol, chèvre noir, paillot de chèvre and many others. You'll also discover a wonderful range of seasonal cheeses from *la belle province* and its French cousin!

WHITEHOUSE MEATS

2978 Bloor Street West (East of the Royal York subway) ☎ 416 231-5004

Closed Sunday-Monday; Tuesday-Wednesday 9-6; Thursday 9-8; Friday 9-6; Saturday 8-6

Subway: ROYAL YORK

Whitehouse Meats not only stocks some of the best cuts of meat in the city, it also offers its west-end clients a variety of French cheeses to go with them. You'll find a small selection of classic favourites such as st andré, st agur, brie, camembert, roquefort and st albray (during the Christmas holidays only).

cheese shops & crème fraîche

WHOLE FOODS MARKET

87 Avenue Road (North of Bloor Street)
☎ 416 944-0500
Monday–Friday 9–10, Saturday 9–9,
Sunday 9–9
Subway: BAY or MUSEUM
www.wholefoodsmarket.com

A trip down Whole Foods Market's
cheese aisle reveals an incredible selection of French cheese – fourme d'ambert, comté, tomme de savoie, chaumes,
munster, cantal, crottin de chavignol,
saint-aubin, explorateur, chaource,
montagnou and petit livarot from
Normandy, to name a few. Most cheese
shops in Toronto only import one variety of Swiss gruyère, but at Whole
Foods Market, you'll find three different types! Each has a distinct taste, so
the best way to fully appreciate their
differences is to try them all. Other
Swiss imports include appenzeller,
vigneron and mostkäse. Closer to
home, Whole Foods Market offers an
outstanding (and constantly growing)
variety of rare cheese from Quebec. You
may be surprised to discover a limited
range of hard cheese from New
Brunswick at Whole Foods Market –
Sieur de Duplessis and tomme de
champ doré, both of which are surprisingly good. There are numerous reasons
for a French cheese lover to shop at
Whole Foods Market, but perhaps the
best one is the knowledgeable employees. They will spend the necessary time
to ensure you select the perfect cheese
to match your palate, which makes a
considerable difference when trying
something new.

Did you know?

Crème fraîche is not as fattening as
many Torontonians may think.
According to a study conducted by
French food magazine Elle à table,
crème fraîche is actually much less
fattening than other lipids. Crème
fraîche at 30-35% MF (milk fat) contains only 300 calories, while crème
fraîche at 40% MF contains only 325
calories. Compare these numbers to
some lipids readily found in most
kitchens: butter at 82% MF contains
760 calories, cooking oil at 90% MF
contains a whopping 900 calories
and mayonnaise contains 718 calories. Most of us were happy to
indulge in crème fraîche long before
Elle à table came out with this report!

Crème fraîche

Crème fraîche is a staple in any respectable French kitchen. Unlike the liquid, milky whipping cream readily found in local supermarkets, *crème fraîche* is thick in texture and sour in taste. It is also indispensable in many French soups and desserts. *Crème fraîche* isn't easy to find in Toronto, but there are a few locations that stock it:

ALEX FARM PRODUCTS: Carries bona fide *crème fraîche* from Normandy.

ALL THE BEST FINE FOODS: Stocks a homemade variety of *crème fraîche*.

CHEESE BOUTIQUE: Carries *crème fraîche* imported from France.

CHRIS' CHEESEMONGERS: Located inside the St. Lawrence Market, Chris' Cheesemongers imports its *crème fraîche* from Normandy.

LOBLAWS: This food giant carries *crème fraîche* from England.

MAX'S MARKET: This Bloor West Village shop carries *crème fraîche* from Quebec.

OLYMPIC CHEESE MART: Stocks *crème fraîche* imported from Quebec.

PUSATERI'S FINE FOODS: Carries Quebecois *crème fraîche*.

SCHEFFLER'S DELICATESSEN: Stocks *crème fraîche* from both France and Quebec.

SOBEYS: Due to repeated requests from customers, Sobeys now carries *crème fraîche* from Ontario.

SUN VALLEY FINE FOODS: Located on the Danforth, this is another great source for *crème fraîche* in Toronto.

WHOLE FOODS MARKET: This Yorkville shop carries Ontario-produced *crème fraîche*.

french food shopping

meats, pâtés & terrines

Most local butchers already offer the basics – beef, chicken, veal, lamb and pork – in a variety of cuts, so for our purposes, the focus of this section is strictly on the specialties of the house as well as the essential meats for many French dishes.

meats, pâtés & terrines

ALEX FARM PRODUCTS

Please refer to our directory on page 132 to find all locations for this merchant.

www.alexcheese.com

This cheese empire stocks a decadent treat in its freezers: *merguez* (Moroccan) sausages!

BLOOR MEAT MARKET

2283 Bloor Street West (West of Runnymede Road) ☎ 416 767-2105

Closed Monday; Tuesday-Friday 9-6; Saturday 9-6; Sunday 9-5

Subway: RUNNYMEDE

The majority of the meats and kebabs at Bloor Meat Market have been marinated in a tantalizing house blend of herbs and spices. Even plain chicken breasts are available in dressed-up versions, such as Florentine, Kiev and Cordon Bleu. When it comes to francophone dishes, Bloor Meat Market is the ideal place to find (frozen) Cornish hens, ground bison meat, duck breast, game meat sausages and cuts of meat for Chinese (using beef bouillon instead of oil) and *bourguignonne* (using oil) fondues.

BRANDT MEAT PACKERS LTD.

1878 Mattawa Avenue, Mississauga (South of Dundas Street East) ☎ 905 279-4460

Closed Sunday-Monday; Tuesday 8-6; Wednesday 9-6; Thursday-Friday 8-7; Saturday 7-3

Although Brandt Meat Packers caters mostly to German-Canadians, you'll still find many of the meats needed for French cuisine; including: veal sausages, tongue, kidney and liver, tripe, chicken liver, blood sausages, pheasant thighs, smoked pheasant thighs and whole smoked pheasant. You'll also find the type of ground meat necessary for a real *tartare*. In terms of frozen fare, Brandt Meat Packers offers goose, duck, Cornish hen, pheasant, veal liver and pork fat.

BROWN BROTHERS MEATS

93 Front Street East (St. Lawrence Market) ☎ 416 364-7469

Closed Sunday–Monday; Tuesday– Thursday 8–6, Friday 8–7, Saturday 5–5

Subway: UNION

Brown Brothers Meats sells veal liver, milk-fed veal, filet mignon, cuts of meat for Chinese and *bourguignonne* fondues, and "AA" and "AAA" cuts of beef from Ontario – perfect for your French culinary needs!

CAVALLINO

2995 Islington Avenue (South of Steeles Avenue West) ☎ 416 749-1633

Monday-Sunday 6-7

Subway: ISLINGTON + bus

Leonardo Lorusso is the master butcher behind this well-kept Toronto secret. Cavallino carries a wide selection of well-cut Canadian horse meat. For many French- and Italian-Canadians, horse meat is just another staple ingredient in a fantastic meal. However, horse meat is not very popular amongst Canadians, which is why many Torontonians of French origin often have a tough time finding this rare delicacy. Look no further!

Did you know?

Foie gras is another example of how the French are able to take a technique from another nation or culture, and perfect it to the point where no one could ever imagine it didn't actually originate in France. The technique behind *foie gras* was discovered in ancient Egypt, at the dawn of the third millennium BC. Egyptians, who had long been observing wild geese prepare for the long migration to spend winter in the Nile Delta marshes, noticed with amazement how different the size and taste of these geese livers were compared to the geese they hunted at any other time of the year. Egyptians quickly understood the animals naturally fattened their livers by overfeeding in order to accomplish long migratory flights. One only had to reproduce this operation to discover *foie gras* year-round.

Jews in central Europe inherited these Egyptian techniques and quickly developed a reputation for the delicate taste and perfect size of the liver they raised and sold. In fact, Jews who were in the business of *foie gras* between the fifteenth and eighteenth century became prolific at their craft because they were not allowed to raise pork; therefore, they could rely only on duck and geese farming as a viable business. During the same period, the French in the South of France were renowned across the country for raising the finest *foie gras*. However, many historians claim these Jews and Frenchmen did not influence each other because they had no relationship with each other. *Foie gras* was a favourite amongst royalty, including King Louis XVI, who was especially particular to *foie gras en croûte* (*foie gras* covered with pastry).

CUMBRAE'S NATURALLY RAISED FINE MEATS

481 Church Street (South of Wellesley Street) ☎ 416 923-5600

Monday–Friday 9:30–7, Saturday 9–6, Sunday 11–5

Subway: **WELLESLEY**

Cumbrae's Naturally Raised Fine Meats offers an impressive selection of meats that would make any French dinner memorable – deer, rabbit, duck, quail, sweetbreads, blood sausages, *poussin* (chick), squab, goose, Guinea fowl and pheasant. Depending on the item, you may want to place a special order as many of Cumbrae's meats are imported from Quebec. Cumbrae's also sells duck confit, fat and breast (smoked and non-smoked), chicken and veal kidneys, cuts for fondues, lamb from Quebec and *merguez* sausages, and is also well-known for its pre-seasoned and pre-marinated meats – a wonderful practical solution when you don't want to do all the work yourself! It's also nice to know that the high level of service and knowledge of Cumbrae's staff is as outstanding as its products.

Dried Meats, Pâtés & Terrines

ALEX FARM PRODUCTS This merchant imports a diverse selection of rich delicacies from France such as *foie gras* flavoured with truffles or port wine, as well as duck breast, mousse, confit and *rillettes* (a coarse, highly spiced cold spread made from meat or poultry). From Quebec, you'll find 15 or so flavours of pâté. You'll also find *foie gras* from La Ferme Périgord available in mousse, *rillettes* or pâté.

ALL THE BEST FINE FOODS An exotic assortment of pâtés, *terrines* and mousses from Quebec and Ontario awaits you at All the Best Fine Foods. Be sure to try the green pepper and quail or pepper pâté, the duck and pistachio *terrine* and the truffle or quail and truffle mousse. You'll also find La Ferme Périgord *foie gras* imported from France.

BRANDT MEAT PACKERS LTD. Although this supermarket caters mostly to Canadians of German and Eastern European descent, it has an impressive counter of dried meats that is sure to please most francophiles.

CHEESE BOUTIQUE This cheese shop offers authentic French and Quebecois *foie gras*. There's also six flavours of pâté from Quebec's La Maison du Gibier, a Quebecois *mousse de foie gras* (which makes for a very acceptable substitute at a quarter the price of French *foie gras*) and a decent selection of dried meats.

CHRIS' CHEESEMONGERS Cheese isn't all Chris sells from *la belle province* – you'll also find pâtés and *terrines* from La Ferme Périgord and La Maison du Gibier, as well as a small assortment of duck breast and confit.

CUMBRAE'S NATURALLY RAISED FINE MEATS This is a great place to buy pâtés and *terrines* from Quebec, in the most delicious combination of flavours: pork from Toulouse, duck and green pepper, duck and pink peppercorn, pheasant and pistachio, *pâté de campagne* and wild mushrooms and duck *rillettes*. Cumbrea's Naturally Raised Fine Meats also sells dried sausages *comme les français*, and *foie gras*.

DANIEL ET DANIEL – FOOD SHOP Only a few varieties are available, but the flavours are traditionally French – *pâté de campagne*, pepper and duck *rillettes*.

DINAH'S CUPBOARD This charming gourmet boutique located on Cumberland Street stocks a dozen or so *rillettes*, pâtés and *terrines* from Quebec and a few that are made in Dinah's own kitchen. Choose from *rillettes du Mans*, duck *rillettes*, rabbit *terrine* with pistachios, venison *terrine*, boar *terrine* with apricots and *foie gras*.

GLOBAL CHEESE In this world of cheeses, there's also room for a few pâtés and *foie gras* from Quebec and France!

MAX'S MARKET This shop has an incredibly impressive selection of 15 or so pâtés and *terrines* from Quebec. There's something for every palate, from the traditional to the adventurous, but here's the short list of must-try pâtés: ostrich and blackcurrant, pork and truffle, duck and pistachio, quail, Grand Marnier and pink peppercorn.

MEAT ON THE BEACH This butcher's exotic flavours of *terrines* from

France include pheasant and Corinthian raisin, deer and Cognac and hare – *ooh la la!*

MENDEL'S CREAMERY N' APPETIZER A small selection of pâtés from France and Quebec is available at Mendel's, in rosemary and mushroom, Grand Marnier and pepper and Cognac flavours. There's also *foie gras* from Quebec and France.

OLYMPIC CHEESE MART You'll find an assortment of pâtés and *cretons* (pork pâté) from Quebec. You'll also find *foie gras* from France.

PATACHOU This *pâtisserie* is becoming as well-known for their excellent homemade pâtés as its excellent homemade pastries! Choose from the chicken liver pâté, *pâté de campagne* or duck *foie gras* paté.

PUSATERI'S FINE FOODS Upscale Pusateri's has a reputation for excellence that extends to its pâtés, *terrines* and *foie gras*. For the discerning gourmand, *foie gras* is sold in blocks, in a butter-like pâté spread, with truffles, as a mousse and as a jelly. The selection of pâtés is just as elaborate – you can find duck and orange, cranberry and pheasant, salmon and spinach, smoked trout, Florentine veal and, for traditionalists, pepper cognac.

SCHEFFLER'S DELICATESSEN This merchant imports their pâtés and *terrines* from Quebec, their duck breast and duck *confit* from France, and their *foie gras* from both places. Their selection of pâtés includes about 10 or so exotic flavours such as rabbit and walnut, duck *rillettes*, quail and pear, duck and pistachio, rabbit, pork, blueberry and maple syrup, and caribou and fig.

SOBEYS This supermarket imports exquisite Quebecois pâtés, *terrines* and *foie gras* in a variety of unusual flavours which are sure to pique your curiosity. Be sure to try the ostrich and Corinthian raisin *terrine*, wild meat *terrine* (ostrich, deer, pheasant, bison and boar) and pork and cranberry pâtés.

THE BUTCHER BLOCK CAFÉ This butcher sells *foie gras* from Quebec.

THE BUTCHERS Quebecois *foie gras* and a small selection of pâtés – pheasant, duck and pistachio, deer and smoked trout – can be found at The Butchers.

THE VILLAGE BUTCHER This butcher carries several kinds of pâtés and *foie gras* mousses.

WHITEHOUSE MEATS In this butcher's shop, you'll find a small but respectable selection of pâté, including three different kinds of *foie gras* – mousse, *bloc* (denser texture) and *foie gras de canard entier* (whole pieces). You can also buy duck fat, fatty duck legs for *confit, confit de canard* and *magret* (duck breast).

WHOLE FOODS MARKET This upscale supermarket sells a small assortment of domestic and wild meats preservative-free pâtés from Quebec that are absolutely divine. Whole Foods Market intends to increase the number of Quebecois pâtés they carry, but for now, you'll have to be content with caribou, pork and fig, pork and pistachio, and duck, pork and pistachio flavours.

meats, pâtés & terrines

DI LISO'S FINE MEATS

93 Front Street East (St. Lawrence Market)
☎ 416 601-9780

Closed Sunday–Monday;
Tuesday–Thursday 8–6, Friday 8–7,
Saturday 5–5

Subway: UNION

Delicious French dinners start at Di
Liso's, where you'll find filet mignon,
rabbit, pheasant, quail, goose, duck,
Cornish hen, many cuts of lamb and
cuts of meat well-suited for fondues.

EUROPEAN QUALITY MEATS & SAUSAGES

Please refer to our directory on page 132
to find all locations for this merchant.

The house specialty – very reasonable
prices. Cuts are simple, and easily
adaptable to most types of cuisine.
Unfortunately, in the best Kensington
Market tradition, lineups at European
Quality Meats & Sausages are impres-
sively long. An important criterion is
patience, as the service-by-number system is in operation – but it's well worth
the wait!

GRACE MEAT MARKET

644 College Street (corner of Grace Street)
☎ 416 534-7776

Monday–Wednesday 8–6, Thursday–Friday
8–7, Saturday 8–6, Sunday 10–4

Subway: QUEEN'S PARK + streetcar

This Little Italy butcher serves up
beautiful cuts that will create spectacular francophone dishes. You can buy
rabbit, *poussin*, Guinea fowl and deer
on special order, while readily available
selections include smoked turkey, filet

mignon, Cornish hen, frozen quail,
milk-fed veal, sweetbreads, lamb
sausages, liver, kidney and cuts for fondues.

HIGHLAND FARMS

4750 Dufferin Street (North of Finch
Avenue) ☎ 416 736-6606

Monday–Saturday 7–10, Sunday 8–8

Subway: DOWNSVIEW + bus

Highland Farms offers a selection of
meat that is incomparable to most
supermarkets and rarely seen outside a
butcher's shop, including rabbit, beef
tripe, veal liver, capon and a multitude
of cuts of veal and lamb.

LA BOUCHERIE FINE MEATS INC.

93 Front Street East (St. Lawrence Market)
☎ 416 363-0062

Closed Sunday-Monday; Tuesday-
Thursday 8-6, Friday 8-7, Saturday 5-5

Subway: UNION

La Boucherie Fine Meats has a terrific
selection of AA, AAA and Black
Angus beef from Ontario, as well as
veal kidney, filet mignon, milk- and
grain-fed veal, cuts of meat for Chinese
and *bourguignonne* fondues and numerous cuts of lamb.

MANOS MEATS

93 Front Street East (St. Lawrence Market)
☎ 416 364-2652

Closed Sunday–Monday;
Tuesday–Thursday 8–6, Friday 8–7,
Saturday 5–5

Subway: UNION

Manos Meats carries a small assortment of essentials for French cuisine including veal, liver, filet mignon and cuts of meat for Chinese and *bourguignonne* fondues.

MEAT ON THE BEACH

1860 Queen Street East (West of Rainsford Road) ☎ 416 690-1228

Monday–Friday 7-7, Saturday–Sunday 7-6

Subway: QUEEN + streetcar

Many of the all-grain-fed meats you'll find here are perfect for francophone dishes, including a good selection of game (duck, goose, and squab), smoked turkey, blood sausages, Guinea fowl and rabbit year-round (by special order). Unlike many other butchers in the city, Meat on the Beach carries a full range of offal (organ meats), considered to be a French delicacy. Meat on the Beach also carries *merguez* sausages, multiple cuts of lamb, an incredible assortment of homemade sausages, filet mignon and cuts of meat for Chinese and *bourguignonne* fondues. During the Christmas season, you'll even find pheasant and capon. If you are looking for a change from the everyday, try their bacon-stuffed specialties.

NICOLA'S FINE FOODS

298 Eglinton Avenue West (corner of Avenue Road) ☎ 416 485-4429

Closed Sunday; Monday 11-5; Tuesday-Friday 7-7, Saturday 7-5

Subway: EGLINTON + bus

Nicola's Fine Foods is as discerning about its meats as its customers are. Many of Nicola's meats have received the coveted Honour for Excellence and Quality award from the Royal

We finally found it!

Many Toronto francophiles have been searching high and low for proper French *saucisson* (dried salami-style meat). Admittedly, we, too, have had little luck finding this much sought-after meat – until now. We found two merchants who carry this incredible Quebecois import: Cumbrae's Naturally Raised Fine Meats and Olliffe. Hopefully, they'll be able to keep enough in stock to meet the demand we predict for this must-have product!

Agricultural Winter Fair. When it comes to meat for French cuisine, you can expect to find rabbit, blood sausages, veal liver, mutton, quail, pheasant, goose, duck and cuts of meats for Chinese and *bourguignonne* fondues, as well as a good selection of offal.

OLLIFFE

1097 Yonge Street (North of Roxborough Street) ☎ 416 928-0296

Monday–Thursday 8:30–6:30, Friday 8:30–7, Saturday 8:30–6, Sunday 10–5

Subway: SUMMERHILL

The quality and the high standards at Olliffe are befitting of its Rosedale location. Choice cuts suited to complement any francophone dish include milk-fed veal, *merguez* sausages, duck breast, rabbit, blood sausages, veal liver, pheasant, squab, Cornish hen, poussin, Guinea fowl, fondue meats and quail (fresh during the winter months and frozen the remainder of the year). Some items are available through special order only. During the Christmas holiday season, Olliffe also imports duck *foie gras* and goose from France and Quebec. Olliffe sells a beautiful selection of well-cut meats, but be warned – this butcher is so upscale, prices are not even displayed. In fact, chances are if you have to ask, you probably can't afford it.

Pusateri's Fine Foods

Please refer to our directory on page 132 to find all locations for this merchant.

www.pusateris.com

Pusateri's offers an elegant selection of perfectly marinated and prepared meats. Selections that are sure to please Francophiles include cranberry and fig stuffed quail, Mediterranean quail (wrapped in bacon and stuffed with goat cheese, chipotles and arugula) and the Cornish hen with cranberries. It's never been so easy to serve a French-inspired meal with little or no effort on your part – you only need to choose whether to grill, bake or sauté! Pusateri's is also one of the rare places in Toronto where you'll find Guinea fowl.

Royal Beef

1968 Danforth Avenue (West of Woodbine Avenue) ☎ 416 421-1029

Closed Monday; Tuesday–Wednesday 9–6, Thursday–Friday 9–7, Saturday 9–6, Sunday 10–4

Subway: WOODBINE

Royal Beef meats are sold the same day they are cut – now that's fresh! Another fresh twist is its range of healthy offer-

ings – herb-fed veal scallops and free-range chicken. When it comes to meats that match most French dishes, you'll find rabbit, duck, pheasant, filet mignon, offal, quail, Cornish hen and cuts of meat for Chinese and *bourguignonne* fondues. Blood sausages and Guinea fowl are available by special order, while geese are available exclusively at Christmastime.

Where to buy merguez sausages

Most of the places listed here import these spicy Moroccan sausages from Quebec.

1. Alex Farm Products
2. Cumbrae's Naturally Raised Fine Meats
3. Meat on the Beach
4. Olliffe
5. Scheffler's Delicatessen
6. The Butchers
7. The Village Butcher
8. Whitehouse Meats

St. Lawrence Upper Cut

93 Front Street East (St. Lawrence Market) ☎ 416 362-3142

Closed Sunday–Monday; Tuesday–Thursday 8–6, Friday 8–7, Saturday 5–5

Subway: UNION

Rabbit, milk-fed veal, pheasant, Cornish hen, squab and great cuts of filet mignon are just some of the meats available at St. Lawrence Upper Cut. It's also an excellent place to buy cuts of meat for Chinese and *bourguignonne* fondues (by special order only).

SCHEFFLER'S DELICATESSEN

93 Front Street East (St. Lawrence Market)
☎ 416 364-2806

Closed Sunday–Monday;
Tuesday–Thursday 8–6, Friday 8–7,
Saturday 5–5

Subway: UNION

Scheffler's is one of a handful of places in Toronto that sells Moroccan *merguez* sausages.

SOBEYS

81 St. Clair Avenue East (East of Yonge Street) ☎ 416 413-0594

24 hours a day, 7 days a week

Subway: ST CLAIR

If you live in the Yonge and St. Clair neighbourhood, look to Sobeys for the following French favourites – rabbit, deer medallions, quail and Cornish hen. More game meats are promised to be available in the future.

THE BUTCHER BLOCK CAFÉ

3251 Yonge Street (North of Lawrence Avenue) ☎ 416 544-1729

Monday-Friday 10-7; Saturday 10-6; Sunday 11-6

Subway: LAWRENCE

The ideal shopping spot for barbecue lovers! Not only can you buy the most succulent meats for the grill (including AAA Canadian Black Angus), you can buy the grill itself – The Butcher Block Café also sells top-range barbecues. Another unique feature of The Butcher Block Café is its chef-for-hire service.

Order a chef for an evening or just a few hours to come to your home and cook your meats to perfection. That's sure to impress your guests! Here's something else that's impressive – the selection of AA and AAA Black Angus cuts, rabbit, milk-fed veal, quail, Cornish hen, filet mignon and cuts of meat for Chinese and *bourguignonne* fondues. You'll also be able to find deer, offal and Guinea fowl (by special order). Horse meat is available through very special order (Health Canada has stringent regulations about the sale of horse meat where meat from cows is also sold, due to potential blood contamination; as a result, ordering horse meat is an expensive and often laborious process).

THE BUTCHERS

2636 Yonge Street (North of Eglinton Avenue) ☎ 416 483-5777

Monday–Wednesday 9–6, Thursday–Friday 9–7, Saturday 9–6, Sunday 11–5

Subway: EGLINTON

The name is simple, but the selection is diverse! At The Butchers, you'll find organic AA and AAA lamb, pork and beef, all from Ontario's Beretta Farm, as well as several wild game and fowl including Canadian venison. You'll also find many meats that are sure to please francophiles, such as duck *confit*, duck breast, Cornish hen, deer, rabbit, milk-fed veal and cuts of meat for Chinese and *bourguignonne* fondues. A variety of other meats can be purchased by special order, including squab, duck, goose, Guinea fowl, offal and quail – you can even order horse meat. *Merguez* sausages are another house specialty, for those who like to make Moroccan *tajine* (a stew of veal, lamb, chicken or squab with vegetables).

THE VILLAGE BUTCHER

2914 Lakeshore Boulevard West (near Islington Avenue) ☎ 416 503-9555

Closed Sunday-Monday; Tuesday-Friday 7:30-6; Saturday 7:30-5

Subway: ISLINGTON + bus

Here is a butcher who loves his job! Rupert Grigull, The Village Butcher himself, offers service that is as impeccable as his meats. His selection of French favourites is outstanding – superb cuts of filet mignon, fresh rabbit, milk-fed veal, duck liver, quail, pheasant, deer, Cornish hen, buffalo, blood sausages, squab, liver, kidney (other offal can be bought by special order) and cuts of meat for Chinese and *bourguignonne* fondues. Rupert notes that certain game meats are only available by special order and advises ordering these meats up to three weeks in advance due to the long tenderisation period needed. You'll also want to try The Village Butcher's specialties of the house – organic chicken, and homemade pork, veal, turkey and lamb sausages. As if all this wasn't enough, when asked if The Village Butcher carries hard-to-find *merguez* sausages, Grigull told us that not only does he carry them, he makes them himself!

WHITEHOUSE MEATS

Please refer to our directory on page 132 to find all locations for this merchant.

Whitehouse Meats is the ideal place for lovers of unusual meats, and it only takes one look at their large selection to understand why. House specialties include ostrich, buffalo and venison, while choices of poultry and fowl include *poussin*, Cornish hen, goose, Guinea fowl, duck breast, fresh and frozen pheasant and even squab. They are also one of the few butchers in Toronto to carry game bird (duck, pheasant, quail) and big game (venison, buffalo, elk) stocks. For French dishes, you'll find fabulous cuts of filet mignon and lamb, rabbit, milk-fed veal, sweetbreads and liver sausages (Bayview location only). Whitehouse Meats also carries hard-to-find *merguez* sausages, imported from Quebec, as well as cuts of meats for Chinese and *bourguignonne* fondues and Quebecois black and white blood sausages (both by special order). The staff get high marks for customer service and are happy to offer advice about cuts and selection.

WITTEVEEN MEATS LTD.

93 Front Street East (St. Lawrence Market) ☎ 416 363-6852

Closed Sunday-Monday; Tuesday-Thursday 8-6, Friday 8-7, Saturday 5-5

Subway: UNION

www.witteveens.com

Witteveen Meats offers these great selections: stuffed flank steak, filet mignon, three variations of French pork loin roasts, Black Angus steak, leg of lamb, many varieties of marinated and stuffed chicken and 10 different kinds of kebobs.

fishmongers &
oyster specialists

Breaded, fried, poached, grilled, smoked or raw ... there are almost as many ways to prepare fish as there are varieties. Although seafood is a staple ingredient in French cuisine, a good fishmonger can be as hard to come by as a good hairdresser. The following list should help tremendously.

fishmongers & oyster specialists

AVENUE SEAFOOD

302 Eglinton Avenue West (corner of
Avenue Road) ☎ 416 481-2288

Monday 12-7; Tuesday-Saturday 9:30-7;
Sunday 12:30-6

Subway: EGLINTON + bus

You'll find a good diversity of treasures
from the sea at Avenue Seafood,
including fresh tuna, trout, Alaskan
crab legs, Cuban lobster tails, octopus,
sardines (by special order) and a variety
of salmon, including some from the
West Coast.

BIG FISH MARKET

765 The Queensway (West of Royal York
Road) ☎ 416 259-1585

Closed Sunday–Monday;
Tuesday–Wednesday 10 –6,
Thursday–Friday 10–8, Saturday 10–6

Subway: ROYAL YORK + bus

Big Fish Market has a wonderful selection of fish, shrimp and exotic seafood,
such as Peruvian scallops, lobsters from
Nova Scotia, New Zealand green mussels and several kinds of oysters from
Prince Edward Island and the United
States. They also carry shrimp, craw-
fish, fresh cod and fresh tuna.

BILL'S LOBSTER

599 Gerrard Street East (East of Broadview
Avenue) ☎ 416 778-0943

Monday-Sunday 9:30-7:30

Subway: BROADVIEW + streetcar

Lobster may be Bill's main specialty,
but it is not his only one! He also sells a
wide variety of conventional and exotic
seafood including frog's legs, sea
urchins, clams, trout, crab, a variety of

shrimp and oysters from Canada's East
and West Coasts.

BRANDT MEAT PACKERS LTD.

1878 Mattawa Avenue, Mississauga
(South of Dundas Street East)
☎ 905 279-4460

Closed Sunday-Monday; Tuesday 8-6;
Wednesday 9-6; Thursday-Friday 8-7;
Saturday 7-3

Specialties from the sea include fresh
eel, canned escargots, smoked fish and
preserved or canned fish fillets – Brandt
Meat Packers carries a wide variety,
ranging from sardines to mackerel.

CAVIAR CENTRE

220 Duncan Mills Road (West of Don Mills
Road) ☎ 416 441-9788

Monday-Friday 11-6; closed Saturday-
Sunday (will open by appointment only)

Subway: YORK MILL + bus; PAPE + bus

www.caviarcentre.com

Arguably, caviar is an acquired taste.
But if you enjoy this delicacy of raw
fish eggs, visit Caviar Centre for the
most extensive selection in Toronto. In
addition to French caviar, they also sell
Beluga, Osetra and Sevruga varieties.

CAVIAR DIRECT

93 Front Street East (basement of
St. Lawrence Market) ☎ 416 361-3422

Closed Sunday–Monday;
Tuesday–Thursday 8–6, Friday 8–7,
Saturday 5–5

Subway: UNION

www.caviarforsale.com

Here's a little shop where you'll discover big surprises. Caviar Direct
imports large quantities of Beluga,

Did you know?

Just like wine, oysters require breathing time – you should open oysters half an hour before eating them. It's also recommended that you drain the oysters once you have opened them, because they will secrete juices that are far more fragrant.

Just-bought oysters should not be put in the fridge; instead, place them on ice to keep them fresh. Putting them in the fridge will keep them at a temperature that is too low, and they will lose their flavour.

If you like your oysters raw, you can bring out their flavour by using white pepper. (Purists will tell you not to use shallot vinegar or lemon to flavour oysters, as this will change their true flavour). Of course, the best accompaniment for oysters is a glass of chilled white wine – *magnifique!*

Osetra and Sevruga caviar, as well as a few "Black Label" selections from Iran. Caviar Direct also carries a good assortment of dried and smoked fish, including smoked salmon from Scotland and Canada, smoked trout and smoked mackerel.

CITY FISH MARKET

2929 Dufferin Street (South of Lawrence Avenue) ☎ 416 256-7373

Monday 7:30-3; Tuesday-Thursday 7:30-6; Friday 7:30-7; Saturday 7:30-6; closed Sunday

Subway: LAWRENCE WEST + bus; WILSON + bus

Jovial owner Gus Nikoletsos won't hesitate to do whatever it takes to ensure his patrons leave his shop with the catch of the day – and a smile! Nikoletsos imports many treasures from the sea that are sure to satisfy francophiles' palates. Selection varies depending on the season, but as a rule of thumb you'll find tuna, cod, octopus, clams, oysters, escargots, sea urchins, eel (at Christmastime only), fresh sar-

dines and fresh anchovies. A massive freezer also contains a number of frozen selections: shrimp, giant scallops, mussels, whole crabs and frog legs. Many of the city's sushi chefs have made City Fish Market their sole supplier for tuna – Nikoletsos imports 10 whole fresh tunas of the highest quality every week. Weekends are hopping at City Fish Market, therefore selections tend to disappear quickly.

DIANA'S SEAFOOD

2101 Lawrence Avenue East (near Warden Avenue) ☎ 416 288-9286

Monday 9–7, Tuesday–Friday 9–6, Saturday 9–6, Sunday 10–5

Subway: LAWRENCE + bus; KENNEDY + bus

The best oysters from Canada's East and West Coasts await you at Diana's Seafood.

DOMENIC'S FISH MARKET

93 Front Street East (St. Lawrence Market) ☎ 416 368-1397

Closed Sunday–Monday;

fishmongers & oyster specialists

Tuesday–Thursday 8–6, Friday 8–7,
Saturday 5–5

Subway: UNION

The perfect choices for popular French fish dishes are available at Domenic's Fish Market, including octopus, clams, oysters, fresh tuna and cod and even fresh sardines.

DOMINO FOODS LTD.

93 Front Street East (far end of the basement level of St. Lawrence Market)
☎ 416 366-2178

Closed Sunday–Monday;
Tuesday–Thursday 8–6, Friday 8–7,
Saturday 5–5

Subway: UNION

Domino Foods carries many varieties of canned and preserved fish.

GLOBAL CHEESE

76 Kensington Avenue ☎ 416 593-9251

Monday–Friday 9–7, Saturday 8–6,
Sunday 9–5

Subway: SPADINA + streetcar;
        QUEEN'S PARK + streetcar

Cheese isn't all you'll discover here – there's also several varieties of imported marinated fish, including herring, trout and mackerel.

HIGHLAND FARMS

4750 Dufferin Street (North of Finch Avenue) ☎ 416 736-6606

Monday–Saturday 7–10, Sunday 8–8

Subway: DOWNSVIEW + bus

Tucked away in Highland Farms' freezers, you'll find salmon, tuna, trout, eel, swordfish and sprats (from Belgium).

KENSINGTON MARKET'S FISH HOUSES

Subway: SPADINA + streetcar;
        QUEEN'S PARK + streetcar

► CORAL SEA FISH MARKET

198 Baldwin Street ☎ 416 593-9656

Monday–Saturday 8–6, Sunday 7-7:30

► NEW SEAWAY

195 Baldwin Street ☎ 416 593-5192

Monday-Saturday 7-7; Sunday 8-5

► SEA KINGS

189 Baldwin Street ☎ 416 593-9949

Monday-Sunday 7-6

SEVEN SEAS FISH

196 Baldwin Street ☎ 416 593-9875

Monday-Saturday 8-6; Sunday 9-5

These four neighbouring fishmongers receive their goods from the same supplier, so their prices are in the same (very reasonable) range. As a result, their stores are often incredibly busy and line-ups can be long, particularly on Saturday mornings. Impatient souls may want to consider waiting until the afternoon, Sundays or during the week to do their shopping. When it comes to finding the perfect catch for your French-inspired cooking, the fishmongers in Kensington Market offer scallops, red snapper, sole, crab, mussels, octopus, many varieties of shrimp, fresh and frozen sardines and fresh tuna and cod. Most varieties of fish are fresh; however, many of these shops also have large freezers with ample selections. Most of these shops also carry smoked and dried fish, as well as fresh eel during the winter months. Sea Kings and Coral Sea Fish Market sell sea urchins during the Christmas season.

LOBSTER ISLAND

27 Milliken Boulevard (East of Kennedy
Road) ☎ 416 591-6488

Monday–Saturday 9–5, Sunday 9–noon

Subway: FINCH + bus

Lobster Island sells an impressive array
of lobsters and an equally impressive
assortment of other treasures from the
sea, including oysters from Canada's
East and West Coasts.

MENDEL'S CREAMERY N'APPETIZER

72 Kensington Avenue (inside Kensington
Market) ☎ 416 597-1784

Monday–Friday 8:30–7, Saturday 8–6,
closed Sunday

Subway: SPADINA + streetcar;
QUEEN'S PARK + streetcar

Mendel's carries a small selection of
marinated seafood — herring,
anchovies, mackerel in olive oil and
smoked mackerel and oysters.

MIKE'S FISH MARKET

93 Front Street East (St. Lawrence Market)
☎ 416 368-0876

Closed Sunday–Monday;
Tuesday–Thursday 8–6, Friday 8–7,
Saturday 5–5

Subway: UNION

Mike's Fish Market imports many
items that are sure to please francophones and francophiles. In addition to
their large freezer containing many
varieties of fish and seafood, there is
also fresh tuna, octopus, mussels, red
snapper, clams and oysters. Fresh sardines are available on a monthly basis.
If you're looking for a quick and delicious meal, why not try one of Mike's

Fish Market's varieties of marinated
fish?

NEWPORT FISH IMPORTERS

1140 Dupont Street (East of Dufferin
Street) ☎ 416 537-1278

Monday 7-5; Tuesday-Wednesday 7-6;
Thursday-Friday 7-7; Saturday 7-4;
closed Sunday

Subway: DUFFERIN

If you can't find it at Newport Fish
Importers, it probably doesn't exist!
Choose from about 50 different varieties of fish fillets (!), and about 20
freezers crammed with every kind of
seafood imaginable – shrimp, sole,
giant scallops, lobster and crab are just
a few items offered. You'll also find
salted fish and canned clams. If you're
planning a trip, come on a Tuesday.
That's the day Newport Fish Importers
receives its weekly shipment of fresh
fish and seafood, many of which are
perfect for French-inspired cuisine.
There's fresh cod, sardines and tuna,
octopus, eel, crab, red snapper and
shrimp that are generous in quantity
and size. A rare French delicacy found
here is a bucket of fresh escargots
(escargots has been spotted in other fish
shops in Toronto, however its only purpose was to keep the fish tanks clean –
obviously those fishmongers were not
au courant in the ways of French
seafood!).

OSLER FISH WAREHOUSE

16 Osler Street (corner of Dupont Street)
☎ 416 769-2010

Monday 10–5, Tuesday–Friday 8–7,
Saturday 8–5, closed Sunday

Subway: DUNDAS WEST

fishmongers & oyster specialists

Oyster Specialists

If you're craving oysters, the following are some of Toronto's best suppliers. Most fishmongers sell only one kind of oysters; however, these merchants carry a wide variety of fresh fare straight from Canadian and many other international coasts.

1. Big Fish Market
2. Bill's Lobster
3. Diana's Seafood
4. Lobster Island
5. Oyster Boy
6. Rodney's Oyster House

The variety is plentiful, the service incomparable and the prices reflect the high standards of the shop. Among the selections, you'll discover fresh cod, tuna and sardines, trout, clams, octopus, smoked trout and oyster meat (sold without the shells). If you don't want to spend a lot of time on meal preparation, Pisces's medley of marinated fish kebabs are a tasty alternative and can be ready in just a few minutes. There's also a pre-made, heat-and-serve *bouillabaisse* (traditional French fish soup). As a bonus, you'll receive a lemon to fragrance and flavour your dish with each purchase. *Génial!*

Osler is *the* expert when it comes to fish and seafood imported from Portugal. That said, francophiles will find many items they'll need to prepare their favourite fish dishes, too. Fresh tuna, sardines and cod, octopus from Morocco, salted cod, red snapper, trout, eel and even sea urchins are just some of the things available.

OYSTER BOY

872 Queen Street West ☎ 416 534-3432

Monday–Sunday after 5

Subway: QUEEN + streetcar

Depending on the season, Oyster Boy stocks up to six different varieties of oysters.

PISCES GOURMET

1103 Yonge Street (North of Roxborough Street) ☎ 416 921-8888

Monday 9:30–6:30, Tuesday–Thursday 9–6:30, Friday 9–7, Saturday 9–6, closed Sunday

Subway: SUMMERHILL

Pisces Gourmet has beautiful cuts of fish.

PUSATERI'S FINE FOODS

Please refer to our directory on page 132 to find all locations for this merchant.

www.pusateris.com

Pusateri's offers fresh cod, red snapper, trout, scallops, octopus and many varieties of giant shrimp. The Avenue Road location also has a freezer full of crab, lobster, shrimp and scallops. You'll also find many varieties of canned fish fillets, and Beluga, Osetra and Iranian Sevruga caviar.

RODNEY'S OYSTER HOUSE

469 King Street West (West of Spadina Avenue)
☎ 416 363-8105

Monday–Saturday 11–1 a.m., closed Sunday

Subway: KING + streetcar

www.rodneysoysterhouse.com

Rodney's imports many varieties of oysters from the four corners of the world — Europe, Japan, and Canada's East and West Coasts. Don't be surprised to

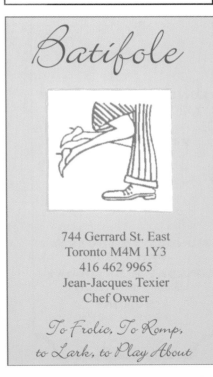

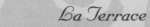

find up to a dozen varieties at any given time, but as a general rule of thumb, you'll find eight or nine kinds in the summer and up to 20 (!) in the winter. Best of all, Rodney is open until 1 a.m. six nights a week to satisfy your late night cravings.

SEAFRONT FISH MARKET

93 Front Street East (St. Lawrence Market) ☎ 416 365-0086
Closed Sunday–Monday; Tuesday–Thursday 8–6, Friday 8–7, Saturday 5–5
Subway: UNION

You'll find fresh tuna and cod, fresh sardines (on occasion), salmon, scallops, clams and mussels, among many other varieties of seafood, at Seafront Fish Market. Check their large freezer when your favourite fish or seafood item is no longer in season – you'll be surprised at what you can find!

SNAPPERS FISH MARKET

263 Durie Street (North of Bloor Street West) ☎ 416 767-4083
Monday–Friday 10–6:30, Saturday 9–6, Sunday 12–5
Subway: RUNNYMEDE

Snappers Fish Market is a haven for those looking for high-quality seafood in the High Park area. Among the varieties in stock are fresh tuna and cod, sole, haddock, red snapper and scallops. Frozen Alaskan crab, escargots, octopus, sardines and lobster tails are also available, as well as a large selection of canned fish fillets. All varieties of fish are readily available at Snappers Fish Market, but if you have a penchant for something a little more out of the ordinary, simply place a special order.

THE VILLAGE BUTCHER

2914 Lakeshore Boulevard West (near Islington Avenue) ☎ 416 503-9555
Closed Sunday-Monday; Tuesday-Friday 7:30-6; Saturday 7:30-5
Subway: ISLINGTON + bus

Seafood at a butcher's? Although you'll only find a small selection of fish at The Village Butcher, it is delivered three times a week to guarantee freshness. Choices include salmon, halibut, scallops, shrimp and tilapia (an Oriental fish that lives off algae — ideal for *meunière* recipes). You can also purchase different kinds of seasonal fish throughout the year.

other french specialties

Though many epicureans and food enthusiasts prefer to buy their items fresh or make them from scratch whenever possible, today's frantic lifestyle doesn't always make this possible. In this section, you'll discover a multitude of shops throughout the Greater Toronto Area that stock the ultimate in convenience and quality – frozen, canned, preserved and ready-to-serve French foods. For added ease, shops that offer frozen French goods have been flagged to stand out at a glance. Take advantage of the wonderful shops and products mentioned here to make your life a little easier on those days when everything is hectic.

other french specialties

ALEX FARM PRODUCTS

Please refer to our directory on page 132 to find all locations for this merchant.

www.alexcheese.com

Just a few of the things found on the shelves at Alex Farm Products – walnut, hazelnut, almond, white and black truffle oils, *Maille* vinegars, preserved *béarnaise* and hollandaise sauces from France's *Delouis Fils* and both natural and *herbes de Provence, fleur de sel,* sold at very reasonable prices. We also spotted a rarity in Toronto: butter made from goat's milk.

FROZEN FRENCH GOODS Alex Farm stocks an impressive assortment of frozen dinners from *La Maison du Gibier.* Among the many delicious delights prepared by this famous Quebecois culinary house you will find: red deer stew, bison *bourguignonne,* stuffed chicken *ballotine,* stuffed boneless duck and duck *magret. La Maison du Gibier* truly triumphs when it comes to adding a touch of sophistication to frozen dinners.

ALL THE BEST FINE FOODS

1099 Yonge Street (North of Roxborough Street) ☎ 416 928-3330

Monday–Wednesday 8:30–6:30, Thursday–Friday 8:30–7, Saturday 8:30–6, Sunday 10–5

Subway: SUMMERHILL

www.allthebestfinefoods.com

This Rosedale shop carries an abundance of gourmet French specialties, including chestnut purée, whole preserved chestnuts, hazelnut and olive oils, nut oil from Périgord, dried chanterelle mushrooms, *cornichons* (small gherkins), Niçoise olives, olives from Nyons, canned *flageolets, Meaux Pommery* mustard, *fleur de sel* from Guérande, *Vilux* and *A l'Olivier* vinegars, and chestnut honey and lavender honey from Provence.

FROZEN FRENCH GOODS Finally, an alternative to the commercial frozen pastry found in grocery stores! All the Best Fine Foods carries exceptional *pâte feuilletée* (flaky pastry) from Rahier.

ARARAT INTERNATIONAL FINE FOODS

1800 Avenue Road ☎ 416 782-5722

Monday-Saturday 9:30-6; closed Sunday

Subway: EGLINTON + bus

Since 1969, Peter and Aurora Kashkarian have been greeting patrons with their warm and engaging personalities. It's almost impossible not to feel an immediate connection with these shop owners, who will gladly help you find spices that aren't always easy to locate elsewhere. Ararat stocks many ingredients essentials for the preparation of your Moroccan dishes. For instance, you'll find three different types of *zataar,* as well as preserved whole lemons, which are the ideal accompaniment to any good *tajine.*

Did you know?

In April 2004, the prestigious *Food & Wine* magazine declared the 200+ year old St. Lawrence Market one of the world's best markets, along with 24 others from cities such as Paris, Milan and Tokyo.

Markets

The experience of market shopping is full of old-world nostalgia, and for convenience and selection, it can't be beat. Most of the products sold in Toronto markets are local or come from Ontario's interior. Frequent visits almost guarantee the vendors will become accustomed not only to your face, but to your personal tastes. In terms of large-scale offerings, Toronto is doubly blessed with the sights, sounds, smells, tastes and textures of both St. Lawrence and Kensington Markets. During the summer months, the city and the Greater Toronto Area play host to a variety of smaller specialty, farmers and organic markets (consult your local newspaper for further information).

HIGHLAND FARMS
☎ (416) 736-6606
Subway: DOWNSVIEW + bus

Highland Farms is definitely a "super market" – the selection of breads, meats, fruits and vegetables (many from Ontario) is ample and diverse enough to rival the St. Lawrence or Kensington. Not to mention, Highland Farms carries a lot of seasonal fruits and vegetables that you simply won't find anywhere else (for example, yellow beets and red carrots during Christmastime). The abundance of fresh herbs available during the summer months is also impressive. Best of all, the prices at Highland Farms are more than reasonable, which makes it tempting to try many things that you might not try otherwise. Highland Farms also carries several of the most common varieties of cheese from France and Quebec, as well as an assortment of breads of diverse ethnic origins. If you're

an olive lover, Highland Farms has enough types in stock to make you feel like a kid in a candy store.

KENSINGTON MARKET
Subway: SPADINA + streetcar;
　　　　QUEEN'S PARK + streetcar

Baldwin Street and Spadina Avenue mark the spot for this Toronto treasure that carries everything from meat to cheese to spices. Kensington Market has a dual attraction – not only are all the goods for classical and nouvelle French cuisine readily available, but the market is only steps away from Chinatown ... even the most ardent French food lover needs a little variety once in a while! Perhaps the only drawback to Kensington Market is Toronto's chilly winter – outdoor shopping in icy winds and snow definitely isn't for everyone!

ST. LAWRENCE MARKET
Subway: UNION
www.stlawrencemarket.com
The St. Lawrence Market is an ideal one-stop shopping destination for essentials from France, Morocco and Quebec. Permanent vendors are located in the South building – here you can find butchers, cheese shops, fishmongers and bakers that will supply most of the staples for your next French, Moroccan or French-Canadian meal. On Saturdays, the North building hosts a farmers' market, featuring local goods such as fruits, vegetables, honey, maple syrup, fruit tarts and cheese. The selection is always fresh and delicious, so it's no wonder regulars make the St. Lawrence Market a weekly pilgrimage!

other french specialties

We also found juniper berries for your sauerkraut. Ararat was one of the first places in Toronto to carry imported chocolates from France – indeed, many sugary and chocolatey French treats await you here.

ARZ BAKERY

1909 Lawrence Avenue East (between Warden Avenue and Pharmacy Avenue)
☎ 416 755-5084

Monday-Saturday 8-9:30; Sunday 8-7; statutory holidays 8-5

Subway: LAWRENCE + bus

The Lebanese and Middle Eastern goods at Arz Bakery make it a great place to discover a more exotic side to French culture. France's history with Lebanon in the nineteenth and twentieth centuries resulted in many aspects of French culture being integrated into Lebanese culture – including food. Regulars insist the pita bread at Arz Bakery is the best in the city. You'll also find many varieties of bulgur wheat and couscous, as well as *harissa* paste to flavour your Lebanese or Moroccan dishes and a diverse assortment of nuts and seeds. There's a generous olive counter, including Tunisian olives sold in packages, and a large selection of olive oils from Lebanon, Italy, Spain and Greece. The rose and orange blossom waters sold at Arz Bakery are rare finds in Toronto (orange flower water is one of the ingredients needed to make *madeleines*). Take heed, Mediterranean-cuisine lovers: a dozen types of saffron line the shelves of Arz Bakery. Not only will you be satisfied with the wide variety, you'll also be pleased with the range of prices for this exclusive spice.

Did you know?

The first espresso machine was not invented in Italy, as many may be inclined to believe, but in France by a Monsieur Lebrun in 1838. This indispensable machine was then manufactured in Italy, and presented for the first time at the Paris EXPO in 1855.

Source: Balzac's Coffee House

BALZAC'S COFFEE HOUSE

Please refer to our directory on page 132 to find all locations for this merchant.
www.balzacscoffee.com

Honoré de Balzac was one of the most prolific French writers of his time. He was also an avid coffee drinker. Balzac's love of coffee was one of the motivating factors that inspired owner and coffee connoisseur Diana Olsen when it came time to find a name for her coffee house. Balzac's Coffee House is one of the only coffee houses in Toronto to roast its beans using the French method rather than the Italian method, resulting in a coffee that is richer and more intense in flavours. Alongside the outstanding coffee, this coffee house also serves exceptional tea. It's true you can purchase *Mariages Frères* tea in a few stores in Yorkville, but only here can you order a cup of this luxurious brewed tea for your enjoyment. To learn more about the many flavours of coffee and tea served at Balzac's, visit their Web site.

BONJOUR BRIOCHE

812 Queen Street East (East of Broadview
Avenue) ☎ 416 406-1250

Closed Monday, Tuesday–Friday 8–5,
Saturday 8–4, Sunday 8–3

Subway: QUEEN + streetcar

Bonjour Brioche's signature vinaigrettes
and homemade jams – the very same
ones that accompany their salads and
baguettes – are now available to take
home!

BRANDT MEAT PACKERS LTD.

1878 Mattawa Avenue, Mississauga
(South of Dundas Street East)
☎ 905 279-4460

Closed Sunday-Monday; Tuesday 8-6,
Wednesday 9-6, Thursday-Friday 8-7,
Saturday 7-3

Diverse treasures from around the
world await you at Brandt Meat
Packers. Look no further for hard-to-
find whole and puréed chestnuts, several varieties of French mustard,
preserved sauerkraut, dried and canned
mushrooms, whole preserved cherries
in syrup, *pain d'épices* (ginger bread)
and – *quelle surprise!* – canned *bouillabaisse.* Flavoured syrups are another
specialty of Brandt Meat Packers.
Choose from the well-known French
brand, *William*, or brands from Eastern
Europe, available in many flavours.

CHEESE BOUTIQUE

45 Ripley Avenue (South of South
Kingsway and North of The Queensway)
☎ 416 762-6292

Monday–Friday 8–9, Saturday 8–8,
Sunday 10–6

Subway: RUNNYMEDE + bus

www.cheeseboutique.com

There's more to Cheese Boutique than
just cheese! *William* syrups, canned *flageolets*, canned Dupuy lentils, multiple
brands of canned fish and French mustard, AOC oils from Provence, *herbes de
Provence,* truffles, nut and hazelnut oils,
fleur de sel from Guérande, fresh
chanterelle mushrooms, numerous
flavours of vinegar from *Vilux* and vinegar and vinaigrettes from *Maille* are just
some of the French fare offered here.
You'll also be able to buy your cheese
girolle. Prices may be slightly higher
than elsewhere in the city, but the quality and selection more than compensates.

CHRIS' CHEESEMONGERS

93 Front Street East (St. Lawrence Market)
☎ 416 368-5273

Closed Sunday–Monday;
Tuesday–Thursday 8–6, Friday 8–7,
Saturday 5–5

Subway: UNION

Chris' Cheesemongers sells nut oils
from the French *huilerie Lapalisse*, preserved truffles, French mustard, almond
oil and imported champagne vinegar.

CLAFOUTI

915 Queen Street West (East of Strachan
Avenue, across from Trinity Bellwoods
Park) ☎ 416 603-1935

Closed Monday; Tuesday–Saturday 8–6,
Sunday 9–5

Subway: OSGOODE + streetcar

Clafouti carries a few essential French
specialties, including whole preserved
and canned chestnuts, canned *flageolets*
(French beans), preserved white asparagus, jams from France and Belgium,

other french specialties

William syrups and *fleur de sel*. You'll also find many French specialties prepared by pastry chef Boris Dosne such as savoury ham, cheese or asparagus croissants, sandwiches served on baguettes or croissants, quiches and a traditional favourite, *croque-monsieur* (open-face toasted sandwich made with egg, cheese and ham). Clafouti also sells an impressive selection of *Bonne Maman* jams and *compote* (stewed fruit).

DANIEL ET DANIEL – FOOD SHOP

248 Carlton Street (corner of Parliament Street) ☎ 416 968-9275

Closed Sunday; Monday–Saturday 7:30–6

Subway: CASTLE FRANK + bus;
             COLLEGE + streetcar

www.danieletdaniel.ca

The wide selection of gourmet and imported French food items found at Daniel et Daniel include rose and violet petal confit, packaged chestnuts, several varieties of vinegar and a large assortment of flavoured *William* syrups. As one of Toronto's premier caterers, we strongly suggest you try the following dishes: quiche, baguette sandwiches, chicken *en croûte* (wrapped in flaky dough), *pissaladière* (a French pizza-like dish made with caramelized onions, tomatoes and black olives), *tourtière* (meat pie), *cassoulet* (casserole of white and several kinds of meat and poultry), *boeuf bourguignon*, crêpes and creole shrimp. Then again, it really doesn't matter what you choose at Daniel et Daniel – these caterers master every dish!

DINAH'S CUPBOARD

50 Cumberland Street ☎ 416 921-8112

Monday–Friday 8–7, Saturday 9–6; closed Sunday (open Sundays in December)

Subway: YONGE or BAY

Dinah stocks her Cupboard with these specialty items from France – *Vilux* vinegars, *Meaux Pommery* mustards, *fleur de sel* from Guérande, preserved truffles and truffle oil.

DOMINO FOODS LTD.

93 Front Street East (far end of the basement level of St. Lawrence Market) ☎ 416 366-2178

Closed Sunday–Monday; Tuesday–Thursday 8–6, Friday 8–7, Saturday 5–5

Subway: UNION

Domino Foods is one of the city's hidden gems. This tiny, out-of-the-way shop is a treasure trove of rare and exclusive French gourmet products. For starters, you'll find what is likely the most complete selection of St. Dalfour jams in Toronto. Domino Foods also stocks wine vinegar from the Champagne region, canned chestnut purée, vanilla oil from Tahiti, *fleur de sel* and many flavours of *William* syrups. Rarer finds include cognac and violet mustards, walnut vinegar and about 16 kinds of dried mushrooms, such as chanterelles, morels, porcini, portobello and white truffles.

EPICUREAL

☎ 416 244-1177 • 1-800-206-1177
www.epicureal.com

Epicureal is one of Canada's largest online source for gourmet specialty foods. You'll find more than 800 hand-selected products from around the world. Among the vast assortment of French favourites to choose from are *Valrhona* chocolates, chestnuts, truffles, *foie gras,* caviar, mustards, escargots, *fleur de sel, cornichons,* canned *flageolets,* specialty oils and vinegars. Epicureal.com makes shopping for these essential but often hard-to-find gourmet items an easy and convenient experience. While the epicureal.com Web site is new, the company and the people behind it have been importing high quality products for almost 50 years. *Bon appetit!*

GREAT COOKS

Please refer to our directory on page 132 to find all locations for this merchant.
www.greatcooks.ca

Forfeit boring and tasteless food courts for the delicious and satisfying fare at Great Cooks. Although Great Cooks is a cooking school, the chefs also prepare a variety of diverse dishes from around the world. French specialties prepared by chef Jean-Pierre Challet include goat cheese tarts and poached salmon. Quality and freshness are evident with every bite, and prices are quite reasonable – although if you don't get there early, you may be out of luck. Luckily, owners Esther and Maggie recently opened a chic eatery whre they serve innovative dishes all day long.

HARVEST WAGON

Please refer to our directory on page 132 to find all locations for this merchant.

Harvest Wagon is one of the few places in Toronto that sells chanterelle and morel mushrooms. They also have a nice selection of fresh herbs, canned *flageolets* and *fleur de sel.*

HOLT RENFREW – EPICURE & GOURMET SHOPS

50 Bloor Street West (corner of Bay Street)
☎ 416 922-2333

Monday–Wednesday 10–6,
Thursday–Friday 10–8, Saturday 10–6,
Sunday 12–6

Subway: YONGE or BAY

This luxury Canadian retailer has a French soul, judging by the many Franco-European gourmet goods it carries from brands such as *Fauchon, Neuhaus* and *Mariage Frères.* When it comes to luxury food items, *Fauchon* raises the standards. Holt Renfrew offers a tempting array of their products, like candied chestnuts, vinegars, *fleur de sel,* mustards, cookies and teas,

other french specialties

not to mention a selection of jams in some of the most exotic and original flavours – apricot with jasmine, Calvados apple, Cavaillon melon, clementine, mango and peach, Morello cherry, and pear and vanilla bean. You'll also find other decadent items such as a spreadable hazelnut paste from *Neuhaus* and *Mariage Frères* teas. For tea connoisseurs, Holt Renfrew carries a recipe book from the famous French house of tea *Éloge de la cuisine au thé.*

K.I.S. GLOBAL FLAVORS

☎ 905 477-0024
www.kisglobalflavors.com

K.I.S. Global Flavors' Web site is resplendent with upscale food items from France, Switzerland and Italy. Among the French products you'll find are olive-shaped chocolates, *marrons glacés* (sugar-coated chestnuts), candied

fruits, candied oranges, chocolate-covered lemons, *calissons* (almond treats) from Aix en Provence, nougat, truffles, flower-based jellies and Provence flower honey. K.I.S. Global Flavors also carries many attractive gift baskets – the perfect solution for elegant gift-giving. Just a few clicks and you're all set!

LE GOURMAND

152 Spadina Avenue (South of Queen Street) ☎ 416 504-4494
Monday-Friday 7–8, Saturday 9–6, Sunday 9–4
Subway: OSGOODE + streetcar;
SPADINA + streetcar

Le Gourmand lives up to its name by stocking only the finest French foods, such as white truffle olive oil, grapeseed oil from *Vilux, Meaux Pommery* mustard, walnut oil and vinegar from the house of Clovis. You'll also find French jams, honey and cookies, as well as a few well-chosen selections of Quebecois cheese and *foie gras*. Variety abound at Le Gourmand, but if you're unable to find the French *délice* of your choice, you might want to place a special order for any hard-to-find items.

FROZEN FRENCH GOODS Le Gourmand sells frozen dinners from *La Maison du Gibier*, including red deer stew, bison *bourguignon* and stuffed boneless duck.

LOBLAWS
Various locations across the Greater Toronto Area

This national chain imports many French specialty items like *Maille, Meaux Pommery, Vilux* mustards and vinegars (including cognac and champagne flavours) and an impressive assortment of St. Dalfour jams in flavours that are not easily found elsewhere – black raspberry, royal fig, mirabelle, orange and ginger, and pineapple and mango.

FROZEN FRENCH GOODS True, nothing compares to the real thing, but Loblaws sells a surprisingly good assortment of French-inspired hors d'œuvres, desserts, breakfast and dinner items in their President's Choice® line, including butter croissants, mini chocolate *éclairs*, profiteroles, *cassoulet* and quiche Lorraine.

MA MAISON
4243 Dundas Street West (East of Royal York Road) ☎ 416 236-2234

Closed Monday; Tuesday-Wednesday 8-6; Thursday-Friday 8-7; Saturday 8-6; Sunday 8-4

Subway: **ROYAL YORK** + bus

www.UR2Busy2Cook.com

No time to cook? No problem! Choose one of your favourite containers (they will use your container if you provide it) and head to Ma Maison to have it filled with deliciously prepared French specialties. These ready-to-serve selections are ideal meals for those who may not have time to prepare food from scratch and who want to avoid fast food. There are no compromises here. Chef Patrick Alléguède uses only fresh ingredients to prepare French meals so good, you may never again visit a fast-food chain. *Coq au vin*, veal stew, pork fillet, *cassoulet*, quiches, sandwiches and *tourtières* are just some of the selections you might consider among the 10 or so vacuum-packaged meals. You'll also find a few French cheeses and excellent homemade jams. Homemade pâté is a house specialty (follow the example set by the regulars and opt for at least two or three different flavours at a time). Ma Maison is veritable one-stop-shopping for French food in Toronto's west-end.

Where to find fleur de sel

1. Alex Farm Products
2. All the Best Fine Foods
3. Cheese Boutique
4. Clafouti
5. Dinah's Cupboard
6. Domino Foods Ltd.
7. Harvest Wagon
8. Holt Renfrew
9. Pusateri's Fine Foods
10. Scheffler's Delicatessen
11. Whole Foods Market

other french specialties

Max's Market

2299 Bloor Street West (West of
Runnymede Road) ☎ 416 766-6362

Monday–Wednesday 9–7, Thursday
9–7:30, Friday 9–8, Saturday 9–7,
Sunday 9–6

Subway: RUNNYMEDE

A huge counter of ready-to-serve meals
includes a dozen or so varieties of rich
stuffed crêpes – choose from chicken
and pesto, ham and cheese, mushroom
and salmon and seafood. Max's Market
also sells a dozen flavours of *Vilux* vinegar. Olive aficionados will be excited to
discover more than 20 different kinds
at Max's Market, including several
stuffed varieties.

Did you know?

Dijon mustard sparks thoughts of
fields of yellow blooms somewhere in
the South of France. Indeed, Dijon
mustard was once grown in the Dijon
region (hence the name); however,
the Second World War terminated the
cultivation of mustard seeds in the
region. Many French men and women
who pride themselves on the impeccable quality and taste of their mustard might be disappointed and
surprised to find out that Dijon mustard really started in Canada *(est-ce
possible?)*. Indeed, Saskatchewan is
the world's single largest international producer of mustard seed. In
fact, the Dijon mustard that is served
in some of the finest and most exclusive French restaurants in the world
is as Canadian as maple syrup!

Mercatto

Please refer to our directory on page 132
to find all locations for this merchant.

This Italian merchant has a small but
satisfying assortment of French products, such as walnut and olive oils from
Provence and *herbes de Provence.*

Olympic Cheese Mart

Please refer to our directory on page 132
to find all locations for this merchant.

Truffles, specialty olive oils, vinegars and
vinaigrettes from *Maille* are just some of
the French goods found at Olympic
Cheese Mart. You'll also find a rarity in
Toronto – *Kressi* Swiss vinegar, the ideal
seasoning for hollandaise sauce. Rarer
still – Olympic Cheese Mart has a *girolle*
machine (machine that shaves cheese
from big wheels)! If you're looking for
the perfect item to bring to a pot luck,
shower or party, consider a French
cheese tray from Olympic Cheese Mart.
Ask the staff about this easy, elegant
and tasty solution.

Pain Perdu

736 St Clair Avenue West (West of Christie
Street) ☎ 416 656-7246

Closed Monday; Tuesday-Friday 8-7;
Saturday 8-5; Sunday 8-4

Subway: ST CLAIR WEST + streetcar

www.painperdu.com

When quiches look, smell and taste as
good as the ones at Pain Perdu, why
bother going anywhere else? Or, if
you're after something savoury, try the
onion tart. Hungry regulars are keen to
line up for the terrific quiche and salad
or tart and salad specials. *Le Yannick* is

Spices

Variety is the spice of life, and variety in spices is the key to French cuisine. Most stores in the city cover the basic garden variety, but when you're in need of something specific, nothing but an expert will do. Here are a few locations that offer a more than impressive selection of herbs and spices.

BULK BARN

www.bulkbarn.ca

Spices from around the world ranging from the familiar to the exotic are sold at unbeatable prices at 21 Bulk Barn locations across the GTA.

CASA AÇOREANA

Kensington Market ☎ 416 593-9717

Casa Açoreana boasts a plentiful range of spices sold in bulk. It's the perfect place to visit if you are introducing a new spice to your collection or trying out a recipe for the first time. You'll find everything you need for most of your French-inspired dishes such as honeysuckle, marjoram, sage, tarragon and thyme, as well as Provence herb mix and saffron at very reasonable prices. Casa Açoreana is also a great place to find dried juniper berries – elusive until now! You'll also find yellow and black mustard grains, dried lavender, dried flageolets (small, pale green kidney-shaped beans), four types of lentils and pure vanilla bean extract and vanilla beans imported from Madagascar.

DOMINO FOODS LTD.

St. Lawrence Market ☎ 416 366-2178

Domino Foods sells many herbs essential for French cuisine in bulk including anise, chives, honeysuckle, laurel leaves, marjoram, Provence herb mix, rosemary, saffron, sage, tarragon, thyme and vanilla beans.

HOUSE OF SPICE

Kensington Market ☎ 416 593-9724

This little shop imports spices from all corners of the globe – laurel leaves, Provence herb mix, saffron, tarragon, thyme and yellow and black mustard grains are just a few of the staples you'll find for French dishes. You'll also find vanilla beans from Madagascar and liquorice roots. If you're looking for spices for North African dishes, House of Spice is the perfect place to find harissa, zataar and raz el hanout.

PEROLA

Kensington Market ☎ 416 593-9728

Although Hispanic and Brazilian specialties are the order of the house, French cuisine enthusiasts will be impressed to learn Perola also dries their own bouquets of herbs, including basil, rosemary and sage.

STRICTLY BULK

Various locations across the Greater Toronto Area ☎ 416 766-3319

A veritable Mecca for bulk spices! Variety and selection abound, and the prices are extremely affordable – you can even find notoriously expensive saffron and pure vanilla extract at a reasonable cost.

other french specialties

an absolute must-try. At Pain Perdu, a simple slice of sourdough bread is transformed into an addictive *tartine*. Other popular French specialties include homemade mayonnaise, vinaigrettes and jams, and an organic maple syrup from Lake Erie (the same syrup served with the shop's signature *pain perdu*).

PATACHOU

Please refer to our directory on page 132 to find all locations for this merchant.

In addition to their signature vinaigrettes and homemade jams, Patachou sells flavoured olive oils from France. Choose from the following fragrant blends – chili, basil, *herbes de Provence* and lemon. Patachou also offers a take-out menu and weekend take-out menu. The take-out menu includes *confit de canard* (duck confit served with braised red cabbage and polenta), *bœuf bourguignon* (French beef stew), *agneau navarin* (lamb stew with zucchini, white turnips, carrots, fresh rosemary and thyme), *portobello farcis* (portobello mushrooms stuffed with ratatouille and goat cheese), Israeli couscous (couscous with roasted peppers, black olives, capers and almonds) and *pissaladière*. The weekend take-out menu offers many delicious dishes that are ideal for a dinner *à deux* enjoyed at home. Or, why not try one of Patachou's delicious prepared goods, such as quiches, sandwiches and salads?

PÂTISSERIE D'OR

301 Robinson Street, Oakville (South of Lakeshore Road) ☎ 905 815-8999
Closed Monday–Tuesday;

Wednesday–Friday 8–5:30, Saturday 8–6, Sunday 8–6

Chef Jean-Luc Soulabaille makes one of the best quiches in the Greater Toronto Area – delicate, silky and lighter than air. You'll also want to try the meat and salmon pies, which are equally outstanding.

FROZEN FRENCH GOODS Ingeniously, Soulabaille has created frozen, bake-and-serve versions of many of his most popular items, so you can enjoy them whenever you want! Simply slip these French goodies in your oven and *voilà!* Before you know it, you'll be able to enjoy hot, fresh and delicious pastries and more in the comfort of your home. Choose from baguettes, buns, chocolate croissants, croissants, cookie dough, raisin danishes, *vol-au-vent* (pastry shells) and the house specialty – quiche. Another tempting frozen treat at Pâtisserie d'Or is the extraordinary homemade ice cream, made with fresh ingredients and no preservatives. Flavours are classic and bursting with taste – blackcurrant, caramel, chocolate, coffee, green apple, lemon, pistachio, raspberry, strawberry and, of course, vanilla.

PÂTISSERIE SAINT HONORÉ

2945 Bloor Street West (corner of Grenview Boulevard, East of Royal York Road) Note: no telephone is available

Closed Monday; Tuesday–Thursday 8-7, Friday 8–9, Saturday 8–7, closed Sunday
Subway: ROYAL YORK

Pâtisserie Saint Honoré's house specialties should not be missed – quiche, French onion soup, pâté sandwiches and a mouth-watering *pissaladière*. You'll also find well priced *cornichons* sold in bulk.

PETIT GÂTEAU

2365-B Lakeshore Road, Oakville (West of Bronte Road) ☎ 905 847-1888

Closed Sunday-Monday; Tuesday-Friday 9-6, Saturday 8:30-5

Tourtière is a traditional Quebecois meat pie that tastes even more delicious when someone else has prepared it! Luckily, *tourtières* are a specialty of Petit Gâteau. In addition to the traditional beef and pork variety, Petit Gâteau also offers salmon and chicken *tourtières*. Be sure to order in advance to avoid disappointment!

PUSATERI'S FINE FOODS

Please refer to our directory on page 132 to find all locations for this merchant.

www.pusateris.com

Pusateri's upscale products (with prices to match) may not be suitable for everyday meals, but if you are celebrating a special occasion and willing to splurge a little, this is a shop you simply must visit. Among the French favourites you'll find – sugar-coated and packaged chestnuts, preserved truffles, *fleur de sel*, olive, walnut and almond oils and fresh chanterelle mushrooms (elusive at the best of times!). Pusateri's tempting ready-to-serve dishes are the perfect solution for harried (and hungry) francophiles. French-inspired selections include grilled Cornish hen, *gratin dauphinois* (layered baked potato dish) made with real butter and *salade niçoise*.

Did you know?

Canned food was invented at the end of the nineteenth century in France. The great Emperor Napoleon Bonaparte instigated the canning movement, because he needed a reliable source of nourishment for his troops. Victory is so much easier on a full stomach!

FROZEN FRENCH GOODS Pusateri's Fine Foods carries frozen porcini mushrooms.

QUALIFIRST FOODS

☎ 416 244-1177

www.qualifirst.com

Since 1957, Qualifirst has been importing fine foods from around the world to discerning epicureans who value quality above price. Visit its Web site for the full range of culinary creations, including a diverse and impressive collection of gourmet French goods sure to delight even the most discriminating francophile – Qualifirst carries everything from mustards to black winter truffles.

RAHIER

1586 Bayview Avenue (South of Eglinton Avenue) ☎ 416 482-0917

Closed Monday–Tuesday, Wednesday–Friday 8–5, Saturday 8–4, Sunday 8–3

Subway: EGLINTON + bus

There are always several flavours of delicious quiche on offer at Rahier on the weekends, such as cheese and red pepper, broccoli and cheddar, smoked salmon and asparagus, eggplant and

other french specialties

Where to find flageolets

1. All the Best Fine Foods (canned)
2. Casa Açoreana (dried)
3. Cheese Boutique (canned)
4. Clafouti (canned)
5. Harvest Wagon (canned)
6. Scheffler's Delicatessen (canned)

leek and quiche Lorraine (with ham).

FROZEN FRENCH GOODS Frozen goods that can be found at Rahier include homemade sherbets and ice creams, pastry shells, raspberry coulis, chocolate sauce, and *pâte feuilletée*.

SCHEFFLER'S DELICATESSEN

93 Front Street East (St. Lawrence Market)
☎ 416 364-2806

Closed Sunday–Monday;
Tuesday–Thursday 8–6, Friday 8–7,
Saturday 5–5

Subway: UNION

Scheffler's carries *fleur de sel*, saffron, canned *flageolets*, cream of chestnut dessert spread, preserved morel mushrooms, truffles, *Maille* vinegars, bottled vinaigrettes and Moroccan and French *cornichons*.

THE VILLAGE BUTCHER

2914 Lakeshore Boulevard West (near Islington Avenue) ☎ 416 503-9555

Closed Sunday-Monday; Tuesday-Friday
7:30-6; Saturday 7:30-5

Subway: ISLINGTON + bus

During the Christmas season, The Village Butcher sells traditional French-Canadian *tourtières*. But be warned – this is not a last-minute purchase. You'll have to put your order in ahead of time, as these *tourtières* go like hot cakes!

WHOLE FOODS MARKET

87 Avenue Road (North of Bloor Street)
☎ 416 944-0500

Monday–Friday 9–10, Saturday -
Sunday 9–9

Subway: BAY or MUSEUM

www.wholefoodsmarket.com

Whole Foods Market has a large selection of French specialty items in stock. Add the finishing touches to your French cuisine with olives from Nyons, *Meaux Pommery* mustard, *Delouis Fils* hollandaise sauce, *béarnaise* sauce, garlic and Caesar mayonnaises, a small selection of preserved truffles and dried mushrooms (morel, trumpets and porcini). This is one of the few places in Toronto where you'll find AOC olive oils from Provence. You'll also find other AOC olive oils that have won numerous gold and silver awards of excellence, as well as *fleur de sel* in two flavours – natural and *herbes de Provence*.

ZANE PÂTISSERIE & BOULANGERIE

1852 Queen Street East (West of Woodbine Avenue) ☎ 416 690-2813

Closed Monday, Tuesday–Sunday
7:30–5:30

Subway: QUEEN + streetcar

Every weekend, owner and pastry chef Mo Zane prepares half a dozen scrumptious quiches, including ham and bacon, and vegetarian and smoked salmon.

bistros & fine dining

Is fine dining a thing of the past? Many people mistakenly think that French cuisine can only be a pricey proposition, but nothing could be further from the truth. French cuisine can easily be adapted to suit any palate or budget. Here in Toronto, many chefs and owners of French restaurants have modified their menu to allow a great number of Torontonians and visitors to sample the pleasures of superbly prepared French cuisine at an attractive price. Whether you choose fine or casual dining, French cuisine is all about *savoir-faire*, high-quality ingredients, impeccable presentation and an abundance of love and passion.

We highly recommend you try the some of the numerous French restaurants in our city. Be sure to also try the many delicious Belgian and Moroccan delicacies.

Bon appétit!

bistros & fine dining

ARLEQUIN

134 Avenue Road (corner of Davenport Road) ☎ 416 964-8686

Closed Monday;Tuesday-Saturday for dinner; Friday-Sunday for brunch and lunch

Subway: MUSEUM

Arlequin may have new management, new decor and a new chef, but the cozy and welcoming atmosphere of this neighbourhood bistro has not changed. Chef (and owner) Scott Saunderson's menu is pure Parisian bistro – braised lamb shank, duck confit, *coq au vin, cassoulet* and classic Angus steak and *frites*

served with homemade *aïoli* are just some of the choices. Meats are cooked and seasoned to perfection. For dessert, a velvety crème brûlée, exquisite chocolate cake and tangy lemon tart are worth a look. Wines from many different regions of France are well-represented, notably Burgundy and Alsace. Make sure you reserve in advance because regulars aren't shy to show up several times a month.

– service in French, $$$, PF

AVANT-GOÛT

8 Birch Avenue (corner of Yonge Street, on a side street across from the Summerhill LCBO) ☎ 416 975-9150

Monday-Sunday for dinner

Subway: SUMMERHILL

The combination of French and Moroccan flavours, a retro, kitschy decor and warm, friendly service has made this small Rosedale bistro a hit with locals and out-of-towners alike since it opened in the summer of 2002. Chef and owner Kamal Hani's Moroccan heritage can be tasted in his cuisine. Dishes are savoury and spiced to perfection. For dinner, Hani pulls out all the stops with choices such as pear salad with roquefort, Moroccan stew served on a bed of basmati rice, duck confit served with braised red cabbage, slow-braised lamb shank served with a carrot and white bean ragout and grilled Black Angus steak in a mustard-seed sauce. The dessert menu changes regularly, but one staple is an excellent crème brûlée that will leave you wanting more. Avant-Goût's wine list offers a good selection of whites and reds from various regions in France. – *service in French, $$*

BATIFOLE

744 Gerrard Street East (between Broadview Avenue and Logan Avenue)
☎ 416 462-9965
Wednesday-Sunday for dinner
Subway: **BROADVIEW** + streetcar

Vous mangez, vous buvez, vous batifolez! You eat, you drink and you frolic! What an inviting introduction to a meal. Batifole is another example of excellent French cuisine served with a warm and relaxed attitude. But those won't be the only things that will impress you here – your affordable bill will also make you smile. The one-page menu created by owner and chef Jean-Jacques Texier promises an exceptional culinary journey. Among the many savoury dishes at Batifole, you'll find a *confit de canard* served in a Calvados sauce, flank steak with roasted shallots, oven roasted white bass *Provençale* and pork tenderloin served with a truffle cream sauce. Side dishes should not be overlooked: oven-baked potatoes and onions in white wine and Reblochon cheese, *frites Pont-neuf* and mushroom risotto are truly incredible. Homemade desserts are truly sublime, and chef Texier is not shy in using of Ontario *terroir* (local) ingredients to infuse them with a unique taste. Cointreau and orange blossom *île flottante*, cognac crème brûlée, *clafouti* made with berries from Prince Edward County and four different crêpes are only some of the changing highlights. The *apéritifs* list is incredibly French and incredibly effer-vescent, while the wine list is 100% French! – *bilingual menu, service in French, $$, PF*

BISTRO MATISSE

1710 Lakeshore Road West, Mississauga (Clarkson Village, between Port Credit & Oakville) ☎ 905 822-2222
Closed Monday; Tuesday-Friday for lunch; Tuesday-Sunday for dinner

Since November 2002, Bistro Matisse's delicious menu and reasonable prices have made this small restaurant a hit. Chef and owner Jean Jacques Lemesle is no stranger to French cuisine. A former co-owner and chef at La Maison Benoît, Lemesle's simple aesthetics and artistic presentation only enhance the flavours and textures of his food. The dinner menu offers such tempting specialties as baked chicken stuffed with prosciutto and emmenthal, calf liver coated with Parisian sauce, Black Angus steak with black peppercorn served in cognac sauce, roasted duck, *bouillabaisse* and *merguez* sausages with couscous. Chef Lemesle also makes homemade *andouillettes* (thin French style sausages) and *foie gras*. A small but constantly changing repertoire of desserts (including a silky crème brûlée) round out the menu. Bistro Matisse's wine list is balanced, and represents many regions and varietals. You'll find a few well-chosen reds and whites from France, as well as a pleasant surprise – the inclusion of several kinds of French beer! – *bilingual menu, service in French, $$, PF*

bistros & fine dining

BISTRO TOURNESOL

406 Dupont Street (West of Dupont subway station) ☎ 416 921-7766

Closed Monday; Tuesday-Sunday for dinner

Subway: DUPONT

www.bistrotournesol.com

The three new owners of Bistro
Tournesol know a thing or two about
French cuisine – this dynamic trio were
long-time employees of the bistro when
former owner Yves Robert decided to
return to France. But even though the
management has changed, the winning
formula at Bistro Tournesol hasn't
changed one bit: you can choose any
combination of two dishes from their
$25 prix fixe menu. The menu is often
augmented by the addition of daily
appetiser specials, but don't expect to
find an *à la carte* menu. Each main dish
is accompanied by a bowl of succulent
frites. For dessert, try the lemon tart, a
lovely combination of tartness and
sweetness. Service is very attentive and
welcoming, however reservations are
highly recommended since Bistro
Tournesol is a popular spot for regulars
and theatregoers alike (Tarragon
Theatre is only steps away). – *$$, PF*

BLOOR STREET DINER

55 Bloor Street West (Manulife Centre)
☎ 416 928-3105

Monday-Saturday for lunch; Monday-
Sunday for dinner; Sunday for brunch

Subway: BLOOR or BAY

www.eatertainment.com

The Bloor Street Diner has a genuine
bistro feel, thanks in part to a reason-
able prix fixe menu, the selection of

French classics on the menu – *croque-
monsieur, salade niçoise,* French onion
soup, numerous kinds of quiche, mus-
sels, *steak frites,* and roasted chicken
served with dried tomato *aïoli* – and the
restaurant's signature touch, a warm
half-baguette. – *$$, PF*

BOUJADI

999 Eglinton Avenue West (West of
Bathurst Street) ☎ 416 440-0258

Closed Monday–Tuesday;
Wednesday–Sunday for dinner

Subway: EGLINTON WEST

www.boujadi.com

Marhaba (welcome) to Morocco! Since
1992, Boujadi's chef and owner Charles
Obadia has been serving traditional
Moroccan dishes, many of which are
prepared from recipes passed down by a
long line of ancestors. Boujadi serves up
three *tajine* dishes, six coucous dishes
and half a dozen vegetarian selections.
The dessert menu is short, but typically
Moroccan. Drinks include the traditional sweet mint tea and a signature
lemonade made with rosewater.

Did you know?

Located Southwest of Paris, the city
of Royan hosts a yearly summer festival celebrating *La Belle Epoque* (The
Good Times). This refers to a period
prior to the First World War, where
artisans of cloth, canvas, clay and
food gathered to exchange ideas. An
escape from the busy world of Paris,
Royan was a retreat for artists such
as Picasso and Zolá.

Source: www.royan.ca

Boujadi's warm and relaxing ambience, decor and music is the ideal place to break away from the super-trendy "it" spots and fusion fare found around Bathurst and King. If you stop by on weekends, you may even be lucky enough to watch a performance by authentic belly dancers. Boujadi also offers food to go. – *service in French*, *$$*

BRASSERIE ROYAN

218 Lakeshore Road East, Oakville (West of Trafalgar Road) ☎ 905 845-8623
Monday-Sunday lunch and dinner
www.royan.ca

The creation of brothers Paul and Joe Haskett, Brasserie Royan is quickly becoming a meeting ground for many francophiles in search of a satisfying yet reasonably priced meal. The menu boasts typical brasserie fare alongside many Quebecois adaptations. Steak frites served with a Brandy sauce, duck breast and leg served with port wine jus, chicken *suprême* stuffed with oka cheese and poutine Royan are just some of the selections you'll enjoy. Perfectly seasoned *frites* accompany each dish. Mondays might become your favourite day of the week thanks to Royan's half-price Mussels Madness menu. Desserts are classic, but the *tarte au citron* and the *gâteau au chocolat* (warm chocolate cake) are showstoppers. French-Canadians will also be pleased to find a delicious version of the *tarte au sucre* (Royan calls theirs the Bourbon pecan tart). The wine list is quite fitting for any respectable brasserie, including many selections from France. Service receives high marks! You'd be gravely

mistaken if you thought Brasserie Royan was just the domaine of suburbanites – this quaint brasserie has all the right ingredients to charm any Torontonian. – *$$, PF*

CAFÉ CRÊPE

246 Queen Street West (West of University Avenue) ☎ 416 260-1611
Monday-Thursday 9-10; Friday-Saturday 9-midnight; Sunday 10-10
Subway: OSGOODE

No visit to the City of Lights is complete without sampling the delicious crêpes sold on virtually every street corner. Parisian crêpes are made fresh before your eyes. You wait in mouth-watering anticipation as the heavenly aroma from the special spherical hot plate drifts up towards you, changing your mind at least three times as you contemplate the list of fillings. Perhaps the best part of the ritual is eating your crêpe on the go, savouring every delicious bite while strolling alongside the Eiffel Tower and the banks of the Seine. Torontonians are now able to enjoy the experience of eating one of France's favourite foods *à emporter* (to go), thanks to Café Crêpe. Sweet and savoury menus offer typical Parisian classics, but there are also many flavours created exclusively for Canadian taste buds. Chicken and mushrooms, emmenthal cheese and maple syrup, and tuna and mayonnaise are just some of the options on the savoury menu, while sweet crêpes include honey and coconut, ice cream and rum, and coconut and banana. You can also enjoy one of Café Crêpe's delicious sand-

bistros & fine dining

wiches. To ensure freshness, Café Crêpe prepares only a certain quantity of sandwiches per day, so when they're gone, they're gone. – *$*

CAFÉ MARGAUX

796 College Street (East of Ossington Avenue, on the corner of Roxton Road)
☎ 416 588-7490
Monday–Saturday for dinner
Subway: QUEEN'S PARK + streetcar
www.cafemargaux.ca

Since October 2003, owner Patrice Baron and chef Rob Briden have been dazzling the College Street crowd with a winning formula – great ambience, mellow music, a menu that bursts with flavour from every dish, a remarkable wine list and reasonable prices. Neither is a stranger to the restaurant business – they met whilst working at Quartier bistro and worked together again at Pastis. The menu offers a variety of classic dishes that have been ever so slightly updated, creating a perfect balance of flavours. For dessert, choose from a decadent chocolate marquise, traditional crème brûlée, exotic Armagnac profiteroles or, if you can't decide, the *assiette gourmande* (selections vary). Café Margaux's wine list boasts an impressive 125 labels. There are about 75 reds and about 50 whites, many of which are French. Spoiled-for-choice patrons can consult the wine encyclopedia found at the bar for suggestions and guidance. – *bilingual menu, service in French,* **$$**, *PF*

CAFÉ MOROC

49 Front Street East (West of Church Street) ☎ 416 961-0601

Monday-Sunday for dinner

Subway: UNION

www.thesultanstent.com

Nestled in the downtown core, Café Moroc is an exotic oasis of tastes and aromas. The decor is reminiscent of the home of a well-travelled friend – ceramic tiles, mirrors, lanterns, rich-coloured wood, ebony-coloured round tables, and bamboo ceiling fans. The menu complements the decor and offers many traditional and not-so-traditional Moroccan dishes, such as *merguez* sausages on baguette, a Moroc hamburger (lamb burger served with signature *frites*) and *Keskesu Casablanca* (a couscous *tajine* with vegetables, fruits and nuts). Be sure to end your meal with a traditional Moroccan tea. Café Moroc's wine list reveals many interesting signature drinks. – **$$**

CAFÉ NICOLE

45 The Esplanade (between Yonge Street and Church Street) ☎ 416 367-8900

Monday–Sunday for lunch and dinner

Subway: UNION

Café Nicole is located inside the Novotel hotel. Choose from an impressive and well-prepared selection of French specialties, including *steak frites,* rack of lamb with a fresh herb crust, seared duck breast accompanied by

gratin dauphinois and beef tenderloin with ragout of wild mushrooms in a port wine sauce. Dessert lovers will be torn between a Grand Marnier cake, crème brûlée and crêpes. For theatregoers, Café Nicole's "theatre menu" is an ideal way to enjoy a delicious meal before the curtain rises. – *bilingual menu, service in French,* **$$**, *PF*

CHEZ LAURENT

4965 Yonge Street (North of Sheppard Avenue) ☎ 416 590-0909

Monday–Saturday for dinner; closed Sunday

Subway: NORTH YORK CENTRE or SHEPPARD

Located in a little house, the unpretentious, welcoming atmosphere makes you feel like you've been invited to a friend's home for a casual meal. The hosts and proprietors, the Ferrari family, go out of their way to ensure your dining experience is enjoyable. Chez Laurent's menu is part French and part Italian, but steers clear of fusion; instead, each cuisine is celebrated in its own right. Presentation is simple, without theatrics but with lots of taste. On the French side, starters include *moules marinière* (mussels), escargots, French onion soup and *salade niçoise*. For mains, choose from *veau au citron* (veal in lemon sauce), *suprême de poulet* (chicken breast in creamy paprika sauce), *poulet chasseur* (chicken breast in rose sauce) and *poulet basquez* (chicken breast in tomato sauce), as well as three variations of steak. A simple dessert menu includes the twin staples of *crème caramel* and crème brûlée, both sure bets. – *service in French, bilingual menu,* **$$**

bistros & fine dining

CRÊPES À GOGO

244 Bloor Street West (entrance on Bedford Street) ☎ 416 922-6765

Closed Monday; Tuesday-Thursday 9-7; Friday-Saturday 9-9; Sunday 10-4:30

Subway: ST. GEORGE (Bedford exit)

www.crepesagogo.com

A real French treasure in the heart of the Annex! Considered by many to be the best crêperie in Toronto, Crêpes à GoGo has been creating quite a stir since it opened in May 2003. Regulars swear the crêpes here are as good as their French counterparts, and often stop by daily to get their fix! Crêpes à GoGo makes both sweet and savoury versions. Crêpes à GoGo is also a popular spot for lunch, offering a variety of salads and delicious sandwiches on French bread. This hidden "corner of France" is really worth the detour – the ingredients are fresh, the ambience is charming and the service is welcoming. If you choose to have crêpes for lunch, you might want to arm yourself with bit of patience, but we guarantee the end result is well worth the wait.

– *bilingual menu, service in French*, $

HOLT'S CAFÉ *(second floor)*

50 Bloor Street West (corner of Bay Street) ☎ 416 922-2333

Monday–Wednesday 10–6, Thursday–Friday 10–8, Saturday 10–6, Sunday 12–6

Subway: BLOOR or BAY

The perfect blend of style and substance, Holt's Café is as much a feast for the eyes as the palate. This newly revamped luxurious café features decor that is very modern, very spacious and very upscale, and could easily be mistaken for the lobby of one of Toronto's trendy boutique hotels. But the opulence, aesthetics and good taste extend to the cuisine as well as the atmosphere; indeed, Holt's Café really seduces by conquering your taste buds. The menu, created by chef Corbin Tomaszeski, is a local version of what can be found in the finest Parisian bistros. Exquisite

Did you know?

A March 2004 survey by *Elle à table* (a popular French food magazine) revealed the top three favourite dishes in France: 1) *moules à la marinière* (mussels in white wine and garlic), 2) *blanquette de veau* (veal stew) and 3) *pot-au-feu* (boiled beef). Surprisingly – perhaps shockingly – with all the scrumptious and legendary desserts France has to offer, the locals chose a simple fruit salad as their favourite!

It comes as no surprise, however, that the French still favour their own cuisine at home and when travelling abroad. A staggering 77 per cent picked French cuisine as *tête de peloton* (head and shoulders) above the rest. When it comes to international cuisine, the French prefer the North African dish of couscous and a classic Italian favourite – pizza. Luckily for Franco-Torontonians, there is no shortage of fantastic French restaurants that offer their top three picks, as well as many other local favourites!

soups and salads start off a meal to please even the most discriminating gourmand. But the real jewels in the crown at Holt's Café are the dozen or so *tartines* (open-face sandwiches) served on sinful bread from Paris's Poîlane bakery – a Toronto exclusive. For dessert, the *tarte au citron*, ginger crème brûlée and bread pudding (also made with Poîlane bread) are all outstanding – and don't forget to treat yourself to one of Holt's Café's fabulous cappucinos to round out your meal. Wine is also available, including a few selections from France. Menus change with the seasons and often highlight certain special events in the city – for instance, Tomaszeski creates dishes exclusively for the Toronto International Film Festival. Of course, the service is as exceptional as the food, but one would expect nothing less from Holt Renfrew. – *$$*

Jacques Bistro du Parc

126-A Cumberland Street
☎ 416 961-1893
Monday–Saturday for lunch and dinner;
Sunday for dinner
Subway: BAY

Jacques Bistro du Parc is a small bistro that offers huge value; the type of place where regulars return to frequently because the price is as outstanding as the quality. Owner and chef Jacques Sorin takes great pride in his menu. Dinners are available *à la carte* or *prix fixe*. Selections include rack of lamb provençale and veal scallops with mushroom. With so many appetizing choices, it's easy to forget to leave room for a sweet treat, but just one look at

the sumptuous mousses, profiteroles and fruit tarts, and you'll remember to pace your efforts. For lighter lunchtime fare, be sure to try Sorin's house specialty – a delicious variety of omelettes. – *bilingual menu, service in French, $$*

L'Escargot Bistro

3185 Yonge Street (North of Lawrence Avenue) ☎ 416 485-8338
Monday-Sunday for dinner
Subway: LAWRENCE
www.lescargot.ca

Owner Max Ballin has gone to great lengths to create an authentic French atmosphere at L'Escargot Bistro, particularly with the menu. Dishes are simply prepared and presented, but full of delightful flavours and fragrances. One could almost dine on the appetizers alone. True to the restaurant's namesake, escargots are the star here, and there are three variations to choose from – garlic butter, tomato with herbs from Provence and phyllo pastry with julienne of vegetables in a cream of garlic sauce. If you can summon enough willpower to refrain from ordering more than one appetiser, there are a number of outstanding mains to choose from, including a fish stew, two variations of *steak frites* and veal medallions. Dessert selections are limited, but include a magnificent *gâteau basque* (rarely seen on Toronto dessert menus). L'Escargot Bistro's wine cellar boasts more than 1,000 bottles, many of which are French. With a selection this extensive, it's easy to find something to suit every palate and price range. – *bilingual menu, service in French, $$, PF*

bistros & fine dining

LA MAISON BENOÎT

1921 Avenue Road (North of Brooke
Avenue) ☎ 416 782-9934

Monday–Saturday for lunch and dinner,
Sunday for dinner

Subway: LAWRENCE + bus

La Maison Benoît's charming atmosphere has just the right amount of retro
chic. Chef Jean Luc Moles adds his
own creative flair to many traditional
French dishes, and the results are dazzling – scallops in Pernod sauce, half-
roasted duck with port and orange
sauce, calf liver served with balsamic
vinegar and shallot confit, port pâté,
and well-prepared *steak frites*. Desserts
at La Maison Benoît are plentiful,
including Cointreau profiteroles, the
house specialty. Many well-priced
selections from France can be found on
the wine list. La Maison Benoît is a
neighbourhood favourite, and reservations are highly recommended. – *bilin-
gual menu, service in French, $$, PF*

LA PALETTE

256 Augusta Avenue (West of Spadina
Avenue) ☎ 416 929-4900

Monday–Sunday for dinner

Subway: SPADINA + streetcar;
QUEEN'S PARK + streetcar

This unpretentious little bistro in
Kensington Market offers a selection of
classic, well-prepared dishes at reason-
able prices. The decor is simple (colour-
ful tablecloths and French posters on
the walls) and the service is easygoing,
making La Palette a great choice for a
casual meal. – *service in French, $$*

LA PETITE FRANCE

3317 Bloor Street West (East of Islington
Avenue) ☎ 416 234-8783

Monday–Friday for lunch and dinner,
Saturday for dinner; closed Sunday (will
open Sundays for large groups)

Subway: ISLINGTON

www.lapetitefrance.ca

Chef Gilbert Letort prepares simple
classics that are rich with flavour, and
to keep things fresh, the seasonally
themed menu is changed every six
months. Selections from the winter
menu may include beef tenderloin with
béarnaise sauce, duck with green peppercorn sauce, shrimp and scallop *fricassée* served in a Pastis sauce, and pork
tenderloin with a Calvados sauce.
Desserts include profiteroles, crêpes,
galette bretonne (a Brittany-style flat
cake), *Marjolaine* cake (made with
chocolate, almond and hazelnut) and a
vanilla crème brûlée that can only be
described as a masterpiece. La Petite
France's wine list comprises 60 or so
bottles, including a generous selection
of French reds, with a different wine
region being celebrated each month. In
fact, the eatery regularly hosts numerous food and wine events that should
not be missed! La Petite France's catering service is an ingenious way to share
the flavourful menu prepared by chef
Letort, who will prepare a French
menu, or any other cuisine, for the
enjoyment of your guests. – *bilingual
menu, service in French, $$, PF*

LE PAPILLON

16 Church Street ☎ 416 363-3773

Closed Monday; Tuesday–Sunday for lunch and dinner

Subway: UNION

www.lepapillon.ca

Brittany meets Quebec at Le Papillon, where rustic comfort food is served in a charming, warm atmosphere. A large brick fireplace makes for a cozy and relaxing setting for winter dinners. Le Papillon has amassed many awards of excellence, and, in the process, has also amassed quite a following. Regular diners savour selections like the chicken and peach dish served with Brandy sauce, or pork *bordelaise* and seafood served in a creamy sauce. However, it's the house specialty that wins high marks – a succulent collection of two dozen varieties of *crêpes bretonnes – superbe!* For dessert try the French-Canadian sugar pie or *poudding chômeur. – service in French, $$*

LE PARADIS

166 Bedford Road (South of Dupont Street) ☎ 416 921-0995

Tuesday–Friday for lunch and dinner, Saturday–Monday for dinner

Subway: MUSEUM or ST GEORGE

www.leparadis.com

Le Paradis offers a stellar mix of originality, flavour and value that can't be beat. The ever-changing main menu subtly blends flavours from Morocco and France – *tajines*, lamb, *merguez* sausages and couscous are featured side by side with *blanquette au sauvignon* (mixed fish in *sauvignon* sauce), *bavette*

Did you know?

The Cuvée Quetton Saint-Georges is an award-winning AOC red wine that has been acclaimed by oenophiles from France, Quebec, Germany and the United States. It received the gold medal at the 2001 Concours Général Agricole in France. The origins of this stellar wine can be traced back to Toronto.

Read more about this fascinating story courtesy of *La Société d'histoire de Toronto* (Toronto Historic Society) on our Web site (www.franco-toronto.ca).

(marinated beef flank), *entrecôte chasseur* (rib eye steak) and *lapin à la provençale* (rabbit). *Cassoulet* is made from a recipe that was literally imported from France – during a trip there, Le Paradis's owner David Currie found the perfect version of this white bean ragout at a restaurant in Castelnaudary. He had the restaurant's chef send a frozen container to Toronto, where it evolved into Le Paradis's house specialty. *Flageolets* feature prominently as a side dish with most mains. Although Le Paradis's dessert menu is fairly short, you'll still find it difficult to make a choice. Crème brûlée is eschewed in favour of a splendid *crème caramel.* The restaurant's rich cuisine lends itself to a wine list that is equally robust. Offerings include a variety of full-bodied reds and whites from most regions of France, as well as a number of French beers. – *bilingual menu, service in French, $$*

bistros & fine dining

LE PETIT DÉJEUNER

191 King Street East (East of Church Street)
☎ 416 703-1560

Monday-Friday for lunch; Saturday-Sunday for brunch; Thursday-Saturday for dinner

Subway: KING

www.petitdejeuner.ca

Who serves the best Belgian waffles in Toronto? Le Petit Déjeuner, of course! Owner and chef Johan Maes, a native of Belgium, knows a thing or two when it comes to preparing the perfect waffle. Connoisseurs will notice Maes's waffles are remarkably light, making them almost too sinful to eat. Waffles aren't the only selections you'll find on the menu – omelettes, crêpes, eggs, *croque-monsieur* and *croque-madame* (like a *croque-monsieur*, but topped with a fried egg and *béchamel* sauce) are also favourite *petit déjeuner* (breakfast) selections of many regulars. Since September 2004, Maes offers a dinner menu that features a number of well-prepared and savoury Belgian specialties at a reasonable price. Expect to find *moules et frites*, chicken *Archiduc* with *frites*, *ratatouille* and *steak frites*. Chai crème brûlée and poached Bosc pears are perfect sweet notes to end your meal. The short wine list has well-priced selections that won't put a dent in your budget. From breakfast to dinner, Le Petit Déjeuner is a quaint restaurant to enjoy a tasty meal. – *$$, PF*

LE PETIT GOURMET

1064 Yonge Street (near Roxborough Street) ☎ 416 966-3811

Monday–Friday 7:30–7, Saturday 7:30–6; closed Sunday

Subway: ROSEDALE

Le Petit Gourmet is all about comfort food. This Rosedale diner is a great spot to eat simple yet hearty French fare such as quiches, roasted chicken, *bœuf bourguignon, coq au vin* (chicken in red wine) and chicken pie. Typical *plats du jour* (daily specials) include duck with apples, roast lamb and pork roast. Best of all, Le Petit Gourmet offers a catering service so you can enjoy these homestyle dishes at any time. – *$*

LE SAINT TROPEZ

315 King Street West (corner of John Street) ☎ 416 591-3600

Monday–Sunday for lunch and dinner

Subway: ST ANDREW

www.lesainttropez.com

Le Saint Tropez's casual, Mediterranean-style ambience is a favourite with many French Torontonians, who traditionally gather here to celebrate Bastille Day or cheer on the French national football team during European or World Cup matches. Dine to the sounds of live entertainment seven days a week. Le Saint Tropez's menu features many influences from the South of France, such as Toulouse sausages served with *frites*, sautéed shrimp with a twist from Marseille and veal scaloppini with port. For dessert, choose from traditional favourites such as crème brûlée, *tarte au citron* and profiteroles. Naturally, France also has a strong presence on the wine list. – *bilingual menu, service in French, $$*

ARLEQUIN This bistro is the perfect location for an intimate business lunch.

BISTRO 1603 Business types in Mississauga already know Bistro 1603 offers an excellent French lunch without leaving the 905 area code.

BISTRO MATISSE Another Mississauga find, Bistro Matisse serves up one of the most reasonable lunch menus in town.

BODEGA Bodega's lunches are superb, but did you know they cater, too? Catering by Bodega is an ingenious way to mesh business with pleasure, without setting foot outside the boardroom. A catered lunch from Bodega is sure to impress your business associates and clients.

BRASSERIE ROYAN: Here's another great location to savour a delicious lunch within the 905 area code.

HOLT'S CAFÉ For a simple yet satisfying lunch, try Holt's *tartines* (open-faced sandwiches) on Poîlane bread.

LE CONTINENTAL With its perfectly seasoned meats and a mind-boggling selection of more than 35 cheeses, Le Continental just might be the perfect venue to help seal a business deal!

MIDI BISTRO The ambience of this little bistro is a welcome haven for those in the University and St. Patrick area.

PROVENCE DÉLICES: Enjoy a business lunch in one of Toronto's most charming restaurants.

LE SÉLECT BISTRO

328 Queen Street West ☎ 416 596-6406
Monday-Sunday for lunch and dinner
Subway: OSGOODE
www.leselect.com

The decor is very *rive gauche;* the menu oh-so-French and the experience perfectly charming. Le Sélect Bistro holds many Torontonian and American medals and distinction awards, which would explain why so many patrons consistently return to this bistro. If it's hearty French cuisine you are after, Le Sélect Bistro is where you'll find it. *Cassoulet, foie gras* and *escargots* are only a few of the favourites on the elaborate menu, although the *prix fixe* options are also worth a look for their outstanding value. If choosing what to eat isn't difficult enough, it may be even harder to select an accompanying wine – Le Sélect

Bistro's cellar consists of more than 1,000 bottles. – *bilingual menu, $$, PF*

LOLO RESTAURANT

619 Mount Pleasant Road (East of Yonge Street) ☎ 416 483-8933
Monday-Saturday for dinner; closed Sunday
Subway: EGLINTON

A French bistro that serves Italian food? Why not! Owner Louis Ourique is quite partial to blending the best of both worlds. This charming and quaint bistro is usually packed with regulars who appreciate the simple and straightforward menu, including a variety of fish dishes in particular that are stellar. Vegetables are rarely noteworthy in restaurants, but Lolo's are seasoned to such perfection that they stand out on their own merits. Desserts are just as

bistros & fine dining

heavenly – the *tarte au citron* is truly one of the best in the city; however, the *tarte tatin* and the *pain perdu* (Ourique's mother-in-law's recipe) are also excellent alternatives. The wine list offers a few selections from France, but it's the beer list that pleased us the most. Lolo is a very popular eaterie, so reservations are highly recommended. – *$$, PF*

MATIGNON

51 St. Nicholas Street ☎ 416 921-9226
Monday-Friday for lunch and dinner; Saturday for dinner; closed Sunday (will open Sundays for large private functions)
Subway: YONGE
www.matignon.ca

Tucked away from the hustle and bustle of nearby Yonge and Bay Streets, Matignon is located in a lovely little brick house in a residential neighbourhood, making it the ideal place for an intimate *tête-à-tête* dinner. *Maître d'hôtel* and owner Mustapha Amrani

sets the standard for service *par excellence,* and with its elegant dining rooms and a fantastic *prix fixe* menu, Matignon is sure to be a restaurant you'll return to again and again. Menu choices include chicken with basil and cream sauce and a braised lamb shank with sauce *provençale,* while the regular menu offers *steak frites,* peppered Black Angus steak flambéed with cognac and rack of lamb with mustard, honey and mint. To finish your meal, the wonderful orange-flavoured *crème caramel* is highly recommended. Matignon's wine list is both diverse and reasonably priced, and any selection is sure to complement your meal. – *bilingual menu, service in French, $$, PF*

MERLOT

2994 Bloor Street West ☎ 416 236-0081
Monday–Friday for lunch and dinner, Saturday–Sunday for dinner
Subway: ROYAL YORK

Located in the Kingsway Village, Merlot's cuisine is an interesting hybrid of French classics, such as Alsatian-style sauerkraut. Meat features prominently on the menu – everything from the *steak frites* to the lamb is not only well-cooked but very affordable, making it possible to try something new that may be considerably more expensive elsewhere. The trio of sausages (Toulouse, Italian, *merguez*) served with a Merlot sauce is just divine. No meal at Merlot is complete without one of their delicious desserts or selections from the affordable wine list. – *service in French, $$*

MICHELLE'S BRASSERIE

162 Cumberland Street (Renaissance
Court, near the Four Seasons hotel)
☎ 416 944-1504

Monday-Sunday for lunch and dinner

Subway: MUSEUM or BAY

www.labrasserie.ca

Michelle's Brasserie is a typical French
bistro, offering hearty food and good
drinks in a relaxed atmosphere. Inside,
the decor echoes France right down to
the wiring on the wall, which is remi-
niscent of the base of the Eiffel Tower.
Michelle's Brasserie offers live entertainment from Thursday to Saturday
evenings, when you can dine to the
sounds of blues, jazz, and occasionally, a
few francophone artists. The chef's creations are typical bistro fare, which is
particularly well executed and presented
with much flair. Quail served in Bercy
sauce, pork medallions in Calvados jus
and the chef's *foie gras* special are just
some of the many *spécialités de la maison*. For a lighter meal, choose the *salad
niçoise*. Fresh tuna cooked *à point* makes
this salad truly outstanding. As you
would expect, Michelle's Brasserie also
has a remarkable selection of French
wines, spirits and beers from France
and Belgium. – *service in French, $$$*

MIDI BISTRO

168 McCaul Street (between College Street
and Dundas Street) ☎ 416 977-2929

Monday–Friday for lunch,
Tuesday–Saturday for dinner

Subway: ST PATRICK

www.midibistro.com

Another small eatery that is big on
taste, Midi Bistro is one of those

restaurants you'll go back to again and
again for the good food, warm hospital-
ity and relaxing ambience. Midi Bistro's
menu is a pleasant surprise in terms of
both price and variety. Some of the
more unusual starters include *Farçous
Claudine* (southern French spinach
crêpes with onions and bacon), an
intensely flavourful goat cheese and
vegetable *terrine*, grilled goat cheese on
toast and, of course, *moules*. Mains are
also full of surprises – rainbow trout in
a *bouillabaisse jus,* roasted Cornish hen,
roasted duck confit leg with a light
Pommery mustard sauce, pan-seared
salmon with a cinnamon crust and lime
sauce, and striploin steak with a Merlot
sauce. Desserts are ever-changing, but
consistently incredible. Selections
might include homemade ice cream,
tarte tatin, profiteroles filled with
vanilla ice cream, crème brûlée and a
warm chocolate cake (the 20 minute
preparation time is worth every second
of the wait!). – *bilingual menu, service in
French, $$, PF*

MONITZ

352 Melrose Avenue (corner of
Avenue Road) ☎ 416 781-3764

Monday-Friday for lunch and dinner;
Saturday for dinner; closed Sunday

Subway: EGLINTON + bus

Monitz blends the best of Northern
Africa and Southern France in its
diverse menu, which includes *mignon de
bœuf* (beef medallions with three pep-
percorns), duck with Chambord Royal
(blackberry) sauce, medallions of lamb
with minted wine sauce, pork with cassis sauce (blackcurrant), duck breast

bistros & fine dining

with maple syrup and a variety of chicken, fish and couscous dishes. (*Merguez* sausages are also available by special request, although they do not appear on the menu.) These mouth-watering dishes are nicely complemented by an impressive variety of French wines. – *bilingual menu, service in French, $$, PF*

MONTREAL BREAD COMPANY (MBCO)

Please refer to our directory on page 132 to find all locations for this merchant.

Peter Morentzos, the Montreal maestro who orchestrates "mood food" concepts, offers his latest menu of *esprit de vivre* culinary treasures in a rich *comptoir* setting at MBCo. Feast your palate on flavourful baked breads, boutique muffins, gourmet hand-carved sandwiches as artfully prepared as they are presented, or surrender your senses to the selection of sinful desserts and exotic coffee blends. MBCo also caters to the health conscious with a special signature menu. An eclectic list of seasonal wines are available by the glass. For those who can't make the time, MBCo offers catering services as well as a selection of specialty *prêt-à-manger* items. – *bilingual menu, service in French, $$*

NICE BISTRO

117 Brock Street North, Whitby
☎ 905 668-8839

Closed Sunday-Monday; Tuesday-Saturday for lunch and dinner

This Whitby bistro is a real gem! While Torontonians may consider the half-hour drive East of the city a bit far, this is the kind of detour you'll be happy to make. Named after chef Bernard Alberigo's birthplace, Nice Bistro offers warm and friendly service in a rustic atmosphere. Chef Alberigo and hostess Manon Lacroutz are the attentive and joyful owners, who truly care about their guests' dining experience. It might come as a surprise to hear Lacroutz greeting people *en français,* but you'll quickly realize how happy guests are to brush up on their French. Refined and delicious dishes are complements to a cozy ambience. A classic menu prepared by chef Alberigo includes such noteworty fare as *steak frites,* medallions of veal and duck in zesty Grand Marnier coulis. The *bouillabaisse* and shrimp dish are also prepared with the chef's magic touch. Homemade chocolate truffles open a delicious parade of desserts, of which the *tarte tatin* and white chocolate mousse cake are standouts. The wine list features many excellent vintages from France *(bien sûr!).* – *bilingual menu, service in French, $$$*

POURQUOI PAS

63 Sheppard Avenue West (West of Yonge Street) ☎ 416 226-9071

Monday–Friday for lunch and dinner, Saturday–Sunday for dinner

Subway: SHEPPARD

www.toronto.com/pourquoipas

Located in a small house, Pourquoi Pas has a comfortable charm that feels more like a favourite aunt's living room than a restaurant. Egyptian owner Sherif Elkei first opened his doors in

1975, and has since perfected a winning combination of laid-back ambience, attentive service and terrific French cuisine that has made Pourquoi Pas a favourite among locals. The menu offers an assortment of simple, interesting and reasonably priced selections such as *merguez* sausages, *cassoulet*, calf liver sautéed in red wine and shallots, pork medallions served with Calvados and roasted apples, braised lamb shank with a light tomato sauce, *canard à l'orange* (duck in orange sauce), sweetbreads and a melt-in-your-mouth filet mignon. Desserts include several tried-and-true French staples like *crème caramel, saint-honoré* and crêpes Suzette. *– bilingual menu, service in French, $$, PF*

QUARTIER

2112 Yonge Street (between Davisville Avenue and Eglinton Avenue) ☎ 416 545-0505

Monday-Friday for lunch and dinner; Saturday-Sunday for dinner

Subway: **DAVISVILLE** or **EGLINTON**

This elegant neighbourhood bistro combines classic French flavours with international influences. Among the specialties you'll find a perfectly prepared leg of lamb served with Dupuy lentils, rabbit stew, duck confit and Cornish hen with purée. The *steak frites* and fish dishes are also not to be missed, nor is the Monday evening *table d'hôte* dinner menu, which offers an interesting and eclectic selection of mains. Chocolate lovers will want to indulge in Quartier's velvety chocolate cake, which is more than worth the 20-minute preparation time. Quartier's

wine list leans towards French varietals, especially when it comes to whites. *– service in French, $$*

RESTAURANT JULES

147 Spadina Avenue (at Richmond Street West) ☎ 416 348-8886

Monday-Friday 11:30-9; Saturday 12-4:30; closed Sunday

Subway: **SPADINA** + streetcar; **OSGOODE** + streetcar

Located in the heart of the condo district, Restaurant Jules is popular with the lunchtime crowd who want a delicious yet affordable alternative to the abundance of fast-food chains in the area. The standard here is excellence, in both food and value for money. Chef Eric Strippoli and his wife Mahasti Eslahjou have created a French bistro menu which offers an impressive list of classics such as French onion soup, quiche, *bavette steak* (striploin), homemade mayonnaise and *ratatouille* – and don't forget to treat yourself to one of his delicious signature crêpes! The Jules hamburger is cooked to juicy perfection, while fresh tuna served with *frites* and *ratatouille* is also quite tasty. Be sure to end your meal on a sugary high with either the *tarte tatin*, crème brûlée or dessert crêpes. *– service in French, $$*

SAUVIGNON BISTRO

1862 Queen Street East (West of Woodbine Avenue) ☎ 416 686-1998

Monday-Sunday for dinner

Subway: **QUEEN** + streetcar

Owners Stéphane Poquet and Grégoire Godin have created a backdrop suited to a relaxed and comforting meal by

bistros & fine dining

A category of its own!

JOHN & KING
HOT DOG STAND

(Corner of John Street and King Street West, across from the Princess of Wales Theatre)

Open year-round for lunch, dinner and late night

Subway: ST ANDREW

It's hard enough to find places in Toronto to enjoy Moroccan *merguez* sausages, let alone places where you can enjoy them to go – until now! Purely by chance, *The French Side of Toronto* discovered one of Toronto's best-kept secrets – the hot dog stand at the corner of John and King, in the midst of the Theatre District. Moïse, the owner, is a jovial man of North African descent who will be happy to serve you and chat in either English or French.

adding many eclectic touches to their decor. Sauvignon Bistro offers diners the possibility to enjoy their meals in one of three distinctively decorated rooms. Excellence is not only found in the decor, but also on the menu – a subtle blend of French and Asian cuisine. That said, the Angus steak served with Pommery mustard and sweet potato *frites* is outstanding, although this succulent dish is quite a generous portion and intended to satisfy big appetites. You'll definitely want to leave room for the lemon tart, Sauvignon Bistro's most popular dessert. The wine list offers a few selections from France, but it's the champagne menu that caught our attention. – *$$*

fine dining

AUBERGE DU POMMIER

4150 Yonge Street (North of York Mills Road) ☎ 416 222-2220

Monday–Friday for lunch and dinner, Saturday for dinner; closed Sunday

Subway: YORK MILLS

www.aubergedupommier.com

Auberge du Pommier is fine dining at its best. A perennial favourite on multiple top 10 lists, this charmingly elegant restaurant has been honoured with numerous accolades from a variety of organisations, ranging from *Where* magazine *(Most Memorable Meal Award)* to CAA *(Four Diamond Award)*. The interior resembles the type of cozy country inn found in the French countryside and is the perfect setting for a refined and elegantly presented meal, from a menu that mixes flavours from the South of France with Parisian classics and a twist of *nouvelle cuisine*. Choose an artistic dessert that looks almost too good to eat, or finish your meal with a satisfying cheese plate paired with a selection from the exhaustive wine list. Auberge du Pommier's reputation for excellence is reflected in its prices; however, the combination of impeccable service, haute cuisine and charming decor puts this restaurant on the absolute must-try list, even if it's only once a year or for special occasions. – *service in French, $$$$*

BIFF'S

4 Front Street East (East of Yonge Street)
☎ 416 860-0086

Monday-Friday for lunch; Monday to Saturday for dinner; closed Sunday

Subway: UNION

www.biffsrestaurant.com

Biff's offers a joyful and animated dining experience. A fairly classic French menu is offered amid decor that pays homage to a typical French bistro. Perfectly located for a quick bite before a show, Biff's is one of very few restaurants in Toronto that serves frog's legs, *Chateaubriand, boudin blanc* (blood sausages) and *steak tartare* – not to mention cheese fondue as a mains. *Quel coup!* You'll also find two generous seafood menus and an oyster plate, both of which are a delight. The wine list offers a beautiful selection of reds and whites from most French regions. The excellent service should also be noted. Biff's offers a winning combination worth rediscovering as often as possible. – *service in French, $$$, PF*

BISTRO 990

990 Bay Street (West of Yonge Street)
☎ 416 921-9990

Monday-Friday for lunch; Monday-Sunday for dinner

Subway: WELLESLEY

Bistro 990 has a well-deserved reputation as one of Toronto's most elegant and exclusive restaurants. Ingredients, preparation and presentation are all of the highest quality, in the best classic French style. This dedication to excellence is reflected in the price, but if you're looking for the perfect place to

celebrate a special occasion or seal an important deal, Bistro 990 is it. You may even find yourself rubbing shoulders with the Hollywood celebrities who dine here when in Toronto. House specialties include veal liver, grilled salmon infused with Grand Marnier, fresh tuna steak in an oriental sauce, *steak frites* served with a roquefort sauce, and filet mignon served with stilton and port. Desserts are divine, and, as is fitting, Bistro 990 has a very good French wine list. Their cellar comprises about 150 bottles, of which half are French. More than 30 French wines are served by the glass. – *bilingual menu, $$$$*

BISTRO 1603

1603 Clarkson Road, Mississauga
☎ 905 822-5262

Monday-Saturday for dinner; Wednesday-Friday for lunch; closed Sunday

www.bistro1603.com

Mississauga's Bistro 1603 masters the art of blending traditional French dishes with local ingredients to create an outstanding and original haute cuisine menu. Selections include *bouillabaisse* with an Asian twist, a trio of duck breast, foie and confit, calf's liver and *steak frites*. Classic crème brûlée and a chocolate and raspberry mousse with Lindt chocolate ice cream are both exquisite. Possibly the only thing more impressive than the menu is the wine list – Bistro 1603's 250 vintages received the *Wine Spectator Award of Excellence* in 2002 and 2003. – *service in French, $$$*

bistros & fine dining

BODEGA

30 Baldwin Street (West of McCaul Street)
☎ 416 977-1287
Monday–Sunday for lunch and dinner
Subway: ST PATRICK
www.bodegarestaurant.com

So much has changed at one of
Toronto's oldest French restaurants, and
yet so much remains the same. Bodega
has a new owner, new decor and a new
ambience (not to mention a newer
name!) but the restaurant's reputation
for excellence in cuisine and service is
as steadfast as ever. This new facelift
has brought in a younger crowd looking
for sophistication and creativity, and at
Bodega, there's plenty of both.
Bouillabaisse, duck confit, scallops
served with Pinot noir butter sauce,
trout served on a bed of lentils and filet
mignon are just some of the delectable
mains offered. Bodega may be the only
restaurant in the city that offers a *prix
fixe* menu that also includes a wine-
sampling list. Desserts are a combination of the classic and the exotic,
including crème brûlée, profiteroles
with figs served with port ice cream and
warm chocolate sauce, and a white
chocolate and Grand Marnier mousse
with three sauces. – *$$$, PF*

BOUCHON

38 Wellington Street East (West of Church
Street) ☎ 416 862-2675
Closed Sunday–Monday; Tuesday–Friday
for lunch and dinner, Saturday for dinner
Subway: KING or UNION
www.bouchon.ca

One of the best things about Bouchon

is its endless ability to reinvent itself –
each time you visit, you'll find a menu
bursting with new, fresh and original
creations. Chef Jean-Pierre Challet may
have moved on, but the new chef at
Bouchon adds his own unique flair to
Gallic *nouvelle cuisine,* resulting in a
rich mix of tastes and scents that is
nothing short of genius. The best of
Morocco and Quebec are combined in
an out-of-this-world *merguez poutine,*
topped with *chèvre* and served with
frites. Other dishes of note include *foie
gras poutine,* and steak tartare. For those
who need to eat in a hurry, Bouchon
has created a theatre menu that will
help you do just that. Desserts are daz-
zling and change daily, but always
include a fantastic *tarte au citron,* crème
brûlée and an assortment of chocolate-
based treasures. Well-chosen wines
complement the menu. – *$$, PF*

CAFÉ BRUSSEL

124 Danforth Avenue (East of Broadview
Avenue) ☎ 416 465-7363
Closed Monday; Tuesday–Sunday for
dinner
Subway: BROADVIEW

Only in Toronto will you find a restaurant located in the heart of Greektown
that features dozens of varieties of
moules (mussels) prepared in the best
Belgian tradition! Café Brussel is one
of Toronto's hidden treasures. The luxe,
spacious Art Deco decor provides an
almost theatrical backdrop for a menu
that is bold, colourful and dramatic –
more than 30 (!) kinds of *moules et
frites,* an award-winning wine list and
an unbeatable assortment of meat

Brunch

For many Torontonians, brunch is a weekend ritual. Meeting up with friends for a late breakfast/early lunch on weekends is an ideal way to combine the best of both worlds – good food and good company. Granted, brunch is not a French concept, which explains why only a handful of French restaurants have a specific brunch menu. Many of the other places listed in this guide are open during brunch hours, but serve a regular lunch menu instead.

BLOOR STREET DINER The *prix fixe* menu offers a large selection of yummy favourites.

BODEGA Brunch Bodega-style is an experience not to be missed! The menu is simple and delicious, consisting of a few traditionally French items and a few Torontonian favourites with a French twist – *pain perdu* (French toast), eggs Benedict and smoked salmon omelettes. The regular lunch menu is also available.

BONJOUR BRIOCHE Not only is brunch available both Saturday and Sunday, Bonjour Brioche lets patrons enjoy their meals at a leisurely pace and doesn't hurry them out the door (which means lineups are to be expected). Choose from either the special of the day or the regular lunch menu, which is full of other tasty options including mainstays such as quiches, pizzas and vegetable tarts. Don't forget to finish your meal with one of the fantastic pastries or desserts!

JACQUES BISTRO DU PARC Jacques Bistro serves up a simple but delicious brunch on Saturdays only, consisting of lighter fare such as omelettes, quiches and salads.

LA CIGOGNE La Cigogne serves a nice assortment of French classics for brunch. On the menu you'll find many kinds of quiche, crêpes *fourrées* (stuffed crêpes), *croque-madame* (like a *croque-monsieur*, but topped with a fried egg and Béchamel sauce) and omelettes. Don't forget to try the house specialty – *tarte flambée* (Alsatian-style thin-crust pie with bacon, chopped onion and cream cheese), which is only made on weekends. For dessert, La Cigogne offers an enticing array of crêpes!

LA PALETTE Arrive early, because this small Kensington restaurant fills up quickly for weekend brunch. The main attraction? Crêpes! La Palette also offers omelettes, *salade niçoise, salade basques* and *steak frites*.

LE SÉLECT BISTRO Brunch at Le Sélect Bistro is a feast of tastes. Omelettes, French toast, various egg dishes and, of course, crêpes are just some of the items offered. The regular weekend menu is also available.

PROVENCE DÉLICES This charming restaurant offers a tasty *prix fixe* brunch menu including salads and numerous egg dishes, with a side order of perfectly fried and seasoned *frites* accompanying every dish. Be sure to try the heavenly crème brûlée for dessert!

bistros & fine dining

dishes. Lamb, *steak frites,* filet mignon and *bœuf bourguignon* are all exceptional, but the *moules* are the real *pièce de résistance* here, not just in terms of variety, but quantity – each portion is equivalent to one full kilogram (2.2 lbs). The remarkable vintages found at Café Brussel are sure to delight wine aficionados. It's easy to see why *Wine Spectator* magazine awarded the restaurant its *Top restaurant wine list Award of Excellence* for seven consecutive years. Impeccable service only adds to the pleasure of dining at Café Brussel. The staff take your enjoyment seriously and truly do everything they can to make your dining experience as memorable as possible. – *bilingual menu, service in French, $$$*

CÉLESTIN

623 Mount Pleasant Road (corner of Manor Road) ☎ 416 544-9035

Closed Sunday–Monday; Tuesday–Saturday for dinner

Subway: EGLINTON + bus

www.celestin.ca

Located in a former branch of a big-five bank, Célestin has definitely raised the rate of interest in French food around this Mount Pleasant neighbourhood. Chef Pascal Ribreau combines traditional French cuisine, quality ingredients and an abundance of creativity for a result that is nothing short of spectacular. Appetizers are a triumph, while mains are simply seductive. Chef Ribreau is peerless in Toronto for his four prix-fixe menus, ranging from range from $65 to $80. The *à la carte* menu is forever changing

and one should always expect the unexpected. For dessert, Ribreau collaborates with his brother Martial on creations that look too good to eat. Célestin's 20-page wine list is uncommonly good and includes many noted labels from various regions in France. – *service in French, $$$$, PF*

DIDIER

1496 Yonge Street (North of St. Clair Avenue) ☎ 416 925-8588

Closed Sunday-Monday; Tuesday-Friday for lunch and dinner; Saturday for dinner

Subway: ST CLAIR

After a long hiatus and many years managing some of the top kitchens in the city, chef Didier Leroy recently opened his namesake restaurant, and his legion of devoted admirers immediately packed the place solid. Don't expect to find fusion *à la* anything here – the menu is strictly *français!* Didier offers complex flavours devoid of complicated and outlandish combinations. Dishes are so well seasoned, you'll be hard-pressed to find a salt or pepper shaker on the tables – a true testament to chef Leroy's and sous-chef Philippe Cœurdassier's talent. Every evening, several prix fixe menus are offered. For $75, you'll be able to sample a tasting menu and compare notes with your dining partners. Desserts are tempting, especially the warm *Valhrona* chocolate cake, *tarte au citron* and Grand Marnier soufflé. The majority of the wine list is French, offering a wide range of selection and prices. – *service in French, $$$, PF*

GAMELLE

468 College Street (West of Bathurst
Street) ☎ 416 923-6254

Monday-Saturday for dinner; Tuesday-
Friday for lunch; closed Sunday

Subway: QUEEN'S PARK + streetcar;
BATHURST + streetcar

www.gamelle.com

Gamelle's diminutive size may mistakenly give the impression of a bistro, but just one bite of the superb cuisine quickly underscores the restaurant's gourmet status. Chef Sean Moore may not be French, but you could never tell from his refined culinary skills. Amid a casual yet chic ambience, Gamelle offers a menu full of subtle flavours and exquisite choices. Owner Jean-Pierre Centeno is from the South of France, so you know the foie gras is guaranteed to be first-rate. Other specialties include pheasant, *magret* of duck, escargots, vegetable *millefeuille*, sirloin with brandy, French-Canadian leg of lamb and a variety of savoury fish dishes. This is another restaurant where you'll definitely want to leave room for dessert. The *tarte au citron,* crème brûlée and chocolate cake (considered by many francophiles to be one of the best in the city) are not to be missed. France is well-represented on Gamelle's extensive international wine list, which includes many rare selections. You need only visit Gamelle once, and you too will become a regular. – *bilingual menu,* $$$

Did you know?

The upper class in France has long been accustomed to the concept of *la cuisine bourgeoise.* The closest comparison we have in North America to this French indulgence is the personal chef – until now. Chef Didier Leroy has introduced Torontonians to *la cuisine bourgeoise,* although he and his catering service sous-chef Frédéric Hoffman are far more than mere personal chefs. Not only will they shop on your behalf for seasonal ingredients, they will also come to your home on a Sunday and prepare a spectacular meal fit for royalty in front of your guests. Sunday dinners will never be the same!

LE CONTINENTAL

900 York Mills Road (inside the Westin
Prince Hotel) ☎ 416 444-2511

Closed Sunday-Monday; Tuesday-Friday
for lunch and dinner; Saturday for dinner

Subway: YORK MILLS + bus

Le Continental has raised the bar when it comes to celebrating the trilogy at the heart of French cuisine – an impressive selection of cheese, decadent homemade bread and a 10-page wine list. Indeed, cheese aficionados will flock to Le Continental once they discover chef Hans Herzig offers an almost indecent selection of 35 varieties (mostly from France)! Chef Herzig's reputation for cooking with ingredients that are only of the utmost quality is well-justified, because his high expectations produce an outstanding dining experience, complete with impeccable

service. Meats in general are well prepared here, and the filet mignon and
lamb are noteworthy. Game meats are
prepared with precision, bringing out
the rich flavours to perfection. Le
Continental is also only one of a small
handful of restaurants to serve
Chateaubriand. Desserts are literally
impossible to ignore – the first thing
you see on entering Le Continental is a
glass counter displaying an array of
tempting treats – but half-size portions
are an ingenious way to partake in
guilt-free indulgences. – *service in
French, $$$, PF*

LE MONTMARTRE

911 Sheppard Avenue West (East of Allen
Road) ☎ 416 630-3804
Monday–Friday for lunch and dinner,
Saturday for dinner; closed Sunday
Subway: DOWNSVIEW
www.toronto.com/lemontmartre

The wonderfully French ambience at
Le Montmartre is heard through the
music of Edith Piaf playing in the
background, seen in the Van Gogh and
Renoir paintings on the wall (which
pay homage to the restaurant's name-
sake, the nineteenth century Artists'
Quarter in Paris) and tasted in their
authentic and delicious gourmet cui-
sine. Stand-outs on the menu include
mouth-watering cuts of beef, *canard à
l'orange* (duck in orange sauce), frog
legs and *escargots bourguignon.* For a
perfect ending to a perfect meal, opt for
the profiteroles filled with cold custard
and served with ice cream. Wines
include many fine selections from all
over the world, including several inter-

esting choices from France. – *bilingual
menu, service in French, $$$, PF*

LE TROU NORMAND

90 Yorkville Avenue (West of Bay Street)
☎ 416 967-5956
Monday–Saturday for lunch and dinner;
closed Sunday
Subway: BAY

Le Trou Normand gets its name from
the old Normandy custom of drinking
a glass of Calvados (apple brandy) in the
middle of a meal, which slows digestion
and allows the remaining courses to be
tackled with great gusto. It's a tradition
that would be well-served at this
touristy Yorkville restaurant, where the
terroir (from the earth) cooking is the
heart of the menu. Renowned for its
strict adherence to authentic French
cuisine, Le Trou Normand's Normandy-
inspired (Northern France) menu features a number of seafood-based dishes,
with most mains served with potatoes
and cream. *Foie gras,* veal medallions *à
la Normande,* and scallops and shrimp
in a lobster sauce with Grand Marnier
are among the selections, while desserts
include crème brûlée and other French
classics. An extensive wine list, comprised mostly of French vintages, is
priced to accommodate every budget.
– *bilingual menu, $$$, PF*

MARCEL'S BISTRO

315 King Street West (corner of John
Street) ☎ 416 591-8600
Closed Sunday–Monday; Tuesday–Friday
for lunch and dinner, Saturday for dinner
Subway: ST ANDREW
www.marcels.com

With its low-key ambience, refined menu and incredible service, it's easy to see why Marcel's Bistro has been a favourite of Toronto francophiles since 1984. Marcel's celebrates the fresh, light and pure 'cuisine of the sun' found in the South of France, but also spotlights a different region of the country each month to truly reflect France's culinary diversity. The restaurant's philosophy that cooking is a 'living art' is echoed in the creative selections on its menu – *moules poulettes*, pheasant *terrine*, spinach salad with oyster mushrooms, grilled apples and roquefort cheese, *steak frites*, roasted lamb served with pesto mashed potatoes and grilled Alberta beef tenderloin with *gratin Auvergnat*. For dessert, choose from traditional French fare such as crème brûlée, dark chocolate mousse cake, profiteroles and *tarte au citron*. Marcel's Bistro takes its wines as seriously as the cuisine, and offers an extensive range of French-centric vintages, as well as aperitifs like *kir, pineau des charentes* and *Pastis*. – *bilingual menu, service in French, $$, PF*

PASTIS EXPRESS

1158 Yonge Street (North of Roxborough Street) ☎ 416 928-2212

Closed Sunday–Monday;
Tuesday–Saturday for dinner

Subway: SUMMERHILL

A cross between a bistro and a fine dining restaurant, Rosedale's Pastis serves delicious French cuisine in a warm and inviting atmosphere. In 2004, owner George Gurnon opted for a simpler and less-expensive menu but luckily for

When you're just not in the mood for dessert

Some of us would gladly skip dessert in favour of a nice cheese plate – especially cheese from France, Québec or Switzerland. We're thrilled to report most French restaurants in the city offer superb Franco European cheese plates, so you'll be sure to find both old and new favourites. It goes without saying that the combination of a complex French wine and artisanal bread accompanies a cheese plate perfectly.

us, the *foie gras poelé aux poires caramélisées* (pan-seared *foie gras* served on caramelized pears) made the cut. Simpler combinations include *moules et frites*, fish and chips *à la française* and *steak frites*. Desserts at Pastis Express are decadent (the crème brûlée is rumoured to be one of the best in the city). Courageous diners may want to tackle Pastis' *assiette gourmande* – crème brûlée accompanied by a wedge of dark chocolate cake and raspberry purée, topped with a delicate *tuile* cookie – *fantastique!* The wine list is succinct, but the bottles are well-chosen. – *service in French, $$*

PROVENCE DÉLICES

12 Amelia Street (corner of Parliament Street, close to Wellesley Street) ☎ 416 924-9901

Monday–Sunday for lunch and dinner

Subway: COLLEGE + streetcar or
CASTLE FRANK + bus

www.provencerestaurant.com

bistros & fine dining

Cabbagetown's Provence Délices pays careful attention to everything from the attentive service to the charming decor to the cuisine itself, to ensure you enjoy every moment of your dining experience. Since March 2004, owner and chef Élie Benchitrit has returned to the kitchen to create a revamped menu that is far more affordable than the old one. But don't let the new cuisine fool you – Provence Délices continues to deliver simple yet classic French fare, featuring a rich, complex mixture of fragrances and tastes. Grand Marnier crème brûlée remains the central attraction on the dessert menu. Provence's sophisticated wine list has been honoured by *Wine Spectator* magazine from 1999 to 2004 with the *Wine Spectator Award of Excellence*. *– service in French, bilingual menu, $$*

THE FIFTH

(The restaurant is located on the fifth floor)
225 Richmond Street West (corner of Duncan Street) ☎ 416 979-3005
Thursday-Saturday for dinner
Subway: OSGOODE
www.easyandthefifth.com

Thanks to its refined menu, sensual ambience and top-notch service, The Fifth has established itself as the ideal spot for an upscale evening on the town. If money is no object, try the exquisite new five-course menu prepared by chef Jean-Pierre Challet. Conversely, you can opt for the *à la carte* menu, featuring irresistible delicacies such as duck *magret* and confit of duck leg served in *millefeuille*, elk medallions with *foie gras* and tenderloin

with camembert and truffles. Desserts, including *millefeuille* and brioche bread pudding, will leave you wanting more. A 13-page international wine menu boasts numerous worthy selections. During the summer, be sure to take your meal on the Fifth's magnificent terrace. *– bilingual menu, service in French, $$$$, PF*

THE SULTAN'S TENT

49 Front Street East (West of Church Street) ☎ 416 961-0601
Monday-Sunday for dinner
Subway: UNION
www.thesultanstent.com

Looking for a change of scenery? Dining at The Sultan's Tent combines the best of Moroccan culture and cuisine for an unforgettable experience. Located at the rear of Café Moroc, an evening at The Sultan's Tent's pleases not only the palate, but the senses. Dim lights, billowing tents made of luminous, luxurious fabrics and large, plush banquettes create an enchanting, relaxing atmosphere that makes diners feel like they have been transported to Marrakech. Best of all, sensual belly dancers perform nightly to the rhythms of exotic Arabic music. The food is as beguiling as the decor – the four-course menu, including appetisers and desserts, is a simple yet excellent way to savour many authentic Moroccan dishes. Be sure to finish your meal with a cup of sweet mint tea. *–$$, PF*

french cooking

courses & schools

Now that you know the best places in the city to buy the ingredients you'll need for French cooking, it's time to step into the kitchen and start creating a few sensational dishes of your own. Don't know where to begin? The following schools and courses should help unleash the amateur French chef in you!

ACADEMY OF ARTISANS

490 Eglinton Avenue West (West of Avenue Road) ☎ 416 322-9997

Classes: evenings only

Subway: EGLINTON + bus

www.academyofartisans.com

Grab your apron and head to this Forest Hill cooking school to learn a few new skills and techniques in French and Moroccan cuisine.

CALPHALON CULINARY CENTER

425 King Street West (corner of Spadina Avenue) ☎ 416 847-2212

Classes: evenings and Saturdays

Subway: ST ANDREW

www.calphalonculinarycenter.com

Calphalon Culinary Center offers introductory classes that cater to all levels of culinary expertise, from beginners to advanced students looking to update their skills. Once you have mastered the basics, you can choose from classes pairing food and wine, food and Belgian beer, French cooking and even creating the perfect French crêpe.

COOK GOURMET

1204 Clarkson Road North, Mississauga (South of the QEW) ☎ 905 403-0059

Classes: evenings only

www.cookgourmet.ca

This Mississauga-based cooking school offers French cooking classes.

DISH COOKING STUDIO

390 Dupont Street (West of Spadina Avenue) ☎ 416 920-5559

Classes: throughout the day

Subway: DUPONT

www.dishcookingstudio.com

Dish Cooking Studio is a fun and welcoming place to learn the basics of French and Moroccan cuisine. Past classes have included *A French Market Tour of the St. Lawrence Market*, *Great Bistro Cooking at Home*, *French Flair*, *In A French Kitchen*, *Chez Paris*, *Wine Country Casual* and *A Taste of Morocco*.

GEORGE BROWN COLLEGE

300 Adelaide Street East ☎ 416 415-5000

Classes: evenings and weekends

Subway: KING + streetcar

www.gbrownc.on.ca

You'll find an array of choices here that can take your cooking to another level in the span of just one school semester. French cooking classes include *French Cuisine Classic*, *French Cuisine Contemporary and Crêpes* (sweet and savoury). You'll even find a *French Farmhouse* class that will teach all you need to know about *terroir* (from the earth) cooking. Another option is the *Wine and Dine at Our Table* series, which focuses on a specific cuisine each class, including one evening dedicated to French cooking. For more information, visit the Hospitality and Tourism section of George Brown College's Web site.

GREAT COOKS

Please refer to our directory on page 132 to find all locations for this merchant.

www.greatcooks.ca

Great Cooks has been changing the way Torontonians cook since 1989. Owners Esther Benaim and Maggie McKeown offer students unforgettable culinary learning experiences taught by instructors who are "great cooks" in their own right – chef Bouchra Sidali teaches Moroccan cuisine classes while French cuisine is taught by chef Jean-Pierre Challet. Challet even offers a few classes in French. Now that is a *grand coup* in Toronto! Great Cooks was one of the first private cooking schools in Toronto, and has since opened a third location in Mississauga. The school also offers cooking classes as a team-building activity for large corporations and can easily accommodate groups of up to 70 people. Another note of interest: Great Cooks won the 2004 *Toronto Star Eaters' Choice Award* for the best cooking class category in Toronto.

J.S. BONBONS

329 St. George Street, second floor (at Dupont Street) ☎ 416 920-0274

Classes: evenings and Saturdays

Subway: DUPONT

www.jsbonbons.com

If the thought of J.S. Bonbons's chocolates mentioned in the Chocolatiers section of this guide made your mouth water, you'll be delighted to know you can learn how to make these sinful treasures yourself, at the hands of the master no less! Chocolatier Jenn Stone and other masters demonstrate the joys of chocolate-making in a school located above her shop. Apart from a whole evening talking, looking at and playing with chocolate, participants get to eat everything in sight once the class is finished – *fantastique!*

LCBO

Various locations across the Greater Toronto Area ☎ 1 800 668-5226

Classes: evenings

www.lcbo.com

Wines from Alsace, Belgium Beers and *Whites from the Burgundy Region* are just some of the classes you can take at the LCBO to learn more about wines, spirits and beer from French-speaking countries. The LCBO also conducts a few French cooking courses. In the past, a free cheese-sampling class has been offered by Ektor Stroutzas, Managing Director of Alex Farm Products.

LE CORDON BLEU PARIS

453 Laurier Avenue East, Ottawa ☎ 1 888 289-6302

Classes: evenings, weekends and weekdays

www.lcbottawa.com

Although Ottawa might be a little too far for an evening cooking class, it makes the ideal location for a weekend getaway. Le Cordon Bleu Paris teaches amateurs the basics of French cooking, including a wine-pairing class, and has also produced many top-calibre chefs who have mastered the art of French cuisine.

courses & schools

LOBLAWS

Various locations across the Greater
Toronto Area

Classes: evening and Saturdays

More than 30 Loblaws across Ontario
offer cooking classes, usually located in
culinary labs on the second floor.
Several aspects of French cuisine are
covered in various classes. Learn how to
make the perfect *pâté feuilleté* (puff pastry), or discover new Moroccan and
French cuisine techniques. Chef Jean-
Pierre Challet has even taught a class in
oyster sampling!

RICHMOND HILL CULINARY ARTS CENTRE

1550 16ᵗʰ Avenue, Richmond Hill
☎ 905 508-2665

Classes: evenings

www.culinaryarts.ca

If you have a passion for French sweets,
look no further than Richmond Hill
Culinary Arts Centre, where you'll
learn the art of chocolate-making, how
to turn out the perfect crêpe and the
secrets behind delectable crème brûlée.

STREWN WINERY

1339 Lakeshore Road, Niagara-on-the-Lake
☎ 905 468-8304

Classes: weekends

www.winecountrycooking.com

One of Ontario's most picturesque
regions provides the perfect backdrop
to learn all about French cuisine, wine
sampling and the subtle art of pairing
wine and food. This charming Niagara-
on-the-Lake winery offers day classes
on Saturdays and Sundays, as well as
two-day weekend classes.

THE COOKWORKS

99 Sudbury Street, Suite 8 (South of
Queen Street West) ☎ 416 537-6464

Classes: evenings

Subway: OSGOODE + streetcar

www.thecookworks.com

The Brasserie and *French Bistro* are two
cooking classes at The Cookworks that
will have you cooking like Jacques
Pépin in no time.

a cultural adventure

information &
entertainment

The French are passionate lovers of culture. While Toronto
will never be Paris or Montreal, it is still possible to find many
cultural activities for francophiles in the city and around the
Greater Toronto Area. French newspapers, bookstores, movies,
film festivals, theatres, radio stations, opera, gatherings,
festivals of music and culture are not only great ways to meet
other francophones, but excellent venues and resources for
anglophones and francophiles to get a taste of life *comme les
français.*

information & entertainment

NEWSPAPERS

L'EXPRESS

www.lexpress.to

L'Express is the most important French-language weekly in Toronto, covering international and local news, politics, job postings and, of course, culture and the arts. *L'Express* is available at Maison de la Presse Internationale, Librairie Champlain and Indigo-Chapters for a nominal charge; however, you'll also find free copies in many locations across the city, such as Alliance Française de Toronto, Glendon College at York University and the Consulate General of France in Toronto.

LE MÉTROPOLITAIN

www.lemetropolitain.com

Le Métropolitain focuses on francophone lifestyles in Toronto and the Greater Toronto Area. The publication is available free of charge in most locations where *L'Express* is distributed.

BOOKS, COMIC BOOKS & MAGAZINES

À BON VERRE BONNE TABLE

☎ 1 800 682-5226
www.lcbo.com/french/
fooddrink/index.shtml

À Bon Verre Bonne Table is the French version of the LCBO's popular *Food & Drink* magazine. Each edition is packed with great recipes and suggestions for finding the right beverage to accompany a meal or to enjoy alone.

You'll also find an eclectic group of recipes, cocktails and menus, articles about food, ideas for unusual place settings and centrepieces, the newest food gadgets and even the latest musical hits to accompany everything from picnics to parties. The magazines are published several times a year, and are distributed free of charge inside LCBO stores. Their popularity means they have a very short shelf life (this holds especially true of *À Bon Verre Bonne Table,* as each LCBO only receives a small quantity of the French edition) – so be sure to pick yours up early! The next edition's publishing date can always be found in the current edition's masthead. Home-delivery is available for a small charge, call the info line for further details.

AMAZON.CA

www.amazon.ca

The Canadian branch of the world's biggest virtual bookstore carries a lot of classic and contemporary French fiction, as well as French titles in numerous other genres.

ARCHAMBAULT.CA

www.archambault.ca

This well-known Quebec-based site offers a diverse range of books in both French and English, including titles on the arts, biographies, comics, cooking, computers, children's literature, general fiction, health, reference materials, social sciences and travel. Not sure what to get? Archambault.ca features a list of recommended books that makes gift-giving and decision-making easy.

INDIGO-CHAPTERS

Various locations across the Greater Toronto Area

www.chapters.indigo.ca

The Indigo-Chapters group is comprised of the following bookstores: Chapters, Coles Books, Indigo and The World's Biggest Bookstore (20 Edward Street ☎ 416 977-7009). Most of the great classics of Camus, Molière and Voltaire's language can be found at this family of bookstores, as well as a selection of French-language magazines and newspapers.

LIBRAIRIE CHAMPLAIN

468 Queen Street East (East of Parliament Street) ☎ 416 364-4345

Monday–Thursday 9–6, Friday 9–8, Saturday 9–5, closed Sunday

Subway: QUEEN + streetcar

www.librairiechamplain.com

Librairie Champlain is the largest source of French-language books and magazines in Toronto. You'll find classic literature, romance and mystery novels, children's educational and recreational books, cartoons, dictionaries, CDs and educational games, as well as magazines and newspapers from France, Quebec and Ontario. If, by some chance, you *can't* find what you're looking for on the shelves, simply stop by the special order desk and they will try to locate it for you.

MAISON DE LA PRESSE INTERNATIONALE

99 Yorkville Avenue ☎ 416 928-2328

Monday-Thursday 8:30-11, Friday-Saturday 8:30-midnight, Sunday 8:30-11

Subway: BAY or MUSEUM

Did you know?

During the seventeenth century, French royalty indulged in lavish ceremonies where food was centre stage. Since the rule of thumb at the time was to please royalty at all costs, many chefs prepared extravagant feasts that were not only elaborate but also extremely expensive. One of the first cookbooks to document such grandeur was *Le cuisinier royal et bourgeois* by François Massaliot. This culinary time capsule recounts favourite recipes of royalty, many favoured by King Louis XIV. Many French food historians consider this to be the book that launched the haute cuisine movement. *La physiologie du goût*, written in 1825 by Jean Anthelme Brillat-Savarin, is another important book that marks the beginning of the culinary arts in France. We may not have the time or inclination to spend countless hours preparing a meal fit for a king, but we can surely find the inspiration within the pages of these, and other, French cookbooks and magazines.

Loads of great French books, magazines, newspapers and travel guides can be found at Maison de la Presse Internationale, the Toronto location of the popular Montreal-based chain.

PRESSE INTERNATIONALE

Various locations across the Greater Toronto Area

Presse Internationale carries a fantastic selection of French-language magazines and newspapers from around the world. With multiple locations and extended hours, Presse Internationale is tops for Toronto's francophone readers.

(Note: though similar in name, Presse Internationale is not the same as Maison de la Presse Internationale.)

QUÉBEC LOISIRS

☎ 1 800 361-2441
www.quebecloisirs.com

The francophone's answer to Amazon.ca! Québec Loisirs is the Canadian branch of France's France Loisirs Web site (www.franceloisirs.com) and carries much the same content, without the expense of overseas shipping costs. In addition, members are entitled to 20 to 40 per cent off purchases.

RENAUD-BRAY

☎ 1 888 746-2283
www.renaud-bray.com

Quebec-based Renaud-Bray's Web site has a diverse selection of French books covering all genres.

Did you know?

No one spoke English in 1720 Toronto!

In 1720, French was the official language of our multicultural and multilingual city. *Le magasin royal de Toronto* (The Royal General Store), located in Baby Point in West Toronto, was the heart and soul of the fur trade. (If you want to retrace the steps of history, Baby Point is located North of Bloor Street West and Northeast of the Old Mill restaurant, along the Humber River). *Le magasin royal* was built in 1720 inside the Toronto Fort (Toronto's first fort protecting France's interests in Toronto). This trading post was the first building in a city that had, until then, never been considered a grounding point. Up until 1720, Toronto's reputation was that of a transient city, where people came to trade but not to live. *Le magasin royal* changed this notion and quickly become the cradle of French civilization West of the Quebec frontiers.

The trading industry created a high volume of businessmen who mainly negotiated and exchanged *en français*. *Le magasin royal* was not the only location in Toronto where French was the language commonly used – the Red River, located in the city's east-end (at the Scarborough border, an area still known today as the "Rouge"), was another French centre. In fact, French language and culture was predominant in our city until Toronto came under British rule in 1793. Even though not all Torontonians speak French today, the French roots set down here hundreds of years ago will continue to be a presence for many more centuries to come.

If you're a French history buff, contact la Société d'histoire de Toronto at www.sht.ca for more fascinating facts about Toronto.

Story inspired by Donald Jones' story in the *Toronto Star* "Torontonians all spoke French in 1720."

SALON DU LIVRE DE TORONTO

www.salondulivredetoronto.ca

Held annually every autumn at the Metro Toronto Convention Centre (255 Front Street West), Salon du Livre de Toronto offers the largest selection of French books in Ontario. It's also a great forum to meet and talk to French authors and publishers through various scheduled seminars and book-signing sessions.

TALOUA

☎ 416 934-0588

Welcome to the "multicultur-elle" world of *Taloua! Taloua* means "young women" in Agni, a dialect spoken in the Ivory Coast. This Toronto-based, French-language multicultural magazine for women boasts a contemporary style, an eclectic mix of cultures, a diverse range of subjects from contributors all over the world and a pool of talented up-and-coming photographers, graphic designers, illustrators and writers. In fact, *Taloua*'s only drawback is that it is published just twice a year! *Taloua* is available at Maison de la Presse Internationale, Chapters and Indigo. You can also order a copy by phone.

THE BEGUILING

601 Markham Street (West of Bathurst Street, near Honest Ed's superstore)
☎ 416 533-9168

Monday-Thursday 11-7; Friday 11-9; Saturday 11-7; Sunday 12-6

www.beguiling.com

Established in 1987, The Beguiling is perhaps Toronto's most important

Did you know?

The Beguiling organises an annual comic book festival that usually takes place each May. Visit www.toronto-comics.com for more information.

comic book store. Located in the shadow of the gigantic Honest Ed's, this little bookstore hides a huge collection of rare French comics – in fact, half of the first floor is devoted to French, Swiss and Belgian comic books. If you're looking for a rare find, ask owner Peter Birkemoe, who knows all there is to know when it comes to Franco-European comic books. The Beguiling is a colourful bookstore filled with some of the rarest comic books on the market, and the ideal place to find the perfect gift for comic book lovers.

THE FILM REFERENCE LIBRARY

2 Carlton Street (Mezzanine level)
☎ 416 967-1517

Winter and summer hours are posted on the Web site

Subway: COLLEGE (Carlton exit)

libraryservices@torfilmfest.ca
www.filmreferencelibrary.ca

Of the 17,000 or so books about film on the shelves of The Film Reference Library, about 1,200 are in French. Subjects covered include biographies of many pioneers in the world of film, theatre, acting, television, film history, technical aspects of film-making, cinematography and script writing. You'll also find a variety of French-language magazines covering the francophone film industry such as *Trafic* (France), *24 images* (Quebec), *L'avant-scène*

information & entertainment

cinéma (France), *Cahiers du cinéma* (France), *Jeune cinéma* (France) and *Ciné bulles* (France), as well as numerous English-language magazines reviewing films from Latin American, Asia and Europe, including France.

THE HOUSE OF MR. FIGLIO

748 Broadview Avenue (South of Danforth Avenue) ☎ 416 778-9996
call for hours of operation
www.rgalre.com

"The House of Mr. Figlio is a little house to feed the imagination."
— SERGE BENNATHAN

Serge Bennathan is not only the artist director of the famed Toronto dance troupe Dancemakers; he is also an accomplished writer and illustrator of a series of French children's books. These wonderful creative treasures can be found only at The House of Mr. Figlio art gallery.

MUSIC

AMAZON.CA

www.amazon.ca

Amazon stocks both the latest hits and older classics in francophone music.

ARCHAMBAULT MUSIQUE

www.archambault.ca

Archambault Musique has a wide variety of music from Quebec, France and other French-speaking countries.

HMV

Various locations across the Greater Toronto Area
www.hmv.ca

Most HMV stores contain a small selection of the biggest artists in both French and Quebecois music. However, if there's a particular *chanteur* or *chanteuse* you're dying to hear, simply place a special order and HMV will try to find the title.

LIBRAIRIE CHAMPLAIN

468 Queen Street East (East of Parliament Street) ☎ 416 364-4345
Monday–Thursday 9–6, Friday 9–8, Saturday 9–5, closed Sunday
Subway: QUEEN + streetcar
www.librairiechamplain.com

The most popular French titles are available at Librairie Champlain.

QUÉBEC LOISIRS

☎ 1 800 361-2441
www.quebecloisirs.com

From pop-rock to country and Christmas music to francophone

artists … you'll find it all at Québec Loisirs!

RENAUD-BRAY

☎ 1 888 746-2283

www.renaud-bray.com

This Quebec-based site carries all the latest and greatest French music.

SAM THE RECORD MAN

347 Yonge Street (North of Dundas Street)
☎ 416 646-2775

Monday-Thursday 10-9; Friday-Saturday 10-11; Sunday 10-6

Subway: DUNDAS

Sam the Record Man is tops for French music in Toronto – the second floor of this superstore contains one of the city's most impressive and extensive collections of music from France and Quebec. You'll find it all here, from golden oldies to the latest chart-topping hits; from Yves Montand and Patrick Bruel to Gilles Vigneault and Garou. If you are looking for a particular title that is not stocked, ask the staff to place a special order.

FILM FESTIVALS

CINÉFRANCO – TORONTO FRENCH FILM FESTIVAL

☎ 416 928-6595

www.cinefranco.com

C'est vrai? One full week of French films, right here in Toronto? *Mais, oui!* Cinéfranco – the Annual Celebration of French Language Cinema takes place every year at the end of March and beginning of April. All the films

have subtitles, so there is no excuse for anglophones to miss a wonderful week of great films. Thanks to the passion and commitment of founder and artistic director extraordinaire, Marcelle Lean, Torontonians have an extra reason to look forward to spring!

TORONTO INTERNATIONAL FILM FESTIVAL – FESTIVAL INTERNATIONAL DU FILM DE TORONTO

www.e.bell.ca/filmfest

Held at the beginning of September, the Toronto International Film Festival (Festival international du film de Toronto) marks the annual arrival of big movies and even bigger movie stars in the city. Usually, quite a few French films of various genres are screened amongst the festival's dazzling and diverse repertoire.

Did you know?

Francophones commonly refer to film as *le septième art* (the seventh art). Arguably, film is the only art form to not only encompass the other six arts – architecture, dance, music, painting, poetry and sculpture – but effortlessly braid them together to create a harmonious tapestry.

CINEMAS

CARLTON

20 Carlton Street (East of Yonge Street)
☎ 416 598-2309

Subway: COLLEGE

information & entertainment

CUMBERLAND

159 Cumberland Street (corner of Avenue Road) ☎ 416 646-0444

Subway: BAY (Cumberland exit)

These two theatres show a fair number of superb French films throughout the year. Check your weekly paper for current listings.

CINÉ-JEUDI

150 John Street (National Film Board/Office national du film)
☎ 416 973-3012

Subway: OSGOODE

www.alliance-francaise.ca

Now francophiles can experience the latest French and French-Canadian cinematographic hits on a big screen without having to wait for Cinéfranco or the Toronto International Film Festival! The Consulate General of France in Toronto, the National Film Board, Cinéfranco, the Bureau du Québec and Alliance Française de Toronto have teamed up to create Ciné-Jeudi – year-round presentations of French cinema in Toronto. Screenings take place in the viewing room located on the second floor of the National Film Board (Office national du film) on the first Thursday of every month. For more information about upcoming films, visit Alliance Française de Toronto's Web site.

CINEMATHÈQUE ONTARIO

317 Dundas Street (Jackman Hall, Art Gallery of Ontario, McCaul Street entrance) ☎ 416 968-FILM (3456), extension 2

Subway: ST PATRICK

www.e.bell.ca/filmfest

Cinemathèque Ontario is a division of the Toronto International Film Festival Group (Festival international du film de Toronto) focusing on retrospectives and special series. Both well-known and obscure titles are screened from some of the biggest directors in French film – Cocteau, Deray, Godard, Malle, Renoir, Tati and Truffaut, to name but a few. Following the success of the now-defunct Summer in France, Classics of French Cinema program, Cinematheque Ontario has continued to spotlight French films during the months of July and August. All films are subtitled, so anglophones can join in the fun, too. *Bon film!*

THE FILM REFERENCE LIBRARY

2 Carlton Street (Mezzanine level)
☎ 416 967-1517

Winter and summer hours are posted on the Web site

Subway: COLLEGE (Carlton exit)

libraryservices@torfilmfest.ca
www.filmreferencelibrary.ca

The Film Reference Library is a bountiful resource centre for French *cinéphiles!* With more than 8,000 Canadian and international films to choose from (more than 540 of which are French, all with English subtitles), the library offers professionals, scholars and cinema buffs an exhaustive resource of cinematographic reference materials. Films can even be viewed on the premises, in one of two viewing rooms. There's even viewing equipment for European DVDs – a rare find in Toronto! The Film Reference Library is another division of the Toronto International Film Festival Group

(Festival international du film de Toronto). Members can access all the library's services for free (details on their Web site). If you need assistance, just ask one of the library's incredibly knowledgeable employees, who are resources in their own right and will not hesitate to help you in your search.

VIDEO & DVD RENTALS

▸ QUEEN VIDEO

Please refer to our directory on page 132 to find all locations for this merchant.

▸ REVUE VIDEO

207 Danforth Avenue (near Broadview Avenue) ☎ 416 778-5776

Monday–Sunday 11–10

Subway: BROADVIEW

▸ SUSPECT VIDEO

Please refer to our directory on page 132 to find all locations for this merchant.

▸ VERY VIDEO

1375 Yonge Street (South of St. Clair Avenue) ☎ 416 929-8379

Monday-Thursday 10-10; Friday-Saturday 10-11; Sunday 11-10

Subway: ST. CLAIR

This independent video store offer an amazing selection of movies from France and other French-language countries – with lots of titles to choose from! You'll find rare movies, just-released films and older classics from the French New Wave.

VIDEO & DVD SALES

AMAZON.CA

www.amazon.ca

This online superstore features the latest French blockbusters.

ARCHAMBAULT.CA

www.archambault.ca

From Louis de Funès to Vincent Perez and Clint Eastwood to Pierce Brosnan, you'll find it all at Archambault's online store. Archambault.ca features many French and translated films in both video and DVD formats.

LIBRAIRIE CHAMPLAIN

468 Queen Street East (East of Parliament Street) ☎ 416 364-4345

Monday–Thursday 9–6, Friday 9–8, Saturday 9–5, closed Sunday

Subway: QUEEN + streetcar
www.librairiechamplain.com

Librairie Champlain sells numerous French films on video and DVD, as well as a selection of cartoons and movies for younger francophiles.

QUÉBEC LOISIRS

☎ 1 800 361-2441
www.quebecloisirs.com

Québec Loisirs offers an assortment of films and TV series in French. Not sure what to choose? Consult its bestsellers list for popular titles or choose from Québec Loisirs own list of favourites.

RENAUD-BRAY

☎ 1 888 746-2283

www.renaud-bray.com

Some of the best films French cinema has to offer are only a click away at Renaud-Bray's Web site.

SAM THE RECORD MAN

347 Yonge Street (North of Dundas Street)
☎ 416 646-2775

Monday-Thursday 10-9; Friday-Saturday 10-11; Sunday 10-6

Subway: DUNDAS

Sam the Record Man has a good selection of French films on video and DVD. If you can't find what you're looking for, Sam's will be happy to place a special order.

WATCHING FRENCH FILMS AT HOME

TFO

Audience Relations
☎ 1 800 463-6886

Monday–Friday 9–5

www.tfo.org

The celebration of "the seventh art" takes place every night at 9 p.m. on TFO (the French arm of TVO), where you'll discover films from France, Quebec and French Canada, Africa and Belgium (unfortunately for anglophones, films are shown without English subtitles). To keep up to date

on films scheduled for the coming season, consult TFO's *Passeport Cinema* booklet, which includes information about each film aired (synopsis, schedule, critique, length, country of origin, year of production, producer, director and cast). Call Audience Relations to have a free *Passeport* mailed to your home.

ART GALLERIES

ART GALLERY OF ONTARIO (AGO)

317 Dundas Street West (West of McCaul Street) ☎ 416 979-6648

Closed Monday, Tuesday–Friday 11–6, Wednesday 11–8:30, Saturday–Sunday 10–5:30

Subway: ST PATRICK

www.ago.net

From Monet to Cézanne to Degas, the Art Gallery of Ontario is the ideal place to further your education in the world of fine arts – *en français*. All descriptions for special exhibits and permanent collections, as well as audio guides, are available in French and English.

GLENDON GALLERY

2275 Bayview Avenue ☎ 416 487-6859

Closed Sunday–Monday; Tuesday, Wednesday, Friday 12–3, Thursday 11–2, Saturday 1–4

Subway: LAWRENCE +bus

www.glendon.yorku.ca/gallery

The Glendon Gallery is a public art gallery located on the Glendon campus of York University. The gallery features monthly exhibitions, with emphasis on education and contemporary art.

Literature in French and English, as well as guided tours and lectures by artists and curators, complement the program.

ROYAL ONTARIO MUSEUM (ROM)

100 Queen's Park Crescent (corner of Bloor Street) ☎ 416 586-8000

Monday–Thursday 10–6, Friday 10–9:30, Saturday–Sunday 10–6

Subway: MUSEUM

www.rom.on.ca

At the Royal Ontario Museum, treasures from the past and present can be discovered in both French and in English. All the descriptions on the different pieces in the permanent, curated and special exhibits are available in both languages. Thematic guides for special exhibits are also available in French and bilingual guides are on staff to help with French group tours.

THEATRE

THÉÂTRE FRANÇAIS DE TORONTO

26 Berkeley Street (South of Front Street) ☎ 416 534-6604

Subway: KING + streetcar

www.theatrefrancais.com

Created in 1967, Théâtre français de Toronto (TfT) features a variety of quality productions for francophone adults and children. Most plays are adapted from French, French-Canadian or international literature. Performances take place at the Berkeley Street Theatre. A new feature is sure to excite francophiles – since 2005, Théâtre français de Toronto has been

offering several French productions with English subtitles.

THÉÂTRE LA TANGENTE

☎ 416 487-6832

www.theatrelatangente.ca

Accolades for this Toronto-based theatre company have come from as far away as Quebec and Paris. Théâtre La

information & entertainment

Tangente presents only original creative works – no adaptations or translation pieces here. This interesting way of approaching theatre means only one new piece is produced every two years.

Dance Troupes & Opera

CORPUS

805 Dovercourt Road (North of Bloor Street West) ☎ 416 516-4025
www.corpus.ca

CORPUS is a local dance troupe known for its original and creative work for broad audiences, including children. The company combines contemporary dance and physical theatre to create its trademark surrealist humour. Led by co-artistic directors Sylvie Bouchard and David Danzon, CORPUS has toured extensively in Ontario and across Canada. Visit *"What's on!"* on our Web site (www.franco-toronto.ca) for further details about upcoming performances.

DANCEMAKERS

55 Mill Street (Distillery District)
☎ 416 367-1800
www.dancemakers.org

Established in 1974, Dancemakers' contribution to the advancement of dance in Toronto is irrefutable. This avant-garde dance troupe was originally the brain child of a group of independent dancers. Today, the troupe performs under the creative direction of one of its founding members, Serge Bennathan, who also happens to be French. Although Dancemakers is not an exclusively French dance troupe, the troupe has performed many great

French pieces, such as *Le projet Satie, Tziganes, C'est beau ça la vie, La vie invisible* and *Les vents tumultueux.* Dancemakers' performances are usually held at the Harbourfront Centre theatre. For more details on their 2005–2006 performance schedule, visit *"What's on!"* on our Web site (www.franco-toronto.ca).

OPERA ATELIER

☎ 416 703-3767
www.operaatelier.com

Opera Atelier reproduces opera, ballets and dramas from the seventeenth and eighteenth century. The productions draw upon the aesthetics and ideals of the period, featuring soloists of international acclaim, original instruments, elaborate stage decor, exquisite costumes and an imaginative energy that truly sets the company apart. That said, Opera Atelier has always delivered productions infused with a contemporary flair to better suit the reality of a modern audience. The 2005-2006 season promises to be exciting with Henry Purcell's *Dido and Aeneas* and other gems. Opera Atelier's productions take place at the Elgin Theatre (189 Yonge Street), with many English productions subtitled in French. Tickets are available through Ticketmaster (416 872-5555).

Did you know?

Radio-Canada, TV5 and TVA regularly feature a variety of French films. Consult your television guide for showtimes.

Radio

Coopérative radiophonique de Toronto – 105.1 FM

Coopérative radiophonique de Toronto is the only French community radio station covering the Greater Toronto Area.

Radio-Canada – 860 AM

Radio-Canada (Ontario) is the local version of CBC's national French-language radio station, which broadcasts many different cultural, variety and entertainment shows.

Television

RDI (Réseau d'information)

This 24-hour national and international news station presents breaking news much in the same style as CNN.

SRC (Société Radio-Canada)

La Société Radio-Canada's diverse programming includes French-language news, entertainment, information, sitcoms, soap operas and films.

TFO

www.tfo.org

TFO is the French arm of TVO. The station's cultural investment in Ontario's French community is reflected in its vast range of programming, which is mostly centred on the lives of Franco-Ontarians. TFO's local focus includes *Panorama* and

FranCœur, the first Franco-Ontarian soap opera.

TV5

www.tv5.ca

Launched in 1984, TV5 is the only international French television station. Programs vary from news to entertainment and movies from France, Quebec, Switzerland, Belgium, the Antilles and many French-speaking nations in Africa.

TVA-CHOT

www.chot.ca

Montreal-based TVA television station showcases a broad range of entertainment and information-based shows.

French Cultural Events in Toronto

Alliance Française de Toronto

www.alliance-francaise.ca

Alliance Française de Toronto's Web site has a full page detailing Toronto's best French cultural and entertainment happenings.

Bureau du Québec à Toronto

20 Queen Street West, Suite 1504
☎ 416 977-6713

Bureau du Québec represents Quebec's artistic and cultural interests across Canada. The Toronto chapter has always been very active in promoting many talented artists from the province that gave birth to the phenomenonal Cirque du Soleil. To keep updated on artistic performances from Quebec tal-

information & entertainment

ALLIANCE FRANÇAISE DE TORONTO (www.alliance-francaise.ca) is a great place to learn French. You'll also be able to take advantage of the following services:

▸ TOURISM IN FRANCE

Guide books, atlases, maps, albums, CD-ROMs, magazines and more than 50 video tapes to help plan your next holiday to France.

▸ LEARNING TOOLS

Master the French language with more than 30 video tapes, dictionaries, easy-reading books, audiotapes and CD-ROMs.

▸ FRENCH AND FRANCOPHONE MUSIC

Sample a variety of artists and genres on both CDs and tapes.

▸ FRENCH AND FRANCOPHONE LITERATURE

Explore a library of more than 1,800 books, ranging from classic to contemporary authors.

▸ CONTEMPORARY FRENCH PRODUCTIONS

Books, newspapers, magazines and about 100 video tapes focusing on science, the arts and current issues.

▸ FRENCH FILMS

Choose from more than 250 French blockbusters available for rent.

ent, visit *"What's on!"* on our Web site (www.franco-toronto.ca), or consult *L'Express* newspaper.

CENTRE FRANCOPHONE DE TORONTO

20 Lower Spadina Avenue (South of Front Street) ☎ 416 203-1220
Monday–Friday 8:30–4:30
Subway: UNION + streetcar
www.centrefranco.org

Visit Centre francophone de Toronto's *calendrier des évènements* (calendar of events) Web site to find out what's happening around the city. *Note: this Web site is only available in French.*

CONSULATE GENERAL OF FRANCE IN TORONTO

www.consulfrance-toronto.org

The Consulate General of France in Toronto outlines the city's upcoming French events on their Web site.

HARBOURFRONT CENTRE

235 Queens Quay West (West of University Avenue)
www.harbourfrontcentre.com

Each year, Harbourfront Centre presents an extensive agenda of more than 4000 cultural, educational and recreational activities. There are more than a dozen events featuring and highlighting francophone talent from Ontario, France and Quebec. Consult *"What's on!"* on our Web site (www.franco-toronto.ca) to plan your next event.

RADIO-CANADA

www.radio-canada.ca/regions/ontario

This French-only site features a calendar of events put together by Claudette Gravel, host of *Enfin samedi.*

TORONTO-FRANCO

☎ 416 929-3769

www.toronto-franco.com

Finally – a web-based portal for Toronto's francophone community! Since January 2004, the innovators at Toronto-Franco have created a convenient way for francophones living in the city to access the information they need, including local and international news stories, community service announcements and cultural information. Francophiles, take note – a full English version of this portal is also available. *Note: Although Toronto-Franco is a separate entity from* The French Side of Toronto *(www.franco-toronto.ca), the two organisations are accessible from each other's Web sites through a link exchange.*

EVENING ENTERTAINMENT & SOCIAL GATHERINGS

FRANCO FUN WEDNESDAYS

☎ 416 596-8437

Jacques Charette, Coordinator
jacques.charette@sympatico.ca

This is an ideal opportunity for newcomers to Toronto to network and make new friends. Every Wednesday at 6 p.m., francophones and francophiles gather for drinks, laughter and conversation at a central Toronto bar or coffee house. For now, the meeting ground is the Duke of Richmond pub (20 Queen Street West).

FRANCO FUN DINNERS

☎ 416 596-8437

Jacques Charette, Coordinator
jacques.charette@sympatico.ca

One Thursday a month, Franco Fun Dinners holds a French evening at a local restaurant. This is a perfect way to both discover new restaurants and meet new faces. Meals are usually in the $25 range (tax and tip inclusive), even for the most anticipated event of the year – an annual lobster dinner in June!

FRANCOPHONIQUE

☎ 416 763-8535

www.francophonique.com

A networking system for French-speaking individuals in Toronto, Francophonique is *the* French urban connection where up-and-coming young Franco-Torontonians meet. Francophonique organises many fun-filled brunches and ultra-cool social evenings.

TAM TAM CYBER CAFÉ

86 Nassau Street (inside Kensington Market) ☎ 416 603-0007

Monday-Sunday 8:30-7

Subway: SPADINA + streetcar;
QUEEN'S PARK + streetcar

Just say *bonjour* as you walk in the door! A branch of the Centre des Jeunes Francophones de Toronto, Tam Tam Cyber Café opened its doors in March 2004. Like the area and its residents, the atmosphere here is very trendy and multicultural, but also very welcoming.

The attentive staff will help you with whatever you need. Located a few steps away from a youth hostel popular with French globetrotters, Tam Tam Cyber Café offers Internet access, a photocopier and fax services at competitive prices. Every Saturday, there is a French-style breakfast including baguettes and croissants. On weekdays, drop by for animated discussions with guest speakers, live music, art exhibits and more.

ZAZOU

315 King Street West (corner of John Street) ☎ 416 591-8600 or 416 591-3600

5 p.m. until the last customer has left

Subway: ST ANDREW

www.zazoulounge.com

Part of the Marcel's Bistro and Le Saint Tropez family, Zazou is a chic and sophisticated lounge that welcomes thirtysomething and fortysomething crowds in search of an oasis to unwind after a long day at the office. If you're looking for a comfortable setting, cool music and décor that lends itself to total relaxation, then drop by Zazou's for a drink.

FRANCOPHONE ASSOCIATIONS IN TORONTO

The number of francophone associations in and around Toronto continues to grow steadily, much to our delight. However, in order to ensure we could include all these associations and continue promoting them for the benefit of our readers, we regrettably had to trim the descriptions for each. To find out more about each organisation, including links to their Web sites, visit www.franco-toronto.ca and select the *"Francophone Associations"* link.

CULTURAL & SOCIAL ASSOCIATIONS

- Association Marocaine de Toronto
- Centre des Jeunes Francophones de Toronto
- Centre médicosocial de Toronto
- Club Richelieu de Toronto
- Club Richelieu Trillium de Toronto
- Le Cercle de l'Amitié Canadien de Toronto
- La Société d'histoire de Toronto
- Toronto Accueil

BUSINESS ASSOCIATIONS

- Association des femmes d'affaires francophones
- Association francophone des entrepreneurs et des professionnels (AFEP)
- Belgian Canadian Business Association
- Club Canadien de Toronto
- French Chamber of Commerce of Canada
- Regroupement des gens d'affaires africains canadiens

ARTISTS' ASSOCIATIONS

- BRAVO – Bureau des regroupements des artistes visuels de l'Ontario

the french side of toronto by neighbourhood

NEIGHBOURHOOD	BREADS, PÂTISSERIES & FRENCH SWEETS	CHOCOLATIERS	CHEESE SHOPS & CRÈME FRAÎCHE	DRIED MEATS, PÂTÉS & TERRINES
THE BEACH, EAST TORONTO & THE DANFORTH	Bonjour Brioche Zane	Belgian Chocolate Shop Sun Valley Fine Foods	Alex Farm Sun Valley Fine Foods	Alex Farm Meat on the Beach
BLOOR WEST VILLAGE & WEST TORONTO	Cheese Boutique Ma Maison Max's Market Pâtisserie Saint Honoré	Bernard Callebaut Cheese Boutique Max's Market	Alex Farm Cheese Boutique Max's Market The Cheese Dairy Whitehouse Meats	Alex Farm Cheese Boutique Ma Maison Max's Market The Village Butcher Whitehouse Meats
DOWNTOWN	Balzac's Coffee House Daniel et Daniel Mercatto Montreal Bread Co. St. Urbain Bagel Bakery Scheffler's	Chocolates & Creams Daniel et Daniel Domino Foods Eve's Temptations Mercatto Scheffler's The Bay	Alex Farm Chris' Cheesemongers Olympic Cheese Mart Scheffler's	Alex Farm Caviar Direct Chris' Cheesemongers Cumbrae's Daniel et Daniel Olympic Cheese Mart Scheffler's Whitehouse Meats
KENSINGTON, BALDWIN ST. & COLLEGE ST.	Casa Açoreana Harbord Bakery Magnolia	Chocolate Addict	Cheese Magic Global Cheese Mendel's Creamery	Global Cheese Mendel's Creamery
ENTERTAINMENT DISTRICT, KING ST. WEST & QUEEN ST. WEST	Clafouti Le Gourmand Senses	Clafouti J.S. Bonbons Le Gourmand Senses		
YORKVILLE, AVENUE RD., DAVENPORT RD. & DUPONT AVE.	Dinah's Cupboard Frangipane Holt Renfrew Montreal Bread Co. Pusateri's Whole Foods	Dinah's Cupboard Frangipane Holt Renfrew J.S. Bonbons Leonidas Simone Marie Belgian Chocolate Teuscher Whole Foods	Alex Farm Dinah's Cupboard Pusateri's Whole Foods	Alex Farm Dinah's Cupboard Pusateri's Whole Foods

BUTCHERS	FISHMONGERS & OYSTER SPECIALISTS	SPICES	OTHER FRENCH SPECIALTIES	RESTAURANTS
Meat on the Beach Royal Beef	Bill's Lobster	Bulk Barn Strictly Bulk	Alex Farm Bonjour Brioche Zane	Batifole Bonjour Brioche Cafe Brussels Sauvignon Bistro
Bloor Meat Market The Village Butcher Whitehouse Meats	Big Fish Market Snappers Fish Market The Village Butcher	Strictly Bulk	Alex Farm Cheese Boutique Ma Maison Max's Market Pâtisserie Saint Honoré The Village Butcher	La Petite France Merlot
Brown Brothers Meats Cumbrae's Di Liso's Fine Meats La Boucherie Manos Meats Scheffler's St. Lawrence Upper Cut Whitehouse Meats Witteveen Meats	Caviar Direct Domenic's Fish Market Domino Foods Mike's Fish Market Seafront Fish Market	Domino Foods	Alex Farm Chris' Cheesemongers Daniel et Daniel Domino Foods Mercatto Scheffler's Great Cooks Olympic Cheese Mart	Bistro 990 Biff's Bloor Street Diner Bouchon Café Moroc/ The Sultan's Tent Café Nicole Crêpes à GoGo Le Papillon Le Petit Déjeuner Matignon Midi Bistro Montreal Bread Co. Provence Délices
European Quality Meats Grace Meat Market	Coral Sea Fish Market Global Cheese Mendel's Creamery New Seaway Sea Kings Seven Seas Fish	Casa Açoreana House of Spice Perola		Bodega Café Margaux Gamelle La Palette
	Oyster Boy Rodney's Oyster House		Clafouti Le Gourmand	Bloor Street Diner Café Crêpe Le Saint Tropez Le Sélect Bistro Marcel's Bistro Restaurant Jules The Fifth
Pusateri's	Pusateri's		Alex Farm Dinah's Cupboard Holt Renfrew Pusateri's Whole Foods	Arlequin Bistro Tournesol Holt's Café Jacques Bistro Le Paradis Le Trou Normand Michelle's Brasserie Montreal Bread Co.

the french side of toronto by neighbourhood

NEIGHBOURHOOD	BREADS, PÂTISSERIES & FRENCH SWEETS	CHOCOLATIERS	CHEESE SHOPS & CRÈME FRAÎCHE	DRIED MEATS, PÂTÉS & TERRINES
MIDTOWN & SUMMERHILL	All the Best Fine Foods Fleurdelys Pâtisserie Le Petit Gourmet Pain Perdu Patachou St. Urbain Bagel Bakery	Pain Perdu Sobeys	Alex Farm All the Best Fine Foods Sobeys	Alex Farm All the Best Fine Foods Patachou Sobeys The Butchers
BAYVIEW & MOUNT PLEASANT	Le Comptoir de Célestin La Cigogne Rahier The Bagel House	La Cigogne Rahier The Chocolate Messenger	Alex Farm	Alex Farm Whitehouse Meats
UPTOWN	Ace Bakery Pusateri's Senses The Bagel House	Ararat Pusateri's Senses Swiss-Master Chocolatier	Pusateri's	Pusateri's The Butcher Block Café
GREATER TORONTO	Arz Bakery Brandt Meat Packers Ltd. Pâtisserie d'Or Pâtisserie Daudet Pâtisserie Le Papillon St. Urbain Bagel Bakery	Arz Bakery Bernard Callebaut Brandt Meat Packers Ltd. Pâtisserie d'Or Pâtisserie Le Papillon Truffle Treasures	Arz Bakery Olympic Cheese Mart Quality Cheese	Brandt Meat Packers Ltd. Olympic Cheese Mart

BOUCHERIES	FISHMONGERS & OYSTER SPECIALISTS	SPICES	OTHER FRENCH SPECIALTIES	RESTAURANTS
Nicola's Fine Foods Olliffe Sobeys The Butchers	Avenue Seafood Pisces Gourmet		Alex Farm All the Best Fine Foods Harvest Wagon Pain Perdu Patachou	Avant-Goût Boujadi Didier Le Petit Gourmet Pastis Express Quartier
Whitehouse Meats			Alex Farm Rahier	Célestin La Cigogne Lolo Restaurant

Cavallino
Highland Farms
Pusateri's
The Butcher Block
  Café
	Caviar Centre
	City Fish Market
	Diana's Seafood
	Highland Farms
	Newport Fish
	  Importers
	Pusateri's
			Ararat
			Pusateri's
				Auberge du
				  Pommier
				Bloor Street Diner
				Chez Laurent
				La Maison Benoît
				Le Continental
				Le Montmartre
				L'Escargot Bistro
				Monitz
				Pourquoi Pas

Brandt Meat
  Packers Ltd.
European Quality
  Meats
	Brandt Meat
	  Packers Ltd.
	Lobster Island
		Bulk Barn	Arz Bakery
			Brandt Meat
			  Packers Ltd.
			Olympic Cheese
			  Mart
			Pâtisserie d'Or
			Petit Gâteau
				Bistro 1603
				Bistro Matisse
				Brasserie Royan
				Nice Bistro

ALEX FARM PRODUCTS

☎ 1 877 488-7778
(main number)

• 93 Front Street East
(St. Lawrence Market)
☎ 416 368-2415

Closed Sunday-Monday;
Tuesday-Thursday 8-6;
Friday 7:30-7; Saturday 5-5

Subway: UNION

• 377 Danforth Avenue (at
Chester Avenue)
☎ 416 465-9500

Monday-Wednesday 10-7;
Thursday 10-8; Friday 10-8;
Saturday 10-6; Sunday 11-6

Subway: CHESTER

• 1578 Bayview Avenue
(North of Millwood Road)
☎ 416 322-0368

Monday-Thursday 10-7;
Friday 9-8; Saturday 10-6;
Sunday 11-6

Subway: EGLINTON + bus

• 2594 Yonge Street (North
of Eglinton Avenue)
☎ 416 488-8000

Monday-Thursday 10-7;
Friday 9-8; Saturday 9-6;
Sunday 11-6

Subway: EGLINTON + bus;
LAWRENCE + bus

• 55 Bloor Street West
(Manulife Centre)
☎ 416 966-5995

Monday-Thursday 10-7;
Friday 10-8; Saturday 10-6;
Sunday 1-6

Subway: BAY or BLOOR

• 270 The Kingsway (inside
Humber Town Shopping
Centre) ☎ 416 239-1500

Monday-Thursday 10-7;
Friday 10-8; Saturday 9-6;
Sunday 11-5

Subway: ROYAL YORK + bus

• 1965 Queen Street East
(East of Woodbine
Avenue) *opening soon*
☎ 416-690-3600

Subway: QUEEN + streetcar

*A new location in North
Toronto is scheduled to
open in 2005.*

BALZAC'S COFFEE HOUSE

• 55 Mill Street (Distillery
District) ☎ 416 207-1709

Monday-Saturday 7-8;
Sunday 8-8

Subway: KING + streetcar;
PAPE + bus

BALZAC'S COFFEE HOUSE – TOY FACTORY LOFTS

• 43 Hanna Avenue (South
of King Street West) *opening in 2005*

CHOCOLATES BY BERNARD CALLEBAUT

• 4242 Dundas Street West
(East of Royal York Road)
☎ 416 234-0611

Monday-Wednesday 9:30-7;
Thursday-Friday 9:30-8;
Saturday 9:30-6;
Sunday 12-5

Subway: ROYAL YORK + bus

• 194 Lakeshore Road East,
Oakville (near Trafalgar
Road) ☎ 905 339-2100

Monday-Thursday 10-6;
Friday 10-8; Saturday 10-6

EUROPEAN QUALITY MEATS & SAUSAGES

• 176 Baldwin Street (inside
Kensington Market)
☎ 416 596-8691

Monday-Friday 8-6:30;
Saturday 7-6:30; closed
Sunday

Subway: SPADINA + street-
car; QUEEN'S PARK
+ streetcar

• 16 Jutland Road (The
Queensway and Kipling
Road) ☎ 416 251-6193

Monday-Wednesday 8-6;
Thursday-Friday 8-7;
Saturday 8-6; closed
Sunday

Subway: KIPLING

GREAT COOKS

• 176 Yonge Street (The Bay
at Yonge and Queen
Streets, lower level)
☎ 416 861-4727

Monday-Friday 10-6; closed
Saturday-Sunday

Subway: QUEEN

GREAT COOKS ON EIGHT

• 401 Bay Street (West of
Yonge Street), Simpson
Tower, eighth floor
☎ 416 861-4333

Monday 10-6; Tuesday-
Saturday 10-8; closed
Sunday

Subway: QUEEN

HARVEST WAGON

1103 Yonge Street (North of
Roxborough Street)
☎ 416 923-7542

Monday-Wednesday 8-6:30;
Thursday-Friday 8-7;
Saturday-Sunday 8-6

Subway: SUMMERHILL

• 546 Eglinton Avenue West
(West of Avenue Road)
☎ 416 487-0388

Monday-Friday 8-7;
Saturday-Sunday 8-6

Subway: EGLINTON + bus

J.S. Bonbons

- 163 Dupont Street (corner of Davenport Road)
  ☎ 416 920-0274

Closed Monday; Tuesday-Friday 10-6; Saturday 10-7; Sunday 11-5

Subway: DUPONT

- 811 Queen Street West (West of Bathurst Street)
  ☎ 416 703-7731

Closed Monday; Tuesday 11-7; Wednesday 11-6; Thursday-Saturday 11-7; Sunday 11-5

Subway: OSGOODE + streetcar

Leonidas

- 50 Bloor Street West (corner of Bay Street, lower level of the Holt Renfrew Centre) ☎ 416 944-8822

Monday-Thursday 10-6; Friday 10-7; Saturday 10-6; Sunday 12-5

Subway: BLOOR or BAY

- 176 Yonge Street (The Bay at Yonge Street and Queen Street, lower level) ☎ 416 861-6486

Monday-Friday 10-6; closed Saturday-Sunday

Subway: QUEEN

Mercatto

- 15 Toronto Street (East of Yonge Street, one street North of King Street)
  ☎ 416 366-4567

Monday-Friday 7-5; closed Saturday-Sunday

Subway: KING

- 330 Bay Street (North of Adelaide Street)
  ☎ 416 306-0467

Monday-Friday 7-8; closed Saturday-Sunday

Subway: KING

Montreal Bread Company (MBCo)

- 100 Bloor Street West, Unit 7 ☎ 416 961-MBCO (6226)
- Toronto Dominion Centre 66 Wellington Street West (food court) *opening in 2005*

Olympic Cheese Mart

- 93 Front Street East (St. Lawrence Market)
  ☎ 416 363-7602

Closed Sunday-Monday; Tuesday-Thursday 8-6; Friday 8-7; Saturday 5-5

Subway: UNION

- 7780 Woodbine Avenue, Markham (near 14th Avenue) ☎ 905 944-8676

Monday-Friday 10-6; Saturday 10-5; closed Sunday

Patachou

- 1095 Yonge Street (North of Roxborough Street)
  ☎ 416 927-1105

Monday-Friday 8:30-7; Saturday 8:30-6; closed Sunday

Subway: SUMMERHILL

- 835 St. Clair Avenue West (West of Arlington Avenue)
  ☎ 416 782-0122

Monday-Friday 8:30-7; Saturday 8:30-6; Sunday 10-4

Subway: ST. CLAIR WEST + streetcar

Pusateri's Fine Foods

- 1539 Avenue Road (North of Lawrence Avenue)
  ☎ 416 785-9100

Monday-Wednesday 8-8; Thursday-Friday 8-9; Saturday-Sunday 8-7

Subway: LAWRENCE + bus

- 57 Yorkville Avenue (corner of Bay Street)
  ☎ 416 785-9100

Monday-Wednesday 10-8; Thursday-Friday 10-9; Saturday 8-8; Sunday 10-7

Subway: BAY

Queen Video

- 412 Queen Street West (West of Spadina Avenue)
  ☎ 416 504-3030

Monday-Sunday 11-11 (all locations)

Subway: OSGOODE + streetcar

- 480 Bloor Street West (East of Bathurst Street)
  ☎ 416 588-5767

Subway: BATHURST

- 688 College Street (East of Shaw Street)
  ☎ 416 532-0555

Subway: QUEEN'S PARK + streetcar

Senses

- 318 Wellington Street West (inside the SoHo Metropolitan Hotel, corner of Blue Jays Way)
  ☎ 416 961-0055

Monday-Sunday 7-7

Subway: ST. ANDREW + streetcar

• 2901 Bayview Avenue
(inside Bayview Village
shopping mall at
Sheppard Avenue)
☎ 416 227-9149

Monday-Friday 8-9;
Saturday 8-6; Sunday 10-5

Subway: BAYVIEW

• 2 Queen Street East
(inside the Bank of
Montreal building at Yonge
Street) ☎ 416 364-7303

Monday-Friday 7-7; closed
Saturday-Sunday

Subway: QUEEN

St. Urbain Bagel Bakery

• 93 Front Street East
(St. Lawrence Market)
☎ 416 364-8305

Closed Sunday-Monday;
Tuesday-Thursday 8-6;
Friday 8-7; Saturday 5-5

Subway: UNION

• 895 Eglinton Avenue West
(West of Bathurst Street)
☎ 416 787-6955

Monday-Friday 7-6;
Saturday-Sunday 7-4

Subway: EGLINTON + bus

• 7077 Bathurst Avenue
(close to Steeles Avenue)
☎ 905 731-8305

Monday-Friday 7-6;
Saturday 7-5; Sunday 7-4

Suspect Video

• 605 Markham Street (near
Bloor and Bathurst
Streets) ☎ 416 588-6674

Monday-Saturday 12-11;
Sunday 12-10 (both loca-
tions)

Subway: BATHURST

• 619 Queen Street West
(East of Bathurst Street)
☎ 416 504-7135

Subway: BATHURST +
streetcar

The Bagel House

• 1548 Bayview Avenue
(South of Eglinton Avenue
East) ☎ 416 481-8184

Monday-Thursday 6:30-7;
Friday 6-8; Saturday 6-8;
Sunday 6-7

Subway: EGLINTON + bus

• 1722 Avenue Road (North
of Lawrence Avenue)
☎ 416 781-0032

Monday-Saturday 6-7;
Sunday 6-6:30

Subway: LAWRENCE + bus

*A new location in Toronto is
scheduled to open in 2005.*

Whitehouse Meats

• 93 Front Street East
(St. Lawrence Market)
☎ 416 366-4465

Closed Sunday-Monday;
Tuesday-Thursday 8-6,
Friday 8-7, Saturday 5-5

Subway: UNION

• 1539 Bayview Avenue
(South of Eglinton Avenue
East) ☎ 416 488-2004

Closed Monday; Tuesday-
Friday 9-6; Saturday 8-6;
closed Sunday in winter,
open 11-5 in summer

Subway: EGLINTON + bus

• 2978 Bloor Street West
(East of the Royal York
subway) ☎ 416 231-5004

Closed Sunday-Monday;
Tuesday-Wednesday 9-6;
Thursday 9-8; Friday 9-6;
Saturday 8-6

Subway: ROYAL YORK

index

Although we've come to the end of our journey, we hope you have enjoyed discovering the best spots in Toronto for French food and culture. We mostly hope you'll take it upon yourself to discover more of *The French Side of Toronto!*

If you have any comments regarding the information in the guide, or would like to suggest any French merchants or organisations for a future edition, please feel free to e-mail us at **contact@franco-toronto.ca.**

To share *The French Side of Toronto* with friends and family members, please visit our Web site to order additional copies. We are happy to offer discounts on quantities of 10 or more. E-mail us at **contact@franco-toronto.ca** to find out more about discounts and shipping costs for large orders.

Au revoir et à bientôt!

P.S.: Don't forget to visit **www.franco-toronto.ca** on a regular basis to keep up with the latest news on French food, wine, culture and events!

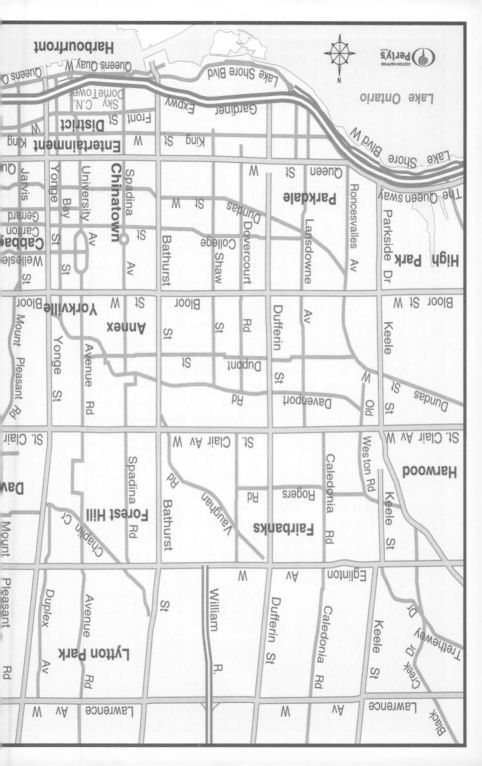

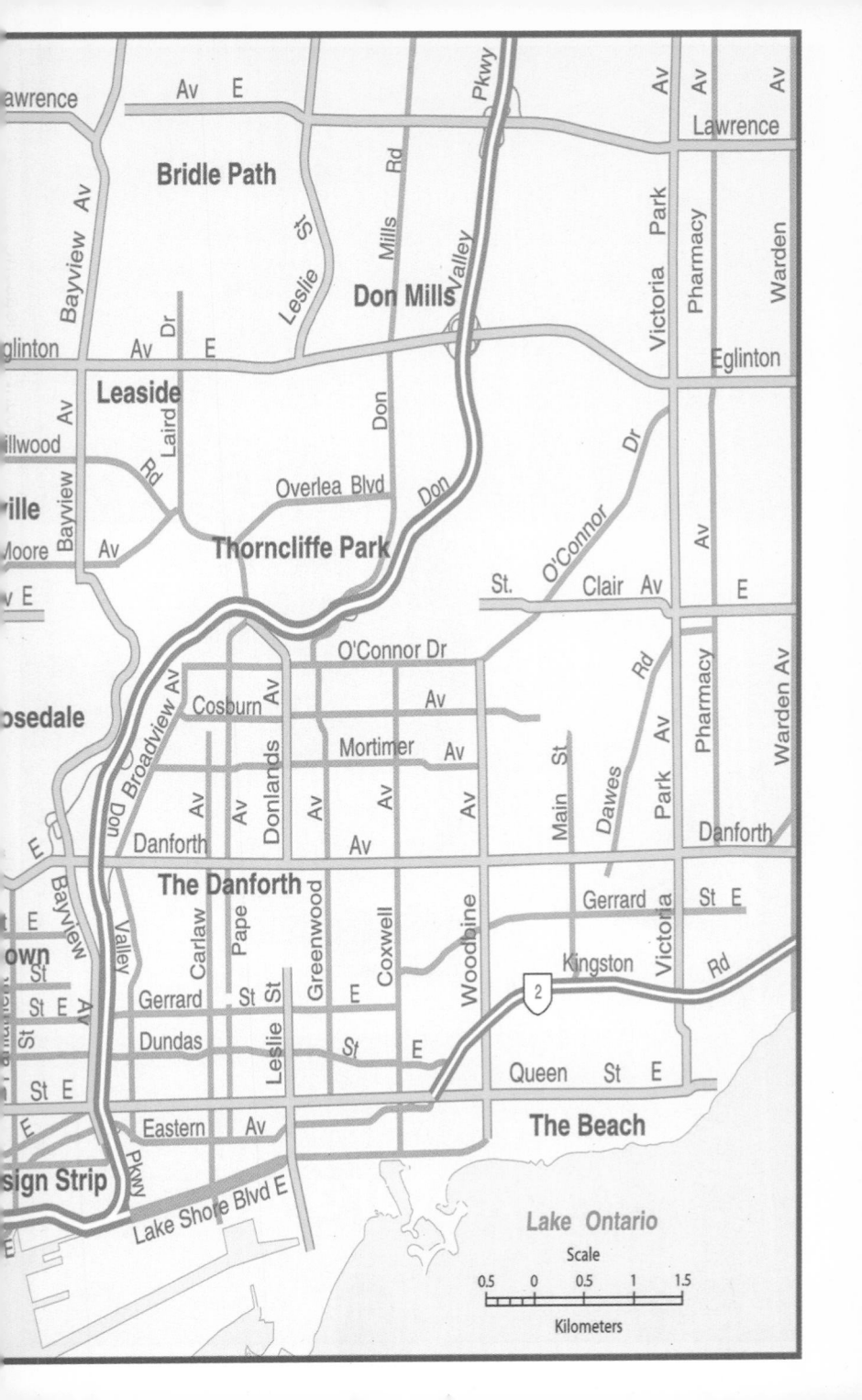

vivre en français à toronto

Le guide incontournable sur l'art de vivre à la française
à Toronto – édition 2006

*franco***toronto**

LES ÉDITIONS FRANCO TORONTO MEDIA & PUBLISHING

ISBN 0-9733020 -2-X

Vivre en français à Toronto/The French Side of Toronto est une propriété de Les Éditions Franco Toronto Media & Publishing.

Les informations publiées sont correctes à l'heure où nous écrivons ces lignes, mais peuvent bien évidemment changer entre le passage de nos rédacteurs et la sortie de notre guide; il est donc recommandé de vérifier auprès des établissements lorsqu'une exactitude totale est exigée. Nous prions nos lecteurs de nous excuser pour les erreurs qu'ils pourraient trouver dans les rubriques pratiques de ce guide.

Maison d'édition :	Les Éditions Franco Toronto Media & Publishing
Commandes :	contact@franco-toronto.ca
Espace publicitaire :	pub@franco-toronto.ca

Commandes en gros : Toutes les corporations, organisations, associations, institutions pédagogiques et tous les organismes à but non lucratif peuvent bénéficier d'une remise.

Imprimé au Canada par :	AGMV Marquis
Cartes de Toronto :	Perly's Maps, www.perlys.com

Consultez notre site Internet : **www.franco-toronto.ca**

table des matières

Voici, pour commencer, quelques témoignages de nos lecteurs :

« *Enfin un guide digne de ce nom sur le Toronto français !* Vivre en français à Toronto *comble un vide, il est rempli d'adresses inattendues et de lieux nouveaux, même pour ceux qui croyaient bien connaître Toronto… comme moi !* »

— MELANIE TSCHUPRUK

« *Je tiens à vous dire le plaisir que j'ai eu à consulter votre livre* Vivre en français à Toronto *que j'ai acheté la semaine dernière. Il est vraiment très bien fait.* »

— SERGE JOTHY, MD, PHD, TORONTO

« *Pour tous les nostalgiques de la France et de ses fromages, de ses vins, de ses foies gras, de ses pâtisseries et de sa baguette, ou tout simplement pour tous les amoureux des bonnes choses.* »

— SÉVERINE BIDERMAN, EX-PARISIENNE

« Vivre en français à Toronto *est la clef magique qui livre les secrets inespérés d'un Toronto épicurien aux offrandes gastronomes et artistiques multiples. C'est un trésor de petites et grandes adresses pour tous ceux qui aiment chiner en français dans les recoins de Toronto. Un guide qui respire le savoir et le plaisir ! Un guide qui inspire le désir de la découverte !* »

— MARCELLE LEAN, DIRECTRICE DE CINÉFRANCO, TORONTO

« *Quelle surprise de découvrir que Toronto a tant de riches dimensions.* Vivre en français à Toronto *met bien en valeur l'importance de la gastronomie et de la culture françaises en Amérique du Nord. Voici enfin un guide en français qui m'invite vraiment à vouloir connaître cette ville cosmopolite. Bien joué !* »

— DÉSIRÉ ALAIN, PARIS

« *Comme j'aurais aimé que ce livre existe en 1992* ! *Européenne traditionnelle, fraîchement arrivée de ma Belgique natale, il m'a fallu des années pour trouver à Toronto de bons croissants, du cramique (terme belge pour pain aux raisins), de vrais fromages français et du pâté comme chez nous. Douze ans plus tard, j'ai retrouvé dans le livre* Vivre en français à Toronto *toutes les bonnes adresses que j'avais mis tant de temps à découvrir, mais bien plus encore… L'équipe de Franco Toronto a fait un magnifique travail et ce guide se doit d'être à portée de main dans tous les ménages qui apprécient la joie d'un bon repas et des mets traditionnels de qualité.* »

— SIMONE MARIE COENEN, PRÉSIDENTE, SIMONE MARIE BELGIAN CHOCOLATE

« *(…) D'autres sections portent sur les bonnes adresses pour qui veut se procurer des ingrédients essentiels à la vie en français, comme les croissants, les baguettes, le fromage et le chocolat. On a pensé aux Européens, bien sûr, mais aussi à ces Québécois qui ne peuvent survivre quelques jours sans leurs bagels et leur oka…* »

— MARIE TISON, *LA PRESSE DE MONTRÉAL.*
EXTRAIT DE L'ARTICLE « TORONTO EN FRANÇAIS »,
PUBLIÉ LE SAMEDI 6 NOVEMBRE 2004
DANS LA SECTION « VACANCES VOYAGES »

« *Ils sont des dizaines de milliers de francophones et francophiles à vivre dans la Ville reine. Ils partagent leurs meilleures adresses dans ce guide intitulé* Vivre en français à Toronto. »

— ARTICLE TITRÉ « À LA FRANÇAISE À TORONTO »,
PUBLIÉ LE MERCREDI 10 NOVEMBRE 2004
DANS LA SECTION « VOYAGE » DE *MÉTRO MONTRÉAL*

remerciements

Les personnes ou organisations suivantes ont joué des rôles clés dans la poursuite de notre rêve et de notre vision. Nous les remercions pour leurs encouragements, conseils et efforts :

Dominic Canazzi, Alexandre Colliex, Jacques Hétu, Rony Israel, Marcelle Lean, Réjean Nadeau, RDÉE Centre Sud Ontario, la Société d'histoire de Toronto, Darren Weeks.

Nous tenons également à remercier de leur soutien tous les commerçants qui ont distribué notre livre.

Enfin, nous témoignons notre reconnaissance à tous nos amis et proches.

L'équipe de *Vivre en français à Toronto* :

Révision texte anglais : Fionna Boyle

Rédaction texte anglais : Fionna Boyle, Mary Nersessian

Révision supports promotionnels : Nicholas Palmer

Révision texte français : Aude Lemoine

Rédaction texte français : Aude Lemoine, Sophie Hautcœur

Rédacteur culturel pour le site Internet : Thomas Chanzy

Directrice artistique : Debi De Santis

Recherche : Krizia de Verdier, Fionna Boyle, Dominic Canazzi, Thomas Chanzy, Derek Lowe, Franck Nanguy, Nicholas Palmer, Prashant Ramesh et Hilda Toh

Vérification des données : Mary Nersessian

Responsable de la mise en page pour la publicité : Ksenia Onosov

Site Internet : Helios Lab Design

Conseiller en édition : Dan Mozersky

Contact : contact@franco-toronto.ca

Publicité : pub@franco-toronto.ca

Maison d'édition : Franco Toronto Media & Publishing

Consultez notre site Internet : **www.franco-toronto.ca**

Note : Afin de faciliter la lecture du présent texte, nous avons employé le masculin comme genre neutre pour désigner aussi bien nos lectrices que nos lecteurs.

introduction

Cette troisième édition s'inscrit dans le prolongement d'un phénomène de grande envergure : la célébration culturelle et gastronomique française et francophone à Toronto.

L'énergie culturelle française se dégage de plus en plus de la ville. La preuve, c'est que nous avons ajouté un grand nombre de nouvelles adresses à la troisième édition de ce guide. C'est un bonheur de constater que les pâtisseries et restaurants français se multiplient à un rythme soutenu à Toronto et dans le grand Toronto. Les francophones ne se regroupent pas au sein d'un seul et même quartier. Leur présence se fait ressentir d'est en ouest et du nord au sud. Cette année, grâce à plusieurs nouvelles adresses du grand Toronto, les habitants de Mississauga, Etobicoke et Oakville auront eux aussi la chance de connaître les richesses franco-torontoises tout près de chez eux.

Cette année encore, nous avons repéré des produits jugés jusqu'ici impossibles à trouver dans une ville anglophone et pourtant importés de France et du Québec par plusieurs commerçants. Votre guide en poche, il ne tient plus qu'à vous, chers lecteurs, de vous les procurer.

Bistros, restos, emplettes, autant de doux sacrifices pour notre équipe qui a dû ingurgiter des calories et des calories pour mieux vous orienter dans vos voyages culinaires et vos envies de culture francophone.

Notre philosophie reste la même. *Vivre en français à Toronto* est un guide qui vous permet d'avoir sous la main les adresses des meilleurs rendez-vous de la francophonie à Toronto. Certaines sont franco-françaises, d'autres sont empreintes d'une touche québécoise, tandis que d'autres encore sont des joyaux bien d'ici, qui sauront satisfaire toutes les envies des Français, francophones et francophiles vivant à Toronto. Nous les avons récoltées dans un seul but : vous faire vivre et revivre des expériences gastronomiques et culturelles « françaises ».

Au plaisir !

Krizia de Verdier
Rédactrice en chef

Note : Notre objectif ne se limitait pas à cibler uniquement les établissements où l'on parle français. Nous voulions mettre à l'honneur les établissements qui célèbrent la culture française à Toronto. Nous cherchions à permettre aux francophiles et francophones de retrouver facilement certains éléments clés de la culture française ici même, dans leur nouvelle ville d'adoption.

pains, pâtisseries et sucreries

On peut croire, à tort, qu'un francophone ou francophile vivant dans une ville anglophone ne serait pas bien gâté lorsqu'il s'agit de se ravitailler en produits français et francophones. Après tout, comment fait-on pour être heureux quand on doit vivre sans bon pain, sans viennoiserie, sans pâtisserie, sans sucreries ni chocolat ? Mais nous, Torontois, sommes particulièrement chanceux puisque l'on n'a pas besoin d'apprendre à se priver de nos produits français, franco-européens et québécois préférés.

Cette section vous prouvera qu'il n'y a plus de raison d'attendre un voyage en France ou au Québec pour satisfaire vos envies gastronomiques françaises. Vous allez vite vous rendre compte que c'est à cette première section que vous aurez sans aucun doute le plus recours, puisqu'elle vous permettra de bien manger (chez vous) à la française, ici à Toronto.

Bonne chasse !

pains, pâtisseries et sucreries

ACE BAKERY

1 Hafis Road (au sud de Lawrence Avenue West et Keele Street) ☎ (416) 241-3600 (bureau général); (416) 241-8433 (pour le Café Ace)

Lundi à vendredi 10h – 16h, samedi 10h – 15h, fermé dimanche

Métro : LAWRENCE WEST + le bus

www.ace-bakery.com

DU BON PAIN Depuis 1993, c'est l'une des baguettes les plus populaires de Toronto. La baguette Ace est tellement populaire que la compagnie d'aviation Air France en a fait sa baguette officielle sur ses vols Toronto/Paris. La baguette Ace est croustillante à l'extérieur et bien moelleuse à l'intérieur. Vous pouvez vous rendre à la source de fabrication même ou encore vous la procurer dans plus de 700 magasins, restaurants et hôtels au Canada (Ontario et Québec) et aux États-Unis (Michigan et New York). En plus de confectionner

d'excellents épis de blé et baguettes, Ace excelle dans l'art de préparer du pain de seigle, du pain aux fruits et aux noix, du pain complet et de la fougasse. Pendant la saison des fêtes, Ace fait preuve de créativité et présente des pains en forme d'oursons et d'énormes pétales de fleurs pour les fêtes de Noël, ou encore de mignons petits lapins pour Pâques. Soyez assuré que vous aurez chez Ace l'embarras du choix et le choix avec embarras. Comment choisir parmi tant de bonnes choses ?

ALL THE BEST FINE FOODS

1099 Yonge Street (au nord de Roxborough Street) ☎ (416) 928-3330

Lundi à mercredi 8h30 – 18h30, jeudi et vendredi 8h30 – 19h, samedi 8h30 – 18h, dimanche 10h – 17h

Métro : SUMMERHILL

www.allthebestfinefoods.com

Le saviez-vous ?

La baguette est sans aucun doute le symbole culinaire français le plus reconnu. Elle fut créée à la demande des consommateurs français à la veille de la Première Guerre mondiale. En France, selon certains experts gastronomiques, les consommateurs du début du siècle dernier n'avaient le choix qu'entre deux formats de pain : la miche ronde et le pain long. Contrairement à la baguette contemporaine, le pain long avait une mie dense et peu délicate. Tout comme la baguette d'aujourd'hui, la croûte était croustillante. La plupart des consommateurs aimaient la croûte, mais étaient un peu moins séduits par la mie. Les boulangers de l'époque s'appliquèrent à répondre aux attentes de leurs clients. Le résultat est ce que l'on connaît aujourd'hui : une longue baguette bien mince à la croûte croustillante et la mie affinée. Légende ou réalité ? Pour en savoir plus sur l'origine de la baguette et sur le pain en général, il vous faudra visiter le Musée national des arts et traditions populaires à Paris ou le Musée de la boulangerie Ismseng et la Maison du blé et du pain à Echallens, en Suisse romande. En attendant, nous vous proposons plusieurs adresses locales pour déguster la baguette et bien d'autres pains savoureux.

DE BONNES PÂTISSERIES All the Best Fine Foods vend des croissants au beurre, des amandines, des pains au chocolat, des tortillons et des danoises au citron en provenance des meilleures pâtisseries françaises de la ville.

DU BON PAIN Le boulanger d'All the Best Fine Foods prépare une série de pains façon artisanale. Le pain au levain et la baguette un peu rustique ne sont que deux des spécialités savoureuses parmi lesquelles vous aurez le choix ici. All the Best Fine Foods vend aussi des bagels de St. Urbain Bagel Bakery.

ARZ BAKERY

1909 Lawrence Avenue East (entre Warden Avenue et Pharmacy Avenue)
☎ (416) 755-5084

Lundi à samedi 8h – 21h30, dimanche 8h – 19h30, les jours fériés 8h – 19h (Arz Bakery ne ferme jamais ses portes)

Métro : LAWRENCE + le bus

DE BONNES PÂTISSERIES Sur la carte de visite de cette pâtisserie libanaise, on lit : « French Cakes and Mediterranean Pastries ». Disons que ce n'est pas de la publicité mensongère. Armand Boyadjian est le chef pâtissier et le frère du propriétaire, Jack Boyadjian. D'origine libanaise, mais de formation française, le chef pâtissier dirige un groupe de pâtissiers qui ont tous fait leurs classes en France. L'équipe d'Arz comprend même un diplômé de l'école culinaire Lenôtre. Cette introduction aura assez clairement dévoilé, nous l'espérons, la qualité de la sélection de pâtisseries que vous trouverez chez Arz. Outre une vitrine pleine de pâtisseries françaises plus tentantes les unes que

les autres, vous découvrirez aussi une vitrine tape-à-l'œil remplie de baklavas de style libanais. L'effet visuel des baklavas étalés sur de larges plaques est spectaculaire. Vous pouvez choisir une pâtisserie pour clore un bon repas à la maison ou vous pouvez vous asseoir et accompagner cette gourmandise d'un café serré au sein du petit café annexé au magasin.

DES SUCRERIES Il y a une grande vitrine de biscuits de styles libanais et français chez Arz. Nous avons reçu plusieurs demandes de la part de lecteurs qui tenaient à se procurer des dragées à Toronto. Arz Bakery vend les fameuses petites amandes enrobées de sucre, et importe différents parfums de dragées de France et d'Espagne, ainsi que du massepain (sucrerie à base de pâte d'amandes) et des pâtes de fruits de Paris.

BALZAC'S COFFEE HOUSE

Veuillez consulter notre répertoire d'adresses multiples à la page 142.

DE BONNES PÂTISSERIES Balzac's Coffee House est avant tout un café situé au cœur du récemment accessible « Distillery District », dans le sud-est de la ville. Heureusement que les propriétaires ont fait appel à deux spécialistes de la viennoiserie française à Toronto pour nous offrir de quoi accompagner notre café sur place ou à emporter. Portant l'emblème français, on retrouve Clafouti et Daniel et Daniel. Avec Clafouti, on a le goût des croissants au beurre et des croissants salés, des chaussons aux pommes, des pains au chocolat et des amandines. Le maître traiteur Daniel et Daniel

pains, pâtisseries et sucreries

propose ses croissants, amandines, pains au chocolat, croissants au fromage et danoises aux fruits. Les viennoiseries signées Daniel et Daniel ne sont vendues que le lundi.

BONJOUR BRIOCHE

812 Queen Street East (un peu à l'est de Broadview Avenue) ☎ (416) 406-1250

Fermé lundi, mardi à vendredi 8h – 17h, samedi 8h – 16h, dimanche 8h – 15h

Métro : QUEEN + le tram

DE BONNES PÂTISSERIES Dès qu'on met les pieds à l'intérieur de ce petit miracle gastronomique, on est accueilli par les parfums alléchants des différentes pâtisseries et viennoiseries. Croissants, brioches, croissants aux amandes et brioches au sucre sont au garde-à-vous. La vedette est sans aucun doute la brioche royale – une brioche fourrée de crème pâtissière parfumée au citron et aux myrtilles (bleuets) ou aux framboises. Bonjour Brioche est une excellente adresse pour déguster une bonne tarte au citron à la française. Vous ne serez pas non plus déçu par le gâteau au chocolat maison, préparé sans farine. Pendant que vous y êtes, essayez donc la tarte aux poires et aux amandes. Inoubliable !

DU BON PAIN Bonjour la baguette ! La recette maison est un secret bien gardé… Pour cause, la baguette de Bonjour Brioche fond dans la bouche. Ceux qui aiment leur baguette un peu moins croustillante seront comblés. Avec un peu de beurre et de confiture, voilà un petit coin de paradis qu'on peut s'offrir régulièrement. La baguette de Bonjour Brioche possède même le pouvoir de convertir les personnes qui

redoutent la consommation de glucides en amateurs invétérés. Nul ne résiste à cette bonne baguette. On peut aussi acheter du pain complet ou multigrains chez Bonjour Brioche. Le week-end, du pain aux olives et au romarin est également en vente. Bonjour Brioche a tout récemment ajouté une petite nouveauté à son menu : une fougasse.

DES SUCRERIES Bonjour Brioche propose une belle sélection de biscuits maison, dont certains sont vendus en sachet et d'autres à l'unité. Au choix : petits sablés, tuiles, biscuits à la noix de coco et palmiers. Idéal pour satisfaire vos petites fringales sur le pouce !

CASA AÇOREANA

235 Augusta Avenue (Kensington Market) ☎ (416) 593-9717

Lundi à samedi 8h30 – 18h30, fermé dimanche

Métro : SPADINA + le tram; QUEEN'S PARK + le tram

DES SUCRERIES Parmi le grand choix de bonbons très prisés des Torontois, vous trouverez sur une étagère, à l'arrière du comptoir de caisse, les fameuses dragées. Celles de Casa Açoreana sont importées du Portugal.

CLAFOUTI

915 Queen Street West (à l'est de Strachan Avenue, en face du parc Trinity Bellwoods) ☎ (416) 603-1935

Fermé lundi, mardi à samedi 8h – 18h, dimanche 9h – 17h

Métro : OSGOODE + le tram

DE BONNES PÂTISSERIES Côté croissants, Clafouti triomphe ! En 2003, après six mois d'activité, le chef pâtissier Boris

Le saviez-vous ?

Le clafoutis se définit traditionnellement comme un entremets rustique à base de cerises noires et de pâte à crêpe. Soit, l'Académie française le compare à une «sorte de flan aux fruits», mais Boris Dosne, copropriétaire et chef pâtissier chez Clafouti bouscule les idées reçues! Il vous propose des parfums étonnants. Figue et Grappa, lychee et caramel, baies sauvages, framboises et pommes grenade font partie de sa liste de saveurs originales.

Dosne, doué d'un génie créatif, a décroché pour ses viennoiseries la mention « meilleur croissant de Toronto » du journal *NOW*. Lorsque nous sommes passés goûter ses fameux croissants, la queue était tellement longue qu'elle allait jusqu'à la porte d'entrée et les visages des clients rayonnaient à l'idée de dévorer l'un de ces sublimes croissants. Cet engouement explique pourquoi les croissants disparaissent très vite chez Clafouti. Passé 11h, il ne reste plus grand-chose. Dès que les employés de cette pâtisserie placent les délices tant convoitées dans les vitrines, elles s'envolent. Non seulement la qualité du croissant de Clafouti est irréprochable, mais son originalité est aussi déroutante. Jusqu'à présent, on n'avait encore jamais entendu parler d'un croissant à la figue ou d'un croissant à la cannelle et au sucre brun à Toronto. Ces deux nouveautés font partie des croissants les plus demandés. On trouve aussi des pains au chocolat et des pains aux raisins succulents. Les brioches aux abricots, à la cerise et à la crème pâtissière ne déçoivent guère non plus. Clafouti excelle dans l'art de préparer tartelettes aux fruits et autres desserts tels que la tarte aux pommes caramélisées et au chocolat, la tarte au citron, le baba au rhum, la tarte à la noix de coco et aux pommes caramélisées, la tarte aux lychees et au caramel, sans oublier le fameux dominus (pommes caramélisées couronnées d'une mousse au chocolat). Autre surprise qui vous attend chez Clafouti : la galette des rois. Pendant les deux premières semaines de janvier, les commandes pour ce délice affluent. Une chose est sûre, que vous habitiez dans le coin ou pas, vous trouverez sans aucun doute toutes sortes d'excuses pour passer chez Clafouti.

DU BON PAIN Le pain, chez Clafouti, longe le mur de gauche et est placé dans de grosses caisses à vins en bois. C'est charmant et à la fois très invitant. Comme presque tout dans cette pâtisserie, les pains sont faits sur place. Au rendez-vous, le pain aux olives, la fougasse au romarin, la fougasse aux épinards, le pain muesli. Clafouti vend aussi les bagels de style montréalais de St. Urbain.

DES SUCRERIES Clafouti nous gâte déjà tellement qu'on aurait presque pu se passer de bonbons et autres sucreries. On a bien dit «presque»… La liste est longue et il ne tient qu'à vous de découvrir la liste complète. Pour ce qui est des biscuits en sachet, Clafouti vous surprendra agréablement avec ses biscuits au Grand Marnier, à la

pains, pâtisseries et sucreries

bergamote, à la noisette et à la vanille. En tout, vous aurez le choix entre huit parfums différents. Chose qu'on voit rarement à Toronto : des langues de chat maison. Clafouti vend des madeleines et du quatre-quarts. Enfin, vous trouverez chez Clafouti des biscuits *Bonne Maman* déclinés en trois parfums.

DANIEL ET DANIEL – FOOD SHOP

248 Carlton Street (au coin de Parliament Street) ☎ (416) 968-9275

Lundi à samedi 7h30 – 18h, fermé dimanche

Métro : CASTLE FRANK + le bus; COLLEGE + le tram

www.danieletdaniel.ca

Le saviez-vous ?

« Entre la baguette et le camembert, au panthéon des gloires supposées du patrimoine gastronomique français se trouve le croissant. » Journal *Le Monde*, 2003. Comme c'est bien dit ! Les Français ont peut-être perfectionné le croissant, mais son origine n'a rien de français. Le croissant désigne un petit pain en pâte feuilletée, abaissée en triangle, roulée et incurvée en forme de croissant de lune. L'origine de cette viennoiserie remonte à l'époque de la guerre entre l'Autriche et la Turquie, au moment où les Turcs s'apprêtaient à assiéger Vienne, la capitale, en 1683. Une nuit, les boulangers de Vienne entendirent le bruit des ennemis dans les sous-sols de leurs cuisines et ils donnèrent l'alarme, repoussant ainsi l'assaut ennemi. Les Ottomans furent vaincus grâce aux 25 000 hommes envoyés en renfort par Jean III Sobieski, roi de Pologne. Pour récompenser ces boulangers vigilants, le souverain leur accorda le privilège de fabriquer une pâtisserie qui immortaliserait l'événement. C'est ainsi que naquit le Hörnchen, « petite corne » en allemand, allusion au croissant qui orne l'étendard turc.

Une autre légende attribue l'invention du croissant à un certain Kolschitski, cafetier viennois d'origine polonaise. En récompense pour son courage pendant le siège turc, il aurait reçu des sacs de café pris à l'ennemi. Il aurait alors eu l'idée de servir ce café accompagné d'une viennoiserie en forme de croissant. C'est en 1770, après un séjour passé en Autriche, que Marie-Antoinette, épouse de Louis XVI, introduisit le croissant à la cour de France. Mais ce n'est qu'au début du siècle dernier, en 1920 pour être plus précis, que les boulangers parisiens créèrent le croissant feuilleté au beurre tel qu'on le connaît aujourd'hui. Le croissant est depuis devenu l'incarnation du bon goût et de l'authenticité française à l'étranger. Tout comme pour du bon pain, l'amateur de croissant peut se déplacer fort loin afin d'être assuré de la qualité de sa viennoiserie préférée. Un peu à l'exemple du bagel montréalais, plusieurs expatriés vivant à Toronto ont continué pendant longtemps à remplir leurs congélateurs de croissants en provenance des meilleures pâtisseries de Montréal. Heureusement que nous avons répertorié toutes les bonnes adresses de Toronto où acheter des croissants et bien d'autres viennoiseries !

DE BONNES PÂTISSERIES Daniel et Daniel, c'est avant tout un maître traiteur – l'un des meilleurs de Toronto soit dit en passant. La boutique de Cabbagetown propose également une petite, mais savoureuse, sélection de viennoiseries d'inspiration française : croissants, amandines, pains au chocolat et croissants au fromage. Les tartes aux fruits et gâteaux sont délicieux et valent vraiment le coup. Chose surprenante, Daniel et Daniel est un des seuls pâtissiers de la ville à vendre de la crème brûlée à emporter. On peut non seulement déguster ce délice chez soi, mais aussi le savourer dans un petit ramequin. Ce genre de tentation facile est très dangereux pour les gens qui raffolent de la crème brûlée. Laissez-vous aller, car tout est bon chez Daniel et Daniel !

DINAH'S CUPBOARD

50 Cumberland Street ☎ (416) 921-8112

Lundi à vendredi 8h – 19h, samedi 9h – 18h, fermé dimanche (à l'exception du mois de décembre)

Métro : YONGE OU BAY

DE BONNES PÂTISSERIES Cette petite épicerie fine permet aux résidents du quartier de Yorkville de savourer les brioches et croissants de chez Patachou sans avoir à aller jusque-là.

FLEURDELYS PÂTISSERIE

2046 Yonge Street (au sud d'Eglinton Avenue) ☎ (416) 545-0509

Fermé lundi, mardi à samedi 8h – 18h, dimanche 9h – 16h

Métro : DAVISVILLE OU EGLINTON

www.fleurdelyspatisserie.com

DE BONNES PÂTISSERIES Le chef pâtissier, Miro Musil, propose une série de gâteaux qui marient certains des meilleurs ingrédients français et belges. Mousse aux noix et chocolat noir belge, mousse au kir royal (cassis et champagne), gâteaux de fromage parfumés au Grand Marnier ne sont que quelques-unes des merveilles préparées chez Fleurdelys. Au total, on compte plus d'une trentaine de gâteaux. L'une des meilleures ventes s'appelle Europa : trois couches de mousse au chocolat sur un gâteau style brownie. Comme diraient les anglophones, *death by chocolate* (mort par overdose de chocolat) assurée ! Autre spécialité décadente : le baba au rhum, au chocolat ou à la vanille. Bien imbibé de rhum, il est servi dans un mignon petit bocal. Disposez-le dans un verre à Martini, parsemé de quelques baies, et arrosez encore généreusement de rhum ! Nul doute que vos convives apprécieront un dessert qui a tant de style (et d'alcool) ! Vous trouverez bien sûr une sélection de viennoiseries classiques. Si vous êtes de passage à Aix-en-Provence en France, poussez la porte de la seconde enseigne de ces maîtres en pâtisserie.

DES SUCRERIES Environ six parfums de biscuits maison. Le sablé marbré a notre préférence et c'est aussi la meilleure vente. À goûter également, les meringues aux parfums de fruits, les pailletés feuilletines et les craquelins caramélisés.

FRANGIPANE PÂTISSERIE

215 Madison Avenue (à quelques pas du métro DUPONT) ☎ (416) 926-0303

Lundi à jeudi 8h – 18h30, vendredi 8h – 19h,

pains, pâtisseries et sucreries

samedi 9h – 18h30, dimanche 10h – 16h

Métro : DUPONT

DE BONNES PÂTISSERIES Les habitants
du quartier de l'Annex ont enfin accès à
un réveil envoûtant. Depuis l'ouverture
de la pâtisserie Frangipane, les effluves
de sucre et de beurre font le bonheur de
tous. Claudia Egger et Mary Skey sont
les divas qui gèrent cette bonne adresse.
Le talent est sans doute héréditaire. La
grand-mère et la mère de Mme Egger
furent elles-mêmes d'excellentes pâtis-
sières. La passion que met Mme Egger à
sa tâche se voit et se mange. Prenez la
tarte façon Frangipane par exemple.
Aux poires, aux pommes, aux baies des
champs ou au citron, elle ravira votre
palais. Goûtez aussi la tarte à la noix de
coco et à l'ananas ou la tarte aux noix
caramélisées et à la frangipane. Les
amoureux du chocolat ne sont pas
oubliés non plus : la tarte au chocolat
noir en fera fondre plus d'un. Vous avez
le choix entre trois formats de tarte.
Pour les gâteaux, il faut passer
commande. Mais nous vous conseillons
une spécialité suisse que vous trouverez
quand même en magasin : le gâteau aux
noisettes. Quant au mélange d'amandes
et de chocolat garni de ganache de la
« Reine de Saba », il vous surprendra.
Pour les petites gourmandises, nous
recommandons les mousses aux fruits et
la sélection de viennoiseries de la
pâtisserie Patachou.

DES SUCRERIES Petits sablés au citron,
florentines, biscuits aux noix et pacanes
et biscuits aux chocolat et espresso vous
attendent chez Frangipane.

Le saviez-vous ?

Fait connu en France, mais très peu
en Amérique du Nord, la fameuse
baguette se décline en plusieurs
variations officielles. Baguépi, Banette,
flûte Gana, rétrodor, campagrain,
baguette tradition, serpentine : faites
votre choix !

FRED'S BREAD

45 Brisbane Road, Unit # 13-14
☎ (416) 736-3733
*Cette boulangerie n'est pas ouverte
au public*

DU BON PAIN Le duo d'artistes Andrea
Damon-Gibson et Steve Gibson se
cache derrière Fred's Bread. Ce couple
crée depuis 1995 une collection assez
impressionnante de pains d'inspiration
artisanale. Le plaisir réside vraiment
dans la variété. La liste des plaisirs est
longue chez Fred's – pain au levain,
pain noir (un mélange de chocolat,
espresso, mélasse et miel), pain aux
raisins, pain aux noix, pain aux olives
noires et vertes, pain aux céréales
anciennes et au miel sauvage, pain de
seigle, trois types de fougasses (pommes
de terre, romarin et tomates), baguette
bien croustillante, pain au fromage,
pain aux herbes et oignons et pain
brioché. Vous pouvez acheter l'une des
confections signées Fred's chez les
marchands suivants : Big Carrot, All
the Best Fine Foods, Pusateri's, Holt
Renfrew, Max's Market, Le Gourmand,
York's Deli et IGA dans le quartier
« the Beach ».

HARBORD BAKERY

115 Harbord Street (à l'ouest de Spadina Avenue) ☎ (416) 922-5767

Lundi à jeudi 8h – 19h, vendredi et samedi 8h – 18h, dimanche 8h – 16h

Métro : SPADINA + le tram

Une pâtisserie juive qui propose un succulent croissant au beurre ? Pourquoi pas, puisque tout est possible à Toronto ! Harbord Bakery est l'une des plus anciennes pâtisseries juives de la ville. Les propriétaires nous ont expliqué que leur recette (au secret bien gardé) est tout à fait française et comparable à celle des pâtisseries franco-françaises de Toronto. Le croissant au beurre est tout simplement délicieux et parfaitement feuilleté, sans pour autant être trop gras. En plus, il est l'un des moins chers de la ville. Un dollar (taxes comprises) à débourser pour dévorer ces petites délices. À savourer également : le pain au chocolat.

HOLT RENFREW – EPICURE AND GOURMET SHOPS

50 Bloor Street West (au coin de Bay Street) ☎ (416) 922-2333

Lundi à mercredi 10h – 18h, jeudi et vendredi 10h – 20h, samedi 10h – 18h, dimanche 12h – 18h

Métro : YONGE OU BAY

À la recherche des sucreries franco-européennes à Toronto !

Les sucreries, on aime se les offrir tout le temps ! Pendant longtemps, on a cru qu'il était impossible de retrouver à Toronto certaines de nos sucreries françaises préférées. Eh bien, notre détermination a porté ses fruits, puisque nous avons rassemblé une longue liste d'adresses où acheter nos goûters préférés, ici même, à Toronto.

Nous avons découvert les grandes marques de sucreries franco-européennes suivantes pour vos ravitaillements : bonbons *Barnier*, bonbons *La Vie de la Vosgienne*, pastilles *Vichy*, cachous *Lajaunie*, bonbons *Anis de L'abbaye de Flavigny*, sucettes *Pierrot Gourmand*, nougats aux amandes *Chabert et Guillot*, réglisses *Haribo*, biscuits *Mère Poulard*, caramels *Carambar*, biscuits *l'Or*, madeleines *Gaillard*, pâte de fruits de Provence et gâteaux *Brossard*.

Où trouver les sucreries franco-européennes à Toronto

1. All the Best Fine Foods
2. Arz Bakery
3. Brandt Meat Packers Ltd.
4. Cheese Boutique
5. Clafouti
6. Daniel et Daniel
7. Dinah's Cupboard
8. La Cigogne
9. Le Comptoir de Célestin
10. Le Gourmand
11. Max's Market
12. Mercatto
13. Pâtisserie d'Or
14. Rahier
15. Scheffler's Delicatessen

pains, pâtisseries et sucreries

DE BONNES PÂTISSERIES Si Holt Renfrew n'importe pas des produits de qualité supérieure, il s'organise pour s'associer avec des maîtres dans leurs domaines de prédilection. C'est ainsi qu'Holt Renfrew vend à sa clientèle très exigeante une sélection de croissants de Patachou.

DU BON PAIN Des milliers de Parisiens achètent le pain au levain naturel de Lionel Poîlane, tous les jours, à la boulangerie rue du Cherche-Midi. Pour nous, Torontois, plus besoin d'attendre un voyage transatlantique pour savourer ce délice parisien. Grâce à Holt Renfrew, les francophones et francophiles d'ici peuvent eux aussi manger du pain Poîlane tous les jours. Holt Renfrew fait acheminer deux fois par semaine par FedEx le pain le plus populaire de France et peut-être même du monde. Vous pouvez acheter le pain Poîlane en boule ou encore en quartier au Gourmet Shop situé au sous-sol du magasin le plus chic de Toronto. La boule et même le quart de boule ne sont pas vendus au rabais, mais si l'envie vous prend et si la monnaie pèse lourd dans vos poches, c'est un plaisir qu'il faut satisfaire.

DES SUCRERIES Holt Renfrew importe les tentations françaises suivantes : des petits beurres, des palets bretons, des crêpes dentelées bretonnes, des bonbons aux marrons, des bonbons aux fruits, trois parfums différents de caramels, des dominos de nougat et les irrésistibles marrons glacés. Lors des fêtes de Noël, de la Saint-Valentin et de Pâques, Holt Renfrew importe plusieurs sucreries, destinées à célébrer l'occasion.

LA CIGOGNE

1626 Bayview Avenue (au sud d'Eglinton Avenue) ☎ (416) 487-1234

Lundi à vendredi 7h30 – 19h, samedi 8h – 19h, dimanche 8h – 17h

Métro : EGLINTON + le bus

DE BONNES PÂTISSERIES Thierry Schmitt, chef pâtissier alsacien bardé de diplômes (affichés sur le mur à l'entrée) en fait craquer plus d'un avec ses pièces montées. Il est presque difficile de croquer dans ses gâteaux et croquembouches à la finition si parfaite. Si vous cherchez à éblouir vos invités, les petits chefs-d'œuvre sucrés de ce propriétaire feront tout à fait l'affaire. La spécialité de la maison ? La tarte flambée d'Alsace

bien sûr. Une fois que vous y aurez goûté, il faudra encore essayer les autres viennoiseries et pâtisseries. Ce n'est pas le choix qui manque – pain perdu (fait avec des pommes, des pêches, de la cannelle et de la brioche), éclair, impérial, mont-blanc, crème brûlée, danoise, croissant, croissant aux amandes, pain au chocolat, chausson aux pommes, palmier et bien d'autres encore.

Vous pouvez également commander des croquembouches et des petits fours. Pendant la saison des fêtes de Noël et de Pâques, le chef Thierry Schmitt prépare d'alléchants desserts qui sauront régaler tous vos convives. Vous n'avez qu'à consulter le menu spécialement réalisé pour l'occasion avant de passer votre commande. Le chef Thierry Schmitt confectionne même la galette des rois !

DU BON PAIN Vous trouverez sur place une baguette maison, ainsi que du pain au levain.

DES SUCRERIES Des madeleines, des langues de chat et des sablés aux noix vendus en sachet vous attendent en magasin.

LE COMPTOIR DE CÉLESTIN

623 Mount Pleasant Road (au nord de Manor Road) ☎ (416) 544-1733

Fermé lundi et mardi, mercredi à samedi 7h30 – 19h, dimanche 8h30 – 17h

Métro : EGLINTON + le bus

www.celestin.ca

DE BONNES PÂTISSERIES Cette pâtisserie jouxte le nouveau restaurant Le Célestin. Les frères Martial et Pascal Ribreau sont les créateurs de ce concept

de resto et comptoir de prêt-à-manger que peu ont adopté ici à Toronto, mais qui est très populaire en France. Côté viennoiseries, le Comptoir propose les immanquables français : brioches Nantaire (brioches à la forme allongée), brioches Bostock et kouglofs. Régalez-vous d'une liste infinie de desserts tous plus alléchants les uns que les autres. Vous retrouvez par ailleurs certains classiques du grand Toronto (tartes aux fruits, tarte Tatin et tarte au citron), mais aussi des incontournables de la pâtisserie française, rarement disponibles à Toronto : le gland (crème pâtissière et kirsch) et la religieuse (crème pâtissière et glaçage au café ou au chocolat). Le diplomate est une autre spécialité française qu'on commence seulement à trouver en ville. Martial Ribreau le prépare avec les ingrédients suivants : brioche, Grand Marnier, crème anglaise et fruits secs. Le millefeuille, très français et pas très évident à trouver à Toronto, est également disponible au Comptoir de Célestin, à condition de passer une commande spéciale.

DU BON PAIN Le pain noir aux sept céréales fait partie des meilleurs pains artisanaux que nous ayons goûtés à Toronto. Il a un goût à la fois riche et intense. Le chef pâtissier, Martial Ribreau, vous propose également une boule au miel et aux raisins, un pain au levain, une baguette classique et une baguette au blé entier. Ce qui est rare à Toronto, c'est la viennoise (baguette de style brioché). Chez Célestin, il y a de la viennoise sucrée et de la demi-viennoise au chocolat. C'est le réveil idéal pour les week-ends !

pains, pâtisseries et sucreries

DES SUCRERIES Contrairement à plusieurs autres pâtissiers de la ville, Martial Ribreau crée des macarons disponibles dans 12 parfums irrésistibles. Parmi nos préférés figurent la framboise, la pistache et le chocolat.

• •

Vous pouvez désormais trouver une grande sélection de croissants, pains et desserts du Comptoir de Célestin chez Cheese Boutique.

• •

Le Gourmand

152 Spadina Avenue (au sud de Queen Street) ☎ (416) 504-4494

Lundi à vendredi 7h – 20h, samedi 9h – 18h, dimanche 9h – 16h

Métro : OSGOODE + le tram;
SPADINA + le tram

DE BONNES PÂTISSERIES Le Gourmand n'a peut-être pas de chef pâtissier sur place, mais la petite variété de croissants et pâtisseries signés Rahier qu'il propose compense largement cette absence. Pour les desserts, la pâtisserie fait appel à Dessert Trends. Le café serré signé Le Gourmand est l'un des meilleurs de la ville, largement à la hauteur des viennoiseries et desserts que propose cette pâtisserie du Fashion District.

Le Petit Gourmet

1064 Yonge Street ☎ (416) 966-3811

Lundi à vendredi 7h30 – 19h, samedi 7h30 – 18h, fermé dimanche

Métro : ROSEDALE

DE BONNES PÂTISSERIES Depuis plus d'une vingtaine d'années, Christian Boniteau s'affaire dans sa cuisine. La

Le saviez-vous ?

Les deux détaillants Mercatto et Magnolia ont un faible pour les produits français. Leurs croissants viennent de la pâtisserie Clafouti. Faites vite, à peine sous cloche et encore tout chauds, les gourmands se les arrachent. Vous travaillez dans le centre-ville ou habitez Little Italy et vous avez découvert que vous ne pouvez plus vous passer de ces croissants ? Ne culpabilisez pas, blâmez plutôt Boris Dosne, le chef pâtissier de Clafouti.

• Magnolia Fine Foods
  548 College Street
  ☎ (416) 920-9927
• Mercatto
  15 Toronto Street
  ☎ (416) 366-4567
  330 Bay Street ☎ (416) 306-046

preuve en est que les viennoiseries disparaissent plutôt rapidement dans sa pâtisserie du quartier de Rosedale. La plupart des habitués n'hésitent pas à acheter une demi-douzaine de croissants à la fois. Aux choix, M. Boniteau propose : croissants au beurre, croissants aux amandes, pains au chocolat, pains aux raisins, pains à la cannelle, chaussons aux pommes et chaussons aux fruits. Plus d'une quinzaine de gâteaux et tartes sont disponibles. Vous reconnaîtrez sans aucun doute le gâteau basque que M. Boniteau prépare également pour L'Escargot Bistro. La tarte au chocolat, aux poires et à la crème est fantastique. Les autres desserts à ne pas manquer sont le gâteau à la ganache et la tarte Tatin.

MA MAISON

4243 Dundas Street West (en face du centre Kingsway Mills) ☎ (416) 236-2234

Fermé lundi, mardi à mercredi 8h – 18h, jeudi à vendredi 8h – 19h, samedi 8h – 18h, dimanche 8h – 16h

Métro : ROYAL YORK + le bus

www.UR2Busy2Cook.com

DE BONNES PÂTISSERIES Comme à la maison ? Pas exactement. De Ma Maison, vous ne partiriez pas. Ma Maison épate par sa gamme très complète de produits gastronomiques français. Les clients de Tournayre reconnaîtront un visage très familier, celui de Michel Longuet. Ce dernier s'est associé au chef Patrick Alléguède afin de créer une pâtisserie dédiée aux fins gourmets. Choisir. Un verbe qu'il faut maîtriser avant de passer chez Ma Maison. Brioches, tartes aux pommes, croissants, danoises n'attendent que vous. Laissez-vous tenter par le pain perdu, préparé avec des croissants et assorti d'une succulente crème anglaise. Ma Maison propose également d'appétissants gâteaux et tartes. Les parfums changent selon l'humeur du chef. La tarte aux pommes, la tarte aux prunes et à la crème pâtissière restent particulièrement irrésistibles.

DU BON PAIN Une belle variété de pains est en vente chez Ma Maison. À part la bonne baguette, vous pourrez acheter du pain aux sept céréales savoureux, du pain au levain, de la fougasse et du pain aux noix et aux raisins. Vous serez ravi d'apprendre que vous partagez l'une de vos passions avec le chef Patrick Alléguède, celle des féculents !

DES SUCRERIES Ma Maison séduit aussi par ses biscuits faits… « Ma Maison ». Une demi-douzaine de grands classiques parmi lesquels madeleines, langues de chat et petits sablés.

MONTREAL BREAD COMPANY (MBCo)

Veuillez consulter notre répertoire d'adresses multiples à la page 142.

DE BONNES PÂTISSERIES Depuis plusieurs années, Montreal Bread Company tient la vedette sur la scène culinaire montréalaise. Aujourd'hui, le phénomène MBCo débarque à Toronto. Envie de bonnes petites pâtisseries au petit-déjeuner ? Rendez-vous aux comptoirs MBCo. Et profitez-en aussi pour vous arrêter quelques minutes sur les desserts. Laissez-vous séduire par le gâteau au chocolat assassin ou par la tarte au citron vert (lime) brûlée. Satisfaction garantie !

PAIN PERDU

736 St. Clair Avenue West (un peu à l'ouest de Christie Street) ☎ (416) 656-7246

Fermé lundi, mardi à vendredi 8h – 19h, samedi 8h – 17h, dimanche 8h – 16h

Métro : ST CLAIR WEST + le tram

www.painperdu.com

DE BONNES PÂTISSERIES On croyait que Pain Perdu était tout simplement un nom original. Il s'avère que les propriétaires (les frères Yannick et Christophe Folgoas) ont fait bien plus que donner un nom à leur pâtisserie, ils lui ont aussi donné un emblème – le pain perdu maison. Il est préparé dans la bonne tradition française et selon une vieille recette de famille, puisque c'est la

pains, pâtisseries et sucreries

baguette de la veille qu'on utilise. Pain Perdu offre un vaste choix de viennoiseries et autres pâtisseries françaises. La découverte chez Pain Perdu se fait par les sens, mais voici, en avant-première, une liste des merveilles ambiantes : opéra, marquise, saint-honoré, paris-brest, religieuse, béret basque (génoise au chocolat, mousse au chocolat et rhum) et millefeuille. Les pâtisseries les plus demandées, selon les propriétaires, sont la tarte au citron et le gâteau basque. Nous devons admettre que leur gâteau basque est le meilleur que nous

ayons goûté. Il va sans doute de soi qu'un pâtissier basque (de la région de Saint-Jean-de-Luz) maîtrise cette recette. Mais vraiment, quelle réussite ! Chez Pain Perdu, il y a aussi trois formats de tarte (petite, moyenne et grande). Les viennoiseries et desserts sont préparés tout au long de la journée, ce qui fait de l'endroit l'une des seules pâtisseries françaises de la ville qui n'écoule pas tout son stock avant 11h.

DU BON PAIN Une nouvelle pâtisserie française symbolise le changement en cours à l'ouest de Bathurst, sur St. Clair

Avenue. Les habitants du coin peuvent maintenant acheter une bonne baguette et un bon pain au levain.

DES SUCRERIES Ça n'en finit plus chez Pain Perdu! Il était déjà difficile de résister aux pâtisseries, mais avec les biscuits en sachet, c'est quasi impossible... Dans de petits paniers en osier, aiguillettes à l'orange, petits sablés, fils aux amandes et palmiers vous lancent des regards aguicheurs. On trouve aussi des bonbons au nougat et au chocolat, ainsi que deux parfums de pâtes de fruits : cassis et framboise.

PATACHOU
Veuillez consulter notre répertoire d'adresses multiples à la page 142.

DE BONNES PÂTISSERIES Depuis 1978, cette boulangerie propose aux habitants de Rosedale les grands classiques de la viennoiserie et de la pâtisserie françaises. Vous y trouverez de nombreuses gourmandises telles que croissants, brioches, croissants aux amandes, pains au chocolat, brioches aux raisins et palmiers. Vous aurez en plus le choix parmi une très bonne sélection de petits desserts et gâteaux. Le gâteau basque (parfumé d'un soupçon d'anis) et la tarte au citron ne font pas de vieux os sur les étalages; mieux vaut, donc, aller faire ses courses tôt, les samedis matins. Patachou prépare des spécialités saisonnières pour célébrer l'Épiphanie, la Saint-Valentin, Pâques, la fête des Mères et Noël. Les spécialités de saison les plus convoitées sont sans aucun doute les petits fours glacés. La petitesse de ces gâteries en fait un vrai péché par excès, puisqu'on peut en manger

trois ou même quatre sans vraiment s'en rendre compte. Vous pouvez passer une commande spéciale pour tous vos plaisirs des fêtes afin de partager avec vos convives les charmes de la pâtisserie française. Si vous avez longtemps cherché des croûtes pour la préparation de vos bouchées à la reine, c'est ici que votre recherche prend fin. Une simple commande passée trois à cinq jours à l'avance vous garantit d'avoir ces belles timbales feuilletées. Patachou offre également une bonne variété de plats prêts-à-manger et prêts-à-emporter.

DES SUCRERIES Patachou vend d'excellents petits macarons sucrés aux trois parfums séduisants. Il propose également des feuilletés au fromage et au thym, des palmiers sucrés et des petits biscuits aux brisures de chocolat.

PÂTISSERIE D'OR
301 Robinson Street, Oakville (au sud de Lake Shore Road) ☎ (905) 815-8999
Fermé lundi et mardi, mercredi à vendredi 8h – 17h30, samedi 8h – 18h, dimanche 8h – 18h

DE BONNES PÂTISSERIES Le chef pâtissier Jean-Luc Soulabaille a ouvert depuis août 2000 sa propre pâtisserie à Oakville. Un simple coup d'œil et l'on comprend très vite que M. Soulabaille a reçu une formation française (il a fait ses classes à Saint-Malo). Nombre de paniers regorgent de viennoiseries qui mettent l'eau à la bouche. Les délices proposées sont de dignes classiques incroyablement savoureux. Croissants au beurre, pains aux raisins, croissants aux amandes et pains au chocolat. Pour sa préparation de danoises aux fruits, le

chef Soulabaille n'utilise que des fruits frais de saison. Une touche particulière parmi des centaines d'autres qui le différencient de la concurrence. En matière de desserts, la liste est longue et appétissante. On trouve des spécialités françaises qui ne sont disponibles que dans un très petit nombre de pâtisseries du grand Toronto, telles que le croquembouche, le saint-honoré, la forêt-noire et le « vrai » millefeuille. Le chef Soulabaille marie astucieusement sa patte franco-française à la tendance du marché et offre à ses clients plusieurs viennoiseries et pâtisseries de saison. Consultez la rubrique « produits surgelés » de ce guide pour connaître les trésors gastronomiques que nous avons découverts dans les congélateurs de la Pâtisserie d'Or. En résumé, le chef Soulabaille témoigne d'une qualité irréprochable.

DU BON PAIN Le chef Soulabaille vous invite à goûter sa baguette classique. Elle est à la fois simple et très bonne.

DES SUCRERIES Les biscuits maison vous séduiront. Que ce soit avec le macaron, le palmier, la cigarette à la vanille ou le biscuit au beurre, impossible d'être déçu par les créations du chef. Enfin, la madeleine est une autre confection maison dont il devient difficile de se passer.

. . . .
Solution ingénieuse et délicieuse !
Un gâteau pour 20 à 30 personnes s'avère souvent être une grande déception tant au goût qu'à la présentation. Le chef Soulabaille de Pâtisserie d'Or propose une solution nettement plus savoureuse. Des créations sucrées préparées avec des ingrédients de choix. Le résultat ? Un gâteau très moelleux. Le chef Soulabaille laisse autant que possible libre cours à son génie créatif dans la présentation finale. Le tout donne une véritable « rhapsodie » de rosettes chocolatées. Vos invités auront le souffle coupé par ces chefs-d'œuvre d'Oakville.
. . . .

PÂTISSERIE DAUDET

4335 Bloor Street West, Markland Wood Plaza (au coin de Mill Road)
☎ (416) 626-6310

Fermé dimanche et lundi, mardi à samedi 8h – 18h

DE BONNES PÂTISSERIES Depuis décembre 2004, le maître Bruno Respecte-Daudet illustre ses prouesses gastronomiques dans sa pâtisserie d'Etobicoke. Depuis qu'il a débarqué de France avec le plus haut diplôme en pâtisserie en poche et sa charmante épouse Pascale à son bras, il offre aux Torontois le plaisir de savourer les pâtisseries et viennoiseries qu'il prépare à la perfection. Un simple coup d'œil suffit à mettre l'eau à la bouche. On ne résiste pas aux amandines, danoises aux fruits, chaussons aux pommes et brioches au chocolat. Les minicroissants et pains au chocolat vous régalent en vous ôtant tout sentiment de culpabilité. Jusqu'à présent jamais vu à Toronto, le pain au lait nous a subjugués. Bien que

les desserts varient tous les jours, le baba au rhum, les petits croquembouches, l'éclair et la marquise au chocolat restent des incontournables du magasin. Le maître Respecte-Daudet prépare de savoureuses tartes aux fruits à des prix défiant toute concurrence. Les gâteaux sont préparés avec tant d'attention et de passion qu'il faut les commander à l'avance. Ajoutons que Bruno Respecte-Daudet sait réaliser pièces montées et gâteaux à thème. Proposez à vos invités des croquembouches façon Bruno Respecte-Daudet. Les proportions de certaines pièces montées s'envolent !

DU BON PAIN Une belle gamme de bons pains est au rendez-vous : baguette, pain au blé complet, pain aux graines de lin, pain au levain et pain de seigle.

DES SUCRERIES Des biscuits maison remarquables. Que ce soit le croquet aux amandes, la tuile, le macaron, la meringue ou le petit sablé au beurre, vous trouverez forcément le biscuit qui vous séduira.

Nouvelle tendance !

Le chef Chang de la Pâtisserie Le Papillon révèle que plusieurs mariées optent désormais pour un assortiment de minimousses à la place du traditionnel gâteau de mariage. Un effet visuel épatant et une variété qui permet de combler tout un chacun.

PÂTISSERIE LE PAPILLON

Ce commerçant rouvrira ses portes dans le nord de la ville en 2005

9425 Leslie Street, Unit #9, Richmond Hill
lundi à jeudi 12h – 20h, vendredi et samedi
12h – 22h ☎ (905) 918-0080
www.finecakes.ca

DE BONNES PÂTISSERIES L'accueil chaleureux de Wilfred et Elizabeth Chang vous assure de passer un agréable moment dans la pâtisserie. Aux fourneaux, Mme Chang en personne. Il y a quelques années, elle décide de suivre un cours à l'école George Brown et tombe amoureuse de la pâtisserie française. Le chef Chang détient quant à lui un diplôme de l'école Cordon Bleu de Paris, située à Ottawa. Retour à Pâtisserie Papillon, où la star de l'étalage s'appelle minimousse. Le chef Chang en prépare un assortiment d'une vingtaine de parfums : mangue, tiramisu, cheesecake au chocolat blanc et myrtilles, pour ne citer que les préférés des gourmands qui fréquentent l'endroit. Il n'y a qu'un problème à offrir les minimousses à vos convives : ces derniers ne vous laisseront rien. Trop alléchantes, les minimousses poussent à l'égoïsme. Vous pourrez quand même vous rattraper en dégustant une belle sélection de pâtisseries au format plus généreux. Au rendez-vous : saint-honoré, opéra, profiteroles et tarte aux amandes.

DES SUCRERIES Le chef Chang propose plus d'une dizaine de petits biscuits maison. Au top des ventes, les biscuits aux parfums citron, café, noix et cassis, ainsi que la tuile aux amandes.

pains, pâtisseries et sucreries

PÂTISSERIE SAINT HONORÉ

2945 Bloor Street West (au coin de Greenview Blvd.

, un peu à l'est de Royal York Road)

Il n'y a pas de numéro de téléphone pour cette pâtisserie

Fermé dimanche et lundi, mardi à jeudi 8h – 19h, vendredi 8h – 21h, samedi 8h – 19h

Métro : ROYAL YORK

DE BONNES PÂTISSERIES Les résidents du Kingsway Village se régalent des pâtisseries et viennoiseries préparées par Jean-Jacques Carlier. La sélection classique est complète : croissants, croissants aux amandes, pains au chocolat, brioches aux raisins et danoises aux fruits. Pour ce qui est des croissants salés, ils sont fourrés au fromage ou au jambon et au fromage. Vous aurez également le choix entre plusieurs sélections adaptées aux goûts du marché comme le croissant à la feta et aux épinards par exemple. Les pâtisseries et gâteaux se font remarquer par leur quantité et par leur variété.

DU BON PAIN La Pâtisserie Saint Honoré permet aux habitants de l'ouest de la ville d'acheter une excellente baguette et plusieurs pains maison tout aussi savoureux.

PUSATERI'S FINE FOODS

Veuillez consulter notre répertoire d'adresses multiples à la page 142.

www.pusateris.com

DE BONNES PÂTISSERIES Pusateri's offre à sa clientèle de luxe les savoureux gâteaux, tartes et viennoiseries de Clafouti, Le Comptoir de Célestin, Patachou et Rahier.

RAHIER

1586 Bayview Avenue (au sud d'Eglinton Avenue) ☎ (416) 482-0917

Fermé lundi et mardi, mercredi à vendredi 8h – 17h, samedi 8h – 16h, dimanche 8h – 15h

Métro : EGLINTON + le bus

DE BONNES PÂTISSERIES Depuis 1996, la pâtisserie Rahier chatouille nos narines et satisfait nos envies avec ses alléchantes confections. Certains ont officieusement déclaré Rahier « la Rolls Royce » de la pâtisserie française à Toronto. Rahier est une bonne adresse en ville pour acheter petits gâteaux, tartelettes et mousses aux fruits de style français. Vous remarquerez qu'ici, ce sont les viennoiseries qui règnent. Et elles sont toutes faites sur place. L'une de nos préférées est la danoise aux pistaches. Pendant les fêtes de Noël, Rahier propose des sélections spéciales qui sauront terminer vos repas de festivités en beauté. La bûche de Noël est en vedette. Il y a autre chose qui nous plaît chez Rahier : certaines nouvelles pâtisseries ayant ouvert leurs portes fin 2002, début 2003 ont attribué leur courage d'aller de l'avant et d'offrir ainsi aux Torontois la possibilité de découvrir toujours plus la pâtisserie et la viennoiserie françaises au succès de Rahier. Grâce à ce dernier, de plus en plus de Torontois peuvent donc découvrir ce que nous, francophiles et francophones, savions déjà : en matière de pâtisserie, les Français dominent largement !

DU BON PAIN En vente sur place, une baguette maison ainsi qu'une petite variété de boules : multigrains, romarin, noix et raisins.

DES SUCRERIES Rahier a un choix exceptionnel de biscuits vendus à l'unité ou encore en sachet.

St. Urbain Bagel Bakery

Veuillez consulter notre répertoire d'adresses multiples à la page 142.

☎ (416) 787-6955 (numéro général d'information)

DU BON PAIN St. Urbain Bagel Bakery est un autre boulanger qui offre aux Torontois la possibilité de vivre une véritable expérience du bagel montréalais. Vous n'aurez donc plus vraiment d'excuse pour continuer à manger ces pains qui essaient de se faire passer pour des bagels… Donnez plutôt dans l'authenticité. Les bagels de St. Urbain Bagel Bakery sont aussi vendus chez Clafouti, My Market Bakery (172 Baldwin St., dans Kensington Market), Cheese Boutique et All the Best Fine Foods.

Senses

Veuillez consulter notre répertoire d'adresses multiples à la page 142.

www.senses.ca

DE BONNES PÂTISSERIES Pâtisserie, traiteur et restaurant, Senses n'est pas un établissement purement français, mais ses pâtisseries sont de style français et elles sont incontestablement délicieuses. Dans le domaine des pâtisseries et viennoiseries, on retrouve les incontournables français : assortiment de croissants, nombreuses tartelettes aux fruits et au chocolat, mousses aux fruits et gâteaux au chocolat. Vous pourrez également découvrir plusieurs créations typiquement locales qui valent

vraiment la peine qu'on les déguste. Le gâteau aux marrons nous a plu en particulier. On dit que réussir, c'est bien choisir. Si c'est le cas, la réussite sera d'autant plus assurée chez Senses par une très grande sélection. Pour augmenter vos chances de succès, choisissez donc plus d'une pâtisserie… Enfin, nous ajouterons que les prix des pâtisseries de Senses sont plus élevés que dans la plupart des autres pâtisseries françaises de la ville, mais ne laissez pas cette réalité vous empêcher de vous offrir une gourmandise de temps à autre.

The Bagel House

Veuillez consulter notre répertoire d'adresses multiples à la page 142.

DU BON PAIN Jessie Sahdra et Sat Chouhan sont les propriétaires de ces « bagel shops » à Toronto. Ces boulangers expatriés, originaires de Montréal, ont entamé leur carrière en 1985 et ont tous deux peaufiné leur art en travaillant dans la plupart des « bagel shops » du quartier des bagels de Montréal (les rues Saint-Viateur et Fairmount). À Toronto, The Bagel House instaure une authenticité dans la préparation des bagels. Le vrai bagel doit se distinguer du simple petit pain par sa texture, son goût et sa préparation. Les bagels de The Bagel House sont tels qu'ils devraient l'être : un peu collants, un peu sucrés, roulés à la main et parsemés de graines de sésame ou encore de graines de pavot. En magasin, vous retrouverez une douzaine de parfums, y compris un bagel allégé en sucre. Les bagels de cet établissement

pains, pâtisseries et sucreries

Le bagel a fait sa première apparition aux États-Unis en 1890. Bien que le bagel fasse partie de la gastronomie juive, il n'a jamais été considéré comme une denrée essentielle ou même de base dans la cuisine juive de l'Europe de l'Est, ou même dans celle des Juifs de la Russie. Mais il est vrai que les immigrants juifs de l'Europe de l'Est en ont fait une partie intégrante de leur gastronomie.

L'histoire du bagel dans le Canada français remonte à près d'un siècle déjà. En 1919, Isadore Shlafman arrive au Canada et ouvre la première boulangerie de bagels à Montréal, dans une allée adjacente au boulevard Saint-Laurent, communément appelée « la Main ». C'est là que les Montréalais ont appris à connaître le bagel. En 1949, Isadore Shlafman ouvre sa boutique sur la rue Fairmount, où il installe un four à bagels.

Ceux qui n'ont jamais eu la chance de goûter à un bagel de style montréalais devront savoir que la particularité du bagel réside dans le fait que le pain est façonné à la main, passé à l'eau bouillante et cuit au four à bois. On ne trouve rien de comparable dans la famille des pains.

Pendant plusieurs années, les expatriés montréalais vivant à Toronto rapportaient de leurs week-ends à Montréal des sacs et des sacs de bagels qu'ils congelaient dans l'espoir de faire perdurer ce plaisir. Une chose était sûre, si un ami ou un collègue passait par Montréal, il fallait impérativement lui demander de passer par la rue Fairmount pour acheter une ou deux douzaines de bagels.

C'est vrai que le bagel n'est pas d'origine française, mais vous trouverez très peu de Québécois de souche française n'ayant pas intégré cette tradition juive importée à leurs habitudes.

Le temps où il fallait acheter des dizaines et des dizaines de bagels de Montréal pour les rapporter à Toronto est révolu. La liste suivante répertorie les endroits où dénicher ce délice juif montréalais ici même.

N'oubliez pas qu'il y a bagel et bagel façon montréalaise. Il ne faut surtout pas confondre les deux. Maintenant, il ne vous reste qu'à choisir le parfum et la garniture de votre choix.

Où trouver les bagels de style montréalais à Toronto

1. All the Best Fine Foods
2. Cheese Boutique
3. Clafouti
4. My Market Bakery (Kensington Market)
5. Pusateri's Fine Food
6. St. Urbain Bagel Bakery
7. The Bagel House

sont considérés comme les meilleurs bagels de Toronto par le *Toronto Star*, la *Montreal Gazette* et *Toronto Life*. Les expatriés montréalais de notre équipe le confirment : ces bagels sont les meilleurs de la ville !

WHOLE FOODS MARKET

87 Avenue Road (au nord de Bloor Street)
☎ (416) 944-0500
Lundi à vendredi 9h – 22h, samedi et dimanche 9h – 21h
Métro : BAY OU MUSEUM
www.wholefoodsmarket.com

DE BONNES PÂTISSERIES Whole Foods Market allège le fardeau de ses clients en leur offrant la possibilité d'acheter plusieurs pâtisseries en provenance de chez Patachou. Bien entendu, le choix est moindre, mais l'accessibilité compense le choix un peu plus limité. Nous avons dernièrement remarqué que Whole Foods Market vend des madeleines. Quelle bonne nouvelle !

DU BON PAIN Une belle variété de pains est cuite sur place, chez Whole Foods Market. Vous y aurez le choix entre des pains aux parfums classiques tels que le pain de campagne, le pain aux raisins et pacanes, le pain aux céréales, le pain aux olives et la baguette, mais vous pourrez aussi sortir de l'ordinaire avec le pain à l'ail rôti par exemple.

ZANE PÂTISSERIE ET BOULANGERIE

1852 Queen Street East (à l'ouest de Woodbine) ☎ (416) 690-2813
Fermé lundi, mardi à dimanche 7h30 – 17h30
Métro : QUEEN + le tram

DE BONNES PÂTISSERIES Les grands classiques de la viennoiserie sont à l'honneur : croissants au beurre, croissants aux amandes et pains au chocolat. Danoises au citron, aux abricots, aux myrtilles (bleuets) et aux noisettes font également partie des viennoiseries que vous pourrez déguster chez Zane. Toujours plus fort : le tortillon à la crème pâtissière et le carré à la crème pâtissière. Le chef pâtissier Mo Zane prépare également une douzaine de gâteaux et près d'une dizaine de tartes, tous plus délicieux les uns que les autres. Vous verrez que faire votre choix risque d'être un peu compliqué. Il y a autre chose d'intéressant chez Zane : les petits fours frais. Zane prépare des tartelettes aux fruits, des tartelettes au chocolat et à la framboise, des tartelettes au citron, des miniéclairs et des minichoux. Zane vend aussi des financiers (les cousins des madeleines). Ces petits gâteaux aux amandes et au beurre de noisette vont vous séduire. Il est vrai que des petits gâteaux de ce genre se préparent facilement à la maison, mais avouez qu'il serait bête de se casser la tête, quand on peut simplement faire un tour chez cette pâtisserie française de Queen Street East. D'autant plus que ces pâtisseries sont absolument succulentes.

DU BON PAIN C'est la résidence incontestée de l'empire de la baguette et du pain dans le quartier « the Beach ». Le chef pâtissier Mo Zane propose une bonne baguette, un pain multigrains, un pain aux noix épatant et un pain aux tomates séchées, romarin et olives noires. Le pain aux tomates

séchées est particulièrement savoureux.
Il se mange bien seul ou en
accompagnement avec une bonne soupe
ou une bonne salade.

DES SUCRERIES Lorsque nous avons
rencontré Mo Zane, il nous a présenté
ses excuses, car il était alors couvert de
farine et de sucre. Nous, on aime bien
la farine et le sucre… On aime même
beaucoup ! Mo Zane mélange farine,
sucre et bien d'autres ingrédients pour
préparer des petits biscuits vendus par
quinzaine en sachet. Au choix, on a :
des tuiles à la noix de coco, des petits
sablés, des nougatines, des pains turcs
et des croques en chocolat.

chocolats

L'amour que nous, mortels, portons au chocolat n'a pas d'équivalent. Le chocolat est toujours bon, en toute occasion, peu importe la saison. Comme pour tout ce qui touche à la gastronomie, les Français ont su faire de ce goûter, véritable élixir velouté, quelque chose d'irrésistible.

Les Français sont tellement passionnés de chocolat qu'ils ont eu la bonne idée de former une association de personnes qui partagent ce penchant. C'est ainsi que le Club des croqueurs de chocolat a vu le jour. Ce groupe parisien très privé du chocolat se rencontre pour déguster et débattre des bienfaits du chocolat.

Attention, en matière de chocolat, les Français ne détiennent pas l'exclusivité, puisqu'ils ont des concurrents assez féroces. La Suisse et la Belgique sont deux autres pays reconnus pour leur passion et leur travail acharné pour faire de la préparation du chocolat un art véritable.

Que ce soit dans le but de former votre propre «Club de croqueurs de chocolat» à Toronto ou pour déguster votre douceur préférée, cette section deviendra sans aucun doute votre section favorite!

chocolats

Le vocabulaire du chocolat

Lors de nos recherches, nous avons réalisé que nous ne connaissions pas le lexique qui convient pour qualifier les différents chocolats que nous aimons tant. Nous avons décidé de faire appel à un expert qui éclairerait notre lanterne. C'est ainsi que Mme Patricia Cohrs, de la boutique Belgian Chocolate Shop dans le quartier « the Beach », nous a fourni les bonnes définitions.

La truffe : On commence d'abord par former le cœur de la truffe. Une fois l'intérieur confectionné et ferme, on l'enrobe de chocolat liquide qu'on roule traditionnellement dans de la poudre de cacao. On peut aussi rouler la truffe dans la noix de coco râpée ou les amandes effilées.

La ganache : La ganache est un mélange de crème faite essentiellement à base de chocolat, soit en général ²/₃ de chocolat et ¹/₃ de crème fraîche bouillante.

La praline : La praline est le nom donné à tout chocolat dont l'intérieur se compose de noisettes grillées ou caramélisées qui ont été broyées pour obtenir une pâte lisse qu'on mélange ensuite à du chocolat.

ARZ BAKERY

1909 Lawrence Avenue East (entre Warden Avenue et Pharmacy Avenue)
☎ (416) 755-5084

Lundi à samedi 8h – 21h30, dimanche 8h – 19h, les jours fériés 8h – 17h (Arz Bakery ne ferme jamais ses portes)

Métro : LAWRENCE + le bus

La vitrine de truffes et pralines importées de France ne déçoit pas.

BELGIAN CHOCOLATE SHOP

2455 Queen Street East (à l'ouest de Victoria Park Avenue) ☎ (416) 691-1424

Fermé lundi, mardi à vendredi 11h – 19h, samedi et dimanche 11h – 17h

Métro : QUEEN + le tram

www.belgianchocolateshop.ca

Nougatine d'amande croquante, poires pochées à la vodka, bergamote, crème au citron, caramel… Qu'ont tous ces parfums en commun ? Ils sont transformés en objets d'art chocolatés dans cette chocolaterie de l'est de Toronto. Depuis 1984, la charmante petite boutique du quartier « the Beach » ne cesse de satisfaire les amateurs, résidents du quartier ou non, en quête de chocolats raffinés. On sait d'emblée que les chocolatiers Éric Smets et Patricia Cohrs sont belges, car on remarque les deux horloges qui sont placées sur le mur à l'arrière de la vitrine. L'une de ces horloges est réglée à l'heure de Toronto et l'autre à l'heure de Bruxelles. Autre indice quant à la nationalité des chocolatiers : l'utilisation exclusive de chocolat importé de Belgique. Les truffes, pralines et ganaches sont préparées ici de façon très artisanale. Les ingrédients sont de grande qualité, la fraîcheur est assurée et l'on n'ajoute pas une goutte de conservateur. Contrairement à plusieurs autres cho-

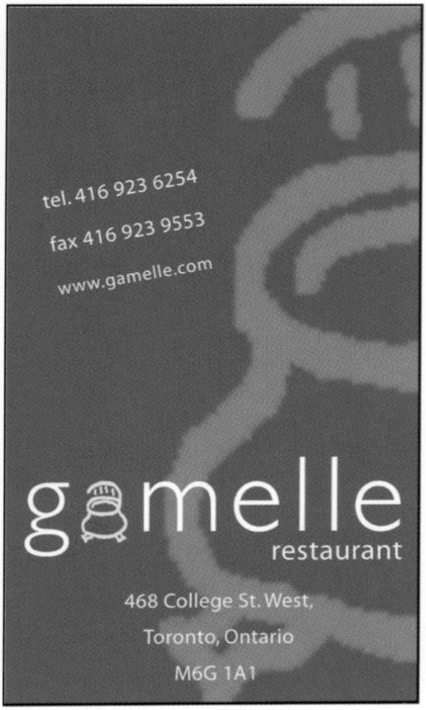
tel. 416 923 6254
fax 416 923 9553
www.gamelle.com
gamelle
restaurant
468 College St. West,
Toronto, Ontario
M6G 1A1

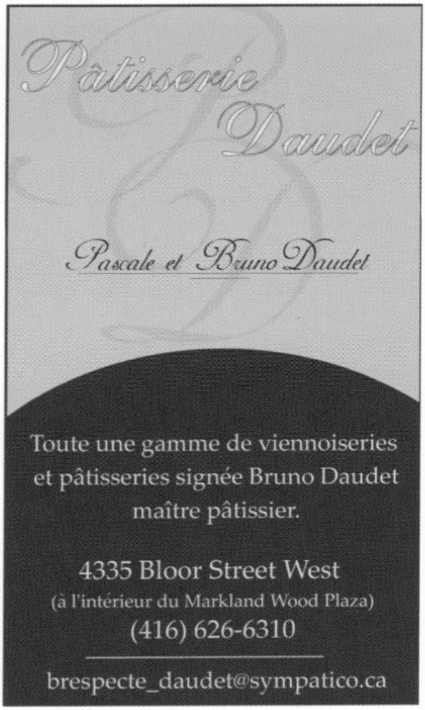
Pâtisserie Daudet
Pascale et Bruno Daudet
Toute une gamme de viennoiseries
et pâtisseries signée Bruno Daudet
maître pâtissier.
4335 Bloor Street West
(à l'intérieur du Markland Wood Plaza)
(416) 626-6310
brespecte_daudet@sympatico.ca

PAIN ♦ PERDU
BOULANGER ET PATISSIER
Découvrez la gamme rustique de
pâtisseries signée du chef
Christophe Folgoas !
Médaillé d'or de la Chambre des Métiers
des Pyrénées-Atlantiques à Bayonne.
736 St. Clair Avenue West
(416) 656-7246
www.painperdu.com
PAIN ♦ PERDU

Pâtisseries Café Sandwiches Salades
Le GOURMAND Cafe
152 Spadina Ave.
(416) 504-4494
Idées Cadeaux Gelato Chocolats

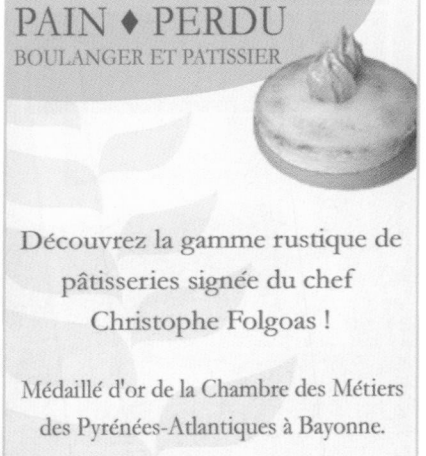

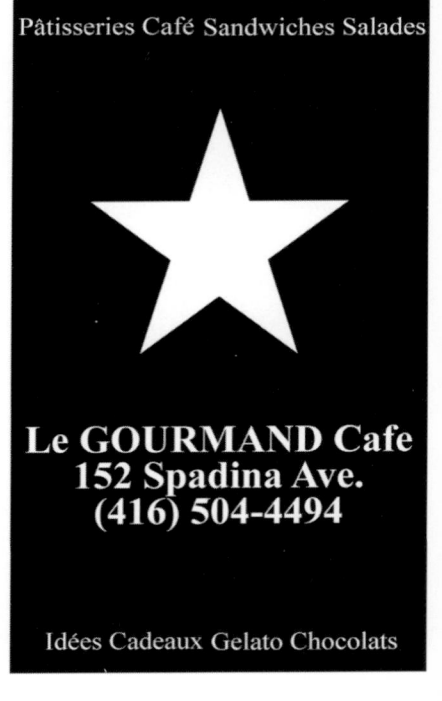

colats importés de Belgique, ceux-ci sont fabriqués sur place. Pour le consommateur, cela signifie pas de mise en entrepôt, pas de soute d'avion et pas de transport par camion. Les parfums sont fort classiques. Ceux qu'il faut à tout prix goûter sont les suivants : Grand Marnier, champagne et caramel.

CHEESE BOUTIQUE

45 Ripley Avenue (au sud de South Kingsway et au nord de The Queensway)
☎ (416) 762-6292
Lundi à vendredi 8h – 21h, samedi 8h – 20h, dimanche 10h – 18h
Métro : RUNNYMEDE + le bus
www.cheeseboutique.com

En marketing, on nous dit souvent que tout réside dans le nom. Cheese Boutique est l'exception qui confirme la règle. Rien, dans le nom de ce magasin, ne laisse deviner une telle sélection de chocolats. Cheese Boutique est l'un des plus grands importateurs de chocolats de la francophonie à Toronto. Il y en a a tellement qu'il a fallu en ranger sur la mezzanine, car le comptoir de devant ne suffisait plus. Non seulement on y trouve les grandes marques du chocolat, mais l'on peut aussi faire l'acquisition de plusieurs boîtes-cadeaux.

• •

Une première à Toronto !
Cheese Boutique vend des roulettes de chocolat suisse. Choisissez parmi la roulette marbrée, chocolat blanc, chocolat au lait ou encore la moitié/moitié. Idéal pour décorer vos desserts avec style et panache.

• •

CHOCOLATE ADDICT

185 Baldwin Street (Kensington Market)
☎ (416) 979-5809
Lundi à samedi 9h – 18h30, dimanche 10h – 18h
Métro : SPADINA + le tram;
QUEEN'S PARK + le tram
www.911chocolate.com

Nous avons déjà dit à quel point le marché Kensington cachait les meilleurs coins pour faire ses emplettes. Ce qu'on ne vous avait pas encore dit, c'est que le marché Kensington cache aussi un petit chocolatier. Chocolate Addict offre aux « mordus » du chocolat une vingtaine de parfums de truffes faites à la main avec du chocolat belge. Parmi les parfums assez classiques de noix, alcool et fruits, on retrouve trois parfums hors du commun : Sambuca, lavande et basilic.

CHOCOLATES & CREAMS

Queen's Quay Terminal, 207 Queen's Quay West ☎ (416) 368-6767
Lundi à dimanche 10h – 18h (l'hiver); lundi à vendredi 10h – 20h, samedi et dimanche 10h – 18h (l'été)
Métro : UNION + le tram
www.chocolatesandcreams.com

La boutique Chocolates & Creams est le seul importateur canadien des chocolats belges confectionnés à la main *Manon*. Les chocolats *Manon* sont bien connus en Europe pour la sélection raffinée de leurs ingrédients et le nombre de prix de qualité qui leur ont été décernés. En 1985, ces chocolats ont notamment remporté le prix d'excellence au concours international qui avait lieu à New York.

chocolats

Les chocolats *Manon* sont préparés de façon entièrement artisanale par Christian Vanderkerken. Vous aurez le choix entre plusieurs créations *Manon* à la boutique Chocolates & Creams. La plus intéressante et renversante reste sans doute le «bouchon» (qui fait partie de la collection des créations de Christian Vanderkerken). Chaque bouchon demande trois jours de préparation. Cette praline est fourrée d'une dizaine de farces sucrées. Une fois créé, le bouchon est trempé à la main dans du chocolat avant d'être recouvert d'or 24 carats. Quel sacré chocolat !

CHOCOLATES BY BERNARD CALLEBAUT
Veuillez consulter notre répertoire d'adresses multiples à la page 142.

www.bernardc.ca

Ici se marie la tradition d'une longue lignée de chocolatiers avec le modernisme contemporain. M. Callebaut, ce chocolatier belge qui a élu domicile à Calgary, s'inspire de différentes cultures et religions pour nous surprendre en matière de chocolat. Ces tendances extraordinaires ne contraignent pas M. Callebault à pourchasser l'excellence absolue; il a dernièrement diminué la part de sucre utilisé dans la préparation de ses chocolats et en a augmenté la proportion de cacao. Cette équation ne signifie qu'une chose pour nous, les amoureux du chocolat : un chocolat nettement supérieur et nettement plus raffiné. Si vous recherchez un chocolat plus simple, vous trouverez aussi votre bonheur dans cette chocolaterie, grâce aux truffes et aux ganaches. Rappelons

que M. Callebaut n'utilise aucun conservateur dans la préparation de ses produits. Conservateur ? Comme si on allait les laisser faire de vieux os, ces chocolats ! On a un petit secret à partager avec vous. Dans le congélateur se cache un goûter divin. Il s'agit d'une banane entière surgelée, trempée dans du chocolat *Bernard Callebaut* !

CLAFOUTI
915 Queen Street West (à l'est de Strachan Avenue, en face du parc Trinity Bellwoods) ☎ (416) 603-1935
Fermé lundi, mardi à samedi 8h – 18h, dimanche 9h – 17h
Métro : OSGOODE + le tram

Clafouti fait uniquement dans le chocolat de tous les jours. Vous trouverez ici aussi le chocolat à boire *Poulain* et le chocolat pour fondue *Mazet*. N'oubliez pas que vous pouvez même commander sur place une bonne tasse de chocolat chaud *Poulain* !

DANIEL ET DANIEL – FOOD SHOP
248 Carlton Street (au coin de Parliament Street) ☎ (416) 968-9275
Lundi à samedi 7h30 – 18h, fermé dimanche
Métro : CASTLE FRANK + le bus; COLLEGE + le tram
www.danieletdaniel.ca

Daniel et Daniel n'a que quelques parfums de truffes en magasin – noisette, chocolat blanc, noix de coco et noix. On y trouve aussi des truffes au champagne importées de France.

Le dictionnaire du chocolat

Ne vous faites pas prendre au dépourvu lors de votre prochain voyage en Europe. Apprenez dès aujourd'hui à demander votre collation préférée dans une douzaine de langues européennes !

Allemand : schokolade

Anglais : chocolate

Danois : chocolade

Espagnol : chocolate

Finlandais : sukiaa

Flamand : chocolade

Grec : sokolata

Italien : cioccolato

Néerlandais : chocolaad

Norvégien : sjokolade

Portuguais : chocolate

Suédois : choklad

Source : site du Salon du chocolat

EVE'S TEMPTATIONS

93 Front Street East (St. Lawrence Market, au sous-sol) ☎ (416) 366-7437
Fermé dimanche et lundi, mardi à jeudi 8h – 18h, vendredi 8h – 19h, samedi 5h – 17h
Métro : UNION

Les truffes et pralines de The Chocolate Messenger y sont disponibles.

FRANGIPANE PÂTISSERIE

215 Madison Avenue (à quelques pas du métro DUPONT) ☎ (416) 926-0303
Lundi à jeudi 8h – 18h30, vendredi 8h – 19h, samedi 9h – 18h30, dimanche 10h – 16h
Métro : DUPONT

Claudia Egger n'utilise que du chocolat des maisons *Lindt* et *Callebaut* dans la préparation de ses pralines et ganaches. Tout comme pour ses tartes et gâteaux, Mme Egger prépare en boutique ses confections chocolatées. Bien entendu, vous aurez le choix entre plusieurs parfums. Permettez-nous de vous suggérer le fondant. Les Italiens l'appellent peut-être *gianduia*, mais nous préférons l'appeler le *sensationnel*!

HOLT RENFREW – EPICURE AND GOURMET SHOPS

50 Bloor Street West (au coin de Bay Street) ☎ (416) 922-2333
Lundi à mercredi 10h – 18h, jeudi et vendredi 10h – 20h, samedi 10h – 18h, dimanche 12h – 18h
Métro : YONGE OU BAY

Placés derrière une vitrine réfrigérée, les chocolats *Neuhaus* de Belgique et *Joseph Schmidt* nous guettent et nous font de l'œil. Holt Renfrew maîtrise l'art de la séduction silencieuse, il n'y a qu'à regarder le décor. Les chocolats *Neuhaus* sont importés de Belgique, tandis que les chocolats *Joseph Schmidt* sont importés des États-Unis, mais ils sont faits uniquement à partir de chocolat belge. Dans les deux cas, vous remarquerez que les parfums sont assez classiques. Lors des fêtes de Noël, de la Saint-Valentin et de Pâques, Holt Renfrew importe plusieurs boîtes-cadeaux de France et de Belgique, destinées à nous faire mieux célébrer l'événement. La sélection de chocolats pour tous les jours est assez limitée. Cela dit, les barres de chocolat *Neuhaus* valent la peine qu'on y pense en cas

chocolats

d'envie pressante de chocolat. Il y a aussi des amandes enrobées de chocolat de la maison *Fauchon*.

Le saviez-vous ?

Une praline se déguste en une seule bouchée. C'est vraiment la seule façon de bien faire ressortir son goût. Vous voilà averti. N'essayez surtout plus de croquer plusieurs fois dans une praline pour en faire durer le plaisir, car tout ce que vous aurez réussi à faire, c'est à saboter partiellement l'expérience.

J.S. BONBONS

Veuillez consulter notre répertoire d'adresses multiples à la page 142.
www.jsbonbons.com

Des truffes aux 30 parfums sous un même toit ! Si cette perspective ne vous séduit pas, c'est fichu ! Et si on vous dit que Jenn Stone, la créatrice qui se cache derrière J.S. Bonbons, peut aussi confectionner un sublime bol en chocolat pour accueillir votre sélection ? Épatant, n'est-ce pas ? Chez J.S. Bonbons, on se donne tout entier à la célébration de ce trésor noir d'Afrique. Les truffes sont en bonne compagnie ici, elles sont généralement alignées parmi de somptueux fruits trempés dans du chocolat. Cette jeune chocolatière n'utilise que du chocolat suisse ou belge pour ses confections. Ce qui place Jenn Stone en tête de peloton, c'est l'originalité et la qualité de ses chocolats. Vous trouverez quelques parfums classiques, mais, évidemment, ce sont les parfums

moins ordinaires que nous vous conseillons. Les spécialités de la maison sont les infusions d'herbes et les infusions de thés. Les parfums de ces infusions vous surprendront : estragon et poivre noir, coriandre et citron vert, lavande, thé chai, bergamote et romarin. La liste peut sembler déroutante, mais le goût est tout simplement sublime et étonnamment subtil.

LA CIGOGNE

1626 Bayview Avenue (au sud d'Eglinton Avenue) ☎ (416) 487-1234

Lundi à vendredi 7h30 – 19h, samedi 8h – 19h, dimanche 8h – 17h

Métro : EGLINTON + le bus

Le chef Thierry Schmitt vous propose de superbes truffes maison. Vous pourrez choisir parmi une dizaine de parfums réalisés à base de chocolat français. Il ne faut surtout pas les rater pendant les fêtes de Noël, la Saint-Valentin, Pâques et la fête des Mères.

LA MAISON DU CHOCOLAT

Commande par avion du magasin de New York ☎ 1 800 988-5632

Lundi à samedi 10h – 19h, dimanche 12h – 18h

Oui, vous avez bien lu. On peut enfin acheter les chocolats de La Maison du Chocolat de ce côté-ci de l'Atlantique. Tous ceux qui ont eu le privilège de visiter les boutiques de Paris, rue du Faubourg Saint-Honoré, rue François 1er et boulevard de la Madeleine, savent à quel point les chocolats de cette maison sont sublimes. Que ce soit à Paris ou à New York, le simple fait de respirer ces parfums merveilleux nous

enivre. Bien que nous n'ayons pas encore la chance d'avoir une boutique de la célèbre enseigne La Maison du Chocolat à Toronto, nous avons tout de même la possibilité de nous offrir cette gourmandise affriolante. Il suffit de téléphoner pour passer commande à la boutique de New York. Attention le luxe se paie : la boîte de 77 joyaux coûte plus de 100 CAD.

LE GOURMAND

152 Spadina Avenue (au sud de Queen Street) ☎ (416) 504-4494

Lundi à vendredi 7h – 20h, samedi 9h – 18h, dimanche 9h – 16h

Métro : OSGOODE + le tram;
SPADINA + le tram

Le Gourmand est un petit bistro-marchand situé en bordure du Fashion District. Voilà une des seules adresses où se procurer du chocolat à boire des marques françaises *Poulain* et *Monbana*. Sur place, vous aurez même la possibilité de déguster une tasse de chocolat *Poulain*.

LEONIDAS

Veuillez consulter notre répertoire d'adresses multiples à la page 142.

La vedette chez Leonidas, c'est la praline à la crème fraîche. Elle est incroyablement riche et onctueuse. Nous la préférons toute simple, dans sa version chocolat au lait et crème fraîche, mais vous pouvez aussi choisir d'autres parfums parmi la gamme de douze pralines à la crème fraîche. Vous aurez également le choix du type de chocolat selon vos préférences : lait, noir ou blanc. Du fait de leur extrême

Chocolats pour tous les jours

Le chocolat est un plaisir qu'on devrait pouvoir s'offrir tous les jours. Voilà pourquoi nous avons répertorié les chocolats de la francophonie qui s'adaptent au budget de chacun. Les grandes maisons du chocolat sont bien représentées à Toronto : *Poulain, Côte D'or, Suchard, Swiss Delice, Alprose, Lindt, Michel Cluizel, Valrhona, Maxim's, Galler, Révillon, Jacques, Suchard, Mazet, Dolfin, Marquise d'Angélis, Petite Périgord Gold, Pierre Ledent* et *Sarments*.

OÙ TROUVER LES GRANDES MARQUES DE CHOCOLATS FRANCO-EUROPÉENS À TORONTO

1. Arz Bakery
2. Brandt Meat Packers Ltd.
3. Cheese Boutique
4. Chocolates & Creams
5. Domino Foods Ltd.
6. Daniel et Daniel
7. La Cigogne
8. Le Comptoir de Célestin
9. Le Gourmand
10. Leonidas
11. Loblaws
12. Max's Market
13. Mercatto
14. Pâtisserie d'Or
15. Pusateri's Fine Foods
16. Rahier
17. Scheffler's Delicatessen
18. Simone Marie Belgian Chocolate
19. Sobeys
20. Sun Valley Fine Foods

chocolats

fraîcheur et de l'absence d'agent conservateur, ces pralines ont une «durée de vie» de huit jours seulement. Nous sommes certains que cela ne devrait pas poser de problème au consommateur gourmand.

PAIN PERDU

736 St. Clair Avenue West (un peu à l'ouest de Christie Street) ☎ (416) 656-7246

Fermé lundi, mardi à vendredi 8h – 19h, samedi 8h – 17h, dimanche 8h – 16h

Métro : ST CLAIR WEST + le tram

www.painperdu.com

Des truffes, des truffes et encore des truffes. Voilà ce que propose le chef Folgoas en matière de gourmandises au chocolat. Un médaillé d'or de la chambre des métiers des Pyrénées-Altanliques à Bayonne ne peut donner que dans l'excellence. Au palmarès des parfums les plus populaires du chef Folgoas : chocolat noir et rhum, chocolat blanc et chocolat noir avec framboise.

PÂTISSERIE D'OR

301 Robinson Street (au sud de Lake Shore Road), Oakville ☎ (905) 815-8999

Fermé lundi et mardi, mercredi à vendredi 8h – 17h30, samedi et dimanche 8h – 18h

Le saviez-vous ?

La première chocolaterie ouvrit ses portes à Paris en 1659, rue de l'Arbre, dans le 1er arrondissement. L'ingéniosité du roi Louis XIV amena cette petite douceur en France lorsqu'il donna le privilège exclusif à l'un des officiers de la reine Anne de vendre du chocolat à Paris.

Quelques savoureux chocolats suisses sont placés dans une vitrine à l'arrière de cette pâtisserie d'Oakville. Au menu des parfums, vous découvrirez les chocolats à l'orange, à la pistache, à la violette, aux pacanes, aux noisettes et à la noix de coco, ainsi que le chocolat blanc.

PÂTISSERIE DAUDET

4335 Bloor Street West, Markland Wood Plaza (au coin de Mill Road) ☎ (416) 626-6310

Fermé dimanche et lundi, mardi à samedi 8h – 18h

Le chef Respecte-Daudet fait non seulement dans la pâtisserie, mais aussi dans le chocolat ! Il utilise le chocolat français *Valhrona* pour confectionner ses délices. Les truffes sont les vedettes de cette pâtisserie et, pendant les fêtes, le chef Respecte-Daudet donne le champ libre à sa créativité. Le résultat est délicieusement original.

PÂTISSERIE LE PAPILLON

Ce commerçant rouvrira ses portes dans le nord de la ville en 2005

9425 Leslie Street, Unit #9, Richmond Hill ☎ (905) 918-0080

Lundi à jeudi 12h – 20h, vendredi à dimanche 12h – 22h

www.finecakes.ca

Une tarte truffée ? Eh bien oui ! C'est ce que nous propose le chef Chang. Tout commence par du chocolat français ou belge qu'on infuse de parfums traditionnels et exotiques. Une fois prêtes, les truffes infusées sont placées au cœur de la pâte à tarte. Il ne reste plus qu'à les déguster !

chocolats

PUSATERI'S FINE FOODS

1539 Avenue Road (au nord de Lawrence Avenue) ☎ (416) 785-9100

Lundi à mercredi 8h – 20h, jeudi et vendredi 8h – 21h, samedi et dimanche 8h – 19h

Métro : LAWRENCE + le bus

www.pusateris.com

Dans un recoin du magasin se cache une vitrine de truffes et ganaches de la maison *Neuhaus*.

SENSES

Veuillez consulter notre répertoire d'adresses multiples à la page 142.

www.senses.ca

Senses a fait appel au chocolatier Thomas Hass de Vancouver pour offrir à ses clients une expérience inoubliable. Le chocolatier de la côte ouest utilise exclusivement du chocolat français *Valrhona* pour la confection de ses truffes et pralines. On découvrira bien sûr des parfums classiques, mais aussi quelques surprises parmi lesquelles la truffe au champagne et à l'espresso, la truffe blanche à la vanille et au rhum, et la truffe aux mûres et au miel.

SIMONE MARIE BELGIAN CHOCOLATE

126 Cumberland Street (au coin de Bellair Street) ☎ (416) 968-7777

Lundi à samedi 10h30 – 18h30, fermé dimanche

Métro : BAY, sortie Cumberland

www.simonemarie.net

Depuis 1993, Mme Simone Marie s'est spécialisée dans l'importation de chocolats artisanaux belges. Vous découvrirez

une sélection de truffes aux parfums d'alcools populaires tels que le champagne, le Cointreau et l'Amaretto. Vous aurez aussi la possibilité d'acheter des truffes fruitées à la crème d'orange, à la crème de citron, à la cannelle, à l'orange et à l'écorce d'orange, enrobée de chocolat noir. N'oubliez surtout pas de demander aux vendeurs quelle est la sélection du mois. En effet, chaque mois, la boutique met en vedette une nouveauté. La spécialité belge, adoptée par les Français et qu'il ne faut pas manquer, c'est le chocolat aromatisé à la liqueur. Eh bien oui, chez Simone Marie on peut acheter des chocolats *Bruyerre*. Cette maison, fondée en 1909, fabrique des chocolats fourrés à la liqueur (la vraie !).

SWISS-MASTER CHOCOLATIER

2538 Bayview Avenue (au coin de York Mills Road, au nord de Post Road) ☎ (416) 444-8802

Lundi à samedi 10h – 18h, fermé dimanche

Métro : YORK MILLS + le bus

www.swissmaster.com

Les chocolats Swiss-Master des Alpes suisses remplissent cette petite boutique. Les parfums sont très classiques puisque la propriétaire, Ingrid Läderach, n'adhère pas au courant de pensée de la fusion. Pour autant, ne croyez surtout pas que classique veuille dire prévisible. Il n'y a rien de prévisible dans plusieurs des chocolats que nous avons goûtés – truffe au Grand Marnier et à la crème fraîche, truffe au rhum et aux raisins, truffe au chocolat noir et à la véritable

chocolats

liqueur de Grand Marnier. Si vous avez quelque chose à exprimer de façon originale, optez donc pour les chocolats en forme de cœur qui portent les inscriptions suivantes : « I love you », « For you » et « Thank you ». La spécialité de la maison la plus prisée est sans aucun doute la truffe pastel. Eh oui, ces petites boules de chocolat blanc et fruits frais colorées dans des tons pastel sont très populaires dans cette boutique. Lors des fêtes de la Saint-Valentin, Noël et Pâques, le magasin se transforme en château de conte de fées plein à craquer sous le poids de figurines en chocolat aux parfums divers.

TEUSCHER CHOCOLATES

55 Bloor Street West (au coin de Bay Street, à l'intérieur du Manulife Centre)
☎ (416) 964-8200

Lundi à mercredi 10h – 18h, jeudi et vendredi 10h – 19h30, samedi 10h – 18h, fermé dimanche

Métro : YONGE OU BAY

Bon nombre d'épicuriens accordent à ces chocolats des éloges qui font des envieux. Le magazine de cuisine américain *Bon Appétit* déclare que les chocolats Teuscher sont « les plus

L'œuvre des « chocoholic » américains (amateurs invétérés de chocolat)

Les vrais connaisseurs du chocolat aux États-Unis ont créé leur propre magazine. *The Magazine for Gourmet Chocolate Lovers* est même imprimé sur un papier parfumé au... chocolat !

Source : site du Salon du chocolat

merveilleuses créations chocolatées jamais réalisées ». Quel compliment ! Il y a plus de 65 ans que ce chocolatier suisse maîtrise l'art de séduire les palets. La fabrique de Zurich confectionne plus d'une centaine de parfums de chocolats en prenant soin de n'utiliser que les produits les plus raffinés. Les chocolats Teuscher qu'on retrouve à la boutique de Bloor West sont importés directement de Zurich chaque semaine. Vous aurez le choix entre plusieurs parfums classiques chez Teuscher, tels que l'orange, l'abricot, la crème de chocolat blanc, le citron, le nougat et le caramel. Enfin, les vœux s'achètent chez ce chocolatier – une étoile filante ou deux en chocolat devraient faire l'affaire...

THE CHOCOLATE MESSENGER

1645 Bayview Avenue (au sud d'Eglinton Avenue) ☎ (416) 488-1414

Fermé dimanche et lundi, mardi à vendredi 10h – 18h, samedi 10h – 17h

Métro : EGLINTON + le bus

www.chocolatemessenger.com

Ce chocolatier d'origine suisse utilise le chocolat *Lindt* pour nous faire craquer. Les truffes et les pralines maison remplissent la vitrine. Les truffes à la crème fraîche sont les spécialités de la maison. Vous aurez le choix entre 20 parfums. Pour les pralines, de même, une vingtaine de parfums vous attendent, tous à base de beurre. Au sommaire des parfums les plus intéressants, voici ceux que nous avons retenus : vodka pêche, vodka orange, thé vert et porto. Nous devons aussi ajouter que ce chocolatier, comme tout chocolatier qui se respecte,

n'ajoute aucun agent conservateur à ses préparations chocolatées. Lors des fêtes de la Saint-Valentin, Noël et Pâques, le magasin regorge de confections chocolatées et de boîtes de truffes. Pendant les fêtes de Noël, vous trouverez enfin des fruits confits et des marrons glacés.

TRUFFLE TREASURES

15751 Island Road, Port Perry
☎ (905) 982-0506

Lundi à samedi 9h – 17h30

www.truffletreasures.com

Lara Vaarré a développé son art en étudiant avec un chocolatier chevronné (70 années d'expérience à son actif!). Après avoir acquis les bases du métier, elle est allée parfaire son éducation à l'école de renommée internationale Lenôtre, à Paris. Aucun doute là-dessus, Lara Vaarré adore son métier. Ça se lit dans la passion qu'elle transmet et ça se goûte lorsque l'on croque ses truffes. Les parfums abondent, si bien qu'il devient difficile de choisir parmi la trentaine de truffes proposées. Il y a quatre façons de déguster les chocolats de Lara Vaarré : on peut aller directement à l'entrepôt de Port Perry, au nord d'Oshawa; certains magasins Fortino en ville les vendent; on peut les commander sur le site; enfin, si vous parcourez les foires gastronomiques de Toronto et du grand Toronto, vous serez presque assuré de tomber sur le point de vente de Truffle Treasures.

WHOLE FOODS MARKET

87 Avenue Road (au nord de Bloor Street)
☎ (416) 944-0500

Lundi à vendredi 9h – 22h, samedi et dimanche 9h – 21h

Métro : BAY ou MUSEUM

www.wholefoodsmarket.com

Ici, vous trouverez les chocolats et le chocolat à cuire de la maison *Callebaut*, ainsi que le chocolat *Valhrona*.

fromages et crème fraîche

Lorsqu'on pense à la France, on pense sans conteste à « la Sainte-Trinité » : du pain, du vin et du fromage. Il n'y a rien de plus français qu'une bonne baguette garnie de camembert et accompagnée d'un verre de vin. La Suisse est un autre pays francophone à la belle sélection de fromages. Si l'on ne doute pas qu'une bonne éducation au monde des fromages se fasse de l'autre côté de l'Atlantique, soyez rassuré d'apprendre qu'on peut très bien parfaire son éducation ici aussi, à Toronto.

À la recherche de plaisirs fromagers ? Les adresses suivantes devraient pouvoir vous satisfaire.

fromages et crème fraîche

ALEX FARM PRODUCTS

Veuillez consulter notre répertoire d'adresses multiples à la page 142.

www.alexcheese.com

La France produit 350 à 400 fromages différents. Vous aurez l'impression de tous les retrouver chez Alex Farm, car cette boutique est celle qui importe le plus grand nombre de fromages français à Toronto. Parmi les fromages qu'on vous y propose : le vacherin Mont-d'Or de Badoz (AOC), le pouligny-saint-pierre, le coulommiers, le pont-l'évêque, l'époisses de Bourgogne, le saint-andré, la fourme d'Ambert, le saint-agur, le rondin du Poitou, le brique de Jussac, le morbier, le fromage *Belle des Champs*, le grand pont-l'évêque, le laguiole (AOC), le chaumes, l'etorki, l'abondance (AOC), le chaource (AOC), et le grain d'orge de Normandie. La gamme de fromages classiques est également impressionnante. Vous pouvez même acheter du p'tit Basque (fromage de brebis pur du Pays basque). Vous y trouverez également une bonne sélection de fromages suisses, parmi lesquels trois variétés d'emmenthal, du gruyère, trois types de fromage appenzeller et de la raclette.

ALL THE BEST FINE FOODS

1099 Yonge Street (au nord de Roxborough Street) ☎ (416) 928-3330

Lundi à mercredi 8h30 – 18h30, jeudi et vendredi 8h30 – 19h, samedi 8h30 – 18h, dimanche 10h – 17h

Métro : SUMMERHILL

La sélection est très intéressante dans cette boutique du quartier Rosedale. Elle inclut des fromages français, québécois et suisses bien connus ainsi que quelques autres moins courants à Toronto. Entre autres, vous trouverez de l'époisses, du comté, du morbier, du camembert Jort, du livarot, du mothais, du selles-sur-cher, du pouligny-saint-pierre et du brie, parmi les fromages les

plus connus. Le fromage de chèvre chabichou du Poitou, le fougerus, le colombier, le fromage de Riblaire et l'édel de Cléron font partie de la liste des fromages plus « extraordinaires ». Du côté du Québec, une bonne sélection de fromages crus tels que le saint-basile, le saint-félicien, le Lechevalier Mailloux, le pied de vent et l'ange cornu sont au rendez-vous.

ARZ BAKERY

1909 Lawrence Avenue East (entre Warden Avenue et Pharmacy Avenue)
☎ (416) 755-5084

Lundi à samedi 8h – 21h30, dimanche 8h – 19h, les jours fériés 8h – 17h (Arz Bakery ne ferme jamais ses portes)

Métro : LAWRENCE + le bus

Cet empire de la cuisine libanaise importe aussi de très bons fromages de France, du Québec et de la Suisse. Vous y découvrirez également un très beau choix de fetas de Macédoine, de Grèce et de Bulgarie.

CHEESE BOUTIQUE

45 Ripley Avenue (au sud de South Kingsway et au nord de The Queensway)
☎ (416) 762-6292

Lundi à vendredi 8h – 21h, samedi 8h – 20h, dimanche 10h – 18h

Métro : RUNNYMEDE + le bus

www.cheeseboutique.com

Avouez que le nom est assez révélateur... et trompeur à la fois ! Nous, on rebaptiserait bien Cheese Boutique « French Cheese Boutique ». En effet, puisqu'on y trouve une très grande sélection de fromages français (plus d'une centaine), québécois (une trentaine) et suisses (une dizaine). On a

décidé de ne pas citer les grands noms du fromage en vente chez Cheese Boutique, puisqu'ils y sont tous. Vous trouverez même des fromages qu'on trouve difficilement ailleurs, comme l'explorateur. La plupart des autres importateurs s'approvisionnent en explorateur à l'époque des fêtes de Noël, mais le propriétaire de Cheese Boutique l'importe tout au long de l'année. Ce qu'on voit par ailleurs peu à Toronto, c'est un si grand nombre de fromages provenant de petits artisans fromagers québécois. Chez Cheese Boutique, on importe également plusieurs fromages de France qu'on affine ensuite sur place. Le propriétaire nous a fait goûter un petit bout d'explorateur venu de France et un petit bout d'explorateur affiné en boutique. Aucune comparaison !

CHEESE MAGIC

182 Baldwin Street (Kensington Market)
☎ (416) 593-9531

Lundi à samedi 8h30 – 19h, dimanche 9h – 18h

Métro : SPADINA + le tram;
QUEEN'S PARK + le tram

Cheese Magic ne propose pas un choix comparable à celui des deux géants du fromage de la francophonie du marché Kensington, mais sa sélection demeure

Le saviez-vous ?

La France produit plus de 160 000 tonnes de camembert par an. Rien d'étonnant ! Ce fromage tient l'une des meilleures places dans le cœur des Français.

tout à fait honorable. De la Suisse, on importe de l'appenzeller, du gruyère, de la raclette et de l'emmenthal. En provenance de France, on a du roquefort, du morbier, du bleu d'Auvergne, du port-salut et de la raclette. Et, arrivés directement du Québec, oka, saint-benoît bleu bénédictin, brie et chèvre.

CHRIS' CHEESEMONGERS

93 Front Street East (St. Lawrence Market) ☎ (416) 368-5273

Fermé dimanche et lundi, mardi à jeudi 8h – 18h, vendredi 8h – 19h, samedi 5h – 17h

Métro : UNION

Voici le petit cousin d'Alex Farm. Si Alex Farm se spécialise dans les fromages en provenance de la France, Chris' Cheesemongers s'en donne à cœur joie dans les fromages en provenance du Québec. Leur liste en est presque étourdissante (une quinzaine de fromages français contre une soixantaine de fromages québécois). Vous trouverez une variété abondante côté Québec : chèvre noir, grand cru de Chaput, double brie aux herbes et double brie au poivre, pied de vent des Îles-de-la-Madeleine, capra et freddo, jeune cœur des Îles-de-la-Madeleine, mi-carême de l'Île aux Grues (un fromage très similaire au camembert de Normandie) et cendré de Warwick (la

Le saviez-vous ?

Le cantal est l'un des fromages les plus vieux de France, avant le roquefort (produit depuis le XIe siècle) et le livarot (produit depuis le XIIIe siècle).

version québécoise du morbier). Vous remarquerez également quelques fromages français tels que le chaumes, le saint-paulin, le brie triple crème, le port-salut, le bresse bleu, le camembert de Normandie, le pont-l'évêque, le boursault, le rouy et le vacherin Mont-d'Or, pour ne citer que ceux-là.

DINAH'S CUPBOARD

50 Cumberland Street ☎ (416) 921-8112

Lundi à vendredi 8h – 19h, samedi 9h – 18h, fermé dimanche (à l'exception du mois de décembre)

Métro : YONGE OU BAY

Dinah's Cupboard importe une très petite quantité de fromages français; environ une demi-douzaine d'entre eux sont parmi les plus populaires.

GLOBAL CHEESE

76 Kensington Avenue ☎ (416) 593-9251

Lundi à vendredi 9h – 19h, samedi 8h – 18h, dimanche 9h – 17h

Métro : SPADINA + le tram; QUEEN'S PARK + le tram

Global Cheese propose les fromages français suivants : morbier, saint-agur, truffier, fourme d'Ambert, champagne, chèvre, saint-andré, saint-paulin, pont-l'évêque, bleu d'Auvergne et roquefort. Ces fromages font partie d'une liste totale d'environ quarante fromages français. Pour ce qui est des fromages du Québec, Global en importe une vingtaine, parmi lesquels le brie, le brie aux herbes, le brie aux poivres, l'oka, l'emmenthal du Québec et le camembert. Enfin, côté Suisse, la liste est plus courte. Vous aurez surtout accès aux plus connus : le gruyère et l'emmenthal.

Par contre, Global Cheese donne à ses clients la possibilité de goûter avant d'acheter. Pas moyen de se tromper!

LOBLAWS

Différentes adresses dans toute la ville

Si vous n'avez pas le temps de rendre visite à votre fromager préféré, vous pouvez toujours vous arrêter chez Loblaws. Le choix y est très satisfaisant pour un supermarché. Vous êtes sûr de trouver plus d'une vingtaine de classiques français, québécois et suisses. Le brie, le camembert, le *Boursin*, le *Caprice des Dieux*, l'emmenthal français, le coulommiers, le comté, le bleu d'Auvergne, l'oka, le bleu et le chèvre figurent, entre autres, sur la liste des fromages disponibles. Loblaws importe également de la raclette et du gruyère de Suisse.

MAX'S MARKET

2299 Bloor Street West (à l'ouest de Runnymede Road) ☎ (416) 766-6362

Lundi à mercredi 9h – 19h, jeudi 9h – 19h30, vendredi 9h – 20h, samedi 9h – 19h, dimanche 9h – 18h

Métro : RUNNYMEDE

On trouve chez Max's Market une quantité raisonnable de fromages de France, du Québec et de Suisse. Au palmarès des grands noms figurent le morbier, la raclette de France et celle de Suisse, l'appenzeller, le bleu d'Auvergne, la fourme d'Ambert, le saint-agur, le roquefort, le chèvre de Riblaire, l'oka et le gruyère.

Où trouver les fromages AOC à Toronto

1. Alex Farm Products
2. All the Best Fine Foods
3. Cheese Boutique
4. Chris' Cheesemongers
5. Global Cheese
6. Mendel's Creamery n' Appetizer (à Noël seulement)
7. Olympic Cheese Mart
8. Pusateri's Fine Foods
9. Scheffler's Delicatessen
10. Whole Foods Market

MENDEL'S CREAMERY N' APPETIZER

72 Kensington Avenue ☎ (416) 597-1784

Lundi à vendredi 8h30 – 19h, samedi 8h – 18h, fermé dimanche

Métro : SPADINA + le tram; QUEEN'S PARK + le tram

Mendel's Creamery n' Appetizer occupe une superficie bien moindre que son voisin, mais en matière de fromages de la francophonie, la taille du magasin n'a plus rien à voir. Selon la saison, Mendel's a en magasin jusqu'à 80 fromages français, une dizaine du Québec et une demi-douzaine de la Suisse. Sur la liste des fromages français, on a le morbier, le roquefort, le saint-paulin, le saint-andré, le fromage de chèvre de Corse et le bleu brie. Au palmarès québécois figurent l'oka, le camblu et le brie. Quant à la Suisse, ses couleurs sont bien représentées avec du gruyère, de la raclette, de l'emmenthal, de l'appenzeller et du vacherin Mont-d'Or.

fromages et crème fraîche

OLYMPIC CHEESE MART

Veuillez consulter notre répertoire d'adresses multiples à la page 142.

Plus de 400 fromages rassemblés sous un même toit ! Les mordus de la fondue au fromage trouveront plusieurs types de raclette sans lait de vache et à faible teneur en sodium. En matière de fromages français, Olympic Cheese Mart propose plus de 100 variétés. On y retrouve les plus populaires, mais aussi certains moins bien connus, tels que le camembert au poivre, le gourmelin, l'époisses, le roquefort papillon, le comté, le beaufort et le *p'tit reblo*. Parmi les fromages les plus connus figurent le brie, le camembert, le brie en brioche, le saint-morgon, le saint-andré, la raclette et le chèvre. Olympic Cheese Mart est un autre marchand qui importe plusieurs variétés du Québec. Parmi celles-ci, on a le mouton noir, le saint-ambroise (un fromage à la bière), le frère Jacques, le moine, le douanier (façon morbier) et la mamirolle. Autres fromages intéressants en provenance du Québec : le Sir Laurier d'Arthabaska, les fromages de la région de Saint-Benoît, le cantonnier et les fromages de la région de Plessisville. Les fromages suisses sont bien représentés ici aussi : gruyère, emmenthal, raclette, vacherin fribourgeois, vacherin Mont-d'Or, maréchal, trois types d'appenzeller, Mont Vully, weinkäse (vieilli au vin) et tête de moine, pour n'en citer que quelques-uns. Olympic Cheese Mart est également approvisionné en fromages au lait cru.

PUSATERI'S FINE FOODS

Veuillez consulter notre répertoire d'adresses multiples à la page 142.
www.pusateris.com

Comme vous pouvez l'imaginer, il y a chez Pusateri's un grand choix de fromages parmi les plus raffinés de la francophonie. En voici donc quelques exemples pour vous inciter à faire un tour au magasin et y découvrir la gamme complète : roquefort, époisses, bleu d'Auvergne, saint-agur, etorki,

tomme de Savoie, morbier, saint-albray et chaumes. Nous avons remarqué la présence de welsche, fromage affiné d'Alsace, de rebloch'art en provenance du Québec et de chimay, fromage belge.

QUALITY CHEESE

111 Jevlan Drive, Vaughan (au coin de Highway 7 et Weston Road)
☎ (905) 265-9991

Lundi à vendredi 8h30 – 18h, samedi 8h30 – 17h, fermé dimanche

La famille Borog fabrique des fromages de qualité « olympique ». Vous recherchez des fromages ayant remporté plusieurs médailles ? Dans la catégorie des fromages français, Quality Cheese vous propose un brie médaillé.

SCHEFFLER'S DELICATESSEN

93 Front Street East (St. Lawrence Market)
☎ (416) 364-2806

Fermé dimanche et lundi, mardi à jeudi 8h – 18h, vendredi 8h – 19h, samedi 5h – 17h

Métro : UNION

Tout comme ses confrères du marché St. Lawrence, Scheffler's met à votre

Le saviez-vous ?

Nous avons consulté un maître fromager afin d'obtenir de bonnes astuces pour choisir un camembert. Ne vous laissez pas séduire par une croûte trop blanche et trop soyeuse, par exemple. Recherchez un camembert velouté, d'un blanc très léger et à la croûte striée de rouge brun. Et sachez que l'appellation « camembert » ne peut qu'être attribuée à un fromage au lait cru de vache.

disposition un vaste choix de fromages du Québec et de France. Côté français, vous trouverez du saint-agur, du camembert, du saint-andré, de l'ermite, du chèvre, du fromage de brebis et du saint-paulin. De ce côté-ci de l'Atlantique, vous aurez le choix entre du camembert, du brie, du chèvre, de l'oka, du frère Jacques et du bleu bénédictin. En provenance de la Suisse enfin, il y a du gruyère et de l'emmenthal.

SOBEYS

81 St. Clair Avenue East (un peu à l'est de Yonge Street) ☎ (416) 413-0594

Tous les jours, 24 heures sur 24

Métro : ST CLAIR

Sobeys est une franchise du grand Toronto et l'on retrouve ses magasins partout en ville. Cependant, le nouveau magasin du quartier de Yonge et St. Clair a su s'adapter au goût un tantinet francophile du coin. Vous y découvrirez une petite sélection de fromages bien connus de la francophonie – saint-aubin, rustique de Normandie, morbier, *p'tit reblo*, saint-paulin, emmenthal, brie et camembert de France ou du Québec, oka et chèvre.

SUN VALLEY FINE FOODS

583 Danforth Avenue (à l'ouest de Pape Avenue) ☎ (416) 469-5227

Lundi à vendredi 8h30 – 21h, samedi 8h – 20h, dimanche 8h30 – 20h

Métro : PAPE

Sun Valley est avant tout un expert de la feta grecque. Cependant, Sun Valley propose aussi les fromages les plus connus de la francophonie. Côté suisse, on a le gruyère et l'emmenthal. Pour les

fromages et crème fraîche

fromages français, le choix est un peu plus varié, avec une quinzaine de variétés de l'Hexagone représentées, parmi lesquelles le morbier, la tomme de montagne, la fourme d'Ambert, le saint-nectaire, le roquefort et le bleu d'Auvergne.

THE CHEESE DAIRY

454 Bloor Street West (à l'ouest de Howland Avenue) ☎ (416) 533-3007

Lundi à vendredi 9h – 19h, samedi 9h – 18h, dimanche 11h – 17h

Métro : BATHURST

www.thecheesedairy.com

Le propriétaire de Michelle's Brasserie nous a mis sur la piste de ce fromager. The Cheese Dairy peut sembler petite de l'extérieur, mais la boutique abrite un très grand nombre de fromages français et québécois. Bien sûr, vous y retrouverez les grands noms du fromage, mais aussi plusieurs variétés plus rares à Toronto telles que le saint-albray, la tomme des Pyrénées, la tomme de Savoie ou le chaumes pour

les fromages français. Le saint-benoît, le victor et le bertol, le chèvre noir et le paillot de chèvre comptent parmi les spécialités fromagères québécoises.

WHITEHOUSE MEATS

2978 Bloor Street West (à l'est du métro ROYAL YORK) ☎ (416) 231-5004

Fermé dimanche et lundi, mardi et mercredi 9h – 18h, jeudi 9h – 20h, vendredi 9h – 18h, samedi 8h – 18h

Métro : ROYAL YORK

Les morceaux de viande de Whitehouse Meats sont parmi les meilleurs de la ville. À la troisième adresse, les résidents de l'ouest de Toronto peuvent se procurer plusieurs spécialités fromagères françaises, parmi lesquelles : saint-andré, saint-agur, brie, camembert, roquefort et saint-albray (uniquement pendant les fêtes de Noël).

WHOLE FOODS MARKET

87 Avenue Road (au nord de Bloor Street) ☎ (416) 944-0500

Lundi à vendredi 9h – 22h, samedi et dimanche 9h – 21h

Métro : BAY OU MUSEUM

www.wholefoodsmarket.com

Whole Foods Market est approvisionné en fromages français et québécois rares à Toronto. Venus de France : la fourme d'Ambert, le comté, la tomme de Savoie, le chaumes, le munster, le cantal, le crottin de Chavignol, le saint-aubin, l'explorateur, le chaource et le montagnou. Whole Foods Market s'est aussi donné pour mission d'initier les Torontois aux fromages recherchés du Québec. La sélection de fromages de la belle province ne cesse de s'agrandir. Les fro-

mages les plus surprenants sont ceux d'influence française en provenance du Nouveau-Brunswick. Là-bas, les producteurs fabriquent des fromages à pâte dure succulents. La gamme en est restreinte, qui permet de tout essayer ! Whole Foods Market importe le Sieur de Duplessis et la tomme de champ doré. Du côté des fromages suisses, le choix ne se limite pas aux plus populaires que sont le gruyère, l'emmenthal et la raclette. Et tandis que la plupart des fromagers de Toronto ne proposent qu'un seul type de gruyère, Whole Foods Market en vend trois. Le magasin distribue des fromages suisses difficiles à dénicher ailleurs à Toronto, tels que le vigneron, l'appenzeller et le mostkäse. Le vaca prino est un autre fromage moins connu qu'il faut absolument goûter. À noter que les vendeurs très qualifiés de Whole Foods Market prennent vraiment le temps d'aider chaque client à faire le bon choix.

La crème fraîche

Elle n'est pas facile à dénicher cette crème fraîche ! À tous ceux qui désespéraient de pouvoir trouver de la véritable crème fraîche à la française à Toronto : votre patience est enfin récompensée, car nous avons repéré les bonnes adresses. Vous pourrez enfin ajouter ce délice crémeux et indispensable à la cuisine française, entre autres, à vos desserts et soupes.

ALEX FARM PRODUCTS Cette boutique met fin à nos recherches de ce délice des dieux. On y trouve de la crème fraîche de Normandie en grande quantité.

ALL THE BEST FINE FOODS On vous propose ici une crème fraîche préparée sur place.

CHEESE BOUTIQUE On vend de la crème fraîche de France dans cette boutique.

CHRIS' CHEESEMONGERS Vous trouverez ici de la crème fraîche de Normandie.

LOBLAWS L'empire de l'alimentation importe de la crème fraîche d'Angleterre.

MAX'S MARKET Voici une adresse, dans le Bloor West Village, où se procurer de la crème fraîche du Québec.

OLYMPIC CHEESE MART Voici une autre bonne enseigne du marché St. Lawrence où l'on vend de la crème fraîche québécoise.

PUSATERI'S FINE FOODS Vous trouverez, chez ce marchand de luxe, de la crème fraîche en provenance du Québec.

SCHEFFLER'S DELICATESSEN Vous pouvez y acheter de la crème fraîche québécoise ou française.

SOBEYS Plusieurs connaisseurs ont poussé ce marchand à avoir de la crème fraîche en magasin. La crème fraîche de Sobeys est un produit de l'Ontario.

SUN VALLEY FRUITS & GROCERY C'est l'adresse à connaître dans le quartier grec quand on est à la recherche de crème fraîche.

WHOLE FOODS MARKET Ce marchand chic met à la disposition des résidents de Yorkville et des quartiers avoisinants de la crème fraîche. Celle-ci est produite en Ontario et on la trouve dans le frigo des spécialités *(specialty cooler)*. Ce frigo n'est pas évident à trouver dans le magasin, donc nous vous conseillons de demander un peu d'aide.

viande, charcuterie, terrines et foie gras

Parmi la sélection de base d'un boucher (veau, bœuf, agneau, porc et, dans bien des cas, volaille), les pièces de viande abondent et l'on peut toujours demander une coupe particulière. Ainsi, nous avons décidé de limiter nos descriptions aux spécialités de la maison. Nous y ajouterons une liste détaillée des viandes les plus prisées des francophones et francophiles. Vous n'aurez donc plus aucune difficulté à trouver les viandes qu'il vous faut pour préparer les meilleurs plats de France et de la francophonie.

viande, charcuterie, terrines et foie gras

ALEX FARM PRODUCTS

Veuillez consulter notre répertoire d'adresses multiples à la page 142.

Cet empire du fromage renferme dans son congélateur des surprises qui réjouiront plus d'un amateur : des merguez !

BLOOR MEAT MARKET

2283 Bloor Street West (à l'ouest de Runnymede Road) ☎ (416) 767-2105

Fermé lundi, mardi à vendredi 9h30 – 18h30, samedi 9h – 18h, dimanche 9h – 17h

Métro : RUNNYMEDE

La spécialité de la maison, ce sont les viandes et kebabs marinés dans des préparations d'épices maison – une dizaine de marinades différentes. Même les poitrines de poulet ont droit à un traitement de faveur et sont entre autres préparées à la florentine, façon kiev ou encore cordon-bleu. Chez Bloor Meat Market, on trouve aussi du poulet de Cornouailles surgelé (petit poulet issu du croisement d'une poule et d'un poulet), de la viande hachée de bison, du magret de canard, des saucisses de gibier et des morceaux de bœuf pour fondue. Notons que ce boucher prend le service à la clientèle très à cœur.

BRANDT MEAT PACKERS LTD.

1878 Mattawa Avenue, Mississauga (près de Dundas Street et Dixie Road) ☎ (905) 279-4460

Fermé dimanche à mardi, mercredi 8h – 18h, jeudi et vendredi 8h – 19h, samedi 7h – 14h

Les Allemands ont décidément fait très fort ! Brandt Meat Ltd. comblera bon nombre de francophiles. Une très grande vitrine de viande révèle divers morceaux de bœuf, porc, volaille et

Le saviez-vous ?

En Égypte, à l'aube du troisième millénaire avant J.-C., les habitants du Delta du Nil auraient découvert un délicieux trésor. Émerveillés par la grosseur et la saveur du foie des oies sauvages migrant pour l'hiver, les Égyptiens auraient compris : l'animal crée naturellement son foie gras en se suralimentant afin d'accomplir de longs trajets migratoires. Il leur suffit de reproduire le procédé pour consommer du foie gras toute l'année. Les Juifs d'Europe centrale, héritiers des vieilles coutumes et recettes égyptiennes, avaient la réputation de connaître la recette d'un foie gras délicat aux dimensions parfaites. En fait, entre le XVIe et le XVIIIe siècle, ils n'avaient pas le droit d'élever de porcs. Par la force des choses, ils devinrent donc les promoteurs de l'élevage des oies et des canards. À cette époque, les paysans du Sud-Ouest de la France savaient déjà comment réaliser de beaux foies gras d'oie. Les cuisiniers connaissaient toutes les vertus d'un foie d'animal engraissé. Un goût bien distinct des simples foies de volaille dont on se régalait à la cour. En France, le foie gras devint célèbre, grâce au roi Louis XVI. Il affectionnait tout particulièrement le foie gras en croûte de son cuisinier.

veau. Au second coup d'œil, on remarque avec surprise les délices suivantes : saucisses de veau, reins de veau, tripes de bœuf, foies de veau, langues de veau, foies de poulet, boudins, cuisses de faisan, cuisses de faisan fumé et faisan fumé entier. Le véritable steak tartare est également en vente dans ce magasin de Mississauga. Un grand congélateur, situé près du rayon des produits de beauté, dévoile d'autres surprises surgelées – oie, canard, poulet de Cornouailles, faisan, foie de veau et graisse de porc.

BROWN BROTHERS MEATS

93 Front Street East (St. Lawrence Market) ☎ (416) 364-7469

Fermé dimanche et lundi, mardi à jeudi 8h – 18h, vendredi 8h – 19h, samedi 5h – 17h

Métro : UNION

Brown Brothers Meats vend les morceaux de viande qui conviennent aux cuisines francophones. Au sommaire : foie de veau, veau de lait, filet mignon (au Canada, c'est le nom pour un filet de bœuf premier choix, et non pas un filet de porc), viande pour la fondue chinoise ou bourguignonne et bœuf d'appellation AA et AAA d'Ontario.

CAVALLINO

2995 Islington Avenue (au sud de Steeles Avenue West) ☎ (416) 749-1633

Lundi à dimanche 6h – 17h

Métro : ISLINGTON + le bus

Leonardo Lorusso est l'expert boucher de cette adresse si bien cachée de Toronto. Cavallino se spécialise uniquement dans la viande de cheval. Les Italiens et les Français ont depuis longtemps intégré la viande de cheval à leurs habitudes alimentaires. Pas étonnant donc, que cet Italien ne vende que de la viande de cheval (canadienne !). À Toronto, très peu de communautés en consomment. Nous avons dû arpenter la ville pour dénicher cet « oiseau rare ».

CUMBRAE'S NATURALLY RAISED FINE MEATS

481 Church Street (au sud de Wellesley Street) ☎ (416) 923-5600

Lundi à vendredi 9h30 – 19h, samedi 9h – 18h, dimanche 11h – 17h

Métro : WELLESLEY

Cumbrae's Naturally Raised Fine Meats impressionne par le choix qu'il propose, son service, ses pièces de viande et la propreté qui y règne. Nous avons déniché de nombreuses viandes qui feront le plaisir des francophones et francophiles. Chez Cumbrae's, il y a plusieurs viandes marinées, du lapin, du canard, de la caille, des rognons, du boudin, du poussin, du pigeon, de l'oie, de la pintade et du faisan (il est préférable de passer une commande spéciale pour certaines viandes).

Sur place, on découvrira aussi du magret de canard, de la poitrine de canard fumée, du foie de poulet, du foie de veau et du confit de canard. Cumbrae's a également en magasin des viandes pour les fondues, de l'agneau du Québec et du cerf. Cumbrae's est l'une des rares adresses en ville où l'on peut acheter des merguez et de la graisse de canard.

viande, charcuterie, terrines et foie gras

Il y a une autre chose bien pratique : Cumbrae's Naturally Raised Fine Meats vend une très bonne sélection de viandes marinées et prêtes-à-cuire.

DI LISO'S FINE MEATS

93 Front Street East (St. Lawrence Market)
☎ (416) 601-9780

Fermé dimanche et lundi, mardi à jeudi 8h – 18h, vendredi 8h – 19h, samedi 5h – 17h

Métro : UNION

Vous trouverez chez ce boucher plusieurs morceaux de viande particulièrement adaptés à vos fondues chinoises ou bourguignonnes, du faisan, de l'oie, du canard, du poulet de Cornouailles, ainsi que du filet mignon, du lapin et divers morceaux d'agneau.

EUROPEAN QUALITY MEATS & SAUSAGES

Veuillez consulter notre répertoire d'adresses multiples à la page 142.

Une spécialité règne ici : des prix très raisonnables. Dans la bonne tradition du marché Kensington, le service est sans façon et la foule afflue. Les pièces de viande sont simples – rien de très sophistiqué – mais elles s'adaptent à toutes les cuisines. Armez-vous de patience, car ici, on fonctionne avec un numéro pour servir les clients.

GRACE MEAT MARKET

644 College Street (au coin de Grace Street) ☎ (416) 534-7776

Lundi à mercredi 8h – 18h, jeudi et vendredi 8h – 19h, samedi 8h – 18h, dimanche 10h – 16h

Métro : QUEEN'S PARK + le tram

Ce boucher, situé dans le quartier italien, vous donne la possibilité d'acheter plusieurs viandes qui conviendront à ravir à la préparation de vos plats. Chez Grace Meat Market, on vend du lapin, du poussin, de la pintade et du cerf sur commande spéciale. À part ça, vous trouverez de la dinde fumée, de la viande pour fondue, du filet mignon, du poulet de Cornouailles, de la caille surgelée, du veau de lait, des rognons, des saucisses d'agneau, du foie et des reins.

HIGHLAND FARMS

4750 Dufferin Street (au nord de Finch Avenue) ☎ (416) 736-6606

Lundi à samedi 7h – 22h, dimanche 8h – 20h

Métro : DOWNSVIEW + le bus

Le rayon boucherie de Highland Farms se démarque des autres grandes surfaces par sa quantité de viandes disponibles à la coupe. Sans compter qu'Highland Farms propose des viandes qu'on voit rarement dans les autres supermarchés, telles que du lapin, des tripes de bœuf et du foie de veau. Vous trouverez également du chapon, ainsi que plusieurs morceaux de veau et d'agneau.

LA BOUCHERIE FINE MEATS INC.

93 Front Street East (St. Lawrence Market)
☎ (416) 869-3251

Fermé dimanche et lundi, mardi à jeudi 8h – 18h, vendredi 8h – 19h, samedi 5h – 17h

Métro : UNION

La Boucherie Fine Meats a en magasin une belle gamme de viandes de bœuf d'appellation AA et AAA d'Ontario, et de bœuf « Black Angus ». Encore un

marchand du marché St. Lawrence qui vend du foie de veau, du veau de lait et du veau nourri au grain. On y trouve aussi plusieurs morceaux d'agneau et de la viande pour fondue chinoise ou bourguignonne.

MANOS MEATS

93 Front Street East (St. Lawrence Market)
☎ (416) 364-2652

Fermé dimanche et lundi, mardi à jeudi 8h – 18h, vendredi 8h – 19h, samedi 5h – 17h

Métro : UNION

Le choix est un peu limité chez Manos Meats, mais on trouve tout de même les éléments de base de la cuisine française, à savoir foie de veau, filet mignon et viande pour fondue bourguignonne ou chinoise.

MEAT ON THE BEACH

1860 Queen Street East (à l'ouest de Rainsford Road) ☎ (416) 690-1228

Lundi à vendredi 7h – 19h, samedi et dimanche 7h – 18h

Métro : QUEEN + le tram

Meat on the Beach a récemment déménagé. La nouvelle boutique offre le même niveau de qualité et de service qu'on connaissait. Les viandes qu'on utilise dans les meilleures recettes de la cuisine française ou francophone sont vendues ici. Il y a une bonne variété de volailles sauvages – canard, oie et pigeon. On y vend aussi de la dinde fumée, du boudin, de la pintade et du lapin (sur commande) pendant toute l'année. On peut s'approvisionner en faisan et en chapon pendant les fêtes de Noël. Contrairement à plusieurs bouchers qui n'ont qu'un ou deux abats

Le saviez-vous ?

Voici enfin deux marchands de saucisson sec (tel qu'on le trouve en France mais importé directement du Québec) : Cumbrae's Naturally Raised Fine Meats et Olliffe. Ces commerçants vont sans doute devoir faire face à une forte demande après la parution de notre guide.

en magasin, Meat on the Beach se distingue par son grand choix. On peut également choisir parmi une bonne quantité de morceaux d'agneau et un large éventail de saucisses maison, de viande pour fondue et de filet mignon. Aux amateurs de nouveauté, nous recommandons les viandes fourrées au lard. Enfin, notons que ce boucher vend les fameuses saucisses merguez et que toutes ses viandes sont nourries au grain.

NICOLA'S FINE FOODS

298 Eglinton Avenue West (au coin d'Avenue Road) ☎ (416) 485-4429

Lundi 7h – 17h, mardi à vendredi 7h – 19h, samedi 7h – 17h, fermé dimanche

Métro : EGLINTON + le bus

La spécialité ici, c'est l'attention particulière qu'on accorde à l'achat des viandes : on les préfère médaillées. Ce boucher a reçu un prix de qualité et d'excellence de la « Royal Agricultural Winter Fair ». Parmi les viandes qui sauront plaire aux francophones, on a : le lapin, le boudin, le foie de veau, le mouton, la caille, le faisan, la viande pour fondue, l'oie et le canard.

viande, charcuterie, terrines et foie gras

Charcuterie, terrines et foie gras

ALEX FARM PRODUCTS Ce marchand importe de la mousse de foie gras truffée, de la mousse de foie gras au porto, de la mousse de canard, du confit de canard, des rillettes de canard et du magret de canard de France. Du Québec, il est approvisionné en pâtés aux parfums tous plus extraordinaires les uns que les autres (environ une quinzaine). Chez Alex Farm, il y a aussi du foie gras de La Ferme Périgord, disponible en mousse, bloc, terrine, rillettes et pâté.

ALL THE BEST FINE FOODS Cette épicerie fine vend des pâtés et terrines de La Ferme (Québec) ainsi que quelques sélections d'Ontario. À notre dernier passage, nous avons pris note des spécialités suivantes : pâté de caille aux poivrons verts, terrine de canard aux pistaches, mousse truffée, mousse de caille et truffes. Vous trouverez aussi du foie gras de La Ferme Périgord.

BRANDT MEAT PACKERS LTD. Chez ce marchand allemand, une grande vitrine dévoile une sélection assez remarquable de viandes séchées et saucissons secs.

CAVIAR DIRECT Il n'y a pas que du caviar et du poisson fumé chez ce marchand. Caviar Direct vend aussi du foie gras du Québec qu'on peut acheter en bloc ou en plus petite portion. Il y a aussi un foie gras d'oie aux truffes français, vendu en bloc. Vos invités vous en diront des nouvelles !

CHEESE BOUTIQUE Chez Cheese Boutique, blocs de foie gras français et blocs de foie gras québécois rivalisent. À vous de trancher. Cheese Boutique vend par ailleurs une mousse de foie gras du Québec au quart du prix du véritable foie gras français ou québécois. On y trouve également six pâtés de La Maison du Gibier, en provenance du Québec.

CHRIS' CHEESEMONGERS Vous découvrirez ici plusieurs pâtés et terrines de deux maisons québécoises fort réputées : L'Élevage Périgord et La Maison du Gibier. On y vend également une petite gamme de blocs de foie gras et de terrines importés de France. Enfin, vous pourrez vous régaler de magret et de confit de canard.

CUMBRAE'S NATURALLY RAISED FINE MEATS Une bonne variété de pâtés et terrines en provenance du Québec vous attendent ici. Au menu, vous aurez le choix entre du porc de Toulouse, du canard au poivre vert, du canard au poivre rose, du faisan aux pistaches, du pâté de campagne aux champignons sauvages et des rillettes de canard. Enfin, voici une bonne adresse pour se procurer du foie gras.

DANIEL ET DANIEL Les pâtés maison sont peu nombreux, mais, comme on le sait, la qualité prime, plutôt que la quantité, dans cet établissement. Daniel et Daniel vous propose deux pâtés (campagne et poivre), ainsi que des rillettes de canard.

DINAH'S CUPBOARD Dans cette charmante épicerie fine, on vend : rillettes du Mans, rillettes de canard, terrine de lapin aux pistaches, terrine de faisan, mousse de truite fumée, terrine de sanglier aux abricots et foie gras ! En tout et pour tout, Dinah's a en magasin une douzaine de pâtés (selon la saison) qui proviennent du Québec ou qui sont faits sur place.

GLOBAL CHEESE Voici une adresse où vous pourrez acheter du foie gras et du pâté importés du Québec et de France.

MAX'S MARKET Ce marchand importe plus d'une quinzaine de pâtés et terrines du Québec. Au programme des réjouissances, on a : le pâté d'autruche au cassis, le pâté de caille, le pâté de porc aux truffes, le pâté au Grand Marnier, le pâté de canard aux pistaches.

MEAT ON THE BEACH Ce boucher vend du foie gras ainsi qu'une gamme originale de pâtés et terrines de France. Voici deux associations surprenantes : le pâté de faisan aux raisins de Corinthe et la terrine de cerf au cognac. La terrine de lièvre que l'on trouve chez Meat on the Beach est assez rare à Toronto.

MENDEL'S CREAMERY N' APPETIZER Mendel's est approvisionné en foies gras du Québec et de France. Les pâtés les plus en vogue sont le pâté au romarin et aux champignons, ainsi que le pâté au Grand Marnier, aux poivrons et au cognac.

OLYMPIC CHEESE MART Cette fromagerie importe quelques foies gras de France. On y trouve aussi du pâté de campagne et du pâté au cognac du Québec. Il y a même des cretons (variété de rillettes de porc) de la belle province.

PATACHOU Cette pâtisserie vend du pâté de foie de volaille, du pâté de campagne ainsi que des blocs de foie gras de canard.

PUSATERI'S FINE FOODS Il y a dans cette épicerie fine une sacrée gamme de pâtés, terrines et foies gras. Le foie gras est disponible sous différentes formes : en bloc, en beurre, truffé, en mousse et en gelée. Le choix des pâtés et saucissons secs est tout aussi varié.

SCHEFFLER'S DELICATESSEN Ce marchand importe du foie gras de France et du Québec. Il propose aussi une bonne dizaine de terrines, toutes en provenance du Québec. Scheffler's vend par ailleurs du magret de canard, du canard tranché et du confit de canard importé de France. Enfin, il y a chez Scheffler's plusieurs saucissons secs.

SOBEYS Ce supermarché importe une bonne quantité de terrines du Québec. La sélection est d'une rareté impressionnante. En témoignent la terrine d'autruche et de porc aux raisins de Corinthe et la terrine de cinq gibiers (autruche, cerf, faisan, bison, sanglier) et porc aux airelles (canneberges). Sobeys vend également du foie gras du Québec.

THE BUTCHER BLOCK CAFÉ Ce boucher propose du foie gras québécois.

THE BUTCHERS On vend ici une petite sélection de pâtés québécois : faisan, canard aux pistaches, cerf et truite fumée. The Butchers vend également du foie gras.

THE VILLAGE BUTCHER Chez ce boucher, on trouve des pâtés et de la mousse de foie gras.

WHITEHOUSE MEATS Il y a en magasin une petite sélection de pâtés, ainsi que des foies gras frais et mi-cuits sous trois formes : mousse de foie gras, bloc de foie gras et foie gras de canard entier. La boutique de Bayview vend plusieurs pâtés de foie québécois. Sur place, vous trouverez également du foie gras de canard, du confit de canard, du magret et des cuisses de canard pour préparer vous-même votre confit.

WHOLE FOODS MARKET Ce supermarché de luxe vous propose quelques variétés de pâtés de viande d'élevage et de gibier. Ces pâtés sans agents conservateurs viennent tous du Québec. On retrouve du pâté de caribou, du pâté de porc aux figues, du pâté de caille, du pâté de porc aux pistaches et, enfin, du pâté de canard et porc aux pistaches.

Où trouver des merguez

La plupart des marchands ci-dessous importent leurs merguez du Québec. Dans tous les cas, soyez assuré que vos saucisses marocaines seront rehaussées en saveur épicée.

1. Alex Farm Products
2. Cumbrae's Naturally Raised Fine Meats
3. Meat on the Beach
4. Olliffe
5. Scheffler's Delicatessen
6. The Butchers
7. The Village Butcher
8. Whitehouse Meats

Chose assez rare, sur place on trouve des rognons d'agneau et beaucoup d'autres abats. Pour les spécialités françaises, il vaut mieux demander, car elles sont souvent conservées à l'arrière du magasin.

OLLIFFE

1097 Yonge Street (au nord de Roxborough Street) ☎ (416) 928-0296

Lundi à jeudi 8h30 – 18h30, vendredi 8h30 – 19h, samedi 8h30 – 18h, dimanche 10h – 17h

Métro : SUMMERHILL

Si connaître le prix avant d'acheter vous intéresse, il y a de bonnes chances pour qu'Olliffe ne puisse être votre boucher attitré. Les prix ne sont pas affichés (et pour cause…), la qualité répond aux « standards » d'exigence du quartier et les viandes sont bien coupées, en même temps que quasiment dépourvues de gras. Vous pourrez acheter des merguez (livrées le jeudi), de la poitrine de canard, du lapin, du boudin, du foie de

veau, de la caille (fraîche pendant l'hiver et surgelée le reste de l'année). Le faisan, le pigeon, le poulet de Cornouailles, le poussin et la pintade sont disponibles sur commande spéciale. Mais Olliffe a toujours en magasin du veau de lait. Il vend aussi de beaux morceaux de viande pour les fondues. À l'époque des fêtes de Noël, Olliffe importe du foie gras de canard et d'oie de France et du Québec. Que ce soit pour une occasion spéciale ou pour vos courses hebdomadaires, Olliffe offre tout ce dont on peut rêver… à condition d'être prêt à payer le prix.

PUSATERI'S FINE FOODS

Veuillez consulter notre répertoire d'adresses multiples à la page 142.

www.pusateris.com

Pusateri's rend la vie plus facile à sa clientèle en lui offrant un grand choix de viandes marinées et assaisonnées, telles que de la caille fourrée aux airelles (canneberges) et aux figues, de la caille méditerranéenne (caille enrobée de lard, fourrée au fromage de chèvre, aux piments et à la roquette) et du poulet de Cornouailles aux airelles. Ces viandes marinées sont incroyablement pratiques, car elles sont toutes prêtes en un tour de main et elles se cuisinent aussi bien au four, à la poêle ou grillées. Vous pourrez également acheter de la pintade et du magret de canard chez Pusateri's.

ROYAL BEEF

1968 Danforth Avenue (à l'ouest de Woodbine Avenue) ☎ (416) 421-1029

Fermé lundi, mardi et mercredi 9h – 17h,

jeudi à samedi 9h – 18h, dimanche 10h –
16h

Métro : WOODBINE

Attention, on ne badine pas ici. Les
viandes sont coupées le jour même. Et
pour être frais, c'est frais ! En plus, vous
trouverez chez Royal Beef des escalopes
de veau nourri à l'herbe et du poulet
élevé en plein air. Au palmarès des
préférences des francophones : lapin,
faisan, boudin (sur commande
spéciale), oie (à Noël), canard, pintade
(sur commande spéciale), viande pour
fondue, filet mignon, rognons, abats,
caille et poulet de Cornouailles.

St. Lawrence Upper Cut

93 Front Street East (St. Lawrence Market)
☎ (416) 362-3142

Fermé dimanche et lundi, mardi à jeudi 8h
– 18h, vendredi 8h – 19h, samedi 5h – 17h

Métro : UNION

St. Lawrence Upper Cut propose de
beaux morceaux de filet mignon, du
lapin, du veau de lait, du faisan et du
poulet de Cornouailles. À notre grande
surprise, St. Lawrence Upper Cut vend
du pigeon. Enfin, voici une adresse en
plus où dénicher de la viande pour
fondue : il suffit de commander.

Scheffler's Delicatessen

93 Front Street East (St. Lawrence Market)
☎ (416) 364-2806

Fermé dimanche et lundi, mardi à jeudi 8h
– 18h, vendredi 8h – 19h, samedi 5h – 17h

Métro : UNION

Voici un rendez-vous dans le marché
St. Lawrence pour les amateurs de
merguez.

Sobeys

81 St. Clair Avenue East (un peu à l'est
de Yonge Street) ☎ (416) 413-0594

Tous les jours, 24 heures sur 24

Métro : ST CLAIR

Si vous habitez dans le quartier de
Yonge et St. Clair, Sobeys est l'adresse
qu'il vous faut pour vos lapins,
médaillons de cerf, cailles et poulets de
Cornouailles. On nous a aussi laissé
entendre qu'il devrait y avoir de plus en
plus de gibier en magasin.

The Butcher Block Café

3251 Yonge Street (au nord de Lawrence
Avenue) ☎ (416) 544-1729

Lundi à vendredi 10h – 19h, samedi 10h –
18h, dimanche 11h – 18h

Métro : LAWRENCE

Les mordus de la grillade ne seront pas
déçus. Sur place, on peut acheter le gril,
la viande et les sauces dans un seul et
même rayon. Le boucher peut même se
déplacer à domicile, se faisant un plaisir
de cuire votre viande à la perfection
dans votre cour ou dans votre cuisine,
histoire d'épater vos convives. Ce service fait partie du service traiteur. Les
appellations AA et AAA du bœuf
Black Angus canadien sont une autre
spécialité chez ce boucher. Côté préférences des francophones et francophiles, on a du lapin, du veau de lait, de
la caille, du poulet de Cornouailles, du
filet mignon et de la viande pour fondue. Vous pourrez aussi acheter de la
viande de cheval, du cerf, des abats et
de la pintade en passant une commande
spéciale.

viande, charcuterie, terrines et foie gras

THE BUTCHERS

2636 Yonge Street (au nord d'Eglinton Avenue) ☎ (416) 483-5777

Lundi à mercredi 9h – 18h, jeudi à vendredi 9h – 19h, samedi 9h – 18h, dimanche 11h – 17h

Métro : EGLINTON

The Butchers est un spécialiste de la viande biologique : on peut acheter du bœuf d'appellation AA et AAA d'Ontario, de l'agneau et du porc biologique. Ces viandes biologiques viennent de l'élevage de la célèbre ferme Beretta en Ontario. The Butchers vend aussi une quantité remarquable de viandes qui sauront plaire aux francophones et francophiles : lapin, veau de lait, viande pour fondue, rognons, filet mignon, poulet de Cornouailles et cerf. Par ailleurs, on y trouve du confit de canard et du magret de canard. Les viandes qui suivent sont disponibles sur commande spéciale : faisan, pigeon, canard, oie, pintade, abats et caille. On peut même passer une commande pour la viande de cheval. Enfin, les inconditionnels du couscous trouveront ici de bonnes merguez !

THE VILLAGE BUTCHER

2914 Lake Shore Boulevard West (près d'Islington Avenue) ☎ (416) 503-9555

Fermé dimanche et lundi, mardi à vendredi 7h30 – 18h, samedi 7h30 – 17h

Métro : ISLINGTON + le bus

The Village Butcher propose les viandes suivantes : lapin, veau de lait, foie de canard, caille, faisan, cerf, poulet de Cornouailles, bison, boudin, pigeon, foie et rognons. Vous pouvez aussi acheter d'autres types d'abats, il suffit de passer une commande spéciale. La viande de cheval et la pintade sont également disponibles sur commande. Chez The Village Butcher, il y a un filet mignon hors pair ainsi que de la viande pour fondue. La spécialité ici, c'est la saucisse maison – porc, veau, dinde et agneau. Encore une chose qui a retenu notre attention chez ce marchand : la vente de poulet de culture biologique. Rupert Grigull, le boucher, nous dit aussi qu'il prépare des merguez maison sur commande. Son conseil : il est préférable de commander certaines viandes jusqu'à trois semaines à l'avance. Rupert les fera vieillir en magasin afin que vous puissiez les savourer aussi tendres que possible.

WHITEHOUSE MEATS

Veuillez consulter notre répertoire d'adresses multiples à la page 142.

Ce boucher remporte la Palme d'or en matière de service à la clientèle. Il n'y a pas à dire, ce duo fraternel a la passion du métier. Les habitués disent que la boutique est un paradis sur terre quand on est amateur de viande. Effectivement, nous avons été épatés par le choix qu'offre ce boucher. En magasin, on trouve plusieurs viandes qui sortent de l'ordinaire telles que les viandes d'autruche, de cerf et de bison. Côté viandes de la francophonie, une sélection impressionnante : morceaux d'agneau, saucisses de foie (à la boutique de Bayview), veau de lait, ris de veau, lapin et superbes morceaux de filet mignon. Quant à la viande pour fondue bourguignonne ou chinoise, là aussi, Whitehouse assure. Si vous

passez commande à l'avance, vous serez
assuré de déguster une fondue inoubliable. La variété de volailles ne laisse pas
non plus à désirer : poussin, poulet de
Cornouailles, oie, pintade, magret de
canard, faisan frais ou surgelé et pigeon.
Ce boucher vend aussi deux autres
pièces rares à Toronto, à savoir la saucisse merguez et le boudin blanc ou
noir (sur commande seulement). Enfin,
chez Whitehouse Meats, vous pourrez
acheter de la graisse de canard ainsi que
des bouillons de bœuf, volaille et gibier
faits maison.

WITTEVEEN MEATS LTD.

93 Front Street East (St. Lawrence Market)
☎ (416) 363-6852

Fermé dimanche et lundi, mardi à jeudi 8h
– 18h, vendredi 8h – 19h, samedi 5h – 17h

Métro : UNION

www.witteveens.com

Si vous cherchez à composer un menu
de brochettes, Witteveen Meats est
l'endroit qu'il vous faut. Le boucher
propose une dizaine de variétés de
brochettes marinées. Il vend également
du filet mignon, de la bavette fourrée,
trois sortes de couronnes de porc à la
française, du bœuf Black Angus, du
gigot d'agneau, ainsi que plusieurs
spécialités de poulet mariné et fourré.

Diversité
Cultures
Dialogue

INFORMATION

ÉVASION

DÉBATS ET
ENTRETIENS

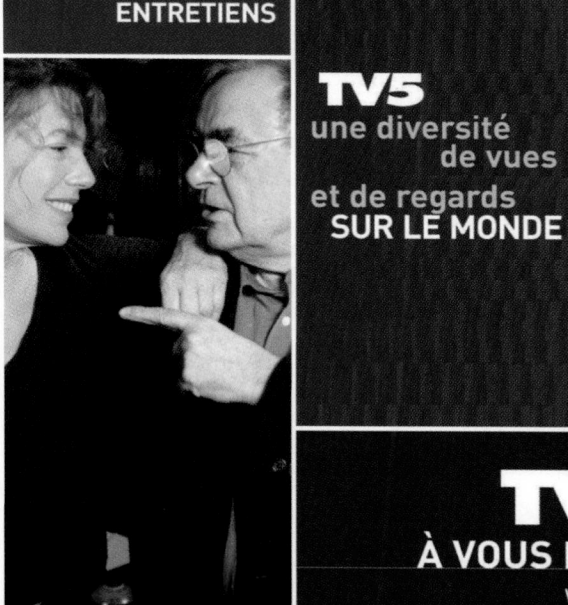

TV5
une diversité
de vues
et de regards
SUR LE MONDE

DOCUMENTAIRES
ET GRANDS
REPORTAGES

TV5
À VOUS LE MONDE
WWW.TV5.CA

LINE
BOILY

dès **12 h 15**

Réalisation : Gabriel Dubé

860 AM

Première Chaîne
R a d i o - C a n a d a

www.radio-canada.ca/radio

TORONTO BALADES

Venez découvrir le Toronto d'hier et d'aujourd'hui en français.

Toronto Balades vous propose des visites guidées de la ville de Toronto en français.

Le Quartier du Marché St Lawrence, son marché coloré, sa galerie et ses diverses expositions sur l'histoire de la ville, la vieille ville de York avec l'une de ses boutiques d'origine, le premier bureau de poste, St Lawrence Hall, la première salle de réception de la ville, le parc et la cathédrale St James, sans oublier la dégustation de produits offerts par les commerçants du marché.

L'Université de Toronto, (Campus de St George) située au coeur de la ville : venez découvrir son histoire, ses *Colleges* à l'architecture gothique, ses bibliothèques, ses manifestations culturelles, son centre sportif.

Hôtel de Ville de Toronto et son quartier, le square Nathan Phillips, Osgoode Hall, Barreau de l'Ontario et Cour d'appel, Old City Hall, ancien Hôtel de Ville reconverti en tribunal, les magasins *The Bay* et Eaton.

À venir :
Le quartier de Yorkville
La balade des trois forts français, son projet de parc historique avec la Société d'histoire de Toronto.

Nos visites sont d'une durée approximative de 2 heures.

Tarifs individuels

Adultes	$20
Étudiants, Seniors	$15
Enfants (-12 ans)	$5

Pour les tarifs de groupe, veuillez nous consulter.

N'hésitez pas à nous contacter pour prendre rendez-vous et passer un agréable moment à découvrir notre ville, son histoire, ses curiosités et ses différentes cultures.
N'hésitez pas à nous faire part des lieux que vous souhaiteriez découvrir à Toronto.

Discover in French the Past and the Present of Toronto.

Toronto Balades offers walking tours of the City of Toronto in French.

St Lawrence Market area with its colorful market, its gallery that offers many different exhibitions about the history of the City, the Old town Toronto, one of its original stores, the first post office, St Lawrence Hall and the first reception Hall, the park and the St James Cathedral. The tour includes visiting local vendors and sampling their products.

The University of Toronto, Discover the St George campus, located in downtown Toronto, the university area, its history, colleges with their gothic architecture, libraries, cultural activities, and the athletic centre.

Toronto City Hall and its area with Nathan Phillips Square, Osgoode Hall, Old City Hall, the Court, Bay and Eaton stores.

Coming soon:
Yorkville area
Three French forts and the location for an historical park with la Société d'histoire de Toronto

Our tours are approximately 2 hours long.

Individual rates

Adults	$20
Students and Seniors	$15
Children (-12)	$5

Please contact us for group rates.

Do not hesitate to contact us to spend an enjoyable moment discovering our city, its history, its particularities and its cultures.
Do not hesitate to let us know of the places you would like to visit in our city.

Développement économique
communautaire

- Développement des ressources humaines
- Croissance économique
- Création d'emplois
- Maintien en emploi des communautés minoritaires de langue officielle

RDEE
Ontario

Jeunes
Rural
Savoir
Tourisme

www.rdee-ont.ca

Canada

poissonneries et spécialistes des huîtres

Pané, frit, poché, grillé, fumé ou en tartare, les façons d'apprêter le poisson sont multiples. Bien que les possibilités de préparation des fruits de mer semblent plus limitées, on raffole tout autant de ces coquillages succulents. Le poisson et les fruits de mer occupent une place importante dans la cuisine française et dans la plupart des cuisines francophones. Ainsi, nous savons à quel point un bon poissonnier est indispensable. Nous vous donnons donc rendez-vous dans tous les endroits qui suivent pour acheter toutes vos délices de la mer préférées.

poissonneries et spécialistes des huîtres

AVENUE SEAFOOD

302 Eglinton Avenue West (au coin d'Avenue Road) ☎ (416) 481-2288

Lundi 12h – 19h, mardi à samedi 9h30 – 19h, dimanche 12h30 – 18h

Métro : EGLINTON + le bus

Vous trouverez en magasin des pattes de crabes d'Alaska, du saumon de la côte ouest canadienne, de la truite et des queues de homards cubains. On y trouve aussi de la sardine (sur commande), du poulpe, du thon frais et plusieurs variétés de saumon.

BIG FISH MARKET

765 The Queensway (à l'ouest de Royal York Road) ☎ (416) 259-1585

Fermé dimanche et lundi, mardi à vendredi 10h – 18h, samedi 9h – 18h

Métro : ROYAL YORK + le bus

Big Fish Market vend une bonne sélection de poissons et fruits de mer « exotiques », tels que des pétoncles péruviens, du homard de la Nouvelle-Écosse, des huîtres de l'Île-du-Prince-Édouard, des moules à coquilles vertes de la Nouvelle-Zélande. La morue fraîche (cabillaud), le saumon fumé, la sardine surgelée ou fraîche, le thon frais et les écrevisses sont parmi les exemples de ce que vous trouverez sur place. Ici, on importe généralement des variétés d'huîtres des États-Unis et de la côte est du Canada.

BILL'S LOBSTERS

599 Gerrard Street East (à l'est de Broadview Avenue) ☎ (416) 778-0943

Lundi à samedi 9h30 – 18h

Métro : BROADVIEW + le tram

Le nom est assez révélateur… Mais chez Bill's Lobster, on vend aussi, entre autres choses, des oursins de mer, des cuisses de grenouilles, des crevettes, de la truite et du crabe. Bill's Lobster importe également des huîtres de la côte est et de la côte ouest du Canada.

BRANDT MEAT PACKERS LTD.

1878 Mattawa Avenue, Mississauga (près de Dundas Street et Dixie Road) ☎ (905) 279-4460

Fermé dimanche et lundi, mardi et mercredi 8h – 18h, jeudi et vendredi 8h – 19h, samedi 7h – 15h

La spécialité ici, c'est le poisson fumé et les filets de poisson en conserve et bocal. Brandt Meat Packers Ltd. a en magasin des filets de plusieurs variétés, qui vont de la sardine au maquereau. Il y a même des escargots en conserve, ainsi que de l'anguille.

CAVIAR CENTRE

220 Duncan Mills Road (au coin de Don Mills Road) ☎ (416) 441-9788

Lundi à vendredi 11h – 18h, fermé samedi et dimanche. Possibilité d'ouverture le samedi sur demande.

Métro : DON MILLS + le bus; PAPE + le bus

www.caviarcentre.com

Pour tous les fous de ce délice russe, Caviar Centre propose du Beluga, de l'Osetra, du Sevruga. Il y a même du caviar de France !

CAVIAR DIRECT

93 Front Street East (St. Lawrence Market, au sous-sol) ☎ (416) 361-3422

Fermé dimanche et lundi, mardi à jeudi 8h – 18h, vendredi 8h – 19h, samedi 5h – 17h

poissonneries et spécialistes des huîtres

Métro : **UNION**

www.caviarforsale.com

Voici un petit comptoir qui vaut son pesant d'or. Caviar Direct importe les grandes variétés de caviars – Beluga, Osetra et Sevruga. Il importe aussi certaines sélections « Black Label » perses. Caviar Direct vous propose également plusieurs variétés de poissons fumés, non seulement du saumon fumé d'Écosse et du Canada, mais aussi de la truite et du maquereau fumés.

CITY FISH MARKET

2929 Dufferin Street (au sud de Lawrence Avenue) ☎ (416) 256-7373

Lundi 7h30 – 15h, mardi à jeudi 7h30 – 18h, vendredi 7h30 – 19h, samedi 7h30 – 18h, fermé dimanche

Métro : **LAWRENCE WEST** + le bus; **WILSON** + le bus

Gus Nikoletsos, le propriétaire incroyablement sympathique fait tout pour vous plaire. En magasin, son étalage est composé d'un large choix de produits de la mer. La sélection varie selon les saisons, mais vous trouverez facilement les poissons et fruits de mer suivants : thon, cabillaud, poulpe, palourdes, huîtres, escargots, oursins, anguilles (à Noël seulement) et même sardine et anchois frais. City Fish Market reçoit une dizaine de thons entiers chaque semaine et vous garantit ainsi une fraîcheur inégalable. Plusieurs chefs spécialisés en sushi n'hésitent pas à qualifier la qualité de ce thon de légendaire. Un grand congélateur garde au frais crevettes, pétoncles géants, moules, crabes entiers, cuisses de grenouilles, chair de crabe et bien d'autres richesses encore. Le week-end, le magasin ne désemplit pas, donc le choix est plus restreint qu'en

Le saviez-vous ?

Comme pour le vin, un temps de repos s'impose pour la dégustation des huîtres. Ainsi, on recommande d'ouvrir les huîtres une demi-heure avant de les déguster. Il est également préférable de jeter la première eau, car les huîtres en sécréteront alors une nouvelle, plus parfumée.

Il est déconseillé de remettre des huîtres ouvertes au réfrigérateur. Mieux vaut les conserver sur un lit de glace. Lorsque les huîtres sont trop froides, elles perdent leur saveur.

Si vous préférez manger vos huîtres crues, faites ressortir leur saveur avec un peu de poivre blanc. D'après les puristes en la matière, il est préférable d'éviter le vinaigre aux échalotes et même le citron, qui dénaturent le goût des huîtres.

Contrairement à la tendance populaire, pour bien manger des huîtres, il faut les mâcher et non pas les gober. En les mâchant, on apprécie beaucoup plus les nuances qu'offre chacune de leurs variétés.

Le vin blanc reste le meilleur nectar pour accompagner des huîtres.

poissonneries et spécialistes des huîtres

semaine. Cela dit, Gus et son équipe feront toujours tout ce qui est en leur pouvoir pour vous satisfaire.

DIANA'S SEAFOOD

2101 Lawrence Avenue East (près de Warden Avenue) ☎ (416) 288-9286

Lundi 9h – 19h, mardi à vendredi 9h – 18h, samedi 9h – 19h, dimanche 10h – 17h

Métro : LAWRENCE + le bus; KENNEDY + le bus

Diana's Seafood vend des huîtres de la côte est et de la côte ouest du Canada.

DOMENIC'S FISH MARKET

93 Front Street East (St. Lawrence Market) ☎ (416) 368-1397

Fermé dimanche et lundi, mardi à jeudi 8h – 18h, vendredi 8h – 19h, samedi 5h – 17h

Métro : UNION

Ce marchand importe plusieurs poissons frais bien connus tels que le thon, le cabillaud, le poulpe, les palourdes, les huîtres et même la sardine fraîche. Domenic's Fish Market possède également ment un congélateur qui regorge de poissons et fruits de mer surgelés.

DOMINO FOODS LTD.

93 Front Street East (St. Lawrence Market, au sous-sol, tout au fond du marché) ☎ (416) 366-2178

Fermé dimanche et lundi, mardi à jeudi 8h – 18h, vendredi 8h – 19h, samedi 5h – 17h

Métro : UNION

Domino Foods n'est pas une poissonnerie, mais vous y trouverez plusieurs filets de poisson en conserve et en bocal.

GLOBAL CHEESE

76 Kensington Avenue ☎ (416) 593-9251

Lundi à vendredi 9h – 19h, samedi 8h – 18h, dimanche 9h – 17h

Métro : SPADINA + le tram; QUEEN'S PARK + le tram

Global importe quelques filets de poisson marinés. Au choix : filets de hareng, de truite et de maquereau.

HIGHLAND FARMS

4750 Dufferin Street (au nord de Finch Avenue) ☎ (416) 736-6606

Lundi à samedi 7h – 22h, dimanche 8h – 20h

Métro : DOWNSVIEW + le bus

Highland Farms vend plusieurs poissons fumés surgelés tels que le saumon, le thon, la truite, l'anguille, l'espadon et les sprats (de Belgique).

KENSINGTON MARKET

Métro : SPADINA + le tram; QUEEN'S PARK + le tram

▸ CORAL SEA FISH MARKET

198 Baldwin Street ☎ (416) 593-9656

Lundi à samedi 8h – 18h, dimanche 7h – 19h30

▸ NEW SEAWAY

195 Baldwin Street ☎ (416) 593-5192

Lundi à samedi 7h – 19h, dimanche 8h – 17h

▸ SEA KINGS

189 Baldwin Street ☎ (416) 593-9949

Lundi à samedi 8h – 18h, dimanche 9h – 16h

▸ SEVEN SEAS FISH

196 Baldwin Street ☎ (416) 593-9875

Lundi à dimanche 8h – 17h

Ces quatre adresses sont proches les unes des autres dans la rue Baldwin, au cœur du marché Kensington. Les marchands s'approvisionnent tous auprès du même distributeur, ainsi les prix et les produits proposés sont plus ou moins les mêmes. Attention, le samedi matin n'est peut-être pas le meilleur moment pour aller y faire ses courses. Les queues sont longues et le niveau d'adrénaline, parfois, monte ! Comme pour la plupart des magasins situés dans le marché Kensington, les prix sont incroyablement abordables et la qualité satisfaisante. La sélection est assez classique, mais on retrouve plusieurs des poissons et fruits de mer prisés des francophones – sardine fraîche ou surgelée, thon frais, morue fraîche (cabillaud), pétoncles, rouget, sole, crabe, moules, palourdes, huîtres, poulpe et plusieurs variétés de crevettes. La plupart des poissons sont vendus frais, cependant certains marchands ont un congélateur en magasin, ce qui vous permet de retrouver certains plaisirs de la mer même lorsque la saison est passée. La plupart des marchands vendent des poissons fumés et séchés. Sea Kings et Coral Sea Fish Market vendent des oursins de mer à l'époque des fêtes de Noël. Enfin, la plupart de ces poissonniers vendent de l'anguille pendant les mois d'hiver.

LOBSTER ISLAND

27 Milliker Boulevard (à l'est de Kennedy Road) ☎ (416) 591-6488

Lundi à samedi 9h – 17h, dimanche 9h – 12h

Métro : FINCH + le bus

Lobster Island est un petit poissonnier spécialisé dans l'importation de fruits de mer. Vous êtes certain d'y découvrir un large choix de vos crustacés préférés. Ce marchand vous propose aussi des huîtres des côtes est et ouest du Canada.

MENDEL'S CREAMERY N' APPETIZER

72 Kensington Avenue ☎ (416) 597-1784

Lundi à vendredi 8h30 – 19h, samedi 7h30 – 18h, fermé dimanche

Métro : SPADINA + le tram; QUEEN'S PARK + le tram

Mendel's a une vitrine de filets de poisson marinés. Vous y découvrirez des filets d'anchois, de maquereau à l'huile d'olive, des filets de maquereau fumés et des filets de hareng, ainsi que des huîtres fumées.

MIKE'S FISH MARKET

93 Front Street East (St. Lawrence Market) ☎ (416) 368-0876

Fermé dimanche et lundi, mardi à jeudi 8h – 18h, vendredi 8h – 19h, samedi 5h – 17h

Métro : UNION

Mike's Fish Market importe une variété de poissons et fruits de mer qui saura plaire aux francophones et francophiles. Au menu : moules, poulpe, thon frais, rouget, palourdes et huîtres. Mike's Fish Market importe aussi de la sardine fraîche tous les mois. Ce poissonnier propose également un bon choix de poissons et fruits de mer surgelés. Si vous cherchez la facilité pour un repas du soir, optez donc pour les poissons marinés, prêts à être dégustés.

poissonneries et spécialistes des huîtres

Newport Fish Importers

1140 Dupont Street (au coin de Dufferin Street) ☎ (416) 537-1278

Lundi 7h – 17h, mardi et mercredi 7h – 18h, jeudi et vendredi 7h – 19h, samedi 7h – 16h, fermé dimanche

Métro : DUFFERIN + le bus

Si vous voulez acheter du poisson très frais chez Newport Fish Importers, n'y allez pas le lundi, car la cargaison n'arrive que le mardi matin. Cela dit, à compter du mardi, vous aurez le choix entre du poulpe, du cabillaud (morue fraîche), de la sardine fraîche, des crevettes (très généreuses par la taille), de l'anguille, du crabe, du thon frais et du rouget. Dans un récipient en plastique près des palourdes, des moules et des huîtres, nous avons trouvé des escargots. Et à Toronto, on n'en voit pas très souvent, puisque la plupart des poissonniers utilisent les escargots pour nettoyer leurs aquariums. De toute évidence, ces poissonniers n'en connaissent pas assez long sur la cuisine française... Il y a deux choses caractéristiques chez Newport : les filets de poisson frais d'une part et la vingtaine de congélateurs qui abritent tous les poissons et fruits de mer qu'on peut imaginer d'autre part. Pour ce qui est des filets de poisson, on en importe plus d'une cinquantaine chez Newport. Quant à la liste de poissons surgelés, elle pourrait s'étendre sur deux chapitres; nous vous en donnons donc un petit aperçu : crevettes, filets de sole, pétoncles géants, homards et crabes. Vous trouverez également chez ce poissonnier du poisson salé et des palourdes en conserve.

Osler Fish Warehouse

16 Osler Street (au coin de Dupont Street) ☎ (416) 769-2010

Lundi 10h – 17h, mardi à vendredi 8h – 19h, samedi 8h – 17h, fermé dimanche

Métro : DUNDAS WEST

Osler est un expert des poissons et crustacés en provenance du Portugal. Il importe aussi d'autres pays les plaisirs de la mer suivants : poulpe du Maroc, thon frais, sardine fraîche, cabillaud, morue salée, rouget, truite, anguille de mer et oursin de mer.

Oyster Boy

872 Queen Street West (à l'ouest de Massey Street) ☎ (416) 534-3432

Tous les jours, à partir de 17h

Métro : QUEEN + le tram

Selon la saison, Oyster Boy peut avoir en magasin jusqu'à six variétés d'huîtres.

Pisces Gourmet

1103 Yonge Street (au nord de Roxborough Street) ☎ (416) 921-8888

Lundi 9h30 – 18h30, mardi à jeudi 9h – 18h30, vendredi 9h – 19h, samedi 9h – 18h, fermé dimanche

Métro : SUMMERHILL

Pisces vend de très beaux morceaux de poisson. Le service est excellent et le prix reflète très bien la qualité des poissons. Aux francophones (et aux autres !), Pisces propose du cabillaud, de la truite, des palourdes, des huîtres (la chair est vendue sans les coquilles), du poulpe, de la truite fumée, du thon frais et de la sardine fraîche. Le sommet du plaisir chez Pisces, ce sont sans aucun doute les très belles brochettes de pois-

poissonneries et spécialistes des huîtres

Les spécialistes des huîtres

Pour déguster des huîtres en toute saison et pour toutes les occasions, ces spécialistes des huîtres vous approvisionneront en ce qu'il y a de meilleur sur les côtes des océans d'ici et d'ailleurs. La plupart des poissonniers vendent des huîtres, mais les adresses que nous vous livrons ci-dessous sortent du lot grâce à la grande variété qu'on y propose.

1. Big Fish Market
2. Bill's Lobster
3. Diana's Seafood
4. Lobster Island
5. Oyster Boy
6. Rodney's Oyster House

son marinées et prêtes-à-cuire. Si vous ne voulez pas vous fatiguer à préparer votre repas du soir, voici un très bon compromis, par ailleurs servi en quelques minutes seulement. Sur place, il y a aussi de la bouillabaisse qu'il suffit de réchauffer. En prime, un petit citron jaune est offert à chaque achat pour parfumer vos délices de la mer…

PUSATERI'S FINE FOODS

Veuillez consulter notre répertoire d'adresses multiples à la page 142.
www.pusateris.com

Au rayon des poissons frais de Pusateri's, vous pourrez acheter du thon, du cabillaud, du rouget, de la truite, des pétoncles, du poulpe et des crevettes géantes. Côté poissons surgelés, on vend du crabe d'Alaska, du homard, des écrevisses, des escargots, du cabillaud, des crevettes et des pétoncles (au magasin d'Avenue Road). Plusieurs filets de

poisson en conserve sont également disponibles. Enfin, Pusateri's vous propose du caviar : Beluga, Osetra et Sevruga d'Iran.

RODNEY'S OYSTER HOUSE

469 King Street West (à l'ouest de Spadina Avenue) ☎ (416) 363-8105
Lundi à samedi 11h – 1h (du matin), fermé dimanche
Métro : KING + le tram
www.rodneysoysterhouse.com

Rodney's importe la plus grande variété d'huîtres à son quartier général de King Street. En fait, il importe ses huîtres des quatre coins du monde – Europe, Japon, côtes est et ouest du Canada. Chez Rodney's, on trouve couramment jusqu'à une douzaine de variétés différentes. En règle générale, comptez 8 à 9 variétés l'été et jusqu'à 20 l'hiver. Eh non, on ne plaisante pas ! Rodney's vous accueille même jusqu'à une heure du matin pour l'achat de vos huîtres.

SEAFRONT FISH MARKET

93 Front Street East (St. Lawrence Market) ☎ (416) 365-0086
Fermé dimanche et lundi, mardi à jeudi 8h – 18h, vendredi 8h – 19h, samedi 5h – 17h
Métro : UNION

Seafront Fish Market importe du thon frais, du cabillaud, du saumon, de la sardine fraîche, des pétoncles, des palourdes et des moules. Bien entendu, cette liste n'est qu'un bref aperçu de la sélection de ce poissonnier. Il a aussi un congélateur qui cache plusieurs poissons et fruits de mer surgelés.

poissonneries et spécialistes des huîtres

Snappers Fish Market

263 Durie Street (au nord de Bloor Street West) ☎ (416) 767-4083

Lundi 10h – 18h, mardi à vendredi 10h – 18h30, samedi 9h – 18h, dimanche 12h – 17h

Métro : RUNNYMEDE

Enfin ! Les habitants du quartier de High Park ne sont plus oubliés : un petit poissonnier local leur propose les incontournables de la mer. Au rendez-vous : thon frais, morue fraîche, sole, haddock, rouget et pétoncles. Dans le congélateur, il y a du crabe d'Alaska, des escargots, du poulpe, de la sardine et des queues de homard. Enfin, on trouvera plusieurs filets de poisson en conserve. Et pour les produits qui sortent un peu de l'ordinaire, on peut toujours passer une commande spéciale.

The Village Butcher

2914 Lake Shore Boulevard West (près d'Islington Avenue) ☎ (416) 503-9555

Fermé dimanche et lundi, mardi à vendredi 7h30 – 18h, samedi 7h30 – 17h

Métro : ISLINGTON + le bus

C'est vrai que The Village Butcher est avant tout un boucher… Cependant, vous découvrirez une petite sélection de poissons frais, acheminés chez ce boucher trois fois par semaine. La gamme est restreinte, mais n'oubliez pas, le mot d'ordre ici est « fraîcheur ». Vous pourrez ainsi acheter du saumon, du flétan, des pétoncles, des crevettes et du tilapia. Le tilapia est un poisson oriental qui se nourrit exclusivement d'algues. Il est vendu en filet et se prête particulièrement bien aux recettes façon meunière. On trouve aussi certains poissons de saison.

autres spécialités françaises

Cette section vous permettra de trouver encore davantage de spécialités françaises. Ces produits sont vendus frais, en conserve, en bocal ou même surgelés. L'important est qu'avec eux, vous avez accès à certains incontournables de la gastronomie française au cœur même de votre ville.

On peut préférer acheter des produits frais, le rythme fou de nos vies ne nous le permet pas toujours pour autant. C'est pourquoi nous avons ajouté une rubrique « produits français surgelés » qui vous facilitera la tâche en cas de besoin. Vous trouverez cette mention sous les adresses où l'on vend des produits surgelés.

autres spécialités françaises

HIGHLAND FARMS

☎ (416) 736-6606

Métro : DOWNSVIEW + le bus

C'est vrai qu'Highland Farms est avant tout un supermarché. Cependant, nous l'avons inscrit sous la section « Marchés » car Highland Farms offre la plus grande concentration de fruits et légumes au mètre carré. Des fruits et des légumes à en perdre la tête, plusieurs provenant de l'Ontario. Les semaines qui précèdent les fêtes de Noël, vous pouvez y trouver des betteraves jaunes ou encore des carottes rouges. Les mois d'été, vous avez le choix entre de multiples herbes fraîches, et des jeunes pousses d'ail frais sont même en vente. Highland Farms est une très grande surface. Au fond du magasin, vous trouverez une vitrine de viande assez impressionnante ainsi qu'un choix d'olives à vous rendre fou si vous en êtes amateur. Vous remarquerez qu'Highland Farms possède aussi un rayon de fromages français et suisses non négligeable. Le magasin importe surtout les variétés les plus connues. La boulangerie est remplie de plusieurs spécialités boulangères des quatre coins du monde. Chez Highland Farms, vous découvrirez peut-être moins de produits de la francophonie que dans les marchés Kensington et St. Lawrence, mais les grands rayons de fruits, légumes et viandes compenseront largement.

KENSINGTON MARKET

Métro : SPADINA + le tram;
QUEEN'S PARK + le tram

Baldwin Street et Spadina Avenue, c'est à cette intersection que prend forme ce « marché » de quartier abritant marchands de fruits et légumes, fromagers, commerces d'épices et céréales en vrac, poissonneries et boucheries. Le marché Kensington a un double attrait : on peut y acheter tout ce qu'il faut pour préparer de nombreux plats de la cuisine française à des prix vraiment très raisonnables et l'on n'est qu'à quelques pas de l'exotisme du quartier chinois. Après tout, on ne peut se satisfaire du même type de cuisine tous les jours ! Il est facile et agréable de faire toutes ses emplettes au marché Kensington pendant les trois quarts de l'année. L'hiver, c'est une autre histoire. En effet, seuls les acheteurs les plus motivés s'aventurent au marché Kensington pendant les longs mois d'hiver rigoureux, car le marché est à ciel ouvert.

ST. LAWRENCE MARKET

Métro : UNION
www.stlawrencemarket.com

Le marché St. Lawrence est vraiment un des joyaux de Toronto. Vous découvrirez toutes les délices de la francophonie sous un même toit. Quelle joie ! Les marchands permanents du marché St. Lawrence sont situés dans le bâtiment sud. Bouchers, fruitiers, légumiers, poissonniers et fromagers importent de vastes gammes de produits bien précieux pour la cuisine des francophones ou francophiles. La proximité des différents marchands, le fait que le marché soit couvert toute l'année et sa facilité d'accès font du marché St. Lawrence une excellente destination pour faire ses courses. Le samedi, le bâtiment nord abrite le marché fermier : fruits et légumes frais de l'Ontario et produits de la ferme comme le miel, le sirop d'érable, les tartes et les fromages maison font le bonheur des nombreux acheteurs qui s'y déplacent le week-end.

ALEX FARM PRODUCTS

Veuillez consulter notre répertoire
d'adresses multiples à la page 142.

www.alexcheese.com

Alex Farm vend des huiles aux noix, aux
truffes noires et blanches, aux amandes
grillées et aux noisettes. Il propose aussi
plusieurs parfums de vinaigre *Maille*.
La fleur de sel, nature ou aux herbes de
Provence, est vendue chez Alex Farm à
un prix fort raisonnable. Le magasin
dissimule également quelques sauces
importées de France (béarnaise et
hollandaise) de la maison *Delouis fils*.
Enfin, nous avons même découvert du
beurre de lait de chèvre.

PRODUITS FRANÇAIS SURGELÉS Alex
Farm a une gamme impressionnante de
produits surgelés de La Maison du
Gibier. Parmi la multitude de plats de ce
grand nom québécois de la distribution
alimentaire, nous avons retenu : civet de
cerf, bourguignon de bison, ballottine de
poulet farcie, canard farci et magret de
canard. Il fallait s'attendre à ce que des
francophones ajoutent une touche de
sophistication à des plats surgelés !

ALL THE BEST FINE FOODS

1099 Yonge Street (au nord de Roxborough
Street) ☎ (416) 928-3330

Lundi à mercredi 8h30 – 18h30, jeudi et
vendredi 8h30 – 19h, samedi 8h30 – 18h,
dimanche 10h – 17h

Métro : SUMMERHILL

www.allthebestfinefoods.com

Vous trouverez, à cette adresse de
Rosedale, les incontournables des
spécialités françaises. Ainsi, nous avons
découvert, sur les étagères d'All the

Best Fine Foods, des trésors culinaires
encore jamais vus à Toronto : de la
purée de marrons, des cornichons, des
marrons entiers en bocal, du miel de
marron et du miel de lavande de Provence, ainsi que de l'huile de noisette,
de l'huile d'olive de France, de l'huile
de noix du Périgord, des chanterelles
séchées, des olives niçoises, des olives
de Nyons, des flageolets en conserve, de
la moutarde de *Meaux Pommery*, de la
fleur de sel de Guérande et des
vinaigres des marques *Vilux* et *À
l'Olivier*.

PRODUITS FRANÇAIS SURGELÉS Surprise,
surprise ! Nous avons trouvé dans le
congélateur de ce magasin une pâte
feuilletée signée Rahier. Voici enfin une
alternative aux pâtes surgelées qu'on
trouve dans les supermarchés. C'est la
solution idéale pour ceux qui peinaient
avec leur pâte !

ARARAT INTERNATIONAL
FINE FOODS

1800 Avenue Road ☎ (416) 782-5722

Lundi à samedi 9h30 – 18h, fermé
dimanche

Métro : EGLINTON + le bus

Avec un grand sourire. Voilà comment
Peter et Aurora Kashkarian accueillent
les habitants du quartier. Impossible,
donc, de ne pas adorer ce couple. Chez
Ararat, il y a tout ce qu'il faut pour
cuisiner vos mets marocains préférés.
Des épices incontournables – telles que
le Raz el Hanout et des variétés de
zataar – aux citrons jaunes confits qu'on
trouve difficilement ailleurs (ingrédients nécessaires à tout tajine). Il y a

autres spécialités françaises

également des baies de genièvre *(juniper berries)* pour vos choucroutes. N'hésitez pas à faire appel à l'expertise des propriétaires si vous recherchez des épices particulières. Ararat fut aussi l'un des premiers importateurs de chocolat français à Toronto. En rayon, du chocolat et du sucre en provenance de France.

ARZ BAKERY

1909 Lawrence Avenue East (entre Warden Avenue et Pharmacy Avenue)
☎ (416) 755-5084

Lundi à samedi 8h – 21h30, dimanche 8h – 19h, les jours fériés 8h – 17h (Arz Bakery ne ferme jamais ses portes)

Métro : LAWRENCE + le bus

Arz Bakery est l'endroit idéal pour trouver certains ingrédients nécessaires aux plats libanais et à ceux du Moyen-Orient. Sur place, vous aurez le choix entre plusieurs sortes de boulgour (blé dur concassé) et de semoule de couscous. Chez Arz Bakery, vous pourrez acheter de la pâte d'harissa qui épicera vos plats. Nous avons par ailleurs remarqué une

---

Les endroits où trouver de la fleur de sel

1. Alex Farm Products
2. All the Best Fine Foods
3. Cheese Boutique
4. Clafouti
5. Dinah's Cupboard
6. Domino Foods
7. Harvest Wagon
8. Holt Renfrew
9. Pusateri's Fine Foods
10. Scheffler's Delicatessen
11. Whole Foods Market

---

vitrine d'olives, ainsi que des olives sous vide en provenance de la Tunisie. Pas d'huiles d'olive importées de France, mais que d'autres pays fournisseurs : Liban, Italie, Espagne, Grèce ! Une dizaine de types de safran sont également disponibles. Arz Bakery est un bon point de vente : vous pourrez encore y acheter de l'eau de rose et de l'eau de fleur d'oranger. Comme vous le savez, l'eau de fleur d'oranger est essentielle à la préparation des madeleines. Elle est aussi très difficile à trouver à Toronto, de même que les céréales et les noix diverses qu'il y a chez Arz bakery. À cette adresse, nous vous promettons une expérience très agréable, un petit dépaysement à s'offrir à tout moment.

BALZAC'S COFFEE HOUSE

Veuillez consulter notre répertoire d'adresses multiples à la page 142.

Honoré de Balzac fut non seulement l'un des auteurs français les plus prolifiques du XIXe siècle. Il fut également un grand amateur de café. Une raison qui a suffi à Diana Olsen pour baptiser ses maisons de café du nom de l'écrivain. Il se pourrait bien que Balzac's Coffee House soit le seul endroit à Toronto où l'on torréfie les grains de café selon les techniques françaises plutôt qu'italiennes. Le résultat tient dans une tasse d'un nectar plus intense et plus riche ! En plus de l'excellent café que l'on savoure dans un décor imprégné d'histoire, on peut aussi siroter un thé *Mariage Frères*. Ce thé prestigieux se vend dans certaines boutiques de Yorkville, mais il n'y a qu'ici qu'on vous le servira. Une gamme de parfums que

Le saviez-vous ?

La première machine à espresso fut bel et bien inventée par un Français. Un dénommé Lebrun eut, en 1838, l'idée de cette machine devenue depuis lors indispensable.

Source : Balzac's Coffee House

vous pourrez aussi apprécier à la maison.

Une leçon sur le café

Depuis 1991, Diana Olsen de Balzac's Coffee House se spécialise dans l'art du bon café à la française. Lors de notre rencontre, elle nous a révélé quelques-uns de ses secrets. Pour Diana Olsen, les Nord-Américains ont une conception erronée de la préparation du café au lait. La plupart croient qu'il s'agit d'un café filtre auquel on ajoute du lait chaud. Le vrai café au lait est un espresso avec du lait chaud. Sans machine à espresso, pas de bon café au lait donc !

BONJOUR BRIOCHE

812 Queen Street East (un peu à l'est de Broadview Avenue) ☎ (416) 406-1250
Fermé lundi, mardi à vendredi 8h – 17h, samedi 8h – 16h, dimanche 8h – 15h
Métro : QUEEN + le tram

Si vous avez déjà eu la chance de déjeuner chez Bonjour Brioche, vous savez combien leur vinaigrette maison est savoureuse. Eh bien, vous pouvez continuer à savourer cette vinaigrette à la maison, en l'achetant dans son format prêt-à-emporter. Côté sucré, vous pouvez aussi ramener la confiture maison

chez vous afin d'en tartiner généreusement votre baguette quand vous le voulez !

BRANDT MEAT PACKERS LTD.

1878 Mattawa Avenue, Mississauga (au sud de Dundas Street et Dixie Road)
☎ (905) 279-4460
Fermé dimanche et lundi, mardi 8h – 18h, mercredi 9h – 18h, jeudi et vendredi 8h – 19h, samedi 7h – 15h

Des marrons, des marrons et encore des marrons ! Ils sont vendus entiers, en purée et en tube dans ce magasin de Mississauga. Brandt Meat Packers Ltd. vend également plusieurs moutardes de France, une variété de champignons séchés et quelques champignons en conserve. Surprise ! Il y a aussi de la bouillabaisse en conserve et une grande quantité de choucroute en bocal. Les sirops *William*, ainsi que des sirops de l'Europe de l'Est, sont également en vente sur place. Ce supermarché allemand vous propose aussi du pain d'épice et des cerises griottes dénoyautées, en bocal dans un sirop léger, pour la préparation de vos desserts.

CLAFOUTI

915 Queen Street West (à l'est de Strachan Avenue, en face du parc Trinity Bellwoods)
☎ (416) 603-1935
Fermé lundi, mardi à samedi 8h – 18h, dimanche 9h – 17h
Métro : OSGOODE + le tram

Des marrons entiers en conserve, des flageolets en conserve, des asperges blanches en bocal, quelques confitures de France et de Belgique, des sirops *William* et de la fleur de sel, voilà les spécialités que l'on peut acheter chez

autres spécialités françaises

Clafouti. Pour le prêt-à-emporter français, Clafouti propose des croissants salés, des quiches, un croque-monsieur traditionnel et un autre végétarien, ainsi que plusieurs sandwichs sur baguette ou croissant. Clafouti propose également une belle gamme de confitures et compotes *Bonne Maman*.

CHEESE BOUTIQUE

45 Ripley Avenue (au sud de South Kingsway et au nord de The Queensway)
☎ (416) 762-6292

Lundi à vendredi 8h – 21h, samedi 8h – 20h, dimanche 10h – 18h

Métro : RUNNYMEDE + le bus

www.cheeseboutique.com

Cheese Boutique regorge de produits de la francophonie (et même de l'Europe entière). Les prix sont un peu plus élevés que ceux d'autres commerçants, mais le choix est grand. En matière de spécialités françaises, nous avons repéré les produits suivants : des sirops *Wil-liam*, des flageolets en conserve, une douzaine de moutardes de France, plusieurs filets de poisson en conserve, des huiles AOC de Provence, des herbes de Provence, des truffes, des huiles de noix et de noisette, de la fleur de sel de Guérande, plusieurs vinaigres *Maille* et *Vilux*, des vinaigrettes *Maille* et des chanterelles fraîches. Enfin, Cheese Boutique vend aussi des girolles.

CHRIS' CHEESEMONGERS

93 Front Street East (St. Lawrence Market)
☎ (416) 368-5273

Fermé dimanche et lundi, mardi à jeudi 8h – 18h, vendredi 8h – 19h, samedi 5h – 17h

Métro : UNION

Chris' Cheesemongers vend des huiles de noix de l'huilerie *Lapalisse*, des truffes en bocal, quelques moutardes de France, de l'huile d'amande et du vinaigre de champagne importé de France.

Le saviez-vous ?

Les Bretons surnomment la fleur de sel le « caviar du sel ». La fleur de sel a un goût incomparable. Certains disent que ses cristaux sont de véritables spectres d'or blanc. Les amateurs iront jusqu'à prétendre que la fleur de sel est un « diamant de la mer ».

La fleur de sel est née de l'océan, du soleil et du vent. Ce trésor de la presqu'île de Guérande renferme des petits cristaux blancs qui se forment à la surface des œillets. Très rare et de qualité exceptionnelle, ce sel non raffiné est cueilli à la main à « fleur d'eau », à l'aide d'une louche en bois. Simplement égouttée au soleil, la fleur de sel révèle toute la saveur des mets, au grand bonheur de nos papilles.

La fleur de sel est idéale avec des légumes crus, des salades et des grillades. Mariée à d'autres épices ou aromates, la fleur de sel de Guérande est divine. Dès que vous l'aurez essayée, vous ne pourrez plus vous en passer pour assaisonner vos plats. Pour les fêtes, n'oubliez pas d'en saupoudrer vos toasts de foie gras... Vous pouvez même l'ajouter à la vanille, car elle convient à merveille aux pâtisseries.

DANIEL ET DANIEL – FOOD SHOP

248 Carlton Street (au coin de Parliament Street) ☎ (416) 968-9275

Lundi à samedi 7h30 – 18h, fermé dimanche

Métro : CASTLE FRANK + le bus; COLLEGE + le tram

www.danieletdaniel.ca

Chez Daniel et Daniel, plusieurs produits valent la peine qu'on s'y attarde, comme le confit de pétales de roses et celui de pétales de violettes en bocal. Vous trouverez également des marrons cuits sous vide signés *Ponthier*, différentes marques françaises de vinaigres et une grande sélection de sirops *William*. Daniel et Daniel est l'un des meilleurs traiteurs de Toronto. Nous vous conseillons de goûter les plats à emporter suivants : quiche, sandwich sur baguette, poulet en croûte, pissaladière, tourtière, cassoulet, bœuf bourguignon, crêpes et crevettes façon créole. Quoi que vous choisissiez, vous ne vous tromperez jamais chez Daniel et Daniel !

DINAH'S CUPBOARD

50 Cumberland Street ☎ (416) 921-8112

Lundi à vendredi 9h – 19h, samedi 9h – 18h, fermé dimanche (à l'exception du mois de décembre)

Métro : YONGE OU BAY

Chez Dinah's Cupboard vous pourrez acheter les spécialités françaises suivantes : des vinaigres de la maison *Vilux,* de la moutarde de *Meaux Pommery,* de la fleur de sel de Guérande, des truffes en bocal et de l'huile de truffe.

Le saviez-vous ?

La « Lunch Box » de Daniel et Daniel est une façon simple et gourmande de prendre un bon déjeuner à l'occasion d'un pique-nique entre amis ou d'un déjeuner d'affaires. Votre repas tient dans la boîte et vous n'avez qu'à choisir parmi ces possibilités : poulet, saumon, sandwich et assiette de crudités. Et comme c'est signé Daniel et Daniel, vous êtes certain de recevoir une « Lunch Box » exceptionelle.

DOMINO FOODS LTD.

93 Front Street East (St. Lawrence Market, au sous-sol, tout au fond du marché) ☎ (416) 366-2178

Fermé dimanche et lundi, mardi à jeudi 8h – 18h, vendredi 8h – 19h, samedi 5h – 17h

Métro : UNION

Les apparences sont souvent trompeuses. Ce dicton s'applique très bien à ce magasin. Si, d'extérieur, il ne paie pas de mine, lorsqu'on y rentre, on découvre un vaste choix de produits français. C'est là que se trouve la gamme la plus complète de confitures *St Dalfour* que nous ayons jamais vue. On a également découvert de la moutarde au cognac et de la moutarde à la violette (attention, l'originalité se paie), quelques vinaigres de vin français, du vinaigre de vin provenant de la région Champagne, de la purée de marrons en conserve et sous vide, des truffes en pot ou en purée, de l'huile de vanille de Tahiti, de la fleur de sel et plusieurs parfums du sirop *William*. Le choix de champignons séchés nous a laissés

bouche bée. Nous en avons dénombré 16, dont les champignons de Paris, les cèpes, les portobellos, les truffes blanches, les chanterelles et les morilles. Qu'est-ce qu'on vous disait déjà au sujet des apparences ?

EPICUREAL

☎ (416) 244-1177 et 1 800 206-1177
www.epicureal.com

Régalez-vous grâce à Internet. Ce site propose un grand choix de produits d'alimentation fine. Plus de 800 produits du monde entier parmi lesquels des chocolats *Valrhona*, des marrons français, des truffes, du foie gras, du caviar, de la moutarde, des escargots, de la fleur de sel, des cornichons, des flageolets en conserve, des huiles et des vinaigres. Fini d'arpenter les rues ! Connectez-vous et trouvez en quelques clics ce qu'il vous manquait. Bien que toute nouvelle, l'équipe du site epicureal.com rassemble des personnes ayant déjà à leur actif cinquante années d'expérience dans l'importation des produits de première qualité.

GREAT COOKS

Veuillez consulter notre répertoire d'adresses multiples à la page 142.
www.greatcooks.ca

Si vous en avez assez des soupes et des sandwichs vite avalés à l'heure du déjeuner, voici une excellente alternative. À ceux qui travaillent dans le centre-ville et qui désespéraient à l'idée de consommer de la «vraie» nourriture le midi, nous suggérons Great Cooks. Il s'agit avant tout d'une école de cuisine, mais tous les jours, les chefs de Great Cooks préparent d'incroyables plats d'origines diverses. Lorsque la France est mise à l'honneur, c'est grâce aux créations du chef Jean-Pierre Challet, comme la tarte au chèvre et saumon poché, par exemple. Tout semble délicieux et l'est effectivement ! Le souci de la qualité est primordial ici et vos papilles le sentiront. En plus, les prix sont très raisonnables. Mais passé 14h, les vitrines du restaurant situé au sous-sol du magasin The Bay se vident. Heureusement qu'on peut maintenant manger toute la journée à la seconde adresse située au 8e étage du même grand magasin.

HARVEST WAGON

Veuillez consulter notre répertoire d'adresses multiples à la page 142.

Les chanterelles et les morilles ne sont pas des champignons très courants à Toronto. On les voit rarement dans les marchés ou les grandes surfaces alimentaires. Harvest Wagon vous aidera à trouver des champignons qui sortent un peu de l'ordinaire. Vous constaterez aussi que Harvest Wagon a une très belle sélection d'herbes fraîches. Enfin, deux autres spécialités françaises vous y attendent : les flageolets en conserve et la fleur de sel.

Le saviez-vous ?

Les origines de la boîte de conserve remontent à la fin du XIXe siècle en France. Napoléon, l'instigateur de cette fameuse invention, utilisa les aliments en conserve pour nourrir ses troupes.

HOLT RENFREW – EPICURE & GOURMET SHOPS

50 Bloor Street West (au coin de Bay
Street) ☎ (416) 922-2333

Lundi à mercredi 10h – 18h, jeudi et
vendredi 10h – 20h, samedi 10h – 18h,
dimanche 12h – 18h

Métro : YONGE OU BAY

On va finir par croire que derrière cette
grande marque canadienne du luxe se
cache un francophile averti ! Holt
Renfrew importe des spécialités de
plusieurs marques de luxe françaises.
Et vous découvrirez ainsi de chez *Fauchon* des marrons glacés, des vinaigres
aux parfums divers, de la fleur de sel,
des moutardes, des biscuits, des confitures et des thés. *Fauchon* fait rarement
dans l'ordinaire, c'est ce qui explique les
parfums de confiture d'une originalité
déconcertante – mangue et pêche, clémentine, poire à la gousse de vanille,
pomme au calvados, cerise de Morello,
melon de Cavaillon et abricot aux fleurs
de jasmin. Vous pourrez également
acheter de la pâte à tartiner aux noisettes *Neuhaus*. Enfin, Holt Renfrew importe le thé *Mariage Frères*. Sur place,
un choix tout à fait satisfaisant vous fera
découvrir ou redécouvrir cette grande
maison du thé, fondée en 1854. Le livre
de recettes *Mariage Frères, Éloge de la
cuisine au thé*, est même en vente.

K.I.S. GLOBAL FLAVORS

250 Shields Court, Unit #19, Markham
☎ (905) 477-0024
www.kisglobalflavors.com

Le site de K.I.S. Global Flavors est une
avalanche des meilleurs produits alimentaires haut de gamme. Cette com-

Les endroits où trouver des flageolets

1. All the Best Fine Foods (en conserve)
2. Casa Açoreana (secs)
3. Cheese Boutique (en conserve)
4. Clafouti (en conserve)
5. Harvest Wagon (en conserve)
6. Scheffler's Delicatessen (en conserve)

pagnie importe des produits fins de
France, de Suisse et d'Italie. Voici donc,
entre vous et nous, un petit aperçu des
produits français proposés sur le site :
chocolats en forme d'olives de Provence, marrons glacés, fruits confits,
oranges confites, citron au chocolat,
calissons d'Aix-en-Provence, nougat,
truffes, gelée de fleur et miel de fleur de
Provence. À noter qu'en quelques clics,
vous pouvez offrir à la personne de
votre choix un panier rempli de superbes produits français grâce au
panier-cadeau.

LE GOURMAND

152 Spadina Avenue (au sud de Queen
Street) ☎ (416) 504-4494

Lundi à vendredi 7h – 20h, samedi 9h –
18h, dimanche 9h – 16h

Métro : OSGOODE + le tram;
SPADINA + le tram

Le Gourmand vend de l'huile d'olive
aux truffes blanches, de l'huile de
pépins de raisin *Vilux*, de la moutarde
de *Meaux Pommery*, de l'huile de noix
et du vinaigre de la maison *Clovis*. Vous
trouverez aussi une belle gamme de
confitures, biscuits et miels français,
ainsi qu'une petite sélection de fro-

autres spécialités françaises

mages et foies gras du Québec. Si vous ne trouvez pas ce que vous cherchez sur les étalages, n'hésitez pas à passer une commande !

PRODUITS FRANÇAIS SURGELÉS On trouve désormais les produits surgelés de La Maison du Gibier chez Le Gourmand. Civet de cerf, bourguignon de bison, ballottines de poulet farcies et canard farci sont parmi les plats disponibles dans ce magasin.

LOBLAWS

Différentes adresses dans toute la ville

Dans les rayons de ce grand nom de l'alimentation, vous trouverez les produits suivants : moutardes *Maille,* moutardes et vinaigres *Vilux* (parmi lesquels le vinaigre de cognac et celui de champagne) et moutardes de *Meaux Pommery.* Vous découvrirez aussi un nombre impressionnant de confitures *St Dalfour* aux parfums peu courants à Toronto : figue royale, ananas et mangue, mirabelle, framboise noire, orange et gingembre.

PRODUITS FRANÇAIS SURGELÉS Loblaws vend plusieurs produits surgelés d'inspiration française. Il est vrai que ces produits ne sont pas aussi raffinés que ceux que l'on trouve chez les maîtres fabricants, mais plusieurs d'entre eux vous surprendront quand même. Sur place, vous découvrirez les produits surgelés de la marque « Le Choix du Président^{MC}/President's Choice® » suivants : les croissants au beurre, les miniéclairs au chocolat, les profiteroles, le cassoulet et la quiche lorraine.

MA MAISON

4243 Dundas Street West (en face du centre Kingsway Mills) ☎ (416) 236-2234

Fermé lundi, mardi et mercredi 8h – 18h, jeudi et vendredi 8h – 19h, samedi et dimanche 8h – 16h

Métro : ROYAL YORK + le bus

www.UR2Busy2Cook.com

Pas le temps de cuisiner ? Vous n'avez qu'à apporter vos propres récipients à Ma Maison. On vous les garnira de bons petits plats mijotés à la perfection. Voici enfin une formule *fast-food* non seulement pratique, mais aussi de qualité. Parmi la sélection d'une dizaine de plats sous vide que prépare Ma Maison, vous trouverez le coq au vin, la blanquette de veau, le filet de porc et le cassoulet toulousain. Ne passez pas non plus à côté des croissants salés, des quiches, des tourtières et des sandwiches. Quelques fromages français et de très bonnes confitures maison compléteront le repas. Le pâté est la spécialité de la maison. Suivez l'exemple des habitués et choisissez-en deux ou trois pour vos repas ou vos en-cas. Ma Maison, c'est le *one-stop-shopping* de la gastronomie française dans l'ouest de Toronto.

MAX'S MARKET

2299 Bloor Street West (à l'ouest de Runnymede Road) ☎ (416) 766-6362

Lundi à mercredi 9h – 19h, jeudi 9h – 19h30, vendredi 9h – 20h, samedi 9h – 19h, dimanche 9h – 18h

Métro : RUNNYMEDE

Max's Market présente une vitrine de prêt-à-emporter impressionnante en matière de choix et de fraîcheur. Côté

Épices

Découvrez tout un monde d'épices :

BULK BARN

www.bulkbarn.ca

Voici rassemblées sous un même toit des épices du monde entier vendues en vrac. Que vous soyez à la recherche d'épices courantes ou exotiques, vous les trouverez à bon prix dans l'un des 21 magasins de ce commerçant.

CASA AÇOREANA

Kensington Market ☎ (416) 593-9717

Casa Açoreana importe du chèvrefeuille, des feuilles de laurier, de la ciboulette, de la marjolaine, de la sauge, de la lavande séchée, du thym et de l'estragon. Voici aussi une bonne adresse pour se procurer des herbes de Provence et même du safran d'Espagne à un prix tout à fait raisonnable. En outre, Casa Açoreana importe de la vanille liquide pure et des fèves de vanille de Madagascar. Ce qui est rare à Toronto, mais qui ne l'est pas dans ce magasin, ce sont les baies de genièvre séchées (la traduction anglaise est *juniper berries*).

DOMINO FOODS LTD.

St. Lawrence Market ☎ (416) 366-2178

Pour acheter vos herbes en vrac au marché St. Lawrence, c'est chez Domino Foods qu'il faut que vous alliez. On y trouve du chèvrefeuille, du thym, de l'estragon, de la ciboulette, du romarin, de l'anis, de la marjolaine, de la sauge, du safran et des feuilles de laurier. Domino Foods vend aussi des herbes de Provence et des fèves de vanille.

HOUSE OF SPICE

Kensington Market ☎ (416) 593-9724

House of Spice importe une quantité extraordinaire d'épices du monde entier, souvent indispensables aux cuisines de la francophonie. Vous trouverez par exemple de l'estragon, du thym, des feuilles de laurier, des graines de moutarde jaunes et noires, des herbes de Provence et du safran. Vous pourrez aussi acheter des fèves de vanille de Madagascar et de la racine de réglisse. Enfin, House of Spices est une adresse où dénicher certaines épices pour vos plats exotiques nord-africains, telles que la harissa, le zataar et le Raz el Hanout.

PEROLA

Kensington Market ☎ (416) 593-9728

Perola est avant tout un marchand d'aliments pour les cuisines hispanique et brésilienne. Cependant, il mérite sa place dans ce guide de la gastronomie française ou francophone grâce à l'ingéniosité de son propriétaire. Ce dernier a en effet eu la brillante idée de sécher des bouquets d'herbes entiers. Vous trouverez des bouquets de romarin, sauge, sarriette et basilic chez Perola's.

STRICTLY BULK

Différentes adresses dans toute la ville
☎ (416) 533-3242

Le choix est incomparable et les prix raisonnables. Tout est vendu en vrac. Vous trouverez la plupart des herbes dont vous pouvez avoir besoin pour mijoter vos petits plats, ainsi que du safran et de l'essence de vanille pure.

autres spécialités françaises

spécialités françaises, nous avons trouvé près d'une dizaine de variétés de crêpes fourrées parmi lesquelles : fruits de mer, jambon-fromage, poulet et pistou, champignons et saumon. Il y a également chez Max's Market une dizaine de parfums de vinaigres *Vilux*. Avis aux amateurs d'olives ! Un comptoir en dévoile plus d'une vingtaine de variétés, dont plusieurs fourrées d'ingrédients aussi inattendus que le gorgonzola.

MERCATTO

Veuillez consulter notre répertoire d'adresses multiples à la page 142.

Huile de noix, huile d'olive de Provence et les fameuses herbes de Provence font partie des spécialités françaises que vous pourrez acheter ici.

OLYMPIC CHEESE MART

Veuillez consulter notre répertoire d'adresses multiples à la page 142.

Vous trouverez ici des truffes, des huiles d'olive de France, des vinaigres et vinaigrettes *Maille*, ainsi qu'un produit peu commun à Toronto : du vinaigre *Kressi* de Suisse. Il paraît que c'est *le* vinaigre qu'il faut pour faire la fameuse sauce hollandaise. Deux autres choses ont attiré notre attention : les girolles sont en vente chez ce marchand et un plateau de fromages français est disponible sur commande pour vos repas entre amis.

PAIN PERDU

736 St. Clair Avenue West (un peu à l'ouest de Christie Street) ☎ (416) 656-7246
Fermé lundi, mardi à vendredi 8h – 19h,
samedi 8h – 17h, dimanche 8h – 16h
Métro : ST CLAIR WEST + le tram
www.painperdu.com

Impossible de ne pas remarquer les bonnes quiches chez Pain Perdu ! En plus, elles rivalisent en saveur les unes avec les autres. La tarte aux oignons est, elle aussi, délicieuse. Le midi, les longues files de clients qui salivent n'en finissent pas. Il faut dire que le menu quiche/salade ou tarte/salade est non seulement très bon, son prix défie aussi toute concurrence. « Le Yannick » est sublime lui aussi. Le chef Folgoas a su faire d'une simple tranche de pain au levain une tartine délicieuse. Autres spécialités françaises : la mayonnaise, la vinaigrette et les confitures maison. La qualité du sirop d'érable dont on arrose le pain perdu est remarquable. On peut même acheter ce sirop biologique en provenance de la région du lac Érié.

PATACHOU

Veuillez consulter notre répertoire d'adresses multiples à la page 142.

Patachou vend des huiles d'olive françaises parfumées au piment, au basilic, aux herbes de Provence et au citron. Sur place, on trouve aussi des vinaigrettes et des confitures maison. Patachou propose également un menu prêt-à-emporter et un menu week-end. La carte des plats proposés pour le prêt-à-emporter comprend un confit de canard sur lit de chou rouge et polenta, un bœuf bourguignon, un agneau navarin, des champignons portobellos farcis à la ratatouille et au chèvre, un couscous façon israélienne et une pissaladière. Avec le menu du week-end, on vous

proposera plusieurs plats très appétissants et parfaits pour les repas en tête-à-tête à la maison ou pour ceux entre amis.

PÂTISSERIE D'OR

301 Robinson Street, Oakville (au sud de Lake Shore Road) ☎ (905) 815-8999

Fermé lundi et mardi, mercredi à vendredi 8h – 17h30, samedi et dimanche 8h – 18h

La quiche à base de pâte feuilletée est la grande vedette de la maison. C'est sans aucun doute l'une des meilleures quiches que nous ayons jamais mangées. Essayez aussi les pâtés à la viande et celui au saumon. Là encore, vous serez épaté !

PRODUITS FRANÇAIS SURGELÉS Le chef Jean-Luc Soulabaille ne le sait peut-être pas, mais il est en train de changer la tendance dans notre ville. En effet, les habitants du grand Toronto pourront déguster de délicieuses viennoiseries françaises préparées par un chef français chevronné quand bon leur semblera. Comment le chef Jean-Luc Soulabaille a-t-il fait pour accomplir cet exploit ? Il a tout simplement installé deux congélateurs à l'arrière de sa pâtisserie et les a remplis de ses spécialités. La sélection est très variée : croissants au beurre, pains au chocolat, biscuits à la cuillère, petits pains, baguettes, danoises au raisin, vol-au-vent et la fameuse quiche maison. Autre douceur à emporter : les pots de glace maison. Leurs parfums sont réalisés grâce à des ingrédients tels que du chocolat belge, des fruits frais, de la liqueur ou des noix grillées. Parmi les variétés de ces douceurs glacées figurent le cassis, la framboise, le citron, la fraise, la vanille, le chocolat, le caramel, le café, la pistache et la pomme verte.

PÂTISSERIE SAINT HONORÉ

2945 Bloor Street West (au coin de Greenview Blvd., un peu à l'est de Royal York Road)

Il n'y a pas de numéro de téléphone pour cette pâtisserie

Fermé dimanche et lundi, mardi à jeudi 8h – 19h, vendredi 8h – 21h, samedi 8h – 19h

Métro : ROYAL YORK

Une dizaine de tables sont à votre disposition pour apprécier sur place quelques-unes des spécialités de la maison : quiche, tourtière, soupe à l'oignon, sandwich au pâté maison et pissaladière. Des cornichons français sont vendus en vrac à un prix fort intéressant.

Le saviez-vous ?

C'est en région Bourgogne que se trouvent les plus grands champs de graines de moutarde du monde ? Détrompez-vous. La Seconde Guerre mondiale a mis un terme à la culture de graines de moutarde dans la région de Dijon. En réalité, la province de Saskatchewan (située dans les prairies canadiennes) a dérobé le titre du plus grand producteur de graines de moutarde au monde. La moutarde Dijon servie dans les meilleurs restaurants est aussi canadienne que le sirop d'érable !

autres spécialités françaises

Petit Gâteau

2365 B Lake Shore Road, Oakville
(à l'ouest de Bronte Road) ☎ (905) 847-1888

Fermé dimanche et lundi, mardi à vendredi
9h – 18h, samedi 8h30 – 17h

Cette pâtisserie permet de savourer une tourtière traditionnelle du Québec sans avoir à déployer tous les efforts requis par la longue préparation de ce plat. À cette adresse, vous trouverez la tourtière traditionnelle de bœuf et de porc, mais vous pourrez aussi essayer quelques variations maison de ce plat – tourtière au saumon et tourtière au poulet. Il est préférable de passer votre commande à l'avance.

Pusateri's Fine Foods

Veuillez consulter notre répertoire d'adresses multiples à la page 142.

www.pusateris.com

Ce supermarché haut de gamme importe les spécialités suivantes : marrons glacés, truffes en bocal, marrons cuits sous vide, plusieurs huiles d'olive françaises de très haute qualité, fleur de sel, huile de noix et huile d'amande. Nous avons également trouvé des chanterelles fraîches (très peu de marchands en vendent). La longue vitrine et la section réfrigérée de plats prêts-à-emporter vous feront sûrement de l'œil, en même temps que gargouiller votre estomac. Les plats franco-français ne sont pas oubliés : gratin dauphinois et salade niçoise vous attendent chez Pusateri's.

PRODUITS FRANÇAIS SURGELÉS Vous trouverez ici des cèpes surgelés.

Qualifirst Foods

☎ (416) 244-1177
www.qualifirst.com

Qualifirst a commencé à distribuer des produits haut de gamme français dans l'Ouest canadien en 1957. Aujourd'hui, Qualifirst dessert tout le territoire canadien. Vous pouvez consulter son site Internet et passer une commande de produits français fins. Vous remarquerez que le choix est assez vaste, puisque ce distributeur passe des bonbons français aux truffes, puis des moutardes aux marrons. Profitez-en bien !

Rahier

1586 Bayview Avenue (au sud d'Eglinton Avenue) ☎ (416) 482-0917

Fermé lundi et mardi, mercredi à vendredi 8h – 17h, samedi 8h – 16h, dimanche 8h – 15h

Métro : EGLINTON + le bus

Rahier vous propose plusieurs variétés de quiches pour le week-end : chèvre et poivrons rouges, quiche lorraine, brocoli et cheddar, saumon fumé et asperges, aubergines et poireaux.

Le saviez-vous ?

Le St. Lawrence Market (qui a déjà 200 ans) a été reconnu comme l'un des marchés les plus raffinés du monde. Cette honorable mention lui a été attribuée en avril 2004 par le magazine américain de cuisine *Food & Wine*. Parmi la liste de 24 finalistes, on retrouve des marchés prestigieux dans les villes les plus chics de la planète : Paris, Milan et Tokyo.

PRODUITS FRANÇAIS SURGELÉS Dans le congélateur de Rahier, vous trouverez les produits suivants : pâte feuilletée, sorbets et glaces maison, timbales feuilletées (type croûtes de bouchées à la reine), coulis de framboise, sauce au chocolat et quelques gâteaux.

SCHEFFLER'S DELICATESSEN

93 Front Street East (St. Lawrence Market)
☎ (416) 364-2806

Fermé dimanche et lundi, mardi à jeudi 8h – 18h, vendredi 8h – 19h, samedi 5h – 17h

Métro : UNION

Vous pouvez acheter chez Scheffler's beaucoup d'ingrédients essentiels à la cuisine française ou francophone tels que de la fleur de sel de Camargue, du safran, des flageolets, de la crème de marrons, des morilles en bocal, des truffes et des cornichons du Maroc et de France. On y trouve également une large gamme de vinaigres et vinaigrettes *Maille*.

THE VILLAGE BUTCHER

2914 Lake Shore Boulevard West (près d'Islington Avenue) ☎ (416) 503-9555

Fermé dimanche et lundi, mardi à vendredi 7h30 – 18h, samedi 7h30 – 17h

Métro : ISLINGTON + le bus

Si vous voulez régaler vos invités d'une traditionnelle tourtière québécoise pendant les fêtes de Noël, sachez que ce boucher en vend. Pensez à passer commande, car les fameuses tourtières partent extrêmement vite.

WHOLE FOODS MARKET

87 Avenue Road (au nord de Bloor Street)
☎ (416) 944-0500

Lundi à vendredi 9h – 22h, samedi et dimanche 9h – 21h

Métro : BAY OU MUSEUM

www.wholefoodsmarket.com

Whole Foods Market propose les produits français suivants : huile d'olive de Provence (AOC), huiles de Provence médaillées AOC (l'une d'or, l'autre d'argent), olives de Nyons, fleur de sel nature, fleur de sel aux herbes de Provence, moutarde de *Meaux Pommery* et sauces *Delouis fils* – hollandaise, béarnaise, mayonnaise à l'ail et mayonnaise césar. Enfin, une petite sélection de truffes en bocal ainsi que des champignons séchés (morilles, trompettes et cèpes) sont disponibles sur place.

ZANE PÂTISSERIE ET BOULANGERIE

1852 Queen Street East (à l'ouest de Woodbine) ☎ (416) 690-2813

Fermé lundi, mardi à dimanche 7h30 – 17h30

Métro : QUEEN + le tram

Tous les week-ends, Mo Zane prépare une demi-douzaine de quiches. Au palmarès des variétés les plus demandées figurent la quiche végétarienne, la quiche au jambon et au lard, et la quiche au saumon fumé.

bistros et restos

La haute cuisine française a-t-elle toujours sa place ? Dans certains cas, un repas élaboré est la meilleure façon de célébrer un événement important. Les mille et une facettes de la cuisine française se prêtent à merveille tant à un repas élaboré et onéreux qu'à un repas plus simple, au prix plus abordable.

À Toronto, plusieurs chefs et propriétaires de restaurants français ont tranché. La nouvelle tendance est de proposer un menu haut de gamme, mais pas cher et sans chichi. Les chefs de la ville spécialistes de la cuisine française utilisent des techniques classiques qu'ils adaptent aux ingrédients locaux. Ils nous offrent ainsi de superbes expériences gastronomiques à des prix raisonnables.

La cuisine française n'existerait pas sans le savoir-faire de chefs experts, des ingrédients de qualité, une présentation soignée et un zeste de passion.

Nous vous invitons à découvrir le menu des restaurants français de Toronto. Un bonheur pour les habitants de la ville comme pour les visiteurs. À essayer également : les restaurants belges et marocains !

Bon appétit !

FOURCHETTES DE PRIX

Pour vous faciliter la tâche et trouver un repas adapté à votre budget, nous avons ajouté les symboles suivants :

PF Indique les restaurants qui proposent un menu à prix fixe. La plupart de ces menus coûtent entre 30 et 35 CAD (taxes et pourboire non compris). Le plus souvent, on vous sert deux plats mais dans certains cas, le dessert et le café sont également inclus dans le prix.

$ Indique la fourchette de prix par personne du dîner à la carte de chaque restaurant (prix pour un dîner comprenant trois plats, taxes et pourboire compris, sans les boissons alcoolisées).

$ moins de 25 CAD

$$ 26-50 CAD

$$$ 51-75 CAD

$$$$ 76 CAD et plus

ARLEQUIN

134 Avenue Road (au coin de Davenport Road) ☎ (416) 964-8686
Fermé dimanche et lundi, mardi à samedi pour le dîner, vendredi et samedi pour le déjeuner et le brunch
Métro : MUSEUM

La nouvelle direction, le nouveau décor et le nouveau chef et propriétaire (Scott Saunderson) n'ont rien changé à l'essence même de ce bistro de quartier. Il reste un endroit sympathique, à l'ambiance chaleureuse. Arlequin propose un vaste menu, reflet d'une cuisine typique d'un bistro parisien. Ici, on vous sert du gigot d'agneau, du confit de canard, du coq au vin, du cassoulet ou un steak Angus accompagné de frites et aïoli. Les viandes sont particulièrement bien apprêtées. Leur cuisson toujours parfaite les fait fondre dans la bouche. Ne partez pas avant le dessert ! Laissez-vous séduire par la crème brûlée veloutée, l'exquis gâteau au chocolat ou encore la tarte au citron. La carte des vins regorge de bonnes surprises, avec notamment des vins de Bourgogne et d'Alsace. Dans l'ensemble, le menu permet de déguster un bon repas à prix moyen. – *service en français, $$$, PF*

AVANT-GOÛT

8 Birch Avenue (au coin de Yonge Street, près du métro SUMMERHILL)
☎ (416) 975-9150
Lundi à dimanche pour le dîner
Métro : SUMMERHILL

Le chef et propriétaire, Kamal Hani, est d'origine marocaine et il s'est donné pour mission de bouleverser complètement l'expérience gastronomique des résidents de Rosedale. Avant-Goût propose un vaste choix de plats d'influence française, mais aussi marocaine. À l'heure du dîner, voici à peu près ce qui figurera au menu : soupe du jour (toujours très savoureuse, à goûter absolument), salade de poires et roquefort, steak Black Angus et frites, ragoût de bœuf à la marocaine, magret de canard et choux rouge, gigot

Le saviez-vous ?

Selon les historiens, les Belges faisaient déjà cuire des frites au XVIIe siècle. On a tendance à croire que celles-ci sont d'origine française et non wallonne. La confusion est née d'un fait historique. Des frites furent servies au lendemain de la Révolution de 1789 sur les ponts de la Seine, sous l'appellation de « pommes Pont-Neuf »*. Cette anecdote entraîne, à tort, des Français à revendiquer la paternité de la frite. Mais alors, pourquoi les « French fries » et non pas les « Belgian fries » ? Il y a deux explications possibles. La première remonte à la Première Guerre mondiale. Lorsque les troupes américaines, anglaises et canadiennes débarquèrent en Flandre occidentale, la population locale ne tarda pas à leur faire goûter leur spécialité culinaire. Puisque le français était alors la langue de l'armée belge, les anglophones ont tout simplement baptisé ces bâtonnets frits les « French fries ». L'autre explication remonte à la fin du XIXe siècle. Certains historiens disent que le terme « French fries » faisait partie du vocabulaire culinaire américain. À cette époque, le terme argotique « to french » signifiait « couper en bâtonnets ». Qu'elles soient belges ou françaises, de bonnes frites cuites à point, bien salées et servies avec de l'aïoli, de la mayonnaise ou même du Ketchup, restent tout simplement irrésistibles.

*Les pommes « Pont-Neuf » ont 1 cm de large sur 6 ou 7 cm de long, c.-à-d. qu'elles sont deux à trois fois plus épaisses que les frites allumettes.

d'agneau accompagné d'une purée de pommes de terre et ragoût de haricots blancs. Quant au dessert, laissez-vous tenter par une très bonne crème brûlée. La carte des vins vous emporte dans plusieurs régions de vignobles, avec quelques bouteilles de vins blancs et de vins rouges français. Vous apprécierez de manger dans un décor un peu rétro. Avant-Goût... c'est le goût avant tout !
– *service en français, $$*

BATIFOLE

744 Gerrard Street East (entre Broadview Avenue et Logan Avenue)
☎ (416) 462-9965
Lundi à dimanche pour le dîner (fermé le mardi soir)
Métro : BROADVIEW + le tram

Vous mangez, vous buvez, vous batifolez ! Voilà un slogan qui donne envie d'aller au restaurant. Pour un repas copieux, aux saveurs délicieusement subtiles, pris dans une atmosphère détendue, rendez-vous chez Batifole. Le menu, préparé par le chef et propriétaire Jean-Jacques Texier, promet ! Une dégustation agréable, à prix raisonnable, adaptée aux petites faims comme aux gros appétits. Parmi les délicieux plats proposés : le tartare de filet de bœuf épicé, le confit de canard au calvados, la bavette sautée à l'échalote, le filet de bar blanc rôti à la provençale et le filet mignon de porc à la crème de truffe. Les plats servis en accompagnement méritent d'être mentionnés, comme la tartiflette au reblochon, les frites « Pont-Neuf » maison et le risotto aux champignons.

bistros et restos

Vous vous régalerez également avec les desserts. Le chef Texier utilise sans compter les produits du terroir ontarien et invente régulièrement de nouvelles gourmandises. Vous pourrez ainsi tomber sur l'un des desserts suivants : l'île flottante au Cointreau et à la fleur d'oranger, la crème brûlée au cognac, le clafoutis ou encore quatre suggestions de crêpes différentes. La carte des apéritifs pétille d'originalité. N'hésitez pas à jeter un œil à la carte des vins 100 % française ! – *service en français, menu bilingue, $$*

BISTRO MATISSE

1710 Lake Shore Road West, Mississauga (à l'intérieur du Clarkson Village, entre Port Credit et Oakville) ☎ (905) 822-2222

Fermé lundi, mardi à vendredi pour le déjeuner, mardi à dimanche pour le dîner

Le visage du grand Toronto a sans aucun doute changé avec l'ouverture du Bistro Matisse. Le chef et propriétaire, Jean Jacques Lemesle, sert depuis novembre 2002 des petits plats bien mijotés dans un coin de Toronto qui ne compte qu'un seul autre restaurant français. Le menu du soir vous présente une myriade de plats à prix raisonnables, tels que le suprême de poulet cordon-bleu, le foie de veau à la parisienne, les coquilles Saint-Jacques, le steak au poivre, le canard, la bouillabaisse et les merguez grillées servies avec du couscous. Nous avons entendu dire que le chef préparait aussi des andouillettes et du foie gras maison. Les desserts sont assez irrésistibles. Leur liste n'est pas très longue, mais elle change régulièrement, sauf dans le cas de la crème brûlée, indétrônable. La

Le saviez-vous ?

Après la parution de notre premier guide, nous avons reçu beaucoup de commentaires de la part de lecteurs franco-européens et québécois disant ne pas maîtriser suffisamment l'anglais pour pouvoir bien comprendre un menu. C'est vrai qu'il est parfois assez difficile de repérer un restaurant au service en français dans une ville anglophone. Nous avons donc décidé d'aiguiller un peu mieux nos lecteurs. Lorsque vous voyez la mention **menu bilingue,** cela indique que le menu est disponible en français et en anglais à cette adresse. Avec la mention **service en français,** vous saurez que le chef ou certains serveurs peuvent vous servir en français.

liste des vins comporte quelques bouteilles de régions vinicoles françaises. On pourra également se rafraîchir avec diverses bières françaises. Vous reconnaîtrez peut-être la touche spéciale du chef Lemesle puisqu'il est l'ancien copropriétaire et chef du restaurant La Maison Benoît. – *menu bilingue et service en français, $$, PF*

BISTRO TOURNESOL

406 Dupont Street (à l'ouest du métro DUPONT) ☎ (416) 921-7766

Fermé lundi, mardi à dimanche pour le dîner

Métro : DUPONT

www.bistrotournesol.com

Les trois nouveaux propriétaires de Bistro Tournesol connaissent bien la

gastronomie française. Ils travaillaient déjà dans ce petit bistro avant que l'ancien patron français, Yves Robert, ne retourne dans l'Hexagone. La formule demeure la même : une ambiance chaleureuse et un menu à prix fixe. L'ensemble de deux plats vous est proposé pour 25 CAD. Ce menu est complété avec quelques entrées du jour. Pas de menu à la carte. Chaque plat arrive accompagné d'un bol de frites. Côté desserts, essayez la tarte au citron façon Bistro Tournesol. Une agréable combinaison de saveurs sucrées et acidulées. Le service est à la fois courtois et amical. Réservez à l'avance car les habitués et les détenteurs de billets du théâtre Tarragon ont fait de Bistro Tournesol leur « cantine ». – *$$, PF*

BLOOR STREET DINER

On y sert le petit-déjeuner, le déjeuner et le dîner.

55 Bloor Street West (Manulife Centre) ☎ (416) 928-3105

Métro : BLOOR

www.eatertainment.com

Deux ambiances (bistro-resto) pour cet établissement proposant une large sélection de « classiques » à prix très raisonnables. Croque-monsieur, salade niçoise, soupe à l'oignon, quiche, moules marinière, steak frites, poulet rôti à l'aïoli de tomates séchées et foie de veau sont quelques exemples de ce qui figure sur la carte. Des plats de tous les jours qu'on peut s'offrir souvent ! Le menu est une bonne affaire et l'on ne résiste pas à la petite touche finale du Bloor Street Diner : une demi-baguette toute chaude. – *$$,PF*

BOUJADI

999 Eglinton Avenue West (à l'ouest de Bathurst Street) ☎ (416) 440-0258

Fermé lundi et mardi, mercredi à dimanche pour le dîner

Métro : EGLINTON WEST

www.boujadi.com

Marhaba (« bienvenue ») à la cuisine marocaine ! Le chef et propriétaire, Charles Obadia, exécute depuis 1992 des recettes de plats traditionnels marocains que lui ont transmises ses aïeux. À l'opposé des cuisines « fusion » ou « nouveau genre », Boujadi vous propose trois plats de tajines, six plats de couscous et une demi-douzaine de plats végétariens. Au menu, vous retrouverez également le fameux thé vert à la menthe marocain ainsi qu'une limonade (façon nord-américaine) parfumée à l'eau de rose. La liste des desserts est limitée, mais bien représentative de la cuisine marocaine. Il va de soi que le décor et la musique marocaine sont au rendez-vous pour créer une ambiance des plus animées. Si vous avez de la chance, vous dînerez lors d'une des soirées où les danseuses sont là (surtout le week-end). S'il vous est impossible de profiter de l'ambiance sur place, commandez donc les plats à emporter de Boujadi. – *service en français, $$*

BRASSERIE ROYAN

218 Lakeshore Road East (à l'ouest de Tragalgar Road) ☎ (905) 845-8623

Lundi à dimanche pour le déjeuner et le dîner

www.royan.ca

Paul et Joe Haskett ont créé une véritable brasserie française à Oakville.

bistros et restos

Brasserie Royan est rapidement devenu le lieu de rencontre des francophiles de l'ouest du grand Toronto qui sont à la recherche d'un très bon menu français à un prix raisonnable. Des mets typiques d'une brasserie ainsi que quelques plats bien québécois vous attendent chez Brasserie Royan. Vous pourrez vous satisfaire d'un steak frites et sa sauce au brandy, d'un confit et d'un magret de canard dans un jus au porto, d'un suprême de poulet fourré au fromage oka ou d'une poutine façon Brasserie Royan. Les frites cuites et salées juste comme il faut ne déçoivent pas non plus. Les lundis, Brasserie Royan propose ses moules à moitié prix. Côté desserts, les classiques comme la tarte au citron et le gâteau au chocolat raviront les gourmands. Les Québécois ont également de quoi se régaler avec une excellente tarte au sucre. Une carte des vins digne de toute brasserie qui se respecte dévoile plusieurs vins français. Avec Royan Brasserie, un petit détour par Oakville vaut vraiment le coup !
– *$$, PF*

Le saviez-vous ?

Royan est une ville située au sud-ouest de Paris qui accueillait le festival de la Belle Époque. Ce festival commémore une grande période de l'histoire française, à la veille de la Première Guerre mondiale. À cette époque, les grands artistes, Picasso et Émile Zola par exemple, se réunissaient et échangeaient leurs idées en rivalisant de créativité.

Source : www.royan.ca

Café Crêpe

246 Queen Street West (à l'ouest de University Avenue) ☎ (416) 260-1611

Lundi à jeudi 9h – 22h, vendredi et samedi 9h – 00h, dimanche 10h – 22h

Métro : OSGOODE

Qui dit balade à Paris, dit dégustation de crêpes vendues par les marchands ambulants. Longtemps, les Torontois ont été privés de ces crêpes. Depuis janvier 2003, Café Crêpe, sur Queen Street West, comble ce manque. Il n'y a pas que la dégustation qui plaise.

Regarder comment on prépare votre crêpe a son charme aussi. Les variétés de crêpes sucrées et salées ont des parfums typiquement français et d'autres plus adaptés aux goûts locaux. Pour vous mettre en appétit, voici un échantillon des crêpes que vous pourrez déguster : poulet et champignons, emmenthal et sirop d'érable ou encore thon et mayonnaise. Côté crêpes sucrées, on a par exemple : miel et noix, glace au rhum, noix de coco et banane. Chez Café Crêpe, on peut manger sa crêpe sur place ou à la française, sur le pouce. Si les crêpes ne vous tentent pas, vous pouvez opter pour l'un des sandwichs grillés ou sur baguette. Les sandwichs, préparés le jour même, ne sont disponibles qu'en quantité limitée, un gage de leur fraîcheur. – *$*

Café Margaux

796 College Street (à l'est d'Ossington Avenue, au coin de Roxton Road) ☎ (416) 588-7490

Mardi à samedi pour le dîner

Métro : QUEEN'S PARK + le tram

www.cafemargaux.ca

Le propriétaire du Café Margaux a la restauration dans le sang. Ses parents détenaient La Maison Benoît. À lui maintenant de faire ses preuves ! Notre repas chez Café Margaux nous laisse penser que Patrice Baron y parviendra sans aucun problème. Le chef Rob Briden est un habitué de la cuisine française puisqu'il a travaillé chez Pastis Express et Quartier avant de rejoindre les cuisines de Café Margaux. À la carte, optez pour des plats classiques ou contemporains. Ils sont tous très bien préparés. Le propriétaire et le chef profitent du menu du jour pour associer leur originalité. Un choix restreint de desserts exquis vous attend : profiteroles à l'armagnac, assiette gourmande (sa composition varie), marquise au chocolat et crème brûlée. La cave à vins de Café Margaux est très impressionnante. On y retrouve une cinquantaine de vins blancs et rouges, pour la plupart français. Et si la longue liste des vins vous complique la tâche pour choisir, vous pouvez toujours consulter l'encyclopédie des vins sur le bar. – *menu bilingue, service en français, $$, PF*

CAFÉ MOROC

49 Front Street East (à l'ouest de Church Street) ☎ (416) 961-0601
Lundi à dimanche pour le dîner
Métro : UNION
www.thesultanstent.com

Comme son nom l'indique, ce restaurant met le Maroc en vedette. Et de quelle façon ! Le décor est absolument splendide. Un vrai souci du détail a été apporté à la décoration pour vous trans-

porter dans une médina. La céramique du mur d'entrée, les miroirs, la riche couleur du bois, les lanternes, les petites tables rondes couleur ébène, la teinte des murs, les affiches et les ventilateurs en bambou, tout, au Café Moroc, contribue au dépaysement. Le menu, bien évidemment, vous plonge encore plus au cœur du Maroc. On y retrouve des spécialités traditionnelles et contemporaines telles que la merguez sur baguette, le hamburger Moroc (un hamburger à l'agneau accompagné des frites Moroc) et la spécialité « Keskesu Casablanca » (tajine de couscous, légumes, fruits et noix). La carte des boissons est assez surprenante, car y figurent plusieurs cocktails signés Café Moroc que vous ne boirez qu'ici. Bien entendu, pensez à terminer votre repas avec le traditionnel thé à la menthe !
— *$$*

CAFÉ NICOLE

45 The Esplanade (entre Yonge Street et Church Street) ☎ (416) 367-8900
Lundi à dimanche pour le déjeuner et le dîner
Métro : UNION

Café Nicole est le restaurant situé à l'intérieur de l'hôtel Novotel, dans le centre-ville de Toronto. Les plats de Café Nicole sont savoureux, la cuisson est parfaite et le service est impeccable. Dans les sélections françaises, on retrouve les incontournables suivants : steak frites, carré d'agneau en croûte, magret de canard avec gratin dauphinois et filet de bœuf servi avec un ragoût de champignons sauvages et une sauce au porto. Le « menu théâtre » est

Le saviez-vous ?

Une enquête publiée en mars 2004 par le magazine de cuisine *Elle à Table* dévoile les plats préférés des Français. La liste comprend quelques sélections qui vous surprendront. Parmi les préférences culinaires des Français figurent les moules marinière, la blanquette de veau et le pot-au-feu. Nous avons été particulièrement surpris par le choix des Français en matière de dessert : ils préfèrent la salade de fruits toute simple à tout autre dessert. C'est une révélation percutante pour tous les francophiles qui adorent les desserts français bien riches. Il va de soi que les Français préfèrent leur cuisine à toutes les autres (à la maison comme à l'étranger). L'enquête révèle que 77 % placent la cuisine française en tête de peloton. Côté cuisine internationale, les Français préfèrent le couscous (d'Afrique du Nord) et la pizza (celle des immigrants italiens). Heureusement pour eux, les Français ne seront pas déçus par la longue liste de restaurants torontois où l'on peut savourer leurs plats préférés ainsi qu'une variété de plats affectionnés des francophiles d'ici.

très intéressant puisqu'il permet aux détenteurs de billets de théâtre de manger un excellent steak frites en très peu de temps. Pour clore un bon repas, offrez-vous l'un des desserts suivants : crème brûlée, crêpes ou gâteau au Grand Marnier. — *service en français, $$, PF*

CHEZ LAURENT

4965 Yonge Street (au nord de Sheppard Avenue) ☎ (416) 590-0909

Lundi à samedi pour le dîner, fermé dimanche

Métro : **NORTH YORK CENTRE OU SHEPPARD**

Chez Laurent est un restaurant sans prétention, situé dans une maisonnette qui donne davantage l'impression d'aller dîner chez des amis qu'au restaurant. L'atmosphère est fort conviviale. La famille Ferrari excelle dans la préparation de plats simples et revigorants. Le menu célèbre les classiques des cuisines française et italienne. Le concept de

fusion ne s'applique pas ici. Qui dit français, dit français. Côté entrées, vous pourrez choisir des moules marinière, des escargots, une soupe à l'oignon ou une salade niçoise. Quant aux plats principaux, la maison vous propose du veau au citron, un suprême de poulet, du poulet chasseur et du poulet basquez. Trois préparations de steak sont également au menu. La liste des desserts est assez courte. La crème caramel et la crème brûlée restent des valeurs sûres. — *menu bilingue, service en français, $$*

CRÊPES À GOGO

244, Bloor Street West (entrée par Bedford Road, au nord-est de Bloor Street West) ☎ (416) 922-6765

Fermé le lundi, mardi à jeudi 9h30 – 19h, vendredi et samedi 9h – 21h, dimanche 10h – 16h30

Métro : **ST GEORGE** (sortie Bedford)

www.crepesagogo.com

Depuis mai 2003, les amateurs de

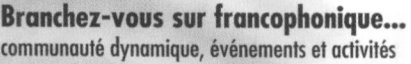

Nous souhaiterions apporter notre contribution

Plusieurs personnes ont contribué au succès de notre guide. Grâce à leur générosité, nous avons pu réaliser notre rêve. C'est pour cela que nous voulons, à notre tour, apporter notre aide à ceux qui en ont le plus besoin. Un pourcentage de nos bénéfices (avant taxe sur les ventes au détail) sera reversé à des organismes qui soutiennent les familles les plus démunies de notre société. L'un des thèmes principaux de notre guide étant la gastronomie, nous avons choisi de soutenir des organisations qui nourrissent tous les jours des milliers de Torontois. En plus d'une contribution financière, nous leur avons offert un espace publicitaire dans notre guide. Les organismes que nous soutenons sont Second Harvest et Daily Bread Food Bank. Merci à nos fidèles lecteurs de nous permettre de faire ce geste.

L'équipe de Franco Toronto

franco **toronto**

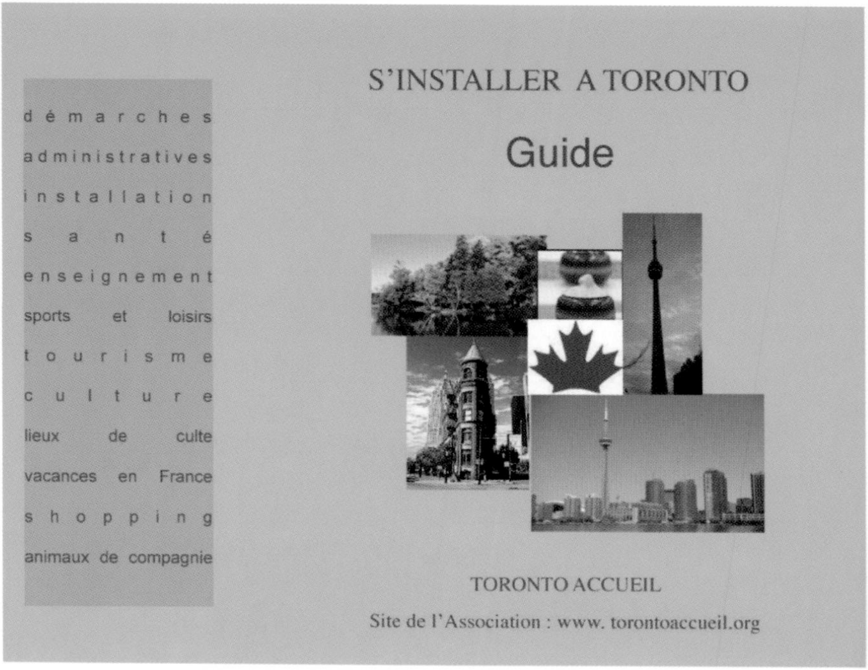

S'INSTALLER A TORONTO
Guide
démarches administratives
installation
santé
enseignement
sports et loisirs
tourisme
culture
lieux de culte
vacances en France
shopping
animaux de compagnie
TORONTO ACCUEIL
Site de l'Association : www. torontoaccueil.org

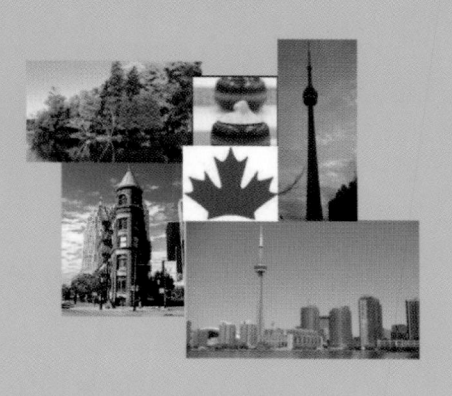

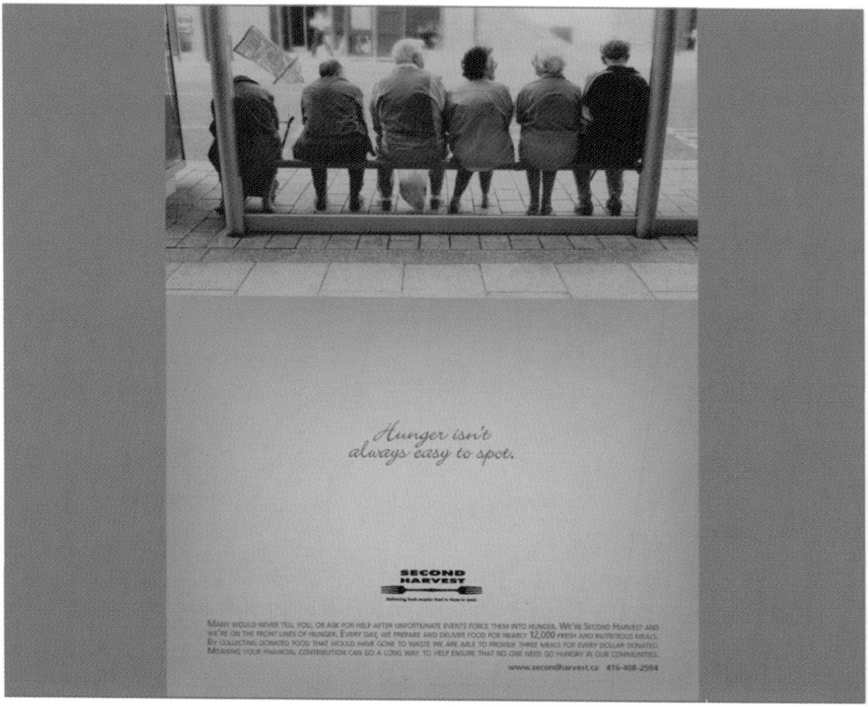

Hunger isn't always easy to spot.
SECOND HARVEST
Many would never tell you, or ask for help after unfortunate events force them into hunger. We're Second Harvest and we're on the front lines of hunger. Every day, we prepare and deliver food for nearly 12,000 fresh and nutritious meals. By collecting donated food that would have gone to waste we are able to provide three meals for every dollar donated. Meaning your financial contribution can go a long way to help ensure that no one need go hungry in our communities.
www.secondharvest.ca 416-408-2594

crêpes courent chez Crêpes à GoGo. Pour beaucoup, ces crêpes sont les meilleures de Toronto ! Des sucrées aux combinées salées/sucrées, elles font sensation (notamment la « Big Ben » et la « Véronique »). Crêpes à GoGo, c'est aussi tout un choix de salades et de sandwichs sur ficelle. L'endroit est difficile à trouver car il n'est pas sur Bloor Street même, mais bien sur Bedford Road. Tendez un peu l'oreille et suivez la musique française. Crêpes à GoGo se situe au-dessus du niveau de la rue. Quelques marches à gravir et vous voilà dans un petit cadre au décor sympathique. Produits frais et naturels à des prix raisonnables garantis (taxes comprises, comme en Europe) ! Quatre petites tables et pas de couverts pour les crêpes ici. Elles se dégustent dans leur sac en papier ! – *menu bilingue, service en français, $*

HOLT'S CAFÉ

50 Bloor Street West (au coin de Bay Street; au 2e étage) ☎ (416) 922-2333

Lundi à mercredi 10h – 18h, jeudi et vendredi 10h – 20h, samedi 10h – 18h, dimanche 12h – 18h

Métro : BLOOR OU BAY

Ce café de luxe situé au deuxième étage jouit d'un décor tout rénové. Le rendu est vraiment très moderne, très aéré et très chic. Contrairement à plusieurs restaurants au décor trop « ultra chic » qui misent avant tout sur les apparences pour séduire leur clientèle, Holt's Café séduit même les plus fins palets de la ville. Le menu, créé par le chef Corbin Tomaszeski, n'est autre que le pendant torontois d'un menu qu'on retrouve dans plusieurs bistros de Paris, au détail près que le chef

Tomaszeski s'est inspiré d'un boulanger assez connu de la rue du Cherche-Midi, à Paris : Poîlane. Eh oui, toutes les tartines du Holt's Café sont composées de pain Poîlane. Oui, oui, vous avez bien lu… du pain Poîlane. Le choix parmi douze tartines environ saura satisfaire les clients les plus indécis. Une tarte au citron, un pain perdu à base de pain Poîlane ainsi qu'une crème brûlée au gingembre figurent sur la liste des desserts. – *$$*

JACQUES BISTRO DU PARC

126 A Cumberland Street ☎ (416) 961-1893

Lundi à samedi pour le déjeuner et le dîner, dimanche pour le dîner

Métro : BAY

Ce tout petit bistro séduira les amoureux de la gastronomie. Jacques Sorin, chef et propriétaire, y prépare des omelettes bien garnies pour le déjeuner. Le dîner se compose à la carte ou au menu. Ni l'un ni l'autre ne vous décevra. En voici quelques exemples : carré d'agneau à la provençale, escalope de veau forestière, médaillons de ris de veau et suprême de poulet fermier. Lorsque le plat de résistance est si bon, on a tendance à oublier de laisser une petite place pour le dessert… Jacques Sorin saura pourtant séduire les amateurs de sucré avec une île flottante, une mousse au chocolat, des profiteroles ou encore une multitude de tartes aux fruits frais. Jacques Bistro est le genre de restaurant où l'on revient régulièrement, car le rapport qualité-prix y est excellent et les plats sont toujours à la hauteur des espérances. En d'autres termes, cette adresse est une

bistros et restos

Hors catégorie !

CAFÉ LA GAFFE

24 Baldwin Street (à l'ouest de McCaul Street) ☎ (416) 596-2397

Lundi à dimanche pour le déjeuner et dîner

Métro : ST PATRICK

Le Café la Gaffe n'est ni un café ni un bistro français. En fait, le menu est assez éclectique et s'inspire de plusieurs cuisines. Cela dit, la crème brûlée qu'on retrouve sur le menu du Café la Gaffe est réalisée grâce à la recette originale de l'artiste Claude Monet. En fait, la recette provient du livre de recettes de l'artiste peintre (il y a une reproduction du livre dans les cuisines du Café la Gaffe). Cette recette date de 1885. Cette crème brûlée est non seulement bonne, elle a aussi une histoire et un passé incontestablement fascinants. Voilà un autre exemple du patrimoine culinaire français à son meilleur, comme il existe à Toronto.

valeur sûre ! – *menu bilingue, service en français, $$*

L'ESCARGOT BISTRO

3185 Yonge Street (au nord de Lawrence Avenue) ☎ (416) 485-8338

Lundi à dimanche pour le dîner

Métro : LAWRENCE

www.lescargot.ca

L'Escargot Bistro tourne bien grâce à Max Ballin. Ce propriétaire astucieux a créé un décor et une atmosphère idéals pour prendre le temps d'un bon petit repas français. Des plats simples, sans chichi, aux saveurs envoûtantes. En entrée, L'Escargot Bistro vous propose trois variations sur son thème : escargots bourguignons, fricassée d'escargots à la provençale et feuilleté d'escargots. Ensuite, vous pourrez découvrir le pot-au-feu de poisson, l'une des deux variétés de steak frites, le magret de canard ou les médaillons de veau au citron. Une courte liste des desserts met quand même le gâteau basque à l'honneur (une première pour un restaurant à Toronto). La cave à vins, majestueuse, renferme plus de 1 000 bouteilles, dont plusieurs françaises. – *menu bilingue, service en français, $$, PF*

LA MAISON BENOÎT

1921 Avenue Road (au nord de Brooke Avenue) ☎ (416) 782-9934

Lundi à samedi pour le déjeuner, lundi à dimanche pour le dîner

Métro : EGLINTON + le bus

La Maison Benoît est un restaurant situé dans le nord du quartier Forest Hill. Un menu typiquement français y est servi dans un décor chaleureux et « rétro ». Laissez-vous surprendre par la note singulière que le chef Jean-Luc Moles apporte aux plats les plus classiques – coquilles Saint-Jacques au Pernod, demi-canard rôti arrosé d'une sauce au porto et à l'orange, et foie de veau servi avec des échalotes confites. Vous pourrez également choisir le steak frites au poivre. La carte des desserts promet une belle aventure. Les profiteroles au Cointreau et la marquise au chocolat sortent du lot. La carte des vins présente quelques crus français. Pour découvrir tous ces plats, on vous

conseille de faire une réservation, le restaurant étant populaire dans le quartier... – *menu bilingue, service en français, $$, PF*

LA PALETTE

256 Augusta Avenue (à l'ouest de Spadina Avenue) ☎ (416) 929-4900

Lundi à dimanche pour le dîner

Métro : SPADINA + le tram; QUEEN'S PARK + le tram

Petit restaurant chaleureux et sans chichi, situé dans le quartier Kensington, La Palette vous propose un menu de plats classiques français, bien préparés et à des prix raisonnables. Le décor est simple (nappes colorées et affiches françaises sur les murs), la terrasse accueillante pendant la saison chaude et le service décontracté. C'est l'endroit idéal pour un bon repas en toute simplicité. Consultez la section «brunch» pour en savoir plus sur les plats alléchants qui figurent alors au menu. On vous donne un indice : le mot *crêpes*! – *service en français, $$*

LA PETITE FRANCE

3317 Bloor Street West (à l'est d'Islington Avenue) ☎ (416) 234-8783

Lundi à vendredi pour le déjeuner, lundi à samedi pour le dîner, fermé dimanche, sauf pour les grands groupes

Métro : ISLINGTON

www.lapetitefrance.ca

Les plats du chef Gilbert Letort sont simples, classiques et particulièrement savoureux. Le menu change tous les six mois pour s'adapter aux saisons. Par exemple, pendant les mois d'hiver, vous pourrez commander un bœuf sauce béarnaise, un canard sauce au poivre vert, une fricassée de crevettes et pétoncles sauce au pastis ou un filet de porc sauce au calvados. L'été, partez à la découverte du tian d'escargots, des timbales de truite fumée, du confit de canard au rhum et aux raisins, du carré d'agneau rôti à la menthe, des cuisses de grenouilles ou du filet de sole meunière. La carte des vins est particulièrement intéressante, avec une soixantaine de bouteilles proposées, la majorité étant des vins rouges français. Attention, pensez à garder une petite place pour le dessert. La crème brûlée à la vanille est renversante! Parmi les autres desserts figurent les profiteroles, les crêpes, la galette bretonne et le gâteau Marjolaine. Les événements mensuels gastronomiques et les dégustations de vins ont particulièrement retenu notre attention. La Petite France propose un service traiteur. Le chef préparera pour vos célébrations un menu français de qualité irréprochable ou encore un menu «cuisine du monde». – *menu bilingue, service en français, $$, PF*

LE PAPILLON

16 Church Street ☎ (416) 363-3773

Fermé lundi, mardi à dimanche pour le déjeuner et le dîner

Métro : UNION

www.lepapillon.ca

Le Papillon, c'est un rendez-vous à mi-chemin entre la France, le Québec et la Bretagne. Au cours des années, ce restaurant a glané les prix d'excellence ainsi qu'un groupe de fidèles. Il est l'un des seuls restaurants de la ville à propo-

bistros et restos

ser des plats typiquement québécois tels que les cretons (rillettes de porc) et la tourtière traditionnelle du Québec. Autres gourmandises à essayer : le poulet aux pêches et au brandy, le filet de porc à la bordelaise et le feuilleté de fruits de mer. Laissez-vous également tenter par l'une des crêpes bretonnes : c'est la spécialité de la maison. Crêpes sucrées en dessert, mais aussi quelques spécialités québécoises comme la tarte au sucre et le pudding chômeur. En bref, Le Papillon vous propose une bonne cuisine servie dans un décor rustique. – *service en français, $$*

LE PARADIS

166 Bedford Road (au sud de Dupont Street) ☎ (416) 921-0995

Mardi à vendredi pour le déjeuner, lundi à dimanche pour le dîner

Métro : **MUSEUM** OU **ST GEORGE**

www.leparadis.com

Le Paradis marie habilement plusieurs cuisines de la francophonie, même si la plupart des plats sont français. Les plats d'inspiration marocaine sont le tajine, l'agneau à la marocaine, les merguez et le couscous. Au sommaire de la longue liste d'incontournables français : blanquette au sauvignon, bavette, entrecôte chasseur, lapin à la provençale, confit de canard. Le cassoulet a déjà fait un grand nombre d'heureux au Paradis. Ayant essayé plusieurs recettes et n'étant toujours pas satisfait du résultat, le chef a, un jour, décidé de remonter à la source de ce mets. Au cours d'un de ses voyages en France, il a demandé au chef d'un restaurant de Castelnaudary de lui

congeler et de lui envoyer le cassoulet qu'il avait mangé chez lui. Et c'est ainsi qu'à Toronto, le chef a peaufiné sa recette pour donner naissance au délicieux cassoulet qu'on connaît. La carte des vins se résume en un mot : franco-française. Les savoureux plats du terroir du Paradis seront merveilleusement rehaussés par ces nectars. – *menu bilingue, service en français, $$*

Les restaurants avec terrasse

1. Bloor Street Diner
2. Bodega
3. Café Margaux
4. La Maison Benoît
5. La Palette
6. Le Saint Tropez
7. Le Trou Normand
8. Merlot
9. Michelle's Brasserie
10. Pourquoi Pas
11. Provence Délices
12. The Fifth

LE PETIT DÉJEUNER

191 King Street East (à l'est de Church Street) ☎ (416) 703-1560

Lundi à samedi pour le petit-déjeuner et le déjeuner, jeudi à samedi pour le dîner, dimanche pour le brunch

Métro : **KING**

www.petitdejeuner.ca

Où peut-on trouver les meilleures gaufres de Bruxelles à Toronto ? Au Petit Déjeuner bien sûr ! Le chef et propriétaire d'origine belge, Johan

Maes, réalise des gaufres d'une légèreté céleste ! Hormis ces spécialités, il y a de quoi faire un bon petit-déjeuner : omelettes, crêpes, œufs, croque-monsieur et croque-madame. Depuis septembre 2004, vous pouvez aussi savourer plusieurs spécialités belges le soir. En créant son menu du dîner, le chef Maes avait un seul but en tête : proposer de bons plats à petit prix. Parmi les incontournables belges, goûtez les moules frites, le poulet sauce archiduc servi avec frites et ratatouille ou le steak frites. Pour terminer le repas en beauté, laissez-vous tenter par la crème brûlée chai ou la poire Bosc pochée. La courte carte des vins présente des crus agréables au palet comme au portemonnaie. Du petit-déjeuner au dîner, on pourrait rester à cette bonne adresse toute la journée ! – *$$, PF*

Le Petit Gourmet

1064 Yonge Street (au sud de Roxborough Street) ☎ (416) 966-3811
Lundi à vendredi 7h30 – 19h, samedi 7h30 – 18h, fermé dimanche
Métro : ROSEDALE

Ce petit bistro du quartier Rosedale est un bon endroit pour déguster un repas en toute simplicité. Quiches, poulet rôti au four, bœuf bourguignon, ragoût de veau, coq au vin et pâté au poulet font partie du menu régulier. Les plats du jour varient, mais les suggestions sont toujours aussi attirantes. Lorsque nous y avons dîné, M. Boniteau, chef et propriétaire, proposait les plats suivants : canard aux pommes, gigot d'agneau et rôti de porc. Les plats simples rappellent la cuisine « comme à la maison ». Enfin, un service traiteur est disponible. – *$*

Le Saint Tropez

315 King Street West (au coin de John Street) ☎ (416) 591-3600
Lundi à dimanche pour le déjeuner et le dîner
Métro : ST ANDREW
www.lesainttropez.com

Le Saint Tropez vous accueille dans une ambiance décontractée et sympathique. C'est souvent le rendez-vous des Français lors de célébrations nationales (14 juillet et coupe du monde de football par exemple). Au menu, vous aurez le choix entre plusieurs plats français, sur un petit air du Sud : saucisses de Toulouse, poêlée de crevettes et escalope de veau au porto avec champignons sauvages et herbes fraîches. Les desserts ne sont pas nécessairement du Sud, mais Le Saint Tropez n'oublie pas certaines des meilleures spécialités françaises, à savoir la crème brûlée, la tarte au citron et les profiteroles au chocolat. La carte des vins nous a impressionnés. Elle couvre toutes les régions françaises. Enfin, signalons que c'est sur un fond musical de jazz que vous mangerez tous les soirs au Saint Tropez. – *menu bilingue, service en français, $$*

Le Sélect Bistro

328 Queen Street West ☎ (416) 596-6406
Lundi à dimanche pour le déjeuner et le dîner
Métro : OSGOODE
www.leselect.com

Voilà une véritable institution à

bistros et restos

Toronto, et ce, depuis plusieurs décennies! Le Sélect Bistro détient un beau palmarès de prix d'honneur et de mentions spéciales attribuées par des chroniqueurs, aussi bien à Toronto qu'aux États-Unis. Les Torontois continuent d'en faire leur bistro de prédilection. Le décor du Sélect Bistro vous emmène rive gauche, à Paris. Le menu? Il est franco-français bien sûr. Si vous voulez manger de la bonne cuisine du terroir comme de la bouillabaisse, du cassoulet, des escargots ou du foie gras, vous avez «frappé à la bonne porte»! Les viandes y sont cuites à la perfection. Le menu est d'un excellent rapport qualité-prix. Il peut s'avérer difficile de choisir le vin qui accompagnera votre repas, car Le Sélect Bistro vous donne à choisir parmi plus de 1 000 variétés. Quelle cave! Le choix des desserts aussi donne un peu le tournis : on aimerait bien tout essayer... En tous les cas, ne manquez pas la banane flambée. – *menu bilingue, $$, PF*

LOLO RESTAURANT

619 Mount Pleasant Road (à l'est de Yonge Street) ☎ (416) 483-8933
Lundi à samedi pour le dîner, fermé dimanche
Métro : EGLINTON

Un bistro français qui sert quelques plats italiens? Pourquoi pas! Le propriétaire Louis Ourique n'y voit aucun inconvénient. Chez Lolo, un charmant bistro de quartier, l'ambiance amicale ajoute au plaisir de déguster des plats savoureux. Les plats de poisson préparés avec soin ont notamment retenu notre attention. Sur la petite carte des desserts, vous pourrez commander l'une des meilleures tartes au citron de la ville. La tarte Tatin et le pain perdu (la recette de la belle-mère de M. Ourique) seront aussi d'excellents choix. Côté boissons, quelques vins de France, et surtout une carte internationale des bières remarquable! – *$$, PF*

MATIGNON

51 St. Nicholas Street ☎ (416) 921-9226
Lundi à vendredi pour le déjeuner, lundi à samedi pour le dîner, fermé dimanche (ouvert dimanche seulement pour les fonctions privées)
Métro : YONGE
www.matignon.ca

Matignon propose un excellent menu à prix très raisonnable et une carte bien variée. On y trouve des plats qui sortent de l'ordinaire, tels que le canard rôti servi sur un coulis de myrtilles, la pièce d'Angus (bœuf) au poivre noir flambée au cognac, le poulet au pistou ou le carré d'agneau à la moutarde, au miel et à la menthe. On peut également commander des plats plus traditionnels tels que le saumon «à la bonne femme», le steak frites, la truite au beurre blanc ou le foie de veau. La cave est pleine de bons vins à petits prix. À ne pas manquer quand vous arriverez au dessert : la crème caramel au parfum d'orange. Matignon est situé dans une maison de briques, dans une rue résidentielle entre Yonge Street et Bay Street, au sud de Charles Street. Le restaurant comporte deux salles élégantes, à l'ambiance tamisée, et propose un service impeccable. – *menu bilingue, service en français, $$, PF*

MERLOT

2994 Bloor Street West ☎ (416) 236-0081

Lundi à vendredi pour le déjeuner, lundi à dimanche pour le dîner

Métro : ROYAL YORK

Le décor, le menu et les œuvres d'art au mur célèbrent bel et bien la France. Merlot est le second restaurant français qui accueille les résidents du Kingsway Village pour déguster de bons petits plats. Vous remarquerez que la viande y est particulièrement mise à l'honneur. Du steak frites à l'agneau, les variations se font sur le même thème : un bon morceau de viande bien cuit. Les prix sont très raisonnables et donnent ainsi la possibilité de goûter à des plats de viande un peu plus chers ailleurs. Le trio de saucisses (toulouse, italienne et merguez) servi dans une sauce signée Merlot ne laisse pas indifférent. Les desserts sont franchement épatants. Quant à la carte des vins à petits prix, vous nous en direz des nouvelles ! *– service en français, $$*

MICHELLE'S BRASSERIE

162 Cumberland Street (Renaissance Court, près du Four Seasons Hotel) ☎ (416) 944-1504

Lundi à dimanche pour le déjeuner et le dîner

Métro : MUSEUM OU BAY

www.labrasserie.ca

Michelle's Brasserie est une brasserie française bien typique où l'on peut manger un excellent repas en sirotant une bonne boisson. Les plats français y sont particulièrement bien présentés, et d'une qualité qui reste irréprochable. Caille servie avec une sauce Bercy,

médaillons de porc sauce calvados et foie gras préparé spécialement par le chef ne sont que quelques-unes des spécialités de la maison. Pour un repas plus léger, choisissez la salade niçoise. Le poisson cuit à point et la touche particulière du chef en font une salade remarquable. Le décor rappelle la France. Si vous y prêtez suffisamment attention, vous verrez que le grillage apposé aux murs est un clin d'œil à la Tour Eiffel. La cave de Michelle's Brasserie est très bien garnie en vins, bières et spiritueux français. Tous les jeudis, vendredis et samedis soirs, vous pouvez profiter du spectacle de jazz et rythm n' blues. Vous aurez même droit à quelques performances d'artistes francophones. *– service en français, $$$*

MIDI BISTRO

168 McCaul Street (entre College Street et Dundas Street) ☎ (416) 977-2929

bistros et restos

Lundi à vendredi pour le déjeuner, mardi à samedi pour le dîner, fermé dimanche
Métro : ST PATRICK
www.midibistro.com

Midi Bistro est un tout petit restaurant qui vous emmène dans une belle aventure gastronomique. L'ambiance feutrée vous permettra de vous détendre et de savourer un repas des plus agréables. Le menu vous surprendra, tant par sa variété que par son montant total vraiment raisonnable. Aussitôt arrivé, vous verrez, à la liste des entrées, que Midi Bistro se distingue par son originalité : Farçous « Claudine » (crêpes aux épinards, oignons et lardons), terrine de chèvre aux légumes, jambon de pays et fromage de chèvre chaud en témoignent. Bien entendu, en bon bistro qui se respecte, Midi Bistro sert aussi des moules. Quant à la sélection de bons petits plats bien mijotés, vous pourrez choisir entre une truite saumonée au jus de bouillabaisse, un coquelet rôti à la mauresque, un confit de canard sauce légère à la moutarde *Pommery*, un faux-filet façon « Pays d'oc » (servi avec une sauce au merlot). La liste des desserts propose les choix suivants : une tarte Tatin, des profiteroles avec glace à la vanille, une crème brûlée et un gâteau tiède au chocolat (vous devrez patienter une vingtaine de minutes pour ce délice chocolaté, mais « le jeu » en vaut vraiment la chandelle, croyez-nous). *– menu bilingue, service en français, $$, PF*

MONITZ

352 Melrose Avenue (au coin d'Avenue Road) ☎ (416) 781-3764
Lundi à vendredi pour le déjeuner, samedi pour le dîner, fermé dimanche

Métro : EGLINTON + le bus

Monitz est un bistro qui marie très judicieusement la cuisine française, la cuisine méditerranéenne et la cuisine nord-africaine. Cela ne s'arrête pas là puisque Monitz vous permet d'accompagner des plats de couscous (servis avec harissa, ils sont d'une originalité surprenante) avec une sélection d'environ 40 vins, pour la plupart français. Les merguez ne figurent pas sur le menu, mais si vous en faites la demande, le chef se fera un plaisir de vous les préparer. Le tarif du menu est très intéressant, vraiment pas très cher. Pour ce qui est des desserts, on vous laisse découvrir par vous-même. *– menu bilingue, service en français, $$, PF*

MONTREAL BREAD COMPANY (MBCo)

Veuillez consulter notre répertoire d'adresses multiples à la page 142.

Peter Morentzos est le maestro montréalais de cette nouvelle adresse de Toronto. L'idée de la Montreal Bread Company (MBCo) consiste en un « menu du marché » qui célèbre l'esprit européen. Dans ces concepts « comptoir », on retrouve la formule complète – du petit-déjeuner au dîner. Levez-vous du bon pied grâce aux pâtisseries et viennoiseries signées MBCo. Terminez une journée de shopping par un bon café exotique et un somptueux dessert. À l'heure du dîner, profitez de l'ambiance détendue. Un menu riche et varié ainsi qu'une carte des vins comportant de bonnes sélections, dont plusieurs servies au verre, ajoutent à l'humeur oisive des clients. MBCo

propose également un service traiteur ainsi qu'un «menu santé» signé Weak Pete. Si votre temps est compté, les plats prêts-à-manger vous faciliteront la vie. – *menu bilingue, service en français,* $$

NICE BISTRO

117 Brock Street North, Whitby
☎ (905) 668-8839
Fermé dimanche et lundi, mardi à samedi pour le déjeuner et le dîner

Belle trouvaille que ce bistro! Il peut sembler inconcevable à un Torontois d'aller aussi loin prendre un bon repas, mais vous verrez qu'on devient très vite un habitué du lieu. C'est sans aucun doute le service qu'on remarque en premier. Bernard Alberigo et Manon Lacroutz sont des propriétaires enjoués et attentifs (lui, c'est le chef et elle, l'hôtesse d'accueil). Manon parle français aux clients anglophones. Une charmante idée. Les clients en profitent pour pratiquer leur français. Dans une ambiance conviviale, on déguste des plats raffinés et délicieux, a priori classiques, mais terminés en beauté par la touche du chef Bernard. Le steak frites, les grenadins de veau et le confit de canard sont particulièrement savoureux. Très appétissantes également, la bouillabaisse et les crevettes à la provençale. Les desserts? Truffes au chocolat maison, tarte Tatin et gâteau à la mousse au chocolat blanc viendront à bout de toutes vos envies sucrées. La carte des vins propose quelques sélections françaises qui accompagneront à merveille vos plats. – *menu bilingue, service en français,* $$$

Hors catégorie !

JOHN & KING
HOT DOG STAND

Au coin de John Street et King Street West, en face du Princess of Wales Theatre
Ouvert presque toute l'année pour le déjeuner et le dîner, et même après 22h
Métro : ST ANDREW

Les merguez sur le pouce s'achètent dans le Theatre District! Vous ne les trouverez pas sur le «menu» de ce kiosque à hot-dogs situé au coin de King Street West et John Street, mais si vous les commandez, on vous les préparera. Le propriétaire se nomme Moïse et il se fera un plaisir de vous servir en français. – *service en français*

POURQUOI PAS

63 Sheppard Avenue West (à l'ouest de Yonge Street) ☎ (416) 226-9071
Lundi à vendredi pour le déjeuner et lundi à dimanche pour le dîner
Métro : SHEPPARD
www.toronto.com/pourquoipas

Pourquoi pas est situé dans une maison sur Sheppard Avenue, un peu à l'ouest de Yonge Street. Le décor a plutôt l'allure du salon d'une grand-tante que celle d'un restaurant. Le propriétaire d'origine égyptienne, Sherif Elkei, n'a pas bougé depuis 1975. Au menu, on vous propose des plats simples, intéressants et à des prix très raisonnables. L'ambiance vous met à l'aise, le personnel fait attention à vous et les plats sont savoureusement mijotés. Au palmarès

Les déjeuners qui valent vraiment le détour !

ARLEQUIN Si vous êtes à la recherche d'un endroit à l'atmosphère un peu plus intime pour vos déjeuners d'affaires, Arlequin est l'endroit qu'il vous faut.

BISTRO 1603 Voici une adresse située dans le grand Toronto qui sert un bon déjeuner à la française.

BISTRO MATISSE Encore une autre adresse du grand Toronto où l'on sert un bon déjeuner à la française. Et les prix défient toute concurrence.

BODEGA Parlez donc au propriétaire de son service traiteur. C'est une excellente façon de vous offrir un délicieux déjeuner d'affaires sans même quitter la salle de réunion. Avouez que ce serait une façon assez astucieuse d'impressionner vos clients.

BRASSERIE ROYAN Les habitants de l'ouest de Toronto apprécieront le bon déjeuner à la française que propose cette charmante enseigne d'Oakville.

HOLT'S CAFÉ Des tartines de pain Poîlane pour le déjeuner, on n'y résiste pas. Et ça, Holt's Café l'a bien compris !

LE CONTINENTAL Si vous êtes amateur de viande et que la perspective de terminer votre repas avec plus de 35 fromages au choix vous attire, optez pour un déjeuner au Continental. Qui a dit que le restaurant de cet hôtel devait être réservé aux touristes ?

MIDI BISTRO Ce charmant petit bistro français à l'ambiance agréable à l'heure du déjeuner sert, entre autres, les professionnels des secteurs académiques et médicaux du quartier de University Avenue et St. Patrick Street.

PROVENCE DÉLICES Et si vous alliez déjeuner dans l'un des restaurants les plus charmants de Toronto ? Faites votre réservation dès maintenant.

---

des plats convoités par les habitués, on trouve les merguez, le cassoulet, le foie de veau à la bordelaise, les médaillons de porc au calvados, l'agneau à la marocaine, le canard à l'orange, les ris de veau et le filet mignon sauce béarnaise. Les plats de viande sont très bien préparés. Ces viandes fondent dans la bouche tant elles sont tendres. Crème caramel, saint-honoré et crêpes Suzette font partie de la courte liste des desserts. La carte des vins référence quelques vins français. – *menu bilingue, service en français, $$, PF*

QUARTIER

2112 Yonge Street (entre Davisville Avenue et Eglinton Avenue) ☎ (416) 545-0505
Lundi à vendredi pour le déjeuner et lundi à dimanche pour le dîner

Métro : DAVISVILLE OU EGLINTON

Quartier est un bistro typique de quartier qui associe les classiques de la cuisine française à d'autres courants gastronomiques internationaux. Ce restaurant est un endroit parfait pour un dîner simple et délicieux, à prix modéré et dans une ambiance détendue. Les spécialités du menu comprennent un civet de lapin, un confit de canard, un gigot d'agneau servi avec des lentilles du Puy et un poulet de Cornouailles

accompagné de purée. Quartier maîtrise aussi la préparation des plats de poisson. Oh ! Et il va sans dire que le steak frites fait également partie des spécialités de la maison. Si vous êtes plutôt d'un naturel patient, nous vous recommandons le velouté au chocolat en dessert (20 minutes d'attente quand même !). Les profiteroles servies avec une sauce au chocolat et l'amandine au citron sur coulis sont d'autres choix tout aussi délicieux. La sélection des vins est assez française, surtout dans la catégorie des vins rouges. – *service en français, $$*

RESTAURANT JULES

147 Spadina Avenue (au sud de Queen Street West ☎ (416) 348-8886

Lundi à vendredi 11h30 – 21h, samedi 12h – 17 h, fermé dimanche, fermé samedi en juillet et en août

Métro : SPADINA + le tram; OSGOODE + le tram

Le chef Éric Strippoli et son épouse Mahasti Eslahjou vous accueillent chez Jules avec une bonne cuisine française à un prix vraiment abordable. En bon bistro français, Jules vous propose une liste impressionnante de classiques simples et succulents : soupe gratinée à l'oignon, quiches, ratatouille et bavette. Le hamburger signé Jules est tout simplement renversant. Commandez aussi l'assiette de thon frais grillé, servi avec frites et ratatouille. Tout simplement délicieux ! La mayonnaise et les croûtons sont même faits maison. Les desserts ne vous décevront pas non plus. Au menu : tarte Tatin, crème brûlée et crêpes. – *service en français, $$*

SAUVIGNON BISTRO

1862 Queen Street East (à l'ouest de Woodbrige Avenue) ☎ (416) 686-1998

Lundi à dimanche pour le dîner

Métro : QUEEN + le tram

Accueillants et décontractés, les propriétaires Stéphane Poquet et Grégoire Godin savent recevoir. Le bistro est composé de trois pièces, trois décors distincts. Ce mélange d'influences se retrouve aussi dans le menu. L'endroit se démarque par sa cuisine française à tendance « fusion », dans laquelle le mariage des ingrédients de différentes origines est particulièrement réussi. Cela dit, c'est avec un plat bien français que Sauvignon régale le plus ses visiteurs : le steak Angus, servi avec une sauce moutarde *Pommery* et accompagné de frites de pommes de terre sucrées, restera gravé dans notre mémoire. Attention, la portion généreuse de ce plat satisfera les faims de loup ! La carte des vins comprend quelques sélections françaises, celle des champagnes propose de grands crus. En dessert, nous avons entendu dire que c'est la tarte au citron qui a le plus de popularité. – *$$*

bistros et restos

repas gastronomiques

AUBERGE DU POMMIER

4150 Yonge Street (au nord de York Mills Road) ☎ (416) 222-2220

Lundi à vendredi pour le déjeuner, lundi à samedi pour le dîner, fermé dimanche

Métro : YORK MILLS

www.aubergedupommier.com

Année après année, l'Auberge du Pommier se voit attribuer le prix d'excellence, décerné par *Where Magazine*, du « Most Memorable Meal Award ». De façon générale, ce restaurant figure parmi les dix meilleurs de la ville. Les prix sont en conséquence plus élevés que la moyenne. Dans cette maisonnette ressemblant à une auberge de campagne française, on propose une cuisine raffinée mélangeant les influences françaises et méditerranéennes aux tendances « nouvelle cuisine ». Pour terminer votre repas, choisissez parmi des desserts à la fois artistiques et savoureux, ou un très bon café alcoolisé. Il faudra aussi vous attarder sur la carte des vins. Le service est vraiment hors pair. Pas de fausse note dans cette Auberge du Pommier, que ce soit au niveau du service, des plats exceptionnels ou du décor particulièrement invitant. Nous vous recommandons d'aller dans ce restaurant, ne serait-ce qu'une fois par an. Vous ne serez jamais déçu de le découvrir ou de le re-découvrir. – *service en français*, $$$$

BIFF'S

4 Front Street East (à l'est de Yonge Street) ☎ (416) 860-0086

Lundi à vendredi pour le déjeuner et lundi à samedi pour le dîner, fermé dimanche

Métro : UNION

www.biffsrestaurant.com

Le décor vous emporte dans un petit restaurant français typique à l'atmosphère dynamique. Biff's, bien situé pour les dîners qui précèdent une soirée au théâtre, propose un menu d'un grand classicisme. Profitez-en, car il est rare de trouver ailleurs certains bons plats de la gastronomie française, comme les cuisses de grenouilles, le chateaubriand, le canard aux cerises, le boudin blanc en choucroute et le steak tartare. Au menu figurent aussi deux copieuses assiettes de fruits de mer et une autre d'huîtres. Biff's est également le seul restaurant français à notre connaissance qui propose une fondue au fromage. La carte des vins impressionne par sa sélection de grands vins français. Toutes ces merveilles gastronomiques s'étendront jusqu'au dessert. Enfin, c'est également le service très soigné de ce restaurant qui vous donnera envie d'y retourner souvent. – *service en français*, $$$, PF

BISTRO 990

990 Bay Street (à l'ouest de Yonge Street) ☎ (416) 921-9990

Lundi à vendredi pour le déjeuner, lundi à dimanche pour le dîner

Métro : WELLESLEY

Bistro 990 possède un répertoire gastronomique classique de la cuisine française. Les ingrédients, la présentation et la préparation des plats reflètent tous la grande qualité ambiante. L'addition n'est pas mince chez Bistro 990, mais vous aurez peut-être la chance d'y voir des célébrités, notamment pendant

le Festival international du film de Toronto. Si vous avez envie de vous faire plaisir et que les prix ne vous arrêtent pas, vous pourrez vous régaler avec les spécialités de la maison suivantes : saumon grillé parfumé au Grand Marnier, filet de thon à l'orientale, steak frites sauce au roquefort et filet mignon au stilton et porto. La carte des vins de Bistro 990 est impressionnante. La cave renferme environ 150 variétés de bouteilles, dont la moitié est française. Parmi les vins français, 30 peuvent être consommés au verre. *– menu bilingue, $$$$*

BISTRO 1603

1603 Clarkson Road, Mississauga
☎ (905) 822-5262

Mercredi à vendredi pour le déjeuner, lundi à samedi pour le dîner, fermé dimanche
www.bistro1603.com

Ce restaurant de Mississauga marie judicieusement la tradition des plats français aux ressources locales en matière d'ingrédients, et crée de ce fait une expérience gastronomique surprenante. Bistro 1603 propose les spécialités suivantes : une bouillabaisse à tendance asiatique, un trio de poitrines de canard, du foie gras et du confit, un foie de veau et un steak frites maison. Il ne faut pas oublier les desserts. La crème brûlée et la mousse au chocolat et à la framboise accompagnée d'une boule de crème glacée au chocolat *Lindt* sont particulièrement savoureuses. Le menu impressionne déjà, mais c'est la carte des vins qui retient encore plus l'attention chez Bistro 1603. Ce restaurant a obtenu trois prix «Wine Spectator

Awards of Excellence» en 2002, 2003 et 2004. Avec plus de 250 bouteilles en cave, vous pouvez comprendre pourquoi. *– service en français, $$$*

BODEGA

30 Baldwin Street (à l'ouest de McCaul Street) ☎ (416) 977-1287

Lundi à dimanche pour le déjeuner et le dîner

Métro : ST PATRICK

www.bodegarestaurant.com

Le nouveau propriétaire, le nouveau décor et la nouvelle ambiance n'ont rien changé à l'essence même de ce restaurant. Le «coup de neuf» a tout simplement amené une clientèle plus jeune qui sait apprécier les charmes d'un plat de cuisine française préparé par une main experte. Eh oui, chez Bodega on peut toujours s'attendre à manger de très bonnes spécialités françaises : bouillabaisse, terrine de foie gras, rognons et pétoncles servis dans une sauce aux beurre et pinot noir, assiette de confit de canard et caille, truite servie avec des lentilles et filet mignon. Bodega est le seul restaurant de cuisine française à proposer un forfait vin pour accompagner le menu à prix fixe du déjeuner et du dîner. Un verre de vin accompagne gracieusement chaque plat ! Ne ratez pas les desserts dont la description suffit à mettre sérieusement l'eau à la bouche. Signalons notamment la crème brûlée, les profiteroles avec des figues accompagnées de glace au porto et de sauce tiède au chocolat et la mousse au chocolat blanc avec du Grand Marnier, servie avec un trio de sauces. *– $$$, PF*

bistros et restos

Brunch

Quoi de plus tentant que de traîner au lit un samedi ou un dimanche matin avant d'aller retrouver des amis pour un brunch ? D'accord, le brunch n'est pas vraiment une institution française, ce qui explique sans doute pourquoi peu de restaurants proposent un autre menu que celui de la semaine à cette occasion. Malgré tout, les restaurants français suivants se sont adaptés à la demande locale et ont créé des menus pour les « lève-tard » du week-end.

BLOOR STREET DINER Le dimanche, au menu du brunch, on vous propose de succulentes suggestions.

BODEGA Quel brunch ! Bodega offre un menu succinct, mais très alléchant. Au rendez-vous : pain perdu, œufs « Bénédicte » (œufs pochés servis sur muffins anglais avec sauce hollandaise) et omelette au saumon fumé. Si ces plats ne vous satisfont pas, vous pourrez choisir un plat dans le menu du déjeuner de la semaine.

BONJOUR BRIOCHE Le brunch est servi le samedi et le dimanche. Délicieuses quiches, omelettes et autres plats du jour viennent compléter la sélection de brioches et pâtisseries. Les plats du jour sont inscrits sur une grande ardoise, mais vous pouvez aussi commander des plats au menu du déjeuner. Avis aux natures impatientes : la popularité du brunch de Bonjour Brioche peut occasionner de longues files d'attente.

JACQUES BISTRO DU PARC On ne sert de brunch que le samedi chez Jacques Bistro. Le menu est simple mais savoureux, avec différentes omelettes, des quiches et des salades.

LA CIGOGNE Les habitants du quartier profitent d'un bon brunch à la française à deux pas de chez eux. À La Cigogne, ils peuvent savourer des quiches aux parfums variés, des crêpes fourrées, des croque-madame et des omelettes. La Cigogne propose des crêpes en dessert ! N'oubliez surtout pas que la tarte flambée n'est servie que le week-end. Profitez-en lors de votre brunch.

LA PALETTE Il est préférable d'arriver tôt, car ce petit restaurant de Kensington se remplit vite pour le brunch. L'attraction principale, ce sont les crêpes bien sûr ! Assez rare à Toronto, La Palette propose plusieurs crêpes fourrées ainsi que des omelettes, une salade basque ou niçoise et un steak frites œuf à cheval.

LE SÉLECT BISTRO Il est ouvert le samedi et le dimanche pour le brunch et vous accueille avec les incontournables de ce repas de fin de matinée : omelettes, œufs « Bénédicte », pain perdu (*French toast* en anglais), œufs brouillés et saucisses, crêpe à la banane avec sirop d'érable.

PROVENCE DÉLICES Le menu du brunch de Provence Délices vous tend les bras le samedi et le dimanche. Le prix de ce menu incluant salade, œufs et crème brûlée est raisonnable. Des frites parfaitement cuites et bien assaisonnées accompagnent tous les plats qui figurent sur le menu du brunch.

BOUCHON

38 Wellington Street East (à l'ouest de Church Street) ☎ (416) 862-2675

Fermé lundi, mardi à vendredi pour le déjeuner, mardi à samedi pour le dîner, fermé dimanche

Métro : KING OU UNION

www.bouchon.ca

Jean-Pierre Challet n'est peut-être plus le chef chez Bouchon, mais la qualité des plats reste indéniable. Le nouveau chef est tout aussi talentueux. Les plats proposés sont bien français, mais ils sont aussi exécutés avec un doigté expert et moderne – poutine de merguez et fromage de chèvre (avec des frites allumettes), steak tartare et frites, poutine de foie gras et fromage de chèvre arrosé d'une sauce bordelaise et côtelettes de porc servies avec une purée agrémentée de truffes. Vous remarquerez, à cette liste, que le chef, chez Bouchon, n'hésite pas à s'inspirer des cuisines de toute la francophonie. Pour déguster rapidement un repas avant une soirée au théâtre, il y a le « menu théâtre ». La carte des vins (à tendance plutôt française) accompagne harmonieusement les plats du restaurant. Quant aux desserts, leur liste est étourdissante. Les immanquables sont la tarte au citron, le gâteau au chocolat et la crème brûlée. – $$, PF

CAFE BRUSSELS

124 Danforth Avenue (à l'est de Broadview Avenue) ☎ (416) 465-7363

Fermé lundi, mardi à dimanche pour le dîner

Métro : BROADVIEW

Cafe Brussels est sans aucun doute un des secrets les mieux gardés de Toronto. Cafe Brussels vous reçoit dans un décor Art déco impressionnant. Le menu est axé sur la viande – agneau, steak frites, filet mignon, bœuf bourguignon. Et bien sûr, vous découvrirez chez Cafe Brussels un menu de 30 variétés de moules frites ! Pour couronner le tout, la portion de moules chez Cafe Brussels équivaut à 1 kg, ce à quoi l'on n'est pas habitué de ce côté-ci de l'Atlantique. La carte des vins est une autre très agréable surprise. En fait, cette dernière fut sélectionnée pendant sept années consécutives parmi la célèbre liste des meilleurs vins « Top restaurant wine list Award of Excellence » du magazine *Wine Spectator*. Enfin, le service irréprochable de Cafe Brussels en fait dans l'ensemble une très bonne expérience gastronomique. – *menu bilingue, service en français*, $$$

CÉLESTIN

623 Mount Pleasant Road ☎ (416) 544-9035

Fermé dimanche et lundi, mardi à samedi pour le dîner

Métro : EGLINTON + le bus

www.celestin.ca

Le chef Pascal Ribreau a peut-être instauré une nouvelle mode en ouvrant son nouveau restaurant dans l'immeuble d'une ancienne banque sur Mount Pleasant Road. Il y prépare une cuisine traditionnelle française, grâce à des ingrédients d'une qualité indiscutable et une créativité culinaire débordante. Dans ce restaurant, les palets les plus fins se régaleront des entrées, des plats principaux et des desserts. Pascal

Ribreau est le seul chef de cuisine française à proposer quatre menus à prix fixe (de 65 à 80 CAD par personne). La carte comme les menus à prix fixe changent régulièrement et s'adaptent merveilleusement aux saisons. Le chef collabore avec son frère Martial pour nous combler au moment du dessert. Célestin met à votre disposition une carte des vins tellement détaillée qu'elle compte une vingtaine de pages !

– service en français, **$$$$**, *PF*

DIDIER

1496 Yonge Street (au nord de St. Clair Avenue) ☎ 416 925-8588

Fermé dimanche et lundi, mardi à vendredi pour le déjeuner, mardi à samedi pour le dîner

Métro : ST CLAIR

Après avoir géré les cuisines les plus réputées de la ville et après une longue parenthèse qui a privé le public de ses délicieux mets, le chef Didier Leroy ouvre enfin sa propre enseigne. Pendant les semaines qui ont suivi l'ouverture, il fallait jouer des coudes pour ne serait-ce qu'entrapercevoir le décor de cet établissement. Les Torontois bien informés avaient envahi l'endroit. Le chef Leroy propose un menu bien étudié de plats français rustiques et savoureux. Des mets si bien assaisonnés que vous ne trouverez ni sel, ni poivre sur votre table. Voilà la signature d'un chef à la confiance absolue en son habileté (et en celle de son sous-chef Philippe Cœurdassier). Didier Leroy propose un menu de dégustation à prix fixe. Pour 75 CAD, embarquez-vous dans cette véritable aventure culinaire. Des vins pour tous les goûts et tous les budgets

Le saviez-vous ?

Contrairement à ce qu'on pourrait croire, la « cuisine bourgeoise » n'appartient pas qu'au passé. Le chef Didier Leroy (chef et propriétaire du restaurant Didier) et son autre sous-chef, Frédéric Hoffman, se font un plaisir de préparer, chez vous, votre repas du dimanche. En plus du spectacle culinaire privé et du repas inoubliable, le chef s'occupe aussi des emplettes pour le repas. Il ne vous reste qu'à recevoir vos convives. Vivement dimanche !

compléteront votre repas. Côté desserts, le gâteau préparé avec du chocolat chaud *Valhrona*, la tarte au citron ainsi que le soufflé au Grand Marnier vous séduiront, c'est sûr. *– service en français,* **$$$**, *PF*

GAMELLE

468 College Street (à l'ouest de Bathurst Street) ☎ (416) 923-6254

Mardi à vendredi pour le déjeuner, lundi à samedi pour le dîner, fermé dimanche

Métro : QUEEN'S PARK + le tram; BATHURST + le tram

www.gamelle.com

Si Gamelle ressemble à un bistro à cause de sa petite taille, il n'en reste pas moins un restaurant. Le chef Sean Moore n'est pas français, mais sa cuisine subtile et élaborée pourrait le laisser penser. Dans une ambiance décontractée chic, Gamelle vous propose des plats d'une grande variété tels que du faisan, du canard fumé, du magret de canard, des escargots, un

millefeuille de légumes, un steak au brandy ou encore du gigot d'agneau québécois. Les poissons sont très bien apprêtés et délicieusement assaisonnés. Le patron, Jean-Pierre Centeno, vient du Sud-Ouest de la France, alors bien sûr, il y a du foie gras au menu! La carte des vins internationale compte plusieurs crus français. Notons que tous les vins ont été méticuleusement choisis par le patron qui sait dénicher les perles rares. N'oubliez pas de penser au dessert! Nous vous recommandons la tarte au citron, la crème brûlée et le gâteau au chocolat (considéré par les francophiles comme l'un des meilleurs de Toronto). Un seul repas chez Gamelle fera de vous un habitué!
– menu bilingue, $$$

LE CONTINENTAL

900 York Mills Road (à l'intérieur de l'hôtel The Westin Prince) ☎ (416) 444-2511

Lundi à dimanche pour le déjeuner et le dîner

Métro : YORK MILLS + le bus

Aux inconditionnels des plaisirs fromagers, le chef Hans Herzig propose plus d'une trentaine de fromages, dont les trois quarts sont français (du jamais vu à Toronto!). Une sélection renversante de fromages, du bon pain fait maison et une carte des vins d'une dizaine de pages : tous les éléments d'un repas réussi sont réunis. Avis aux amateurs de gibier également. Les viandes sont à l'honneur, et le filet mignon ainsi que l'agneau sont vraiment succulents. Le Continental fait parti des rares restaurants de Toronto à servir du chateaubriand. Un comptoir vitré dévoile

plusieurs tentations sucrées pour le dessert. Laissez-vous aller, les demi-portions vous permettent de goûter plusieurs desserts. L'excellente réputation du chef Herzig se confirme : il n'utilise que des ingrédients de très haute qualité, et sa personnalité très exigeante donne des résultats exceptionnels! Le service ? Il est tout simplement impeccable. *– service en français, $$$, PF*

LE MONTMARTRE

911 Sheppard Avenue West (à l'est de Allen Road) ☎ (416) 630-3804

Lundi à vendredi pour le déjeuner, lundi à samedi pour le dîner, fermé dimanche

Métro : DOWNSVIEW

www.toronto.com/lemontmartre

Si vous croyiez que tous les bons restos français se trouvaient au centre-ville, détrompez-vous. Depuis 1991, Le Montmartre accueille chaleureusement une clientèle régulière à l'affût de bons plats préparés avec soin. Ici, les viandes et les abats sont à l'honneur, avec notamment quelques classiques de la cuisine française tels que les cuisses de grenouilles, le canard à l'orange et les escargots à la bourguignonne. N'oubliez surtout pas de consulter le menu qui cache aussi de très bonnes surprises. La carte des vins ne déçoit pas non plus, que ce soit côté France ou côté international. Pour clore un savoureux repas, laissez-vous séduire par les profiteroles fourrées à la crème pâtissière ou à la crème glacée. Le Montmartre vaut sans conteste le détour. *– menu bilingue, service en français, $$$, PF*

LE TROU NORMAND

90 Yorkville Avenue (à l'ouest de
Bay Street) ☎ (416) 967-5956
Lundi à samedi pour le déjeuner et le
dîner, fermé dimanche

Métro : BAY

Dans le quartier de Yorkville, ce restaurant sert une cuisine française authentique. Plusieurs plats sont d'inspiration normande, servis avec des pommes, de la crème ou des fruits de mer. Au palmarès des autres plats du terroir : médaillons de veau à la normande et assiette de coquilles Saint-Jacques, crevettes et homard servis avec une sauce au Grand Marnier. Le Trou Normand propose aussi plusieurs plats de foie gras, sans que les prix flambent pour autant. La liste des vins est longue et bien française, et elle convient à tous les budgets – de 20 à 750 dollars ! Côté dessert, pour ne pas faire dans l'original, mais dans la valeur sûre, nous vous conseillons de commander la crème brûlée. – *menu bilingue, $$$, PF*

MARCEL'S BISTRO

315 King Street West (au coin de John
Street) ☎ (416) 591-8600
Fermé dimanche et lundi, mardi à samedi
pour le déjeuner et le dîner

Métro : ST ANDREW

www.marcels.com

Depuis 1984, Marcel's Bistro vous invite, dans une ambiance feutrée, à choisir parmi un menu raffiné des plats servis de façon impeccable. Moules « Poulette », terrine de faisan, salade d'épinards aux pleurotes, pommes grillées et roquefort ou encore steak frites, noisettes d'agneau servies avec une mousseline de pommes de terre au pistou, filet de bœuf et son jus au cognac, servi avec un gratin auvergnat, sont parmi les plats que vous pourrez déguster sur place. Tous les mois, Marcel's Bistro célèbre la gastronomie d'une région de France. Pour le dessert, les classiques sont à l'honneur : crème brûlée, profiteroles, gâteau à la mousse au chocolat noir et tarte au citron, pour ne citer que ceux-là. La carte des vins illustre l'excellence des vins français et n'oublie pas les apéritifs non plus (kir, pineau, pastis, etc.). – *menu bilingue, service en français, $$, PF*

PASTIS EXPRESS

1158 Yonge Street (au nord de Roxborough
Street) ☎ (416) 928-2212
Fermé dimanche et lundi, mardi à samedi
pour le dîner

Métro : SUMMERHILL

Tantôt bistro, tantôt resto, toujours excellent. Pastis, situé dans le quartier chic de Rosedale, sert des plats d'une simplicité parfaite. En 2004, le propriétaire George Gurnon a opté pour un menu qui fait davantage dans la simplicité et qui est nettement moins cher. On y retrouve toujours du foie gras, des moules frites, un steak frites et une version plus raffinée du « fish and chips » anglais. Heureusement, la carte des desserts permet toujours de déguster l'excellente crème brûlée tant prisée des habitués. L'extraordinaire assiette gourmande reste, elle aussi, au rendez-vous. Si vous vous en sentez l'appétit, essayez cette assiette où la fameuse crème brûlée maison côtoie une pointe de gâteau au chocolat noir, une com-

pote de framboises et une fine tuile. Hum, tout simplement délicieux! La liste des vins n'est pas très longue, mais les bouteilles ont été judicieusement choisies. – *service en français, $$*

PROVENCE DÉLICES

12 Amelia Street (au coin de Parliament Street, près de Wellesley Street)
☎ (416) 924-9901

Lundi à dimanche pour le déjeuner et le dîner

Métro : COLLEGE + le tram;
CASTLE FRANK + le bus

www.provencerestaurant.com

Provence Délices est le restaurant le plus charmant de Toronto. Situé dans le vieux quartier de Cabbagetown, au cœur d'une résidence reconvertie en restaurant, le menu de Provence Délices est à la fois simple, classique et sophistiqué. Depuis mars 2004, le chef et propriétaire, Élie Benchitrit, a repris les rênes de la cuisine et propose désormais un menu moins cher. Les plats n'en sont pas moins soignés du tout. Le chef rehausse la saveur de chaque assiette d'une pointe de parfums riches et complexes. Une nouvelle formule gagnante. Les habitués n'hésitent pas à goûter aux délices du chef Benchitrit plusieurs fois par mois. La cerise sur le gâteau, c'est, bien sûr, le dessert : une crème brûlée au Grand Marnier. La carte des vins est très française et le choix remarquable. Le restaurant a reçu le «Wine Spectator Award of Excellence» tous les ans depuis 1999. Le personnel qui vous sert est attentif et compétent. Consultez le site Internet pour un aperçu du menu. – *service en français, menu bilingue, $$*

Pas envie de dessert ?

Certains gourmands préfèrent terminer leur repas sur une note salée. La plupart des restaurants français de Toronto proposent une belle assiette de fromages français, québécois et suisses. Il ne tient qu'à vous de découvrir ou de retrouver vos fromages préférés. Une bonne bouteille de vin et un bon pain maison accompagneront le tout à merveille.

THE FIFTH

(le restaurant est situé au 5ᵉ étage)
225 Richmond Street West (au coin de Duncan Street) ☎ (416) 979-3005

Jeudi à samedi pour le dîner

Métro : OSGOODE

www.easyandthefifth.com

The Fifth est l'endroit idéal pour sortir «en grande pompe». Le nouveau menu de cinq plats que prépare le chef Jean-Pierre Challet impressionne et régale à la fois. Il faudra débourser un peu plus de 250 CAD à deux, mais si le prix ne vous arrête pas, vous serez comblé. La carte change tous les mois et ne déçoit jamais. Parmi les sélections irrésistibles que nous avons essayées, il y a le magret de canard et son millefeuille de confit, les médaillons de wapiti accompagnés de mousse de foie gras, le filet de bœuf et ses «crosmequis» de camembert et truffes. Les desserts ravissent tout autant les papilles avec une dégustation de chocolat autour de six variations, un millefeuille et un pudding de brioche.

La cave à vins internationale vous permettra de choisir le vin français (ou pas) idéal pour accompagner votre repas. Vous irez également chez The Fifth pour le décor, l'ambiance feutrée et le service irréprochable. L'été, l'atmosphère de la terrasse est magique. — *service en français, menu bilingue, $$$$, PF*

à la menthe, le tableau est complet. Vers 21h, toute la salle s'arrête : c'est le début du spectacle — des jeunes femmes fort séduisantes dansent au son de rythmes arabes. — *$$, PF*

THE SULTAN'S TENT

49 Front Street East (à l'ouest de Church Street) ☎ (416) 961-0601

Lundi à dimanche pour le dîner

Métro : UNION

www.thesultanstent.com

Comment être dépaysé à Toronto ? Pourquoi pas en réservant une table au restaurant The Sultan's Tent qui vous garantira une expérience inoubliable ? Le restaurant est situé à l'arrière du Café Moroc (mentionné dans la section précédente). Tout comme le Café, le décor de The Sultan's Tent est 100 % marocain. La différence ici, c'est que l'on peut savourer des plats plus complexes dans un décor encore plus envoûtant. Tout a été conçu pour ravir tant le palet que les autres sens. D'immenses divans vous permettent de vous mettre à l'aise pour décompresser sous des tentes de tissus aux couleurs chatoyantes. La lumière est tamisée et la musique marocaine fait vibrer. Le menu concourt également très bien à cette aventure magique qui vous emporte au cœur du Maroc. Nous sommes certains que vous serez séduit par les quatre plats proposés par The Sultan's Tent. De l'entrée au dessert, en passant par la théière marocaine de thé

en cuisine avec la francophonie

écoles de cuisine

Maintenant que vous disposez de toutes les adresses pour acheter les ingrédients de vos plats de la francophonie préférés, il est temps de mettre la main à la pâte et de peaufiner vos talents de cuisinier grâce aux écoles suivantes.

écoles de cuisine

ACADEMY OF ARTISANS

490 Eglinton Avenue West (à l'ouest d'Avenue Road) ☎ (416) 322-9997

Cours : en soirée, pas de cours le week-end

Métro : EGLINTON + le bus

www.academyofartisans.com

Vous pourrez parfaire votre éducation en matière de cuisine française ou marocaine dans cette école de Forest Hill.

CALPHALON CULINARY CENTER

425 King Street West (au coin de Spadina Avenue) ☎ (416) 847-2212

Cours : en soirée et le samedi

Métro : ST ANDREW

www.calphalonculinarycenter.com

On vous donnera ici des cours de base en cuisine, idéals pour les débutants ou pour perfectionner les connaissances que vous aviez déjà. Une fois que vous aurez maîtrisé les bases, vous pourrez vous lancer dans l'apprentissage des mystères de la cuisine française. Ensuite, on vous proposera un cours sur l'art de marier le vin et les plats avec finesse. Nous avons aussi remarqué que Calphalon animait un cours sur le mariage des bières belges avec les plats de la même nationalité, ainsi qu'un cours pour apprendre à préparer de merveilleuses crêpes.

COOK GOURMET

1204 Clarkson Road, Mississauga (près de QEW et Highway 10) ☎ (905) 403-0059

Cours : en soirée

www.cookgourmet.ca

Voici une école située à Mississauga qui vous permettra d'élargir vos connaissances en cuisine française.

DISH COOKING STUDIO

390 Dupont Street ☎ (416) 920-5559

Cours : en soirée et le samedi

Métro : DUPONT

www.dishcookingstudio.com

Dish Cooking Studio est une école sympathique où l'on peut appendre les rudiments de la cuisine française ou marocaine.

GEORGE BROWN COLLEGE

300 Adelaide Street East ☎ (416) 415-5000

Cours : en soirée et le weekend

Métro : KING + le tram

www.gbrownc.on.ca

George Brown College propose plusieurs cours de cuisine française : cuisine classique, cuisine contemporaine, crêpes et cuisine du terroir. La série « *Wine and Dine at our Table* » vous permettra de participer à une soirée d'apprentissage. Une fois la leçon terminée, c'est la dégustation qui commence ! Vous trouverez plus de détails sur ces cours sur le site, sous la rubrique « *Hospitality & Tourism* ».

GREAT COOKS

Veuillez consulter notre répertoire d'adresses multiples à la page 142.

www.greatcooks.ca

Les propriétaires de cette école sont elles-mêmes des chefs. Esther Benaim et Maggie McKeown font appel aux plus grands noms de la cuisine franco-

phone de Toronto pour vous emmener dans des aventures culinaires françaises et marocaines. Côté Maroc, c'est le chef Bouchra Sidali qui est aux fourneaux. Tandis que le chef Jean-Pierre Challet vient représenter l'art culinaire français, parfois même en français. C'est une première à Toronto ! Enfin, signalons que Great Cooks est l'une des premières écoles de cuisine privées à avoir ouvert ses portes à Toronto. En 2004, elle a reçu le prix du « Toronto Star Eaters » de la meilleure école de cuisine de Toronto. – *cours de cuisine française dispensé en français*

J.S. BONBONS

329 St. George Street (au coin de Dupont Street), au 2ᵉ étage
☎ (416) 920-0274
Cours : en soirée
Métro : DUPONT
www.jsbonbons.com

Si vous avez déjà lu la section des chocolats de ce guide, vous saurez que nous adorons ceux du chef pâtissier Jenn Stone. D'où notre joie d'apprendre qu'il est possible de prendre des cours avec elle sur l'art de confectionner des chocolats. Tout se passe dans une école de cuisine située juste au-dessus de la boutique. La récompense reste bien entendu la dégustation…

LCBO

Partout en ville ☎ 1 800 668-5226
Cours : en soirée
www.lcbo.com

Vous pourrez suivre plusieurs cours de dégustation de vins avec la LCBO.

« Vins d'Alsace », « Les bières belges » et « Les blancs de la région de Bourgogne » sont des exemples de cours qu'on propose. Il est également possible de prendre des cours de cuisine française. M. Ektor Stroutzas, directeur des fromageries Alex Farm, donne enfin un cours sur les fromages.

LE CORDON BLEU PARIS

453 Laurier Avenue East, Ottawa
☎ 1 888 289-6302
Cours : en soirée ou le week-end, parfois à la journée
www.lcbottawa.com

Il est vrai que lorsqu'on habite le grand Toronto, il est difficilement envisageable d'aller à Ottawa pour un cours de cuisine le temps d'une soirée. Mais si nous avons mis cette adresse dans le guide, c'est parce que cette école propose des cours d'une journée en semaine et même quelquefois le week-end. Voilà une bonne occasion pour s'évader, apprendre, puis déguster les fruits de son labeur. Ici, la cuisine classique française est à l'honneur. Il y a aussi un cours intéressant sur le mariage du vin et des plats.

LOBLAWS

Partout en ville
Cours : en soirée et quelquefois le samedi

Dans plus d'une vingtaine de magasins Loblaws, il y a une école de cuisine. Elle est généralement située à l'étage supérieur. On vous y proposera des cours de cuisine sur différents thèmes tels que la préparation de la pâte feuilletée, la cuisine marocaine et la cuisine

écoles de cuisine

française. Vous aurez également la possibilité de participer à une dégustation d'huîtres et à un cours de cuisine française animé par le chef Jean-Pierre Challet.

RICHMOND HILL CULINARY ARTS CENTRE

1550 16th Avenue, Richmond Hill
☎ (905) 508-2665
Cours : en soirée
www.culinaryarts.ca

Dans cette école de Richmond Hill, vous apprendrez l'art de confectionner des chocolats, de préparer des crêpes parfaites ou encore une savoureuse crème brûlée.

STREWN WINERY

1339 Lake Shore Road,
Niagara-on-the-Lake ☎ (905) 468-8304
Cours : le week-end
www.winecountrycooking.com

Vous avez le choix entre les cours du samedi ou les cours du week-end entier pour apprendre les techniques de la cuisine française ou de la dégustation de vins, et même l'art de marier de bons vins à un bon repas. En plus, les cours ont lieu dans l'une des plus belles régions de l'Ontario.

THE COOKWORKS

99 Sudbury Street, bureau #8 (au sud de Queen Street West) ☎ (416) 537-6464
Cours : en soirée
Métro : OSGOODE + le tram
www.thecookworks.com

Les cours de cuisine française, « French Bistro et Brasserie », dispensés dans cette école, vous permettront de peaufiner vos talents de chef !

aventures culturelles

information et
divertissement

Toronto ne sera jamais Paris ni Montréal. Mais il est tout de
même possible d'y avoir accès à un certain nombre de ressources culturelles en français. Journaux, librairies, cinémas,
films, théâtres, stations de radio, opéra, festivals et soirées
francophones permettent de s'informer et se divertir dans la
langue de Molière. Ces événements et ressources culturelles
sont également une très bonne occasion pour les anglophones
de pratiquer leur français ou même de s'initier à la culture
francophone.

information et divertissement

JOURNAUX

L'EXPRESS

www.lexpress.to

L'Express est l'hebdomadaire canadien-français le plus important à Toronto. Vous serez au courant de l'actualité internationale et locale, mais aussi politique, sociale et économique, sans oublier les événements culturels, les offres d'emploi et les petites annonces. *L'Express* est disponible par abonnement et il est en vente à la Maison de la Presse Internationale, chez Champlain et Indigo. Il est disponible gratuitement dans certains lieux stratégiques tels que l'Alliance Française, le collège Glendon ou le Consulat Général de France.

LE MÉTROPOLITAIN

www.lemetropolitain.com

Le Métropolitain se consacre aux événements qui tournent autour de la vie des francophones du grand Toronto. Il est vendu en kiosque. Il est également disponible gratuitement dans les endroits où l'on trouve *L'Express*.

LIVRES, BD ET MAGAZINES

À BON VERRE, BONNE TABLE

Dans les magasins LCBO
☎ 1 800 682-5226
www.lcbo.com/french/fooddrink/index.shtml

Ce magazine sur la gastronomie, les vins et autres boissons alcoolisées est l'un des magazines préférés des francophones et francophiles torontois. Chaque numéro regorge de recettes, de suggestions en vins, bières et spiritueux,

de conseils d'achat sur les derniers « tubes » musicaux et d'astuces bien utiles. Le magazine est distribué gratuitement dans les boutiques LCBO (société des alcools de l'Ontario). Mais faites vite, car il disparaît très rapidement. L'un des grands attraits de ce magazine, hormis le fait qu'il soit rédigé en français, c'est que les recettes qu'on vous y propose ont été créées à partir d'ingrédients disponibles ici. Si vous ne trouvez pas la version française dans le magasin LCBO le plus proche de chez vous, abonnez-vous pour une modique somme et recevez-le à la maison. Pour plus de renseignements, appelez la ligne d'information.

AMAZON.CA

www.amazon.ca

Cette librairie virtuelle a un large catalogue de livres en français. Commander des livres sur le site d'Amazon est presque un jeu d'enfant. Vous serez étonné de voir à quel point Amazon vous présente une multitude de catégories pour trouver le livre français de votre choix.

ARCHAMBAULT.CA

www.archambault.ca

Archambault est un grand nom des produits culturels francophones au Québec. Nous le mentionnons dans notre guide parce que l'on peut aller sur son site pour effectuer ses achats, même si l'on vit à Toronto. Comme pour toute librairie virtuelle, il suffit de choisir et de cliquer pour commander.

information et divertissement

GROUPE INDIGO-CHAPTERS

Différentes adresses dans toute la ville

www.chapters.indigo.ca

Le Groupe Indigo-Chapters comprend les librairies suivantes : Chapters, Coles Books, Indigo et World's Biggest Book Store (20 Edward Street ☎ (416) 977-7009; lundi à samedi 9h – 22h, dimanche 11h – 18h)

Indigo dispose d'une très petite sélection de livres en français, le choix se limitant surtout aux grands classiques. Côté magazines et journaux français, on retrouve les grands noms. Allez également faire un tour sur le site Internet et dans les autres librairies qui appartiennent au Groupe Indigo-Chapters, car vous y trouverez des journaux, des magazines et des livres en français.

LIBRAIRIE CHAMPLAIN

468 Queen Street East (à l'est de Parliament Street) ☎ (416) 364-4345

Lundi à jeudi 9h – 18h, vendredi 9h – 20h, samedi 9h – 17h, fermé dimanche

Métro : QUEEN + le tram

www.librairiechamplain.com

Voici la meilleure source de Toronto en livres français, académiques, littéraires ou autres. On y trouve tout : BD, dictionnaires, livres de poche, nouvelles parutions, jeux éducatifs, grands classiques, romans à l'eau de rose, romans policiers, traductions de romans étrangers en français, etc. Vous pourrez aussi y acheter plusieurs des journaux de langue française de Toronto, du Québec et de France. La librairie est à votre disposition si vous voulez passer des commandes spéciales.

Le saviez-vous ?

Pendant la royauté française du XVIIᵉ siècle, on préférait les grandes cérémonies à l'heure du dîner. Les menus étaient copieux, élaborés et coûteux. Les grands chefs de l'époque préparaient ces repas somptueux. L'un des premiers livres de cuisine à raconter toutes ces folies culinaires est intitulé *Le cuisinier royal et bourgeois* et signé François Massaliot. Ce livre offre un éventail de recettes élitistes préparées dans les cuisines du roi Louis XIV. Plusieurs historiens considèrent que cet ouvrage est à l'origine de la grande cuisine. Un autre ouvrage illustre avec brio la cuisine du terroir d'antan. Il s'agit de *La physiologie du goût*, écrit en 1825 par Anthelme Brillat-Savarin. D'après les historiens, ce livre marque le début de l'art culinaire. Aujourd'hui, nous avons sans doute moins envie de passer des heures aux fourneaux, mais les livres et les magazines de cuisine française restent une excellente source d'inspiration.

MAISON DE LA PRESSE INTERNATIONALE

99 Yorkville Avenue ☎ (416) 928-2328

Dimanche à jeudi 8h30 – 23h, vendredi et samedi 8h30 – 00h

Métro : BAY OU MUSEUM

Copie conforme des magasins montréalais, on retrouve dans cette maison de la presse des magazines et des journaux français et québécois, des guides touristiques et de nombreux livres français en tout genre.

information et divertissement

En 1720, tous les Torontois parlaient français !*

En 1720, on parlait déjà le français au magasin royal de Toronto situé à Baby Point, dans l'ouest de la ville (Pour se repérer aujourd'hui, Baby Point est situé au nord de Bloor Street West et au nord-est du restaurant Old Mills, le long de la rivière Humber). Le magasin royal, construit en 1720 à l'intérieur du fort Toronto (premier fort de Toronto qui protégeait la Nouvelle-France), fut la première installation dans une ville qui n'était encore qu'un lieu de passage. Cet embryon de la civilisation française était l'un des endroits les plus fréquentés de l'époque. On y gardait les biens qui devaient être donnés aux Amérindiens en échange de fourrures. Une fois achetées, les fourrures canadiennes étaient entreposées au magasin royal avant de faire leur long voyage vers la France. Ce point de rencontre, d'échanges et de négociations représentait le cœur même de la francophonie en 1720. Et il n'était pas le seul endroit de la Ville reine où l'on parlait français. À la rivière Rouge, située à l'est (à la frontière de Scarborough), on pratiquait également le français. Cette prédominance du français dura jusqu'en 1763, quand Toronto devint capitale du Haut Canada. La présence francophone se ressent depuis plusieurs siècles à Toronto et dure toujours, pour notre plaisir à tous.

Si vous êtes un passionné de l'histoire des Français et francophones de Toronto, consultez le site de la Société d'histoire de Toronto à www.sht.ca

*La phrase « En 1720, tous les Torontois parlaient français » est une traduction libre de la phrase « Torontonians all spoke French in 1720 » de Donald Jones, chroniqueur historique de Toronto pour le journal *The Star*.

PRESSE INTERNATIONALE
Différentes adresses dans toute la ville

À ne pas confondre avec La Maison de la Presse Internationale. Vous y trouverez plusieurs magazines et journaux français.

QUÉBEC LOISIRS
☎ 1 800 361-2441
www.quebecloisirs.com

Lorsqu'on devient membre de ce club, on bénéficie de 20 à 40 % de remise sur ses achats ! Québec Loisirs est le cousin canadien de France Loisirs. Si vous consultez les deux sites, vous remarquerez qu'ils se ressemblent. La différence pour nous, Torontois, réside dans les frais de transport. Quand on achète de ce côté-ci de l'Atlantique, on économise beaucoup.

RENAUD-BRAY
☎ 1 888 746-2283
www.renaud-bray.com

Voici un autre grand nom montréalais de la librairie qui permet aux Franco-Torontois d'avoir accès à une multitude de livres de diverses catégories grâce au site Internet. Vous n'avez qu'à consulter ce site pour découvrir votre prochain

coup de cœur ! Vous pouvez également passer une commande par téléphone si vous ne vous sentez pas à l'aise à l'idée d'un paiement électronique sur Internet.

Salon du Livre de Toronto

www.salondulivredetoronto.ca

Ce grand salon annuel se tient en octobre au Palais des Congrès (Convention Centre, 255 Front St. West). Vous pourrez y rencontrer des auteurs et éditeurs de la francophonie et participer à des ateliers, séances de signature, débats, etc. Le Salon offre aussi le plus grand choix de livres français en Ontario et c'est donc l'occasion d'acheter des livres difficiles à obtenir autrement.

Taloua

☎ (416) 934-0588

Multicultur-elle ! C'est la vision de *Taloua,* seul magazine féminin et multi-culturel en français à avoir vu le jour à Toronto (2002). *Taloua* signifie « jeune femme » en agni, dialecte parlé en Côte d'Ivoire. En feuilletant *Taloua,* on se sent « femme taloua » jusqu'au bout des ongles : engagée, ouverte sur le monde, libre et artiste ! Ce qu'on aime chez *Taloua,* c'est le graphisme sensible, l'amalgame de cultures, la place faite aux jeunes talents (photographes, graphistes, illustrateurs, etc.), le traitement original des sujets, les journalistes qui sortent des sentiers battus, l'ouverture internationale (Toronto, Montréal, Paris, Douala, etc.). Ce qu'on regrette, c'est que le jeune magazine ne sorte pas plus souvent : deux fois par an. Vous le trouverez à la Maison de la Presse

Internationale, dans la plupart des magasins Chapters ou Indigo, ou encore en vous abonnant (formulaire disponible en ligne sur le site Internet ou par téléphone).

The Beguiling

601 Markham Street (près du magasin Honest Ed) ☎ (416) 533-9168
Lundi à jeudi 11h – 19h, vendredi 11h – 21h, samedi 11h – 19h, dimanche 12h – 18h

www.beguiling.com

Créée en 1987, The Beguiling est sans doute la plus importante librairie de bandes dessinées de la ville. Situé dans une maison cachée par le gigantesque Honest Ed, l'endroit regorge d'albums rares en français. La moitié du rez-de-chaussée est consacrée aux BD françaises, belges et suisses. Vous trouverez aussi bien les dernières nouveautés que les grands classiques. Peter Birkemoe, le jeune patron, hésite à parler en français, mais n'en reste pas moins un expert de la BD francophone. Il va tous les ans au festival de BD d'Angoulême et connaît ses classiques sur le bout des doigts. Bref, The Beguiling est un lieu original où trouver des cadeaux pour les enfants et (surtout) pour les adultes !

Le saviez-vous ?

The Beguiling organise un festival tous les deux ans, au mois de mai. Consultez le site du festival et jetez un coup d'œil au programme de 2004 : www.torontocomics.com.

information et divertissement

THE FILM REFERENCE LIBRARY

2 Carlton Street (au niveau de la mezzanine) ☎ (416) 967-1517

Les horaires d'hiver et d'été se trouvent sur le site Internet

Métro : COLLEGE (sortie Carlton)

libraryservices@torfilmfest.ca
www.filmreferencelibrary.ca

The Film Reference Library vous permet de feuilleter plus de 1 200 livres et une multitude de magazines en français (au passage, vous trouverez, toutes langues confondues, 17 000 livres sur le monde du cinéma). Bien entendu, le thème de prédilection des ces ouvrages et périodiques reste le cinéma. Vous trouverez des livres sur la biographie des pionniers du cinéma, le théâtre, le métier d'acteur, la télévision, l'histoire du film, les techniques cinématographiques, le scénario et bien d'autres sujets encore. Vous pourrez également consulter les magazines sur le monde du cinéma francophone suivants : Trafic, L'Avant-Scène Cinéma, Les Cahiers du Cinéma, Jeune Cinéma et Ciné Bulles pour la France, 24 images pour le Québec. Vous trouverez aussi plusieurs autres magazines en anglais sur les films de France, de Corée, d'Asie, d'Inde, de Suède, d'Amérique latine et d'Europe.

THE HOUSE OF MR. FIGLIO

748 Broadview Avenue (au sud de Danforth Avenue) ☎ (416) 778-9996

Veuillez téléphoner pour connaître les heures d'ouverture.

www.rgalre.com

« The House of Mr. Figlio est une petite maison pour l'imagination et la poésie. »
— SERGE BENNATHAN

M. Bennathan est non seulement le directeur artistique de la troupe de danse « Dance Makers », il écrit et illustre aussi des contes pour enfants en français. Vous trouverez ses joyaux littéraires et créatifs à la galerie d'art.

MUSIQUE

AMAZON.CA

www.amazon.ca

Vous pourrez commander sur ce site les grands « tubes » du moment, mais aussi vos chansons « rétro » préférées.

ARCHAMBAULT MUSIQUE

www.archambault.ca

Archambault Musique vend les grands succès de la musique française, québécoise ou, plus généralement, francophone.

HMV

Différentes adresses dans toute la ville
www.hmv.ca

La plupart des magasins de cette chaîne nationale vendent des CD français. Ils ont une sélection honorable, principalement les grands noms de la chanson française. S'il y a des artistes en particulier qui vous font frémir et que vous n'arrivez pas à trouver leur dernier album dans les bacs, vous pouvez passer une commande spéciale.

LIBRAIRIE CHAMPLAIN

468 Queen Street East (à l'est de Parliament Street) ☎ (416) 364-4345

Lundi à jeudi 9h – 18h, vendredi 9h – 20h, samedi 9h – 17h, fermé dimanche

Métro : QUEEN + le tram

www.librairiechamplain.com

Vous trouverez ici un très bon choix des plus grands « tubes » de la musique française.

Québec Loisirs

☎ 1 800 361-2441

www.quebecloisirs.com

Québec Loisirs répond aux besoins musicaux des francophones grâce à sa sélection d'albums sur Internet.

Renaud-Bray

☎ 1 888 746-2283

www.renaud-bray.com

Voici une autre enseigne québécoise qui vous permet, grâce à son magasin de disques virtuel, d'avoir accès à la musique que vous préférez.

Sam the Record Man

347 Yonge Street (au nord de Dundas Street) ☎ (416) 646-2775

Lundi à jeudi 10h – 21h, vendredi et samedi 10h – 23h, dimanche 10h – 18h

Métro : DUNDAS

Sam the Record Man est le « roi » à Toronto en matière de musique française. Le deuxième étage de ce très grand magasin de la musique cache la plus impressionnante sélection de musiques française et québécoise que nous ayons vue à Toronto. On y découvre les grands succès d'aujourd'hui et d'hier. Si, si, Sam the Record Man passe d'Yves Montand à Patrick Bruel pour ce qui est de la France, et de Gilles Vigneault à Garou, côté Québec. Nous avons également été très surpris par la grande sélection de musiques africaines. En fait, le deuxième étage est une véritable caverne d'Ali Baba qui

renferme des musiques exotiques des quatre coins du monde. Si vous ne trouvez pas certains albums bien précis, vous pouvez toujours les commander.

Films français – Festivals

Cinéfranco – Festival du film français à Toronto

☎ (416) 928-6595

www.cinefranco.com

Une semaine de films... en français ! Le festival a lieu tous les ans pendant la dernière semaine de mars et/ou la première semaine d'avril. Tous les amateurs, très fidèles, voient l'arrivée du festival comme une superbe occasion de satisfaire leur soif de culture francophone. Tous les films présentés sont sous-titrés en anglais, vous pourrez donc partager votre expérience cinéphile avec vos amis qui ne maîtrisent pas (encore) bien le français. Le dévouement et la passion de la directrice et fondatrice de Cinéfranco, Marcelle Lean, nous donnent une raison de plus d'attendre le printemps.

information et divertissement

Toronto International Film Festival – Festival international du film de Toronto

www.e.bell.ca/filmfest

Le week-end de la fête du Travail est marqué par l'arrivée à Toronto des grandes vedettes du cinéma international. Contrairement à Cinéfranco, le Festival international du film de Toronto ne cible pas une culture en particulier. Mais si l'on prend le temps de bien étudier les horaires des films, on peut certainement en trouver plusieurs en français qui pourraient même entrer dans l'histoire.

Cinémas

Carlton

Rue Carlton, juste à l'est de Yonge Street
☎ (416) 598-2309
Métro : COLLEGE

Cumberland

159 Cumberland Street (au coin d'Avenue Road) ☎ (416) 646-0444
Métro : BAY (sortie Cumberland)

Ces deux cinémas ont souvent un film français récent à l'affiche. Surveillez vos journaux pour en savoir plus.

Le saviez-vous ?

Le 7ᵉ art fait bon ménage avec les six autres. L'architecture, la musique, la sculpture, la peinture, la poésie et la danse sont ultimement regroupées au sein du cinéma, car il est le seul à combiner la science à l'art.

Ciné Jeudi – Cinéma ONF de Toronto

150 John Street ☎ (416) 973–3012
Métro : OSGOODE
www.alliance-francaise.ca

Le Consulat Général de France à Toronto, l'Office national du film, Cinéfranco, le Bureau du Québec et l'Alliance Française ont entrepris un projet ambitieux : promouvoir le cinéma francophone à Toronto pendant toute l'année. Pour ce faire, vous bénéficiez de la projection mensuelle (le premier jeudi du mois) d'un des derniers succès du cinéma de la francophonie. Pour obtenir plus d'informations sur les films à venir, consultez le site de l'Alliance Française à Toronto.

Cinémathèque Ontario

Jackman Hall, Art Gallery of Ontario, entrée rue McCaul ☎ (416) 968-FILM (3456), poste 2
Métro : ST PATRICK
www.e.bell.ca/filmfest

La Cinémathèque est une division du Festival international du film de Toronto (Toronto International Film Festival Group) qui propose des rétrospectives et des cycles spéciaux. On y présente souvent les films connus ou, au contraire, moins connus de grands metteurs en scène français : Truffaut, Tati, Malle, Cocteau, Deray, Renoir, Godard, etc. L'été, on peut « s'en mettre plein les mirettes » avec le cinéma français. Autrefois, la Cinémathèque Ontario présentait le cycle « Summer in France, Classics of French Cinema ». La programmation, en tant que telle, n'existe plus, mais une multitude de films français restent accessibles en

juillet et en août. Voilà une bonne occasion de faire découvrir le septième art à la française à vos amis anglophones, car tous les films sont sous-titrés. Bonne séance !

THE FILM REFERENCE LIBRARY

2 Carlton Street (au niveau de la mezzanine) ☎ (416) 967-1517

Les horaires d'hiver et d'été se trouvent sur le site Internet

Métro : COLLEGE (sortie Carlton)

libraryservices@torfilmfest.ca
www.filmreferencelibrary.ca

The Film Reference Library est une autre division du Festival international du film de Toronto (Toronto International Film Festival Group). Cette bibliothèque a pour mission d'offrir aux professionnels, aux académiciens et aux amoureux du cinéma d'importants ouvrages de référence sur le septième art. The Film Reference Library abrite des collections de films canadiens et internationaux. Les 8 000 films (et plus), dont 541 en français (ils sont tous sous-titrés en anglais), de The Film Reference Library nous ont impressionnés. Vous pouvez regarder ces films sur place, grâce à deux salles mises à la disposition du public. The Film Reference Library est même équipée d'appareils permettant de regarder des cassettes vidéo et des DVD européens. Et ça, ça ne se trouve pas à tous les coins de rue à Toronto ! Vous remarquerez que les bibliothécaires et les employés de The Film Reference Library sont d'une aide précieuse à tout cinéphile. N'hésitez surtout pas à faire appel à eux. En devenant membre, vous aurez gratuitement accès à plusieurs autres services.

CASSETTES VIDÉO ET DVD À LOUER

QUEEN VIDEO

Veuillez consulter notre répertoire d'adresses multiples à la page 142.

REVUE VIDEO

207 Danforth Avenue (près de Broadview Avenue) ☎ (416) 778-5776

Lundi à dimanche 11h – 22h

Métro : BROADVIEW

Lundi à dimanche 11h – 23h pour les deux boutiques

SUSPECT VIDEO

Veuillez consulter notre répertoire d'adresses multiples à la page 142.

VERY VIDEO

1375 Yonge Street (au sud de St. Clair Avenue) ☎ (416) 929-8379

Lundi à jeudi 10h30 – 22h, vendredi et samedi 10h30 – 23h, dimanche 11h30 – 22h

Métro : ST CLAIR

Ces magasins indépendants de location de cassettes vidéo proposent un incroyable choix parmi plusieurs centaines de films français et de langue française : dernières nouveautés, films rares, classiques de la Nouvelle Vague, etc. Pour vous donner une idée de la multitude de films français disponibles, voici quelques chiffres : chez Queen Video, vous trouverez plus de 600 films, dont 500 en cassettes et une centaine en DVD. Suspect Video vous propose entre 100 et 200 films en français. Revue Video vous en propose 250 de la francophonie, y compris l'Afrique française et la Tunisie. Very Video vous en propose une bonne trentaine. Ça, c'est du cinéma !

information et divertissement

CASSETTES VIDÉO ET DVD À ACHETER

AMAZON.CA

www.amazon.ca

Le site Internet d'Amazon vous donne accès à une bonne quantité de films français.

ARCHAMBAULT.CA

www.archambault.ca

De Louis de Funès à Vincent Perez en passant par Pierce Brosnan, on les trouve tous sur le site d'Archambault. Reste à opter pour la vidéo ou le DVD.

LIBRAIRIE CHAMPLAIN

468 Queen Street East (à l'est de Parliament Street) ☎ (416) 364-4345

Lundi à jeudi 9h – 18h, vendredi 9h – 20h, samedi 9h – 17h, fermé dimanche

Métro : QUEEN + le tram

www.librairiechamplain.com

La Librairie Champlain vend plusieurs films français en vidéo ou DVD, pour les petits et les grands.

QUÉBEC LOISIRS

☎ 1 800 361-2441

www.quebecloisirs.com

Québec Loisirs vous permet de faire le plein de films français depuis chez vous.

RENAUD-BRAY

☎ 1 888 746-2283

www.renaud-bray.com

En quelques clics, faites acheminer chez vous les grands noms du cinéma de la francophonie.

SAM THE RECORD MAN

347 Yonge Street (au nord de Dundas Street) ☎ (416) 646-2775

Lundi à jeudi 10h – 21h, vendredi et samedi 10h – 23h, dimanche 10h – 18h

Métro : DUNDAS

Sam the Record Man vend une sélection tout à fait honorable de films français en vidéo et DVD. Cependant, si vous cherchez un film en particulier, vous n'avez qu'à le commander.

FILMS À REGARDER CHEZ SOI

TFO

Service de relations avec l'auditoire ☎ (416) 484-2645 et 1 800 463-6886

Lundi à vendredi 9h – 17h

www.tfo.org

La célébration du 7e art bat son plein tous les jours de la semaine à 21h, sur la chaîne de télévision francophone de l'Ontario. TFO vous propose de découvrir des films français, québécois, africains et belges. Vous pourrez aussi découvrir plusieurs films internationaux ayant été sous-titrés en français (mal-

information et divertissement

heureusement, les films français ne sont pas sous-titrés en anglais). Vous pouvez vous procurer le « passeport cinéma » qui vous donnera la description complète des films (date, durée, pays d'origine, année, noms des producteurs et des acteurs, critiques, etc.). Il vous suffit de téléphoner au Service de relations avec l'auditoire pour en obtenir un exemplaire. On se fera un plaisir de vous l'envoyer gratuitement par la poste à votre domicile.

BEAUX-ARTS

LA GALERIE GLENDON

2275 Bayview Avenue ☎ (416) 487-6859

Fermé dimanche et lundi, mardi à vendredi 12h – 15h sauf jeudi 11h – 14h, samedi 13h – 16h

Métro : LAWRENCE + le bus

www.glendon.yorku.ca/gallery

La Galerie Glendon est une galerie publique située sur le campus de l'université de Glendon. Elle est spécialisée dans l'art contemporain et offre un programme d'expositions mensuelles. Sa mission est d'ordre éducatif. La Galerie Glendon propose de la documentation en français et en anglais, ainsi que des visites guidées et des conférences données par des artistes et des commissaires d'expositions. Pour de plus amples renseignements, consultez son site Internet.

MUSÉE DES BEAUX-ARTS DE L'ONTARIO (AGO – ART GALLERY OF ONTARIO)

317 Dundas Street (à l'ouest de McCaul Street) ☎ (416) 979-6648

Fermé lundi, mardi à vendredi 11h – 18h, mercredi 11h – 20h30, samedi et dimanche 10h – 17h30

Métro : ST PATRICK

www.ago.net

De Monet à Cézanne en passant par Degas, le Musée des beaux-arts de l'Ontario vous propose des expositions permanentes bilingues. Les grandes expositions ainsi que les casques qui les accompagnent sont également en français et en anglais. Au Musée des beaux-arts de l'Ontario, vous vivrez une véritable expérience en français !

MUSÉE ROYAL DE L'ONTARIO (ROM – ROYAL ONTARIO MUSEUM)

100 Queen's Park Crescent (au coin de Bloor Street) ☎ (416) 586-8000

Lundi à jeudi 10h – 18h, vendredi 10h – 21h30, samedi et dimanche 10h – 18h

Métro : MUSEUM

www.rom.on.ca

Le Musée royal de l'Ontario vous permet de découvrir les trésors historiques et contemporains de l'univers des beaux-arts en français. Au ROM, vous pourrez apprécier les œuvres permanentes des différentes galeries du musée, les expositions créées par le musée, ainsi que les expositions spéciales en français (des guides thématiques français sont disponibles pendant votre visite au musée lors des expositions spéciales). N'hésitez surtout pas à contacter le musée pour organiser votre prochaine visite guidée.

information et divertissement

À propos du Musée royal de l'Ontario (ROM)

1. Hors grande exposition programmée, le prix d'admission est réduit de moitié. C'est le bon moment pour visiter les expositions permanentes et les expositions créées par le ROM.

2. Tous les vendredis, on peut visiter les collections permanentes ainsi que les expositions créées par le musée gratuitement. De plus, vous pourrez profiter d'une remise sur les expositions temporaires.

3. Vous trouverez une page en français sur le site Internet du ROM (bouton en haut de la page).

4. Un employé francophone peut répondre à vos questions au téléphone en français.

5. Il y a toujours du personnel bilingue à l'entrée du musée.

THÉÂTRES

THÉÂTRE FRANÇAIS DE TORONTO

26 Berkeley Street (au sud de Front Street)
☎ (416) 534-6604
Métro : KING + le tram
www.theatrefrancais.com

Créé en 1967, le Théâtre français de Toronto (TfT) est un théâtre professionnel de langue française, de répertoire et de création. Il présente des productions de qualité pour adultes et enfants, puisées principalement dans les répertoires canadien et français. Allez applaudir les comédiens au Berkeley Street Theatre, 26 Berkeley Street. Depuis le mois d'avril 2005, le TfT propose des spectacles sur-titrés en anglais.

THÉÂTRE LA TANGENTE

☎ (416) 487-6832
www.theatrelatangente.ca

Le Théâtre La Tangente présente des pièces de création. En d'autres termes, les pièces de théâtre jouées à La Tangente sont originales et inédites. Ce côté insolite oblige ce théâtre à ne présenter qu'une pièce tous les deux ans. Les pièces, produites à Toronto, sont jouées à Toronto, au Québec et même en France.

TROUPES DE DANSE ET OPÉRA

CORPUS

805 Dovercourt Road (au nord de Bloor Street West) ☎ (416) 516-4025
www.corpus.ca

CORPUS est une compagnie de danse torontoise reconnue pour l'originalité et l'humour de ses créations qui s'adressent à un public éclectique d'adultes et d'enfants. Le secret de CORPUS consiste en un univers artistique où la danse, le théâtre et le mime se côtoient avec naturel. Un mariage généreux du comique et du fantasque où l'on utilise le corps pour faire rire et raconter des histoires. Orchestrée par la danseuse et chorégraphe québécoise Sylvie Bouchard et le scénariste et metteur en scène David Danzon, CORPUS compte aujourd'hui un répertoire de sept pièces à son actif. Consultez notre agenda

information et divertissement

électronique afin de connaître les dates de la prochaine représentation.

DANCE MAKERS

55 Mill Street (à l'intérieur du Distillery District) ☎ (416) 367-1800
www.dancemakers.org

Depuis sa création en 1974, cette troupe contribue de façon indéniable au développement de la danse à Toronto. Fondée par plusieurs inconditionnels des arts dont un Français, Dance Makers est aujourd'hui entre les mains du directeur artistique Serge Bennathan. La troupe de danse de M. Bennathan, qui n'est pas exclusivement française, a déjà mis à l'honneur les pièces francophones suivantes : *Le projet Satie, Tziganes, C'est beau ça la vie, La vie invisible* et *Les vents tumultueux.* Pour 2005-2006, M. Bennathan projette de présenter *Tancredi* de Rossini, avec la collaboration du Canadian Opera. Les représentations ont généralement lieu au théâtre du Harbourfront Centre.

OPERA ATELIER

☎ (416) 703-3767
www.operaatelier.com

Cette compagnie artistique produit des opéras, ballets et pièces dramatiques des XVIIe et XVIIIe siècles. Opera Atelier apporte une touche particulière à toutes ses productions et les met au goût du jour. Les décors, les costumes, les instruments et les ballets d'antan, l'expérience théâtrale d'Opera Atelier captent l'imagination de chaque spectateur. Pour la saison 2005-2006, la compagnie présentera *Antéon* au printemps et *Armide* à l'automne

(l'œuvre de Lully sera interprétée pour la première fois en Amérique du Nord). Les pièces d'Opera Atelier sont jouées à l'Elgin Theatre (189 Yonge Street). Commandez vos billets auprès de Ticket Master au (416) 872-5555. Plusieurs pièces anglaises sont sous-titrées en français.

RADIO

COOPÉRATIVE RADIOPHONIQUE DE TORONTO – 105.1 FM

La Coopération radiophonique de Toronto est la radio communautaire des francophones.

RADIO-CANADA – 860 AM

Radio-Canada en Ontario est la station locale de cette radio nationale. Les programmes varient autour de thèmes de l'actualité, de la culture et du divertissement.

TÉLÉVISION

RDI (RÉSEAU D'INFORMATION)

Il s'agit d'une chaîne française d'information nationale et internationale.

SRC (SOCIÉTÉ RADIO-CANADA)

www.radio-canada.ca/regions/ontario

La Société Radio-Canada offre un éventail de programmes très divers avec des bulletins d'information, des émissions de variétés, des romans-feuilletons, des films et bien d'autres choses encore.

information et divertissement

TFO

www.tfo.org

Chaîne de télévision franco-ontarienne, il y a sur TFO plusieurs émissions à vocation culturelle telles que l'émission « Panorama ». Le premier roman-feuilleton franco-ontarien, « Fran-Cœur », passe même sur cette chaîne.

TVA-CHOT

www.chot.ca

TVA est une autre chaîne montréalaise que l'on peut capter à Toronto, avec de nombreuses émissions de variétés et d'actualité.

TV5

www.tv5.ca

TV5 est une chaîne de télévision internationale en français qui propose une programmation variée (journaux télé-visés, reportages, divertissements), grâce au regroupement, depuis 1984, de pro-grammes issus de chaînes françaises, belges, suisses et canadiennes.

ÉVÉNEMENTS CULTURELS FRANCOPHONES À TORONTO

ALLIANCE FRANÇAISE DE TORONTO

www.alliance-francaise.ca

Le site de l'Alliance Française a une page consacrée aux événements franco-phones qui se déroulent à Toronto.

BUREAU DU QUÉBEC À TORONTO

20 Queen Street West, bureau 1504
☎ (416) 977-6713

Le Bureau du Québec promeut très activement les produits culturels et artistiques québécois à Toronto. Consultez le site de Toronto-Franco et le journal *L'Express* afin de profiter des rafales culturelles québécoises qui soufflent de temps à autre sur la ville.

CENTRE FRANCOPHONE DE TORONTO

20 Lower Spadina Avenue
☎ (416) 203-1220
Métro : UNION + le tram
www.centrefranco.org

Pour être mis au parfum des événe-ments francophones de Toronto et planifier votre prochaine sortie, consul-tez ce site Internet.

CONSULAT GÉNÉRAL DE FRANCE À TORONTO

www.consulfrance-toronto.org

Vous trouverez sur le site Internet du Consulat Général de France à Toronto, sous la rubrique « Pleins feux sur la culture », la liste de plusieurs événe-ments culturels francophones.

HARBOURFRONT CENTRE

235 Queens Quay West (à l'ouest de University Avenue)

www.harbourfrontcentre.com

Chaque année, le Harbourfront Centre propose un vaste programme de plus de 4 000 événements axés autour d'activités culturelles, éducatives et récréatives, aussi bien pour les adultes que pour les jeunes. Des dizaines de festivals mettent en vedette les cultures française et québécoise.

RADIO-CANADA

www.radio-canada.ca/regions/ontario

Pour savoir quoi faire, quoi voir et quoi visiter, allez jeter un œil au calendrier de Claudette Gravel « Enfin samedi », sur le site Internet de Radio-Canada.

TORONTO-FRANCO

☎ (416) 929-3769

www.toronto-franco.com

Les francophones de Toronto ont leur propre portail en français ! Depuis janvier 2004, ce portail unique a pour vocation d'offrir aux francophones un accès à l'information rapide et ciblé. Vous y trouverez les nouvelles locales et internationales, ainsi que des informations sur les services et les événements communautaires qui intéressent la communauté francophone de Toronto. Notre site possède un lien vers ce portail d'information.

Le saviez-vous ?

L'ALLIANCE FRANÇAISE est un bon endroit où envoyer vos amis anglophones qui cherchent à apprendre le français; elle offre également les services de location et de prêt des ouvrages de référence suivants :

▸ MATÉRIEL D'APPRENTISSAGE

Plus de 30 cassettes vidéo, dictionnaires, livres en français pour débutants, cassettes audio et CD-ROM.

▸ MUSIQUE FRANÇAISE
  ET FRANCOPHONE

Les meilleurs chanteurs sur CD et cassettes.

▸ LITTÉRATURE FRANÇAISE
  ET FRANCOPHONE

Plus de 1 800 livres, des auteurs classiques aux contemporains, des romans policiers aux essais.

▸ CRÉATION FRANÇAISE
  CONTEMPORAINE

Une centaine de cassettes vidéo sur la science, les arts, la société française d'aujourd'hui, des livres, des journaux et des magazines.

▸ FILMS FRANÇAIS

Plus de 250 grands succès mondiaux du cinéma français y sont disponibles.

Pour plus de renseignements, consultez le site Internet :

WWW.ALLIANCE-FRANCAISE.CA

information et divertissement

Soirées et rencontres branchées

Francophonique

www.francophonique.com

Réseau de regroupements entre francophones et francophiles, Francophonique organise des événements tels que des brunchs et des soirées branchées. Francophonique, c'est le réseau franco-urbain de Toronto où il fait bon se retrouver.

Les Mercredis FrancoFun

☎ (416) 596-8437

Jacques Charrette (coordinateur)
jacques.charrette@sympatico.ca

Chaque mercredi soir, à partir de 18h, des francophones et francophiles se retrouvent pour discuter et prendre un verre. Idéal pour les nouveaux arrivants qui souhaitent rencontrer d'autres francophones ou pour les anglophones qui veulent pratiquer leur français ! Le lieu de rencontre varie de temps en temps. Au moment où nous écrivons ces lignes, il s'agit du pub Duke of Richmond, situé au 20 Queen Street West.

Les Soupers FrancoFun

☎ (416) 596-8437

Jacques Charrette (coordinateur)
jacques.charrette@sympatico.ca

Un jeudi par mois, un dîner est organisé dans un restaurant. Événement populaire, ce dîner est l'occasion de découvrir un nouveau restaurant et de se retrouver entre francophones. Le prix est en général de 25 dollars, ce qui

comprend le repas, les taxes et le service. Le dernier dîner de la saison, qui a lieu en juin, est le plus populaire, car c'est le « dîner homard » !

Tam Tam Cyber Café

86 Nassau Street ☎ (416) 603-0007
Lundi à dimanche 8h30 – 19h
Métro : SPADINA + le tram;
QUEEN'S PARK + le tram

Unique en son genre, Tam Tam Cyber Café a ouvert ses portes en mars 2004. Ce petit coin café accueille tous les internautes au cœur du marché Kensington. Situé à deux pas de l'auberge de jeunesse d'Augusta Street, réputée pour être fréquentée par bon nombre de Français, Tam Tam Cyber Café offre un accès Internet et des services d'impression à petit prix. L'ambiance y est à l'image du quartier et de ses habitants : conviviale et un tantinet bohème. Tous les samedis matins, petits-déjeuners français autour de croissants chauds et tartines de baguette avec beurre et confiture; en semaine, soirées-causeries, concerts et expositions.

Zazou

315 King Street West (au coin de John Street) ☎ (416) 591-3600
Ouvert à partir de 17h, jusqu'au départ du dernier client !
Métro : ST ANDREW
www.zazoulounge.com

Zazou fait partie de la même famille que Marcel's Bistro et Le Saint Tropez. Ce bar chic et sophistiqué accueille les jeunes adultes branchés de la ville. Si vous aimez les ambiances feutrées, la musique cool et un décor qui invite à la

détente, passez prendre un verre chez Zazou. C'est l'endroit idéal pour se relaxer après une longue journée au bureau.

ASSOCIATIONS FRANCOPHONES DE TORONTO

Pour mieux promouvoir la mission des associations suivantes, nous en avons résumé les grandes lignes sur notre site Internet. Nous avons également inclus un lien qui vous permettra d'obtenir des détails pertinents sur chacune d'entre elles. Rendez-vous à l'adresse www.franco-toronto.ca, sous la rubrique « Associations francophones ».

ASSOCIATIONS CULTURELLES ET SOCIALES

- Association Marocaine de Toronto
- Centre des Jeunes Francophones de Toronto
- Centre médicosocial de Toronto
- Club Richelieu de Toronto
- Club Richelieu Trillium de Toronto
- Le Cercle de l'Amitié Canadien de Toronto
- La Société d'histoire de Toronto
- Toronto Accueil

ASSOCIATIONS DE GENS D'AFFAIRES FRANCOPHONES

- Association des femmes d'affaires francophones
- Association francophone des entrepreneurs et des professionnels (AFEP)
- Belgian Canadian Business Association
- Club Canadien de Toronto
- La Chambre de Commerce française de Toronto
- Regroupement des gens d'affaires africains canadiens

ASSOCIATION D'ARTISTES

- BRAVO – Bureau des regroupements des artistes visuels de l'Ontario

les bonnes adresses par quartier

QUARTIERS	PAINS, PÂTISSERIES ET SUCRERIES	CHOCOLATS	FROMAGES ET CRÈME FRAÎCHE	CHARCUTERIE, PÂTÉS ET TERRINES
THE BEACH, L'EST DE TORONTO, DANFORTH AVE. ET BLOOR ST.	Bonjour Brioche Zane	Belgian Chocolate Shop Sun Valley Fine Foods	Alex Farm Sun Valley Fine Foods	Alex Farm Meat on the Beach
BLOOR WEST VILLAGE ET L'OUEST DE TORONTO	Cheese Boutique Ma Maison Max's Market Pâtisserie Saint Honoré	Bernard Callebaut Cheese Boutique Max's Market	Alex Farm Cheese Boutique Max's Market The Cheese Dairy Whitehouse Meats	Alex Farm Cheese Boutique Ma Maison Max's Market The Village Butcher Whitehouse Meats
CENTRE-VILLE (DOWNTOWN)	Balzac's Coffee House Daniel et Daniel Mercatto Montreal Bread Co. St. Urbain Bagel Bakery Scheffler's	Chocolates & Creams Daniel et Daniel Domino Foods Eve's Temptations Mercatto Scheffler's The Bay	Alex Farm Chris' Cheesemongers Olympic Cheese Mart Scheffler's	Alex Farm Caviar Direct Chris' Cheesemongers Cumbrae's Daniel et Daniel Olympic Cheese Mart Scheffler's Whitehouse Meats
KENSINGTON, BALDWIN ST. ET COLLEGE ST.	Casa Açoreana Harbord Bakery Magnolia	Chocolate Addict	Cheese Magic Global Cheese Mendel's Creamery	Global Cheese Mendel's Creamery
ENTERTAINMENT DISTRICT, KING ST. WEST ET QUEEN ST. WEST	Clafouti Le Gourmand Senses	Clafouti J.S. Bonbons Le Gourmand Senses		
YORKVILLE, AVENUE RD., DAVENPORT RD. ET DUPONT AVE.	Dinah's Cupboard Frangipane Holt Renfrew Montreal Bread Co. Pusateri's Whole Foods	Dinah's Cupboard Frangipane Holt Renfrew J.S. Bonbons Leonidas Simone Marie Belgian Chocolate Teuscher Whole Foods	Alex Farm Dinah's Cupboard Pusateri's Whole Foods	Alex Farm Dinah's Cupboard Pusateri's Whole Foods

BOUCHERIES	POISSONS ET HUÎTRES	ÉPICES	AUTRES SPÉCIALITÉS FRANÇAISES	RESTAURANTS
Meat on the Beach Royal Beef	Bill's Lobster	Bulk Barn Strictly Bulk	Alex Farm Bonjour Brioche Zane	Batifole Bonjour Brioche Cafe Brussels Sauvignon Bistro

Bloor Meat Market
The Village Butcher
Whitehouse Meats
	Big Fish Market
	Snappers Fish
	  Market
	The Village Butcher
		Strictly Bulk	Alex Farm
			Cheese Boutique
			Ma Maison
			Max's Market
			Pâtisserie Saint
			  Honoré
			The Village Butcher
				La Petite France
				Merlot

Brown Brothers
  Meats
Cumbrae's
Di Liso's Fine Meats
La Boucherie
Manos Meats
Scheffler's
St. Lawrence
  Upper Cut
Whitehouse Meats
Witteveen Meats
	Caviar Direct
	Domenic's Fish
	  Market
	Domino Foods
	Mike's Fish Market
	Seafront Fish
	  Market
		Domino Foods	Alex Farm
			Chris'
			  Cheesemongers
			Daniel et Daniel
			Domino Foods
			Mercatto
			Scheffler's
			Great Cooks
			Olympic Cheese
			  Mart
				Bistro 990
				Biff's
				Bloor Street Diner
				Bouchon
				Café Moroc/
				  The Sultan's Tent
				Café Nicole
				Crêpes à GoGo
				Le Papillon
				Le Petit Déjeuner
				Matignon
				Midi Bistro
				Montreal Bread Co.
				Provence Délices

European Quality Meats Grace Meat Market	Coral Sea Fish Market Global Cheese Mendel's Creamery New Seaway Sea Kings Seven Seas Fish	Casa Açoreana House of Spice Perola		Bodega Café Margaux Gamelle La Palette
	Oyster Boy Rodney's Oyster House		Clafouti Le Gourmand	Bloor Street Diner Café Crêpe Le Saint Tropez Le Sélect Bistro Marcel's Bistro Restaurant Jules The Fifth
Pusateri's	Pusateri's		Alex Farm Dinah's Cupboard Holt Renfrew Pusateri's Whole Foods	Arlequin Bistro Tournesol Holt's Café Jacques Bistro Le Paradis Le Trou Normand Michelle's Brasserie Montreal Bread Co.

les bonnes adresses par quartier

QUARTIERS	PAINS, PÂTISSERIES ET SUCRERIES	CHOCOLATS	FROMAGES ET CRÈME FRAÎCHE	CHARCUTERIE, PÂTÉS ET TERRINES

MIDTOWN ET SUMMERHILL	All the Best
	  Fine Foods
	Fleurdelys
	  Pâtisserie
	Le Petit Gourmet
	Pain Perdu
	Patachou
	St. Urbain
	  Bagel Bakery
		Pain Perdu
		Sobeys
			Alex Farm
			All the Best
			  Fine Foods
			Sobeys
				Alex Farm
				All the Best
				  Fine Foods
				Patachou
				Sobeys
				The Butchers

BAYVIEW ET MOUNT PLEASANT	Le Comptoir
	  de Célestin
	La Cigogne
	Rahier
	The Bagel House
		La Cigogne
		Rahier
		The Chocolate
		  Messenger
			Alex Farm	Alex Farm
				Whitehouse Meats

UPTOWN	Ace Bakery
	Pusateri's
	Senses
	The Bagel House
		Ararat
		Pusateri's
		Senses
		Swiss-Master
		  Chocolatier
			Pusateri's	Pusateri's
				The Butcher Block
				  Café

LE GRAND TORONTO	Arz Bakery
	Brandt Meat
	  Packers Ltd.
	Pâtisserie Daudet
	Pâtisserie d'Or
	Pâtisserie
	  Le Papillon
	St. Urbain Bagel
	  Bakery
		Arz Bakery
		Bernard Callebaut
		Brandt Meat
		  Packers Ltd.
		Pâtisserie d'Or
		Pâtisserie
		  Le Papillon
		Truffle Treasures
			Arz Bakery
			Olympic Cheese
			  Mart
			Quality Cheese
				Brandt Meat
				  Packers Ltd.
				Olympic Cheese
				  Mart

BOUCHERIES	POISSONS ET HUÎTRES	ÉPICES	AUTRES SPÉCIALITÉS FRANÇAISES	RESTAURANTS
Nicola's Fine Foods Olliffe Sobeys The Butchers	Avenue Seafood Pisces Gourmet		Alex Farm All the Best Fine Foods Harvest Wagon Pain Perdu Patachou	Avant-Goût Boujadi Didier Le Petit Gourmet Pastis Express Quartier
Whitehouse Meats			Alex Farm Rahier	Célestin La Cigogne Lolo Restaurant

Cavallino
Highland Farms
Pusateri's
The Butcher Block
  Café
	Caviar Centre
	City Fish Market
	Diana's Seafood
	Highland Farms
	Newport Fish
	  Importers
	Pusateri's
			Ararat
			Pusateri's
				Auberge du
				  Pommier
				Bloor Street Diner
				Chez Laurent
				La Maison Benoît
				Le Continental
				Le Montmartre
				L'Escargot Bistro
				Monitz
				Pourquoi Pas

Brandt Meat
  Packers Ltd.
European Quality
  Meats
	Brandt Meat
	  Packers Ltd.
	Lobster Island
		Bulk Barn	Arz Bakery
			Brandt Meat
			  Packers Ltd.
			Olympic Cheese
			  Mart
			Pâtisserie d'Or
			Petit Gâteau
				Bistro 1603
				Bistro Matisse
				Brasserie Royan
				Nice Bistro

répertoire d'adresses multiples

ALEX FARM PRODUCTS

☎ 1 877 488-7778 (numéro général)

- 93 Front Street East (St. Lawrence Market)
  ☎ (416) 368-2415

  Fermé dimanche et lundi, mardi à jeudi 8h – 18h, vendredi 7h – 19h30, samedi 5h – 17 h

  Métro : UNION

- 377 Danforth Avenue (au coin de Chester Avenue) ☎ (416) 465-9500

  Lundi à mercredi 10h – 19h, jeudi 10h – 20h, vendredi et samedi 9h – 18h, dimanche 11 h – 18h

  Métro : CHESTER

- 1578 Bayview Avenue (au sud de Millwood Road) ☎ (416) 322-0368

  Lundi à mercredi 10h – 19h, jeudi 9h – 20h, vendredi 9h – 18h, samedi 9h – 18h, dimanche 11h – 18h

  Métro : EGLINTON + le bus

- 2594 Yonge Street (au nord d'Eglinton Avenue) ☎ (416) 488-8000

  Lundi à jeudi 10h – 19h, vendredi et samedi 9h – 18h, dimanche 11h – 18h

  Métro : EGLINTON + le bus; LAWRENCE + le bus

- 55 Bloor Street West (Manulife Centre)
  ☎ (416) 966-5995

  Lundi à jeudi 10h – 19h, vendredi 10h – 20h, samedi 10h – 18h, dimanche 13h – 18h

  Métro : YONGE OU BAY

- 270 The Kingsway (à l'intérieur du Humber Town Shopping Centre)
  ☎ (416) 239-1500

  Lundi à jeudi 10h – 19h, vendredi 10h – 18h, samedi 9h – 18h, dimanche 11h – 17h

  Métro : ROYAL YORK + le bus

- 1965 Queen Street East (à l'est de Woodbine Avenue)
  ☎ (416) 690-3600

  Ce magasin ouvrira bientôt ses portes

  Métro : QUEEN + le tram

  Un autre magasin situé au nord de la ville ouvrira ses portes en 2005

BALZAC'S COFFEE HOUSE

- 55 Mill Street (à l'intérieur du Distillery District)
  ☎ (416) 207-1709

  Lundi à samedi 7h – 20h, dimanche 8h – 20h

  Métro : KING + le tram; PAPE + le bus

BALZAC'S COFFEE HOUSE - TOY FACTORY LOFT

- 43 Hanna Avenue
  L'ouverture est prévue pour 2005

CHOCOLATES BY BERNARD CALLEBAUT

- 4242 Dundas Street West (à l'est de Royal York Road) ☎ (416) 234-0611

  Lundi à mercredi 9h30 – 19h, jeudi et vendredi 9h30 – 20h, samedi 9h30 – 18h, dimanche 12h – 17h

  Métro : ROYAL YORK + le bus

- 194 Lake Shore Road East, Oakville (près de Trafalgar Road) ☎ (905) 339-2100

  Lundi à jeudi 10h – 18h, vendredi 10h – 20h, samedi 10h – 18h, dimanche 12h – 17h

EUROPEAN QUALITY MEATS & SAUSAGES

- 176 Baldwin Street (Kensington Market)
  ☎ (416) 596-8691

- Lundi à vendredi 8h – 18h30, 7h – 18h30, fermé dimanche

  Métro : SPADINA + le tram; QUEEN'S PARK + le tram

- 16 Jutland Road, Etobicoke (près de Queensway et Kipling Avenue)
  ☎ (416) 251-6193

  Lundi à mercredi 8h – 18h, jeudi et vendredi 8h – 19h, samedi 8h – 18h, fermé dimanche

  Métro : KIPLING

GREAT COOKS

- 176 Yonge Street (au sous-sol du grand magasin The Bay, Queen Street)
  ☎ (416) 861-4727

  Lundi à vendredi 10h – 18h, fermé samedi et dimanche

  Métro : QUEEN

GREAT COOKS ON THE EIGHT

- 401 Bay Street (au 8e étage de la Simpson Tower, Queen Street) ☎ (416) 861-4333

  Lundi à samedi 10h – 18h, fermé dimanche

  Métro : QUEEN

HARVEST WAGON

- 1103 Yonge Street (au nord de Roxborough Street)
  ☎ (416) 923-7542

  Lundi à mercredi 8h – 18h30, jeudi et vendredi 8h – 19h, samedi et dimanche 8h – 18h

  Métro : SUMMERHILL

répertoire d'adresses multiples

- 546 Eglinton Avenue West (à l'ouest d'Avenue Road) ☎ (416) 487-0388

Lundi à vendredi 8h – 19h, samedi et dimanche 8h – 18h

Métro : EGLINTON + le bus

J.S. BONBONS

- 163 Dupont Street (au coin de Davenport Road) ☎ (416) 920-0274

Fermé lundi, mardi à samedi 10h – 18h, dimanche 11h – 17h

Métro : DUPONT

- 811 Queen Street West (à l'ouest de Bathurst Avenue) ☎ (416) 703-7731

Fermé lundi, mardi 11h – 19h, mercredi 11h – 18h, jeudi à samedi 11h – 19h, dimanche 11h – 17h

Métro : OSGOODE + le tram

LEONIDAS

- 50 Bloor Street West (au coin de Bay Street, à l'intérieur du centre Holt Renfrew) ☎ (416) 944-8822

Lundi à jeudi 10h – 18h, vendredi 10h – 19h, samedi 10h – 18h, dimanche 12h – 17h

Métro : YONGE OU BAY

- 176 Yonge Street, au sous-sol du magasin The Bay ☎ (416) 861-6486

Lundi à vendredi 10h – 18h

Métro : QUEEN

MERCATTO

- 15 Toronto Street (à l'est de Yonge Street et au nord de King Street) ☎ (416) 366-4567

Lundi à vendredi 7h – 20h, fermé samedi et dimanche

Métro : KING

- 330 Bay Street (au nord d'Adelaïde Street) ☎ (416) 306-0467

Lundi à vendredi 7h30 – 20h, fermé samedi et dimanche

Métro : KING

MONTREAL BREAD COMPANY (MBCo)

- 100 Bloor Street West, Unit # 7 ☎ (416) 961-MBCO (6226)
- Toronto Dominion Centre 66 Wellington Street West (Food Court) *L'ouverture est prévue pour 2005*

OLYMPIC CHEESE MART

- 93 Front Street East (St. Lawrence Market sud) ☎ (416) 363-7602

Fermé dimanche et lundi, mardi à jeudi 8h – 18h, vendredi 8h – 19h, samedi 5h – 17h

Métro : UNION

- 7780 Woodbine Avenue, Markham (au coin de la 14ᵉ Avenue) ☎ (905) 944-8676

Lundi à vendredi 10h – 18h, samedi 10h – 15h, fermé dimanche

PATACHOU

- 1095 Yonge Street (au Nord de Roxborough Street) ☎ (416) 927-1105

Lundi à vendredi 8h30 – 19h, samedi 8h30 – 18h, fermé dimanche

Métro : SUMMERHILL

- 835 St. Clair Avenue West (à l'ouest d'Arlington Street) ☎ (416) 782-0122

Lundi à vendredi 8h30 – 19h, samedi 8h30 – 18h, dimanche 10h – 16h

Métro : ST CLAIR WEST + le tram

PUSATERI'S FINE FOODS

- 1539 Avenue Road (au nord de Lawrence Avenue) ☎ (416) 785-9100

Lundi à mercredi 8h – 20h, jeudi et vendredi 8h – 21h, samedi et dimanche 8h – 19h

Métro : LAWRENCE + le bus

- 57 Yorkville Avenue (au coin de Bay Street) ☎ (416) 785-9100

Lundi à mercredi 10h – 20h, jeudi et vendredi 10h – 21h, samedi 8h – 20h, dimanche 10h – 19h

Métro : BAY

QUEEN VIDEO

Heures d'ouverture pour tous les magasins : lundi à dimanche 11h – 23h

- 412 Queen Street West (à l'ouest de Spadina Avenue) ☎ (416) 504-3030

Métro : OSGOODE + le tram

- 480 Bloor Street West (à l'est de Bathurst Street) ☎ (416) 588-5767

Métro : BATHURST

- 688 College Street (près de Shaw Street) ☎ 416 532-0555

Métro : QUEEN'S PARK + le tram

répertoire d'adresses multiples

St. Urbain Bagel Bakery

- 93 Front Street East
  (St. Lawrence Market sud)
  ☎ (416) 364-8305

Fermé dimanche et lundi, mardi à jeudi 8h – 18h, vendredi 8h – 19h, samedi 5h – 17h

Métro : UNION

- 895 Eglinton Avenue West
  ☎ (416) 787-6955

Lundi à vendredi 7h – 18h, samedi et dimanche 7h – 16h

Métro : EGLINTON + le bus

- 7077 Bathurst Avenue
  (près de Steeles Avenue)
  ☎ (905) 731-8305

Lundi à vendredi 7h – 18h, samedi 7h – 17h, dimanche 7h – 16h

Senses

- 318 Wellington Street West
  (au coin de Blue Jay Way,
  à l'intérieur du SoHo
  Metropolitan Hotel)
  ☎ (416) 961-0055

Lundi à dimanche, 7h – 19h

Métro : ST ANDREW + le tram

- 2901 Bayview Avenue
  (à l'intérieur de la Galerie
  Bayview/Bayview Village)
  ☎ (416) 227-9149

Lundi à vendredi 8h – 21h, samedi 8h – 18h, dimanche 10h – 17h

Métro : BAYVIEW sur la ligne SHEPPARD

- 2 Queen Street East (à l'intérieur de l'immeuble de la Banque de Montréal)
  ☎ (416) 364-7303

Lundi à vendredi 7h – 19h, fermé samedi et dimanche

Métro : QUEEN

Suspect Video

Lundi à samedi 12h – 23h, dimanche 12h – 22h pour les deux boutiques

- 605 Markham Street (à
  l'est de Bathurst Street)
  ☎ (416) 588-6674

Métro : BATHURST + le tram

- 619 Queen Street West
  ☎ (416) 504-7135

Métro : OSGOODE

The Bagel House

- 1548 Bayview Avenue (au
  sud d'Eglinton Avenue)
  ☎ (416) 481-8184

Lundi à jeudi 6h30 – 19h, vendredi 6h – 18h, samedi 6h – 20h, dimanche 6 – 19h

Métro : EGLINTON + le bus

- 1722 Avenue Road (au
  nord de Lawrence Avenue)
  ☎ (416) 781-0032

Lundi à samedi 6h – 19h, dimanche 6h – 18h30

Métro : LAWRENCE + le bus

Un autre magasin ouvrira ses portes en 2005

Whitehouse Meats

- 93 Front Street East
  (St. Lawrence Market)
  ☎ (416) 366-4465

Fermé dimanche et lundi, mardi à jeudi 8h – 18h, vendredi 8h – 19h, samedi 5h – 17h

Métro : UNION

- 1539 Bayview Avenue
  (au sud d'Eglinton Avenue
  East) ☎ (416) 488-2004

Fermé lundi, mardi à vendredi 9h – 18h, samedi 8h – 18h, dimanche 11h – 17h
(fermé le dimanche pendant l'hiver)

Métro : EGLINTON + le bus

- 2978 Bloor Street West
  (à l'est du métro ROYAL
  YORK) ☎ (416) 231-5004

Fermé dimanche et lundi, mardi et mercredi 9h – 18h, jeudi 9h – 20h, vendredi 9h – 18h, samedi 8h – 18h

Métro : ROYAL YORK

VIVRE EN FRANÇAIS À TORONTO

index

VIVRE EN FRANÇAIS À TORONTO

Nous voici à la fin de notre parcours. Nous espérons que vous avez aimé les aventures culturelles et gastronomiques dans lesquelles nous vous avons emportés. Nous espérons surtout que vous continuerez à découvrir par vous-même, si vous ne l'avez déjà fait, les bonnes adresses « françaises » de Toronto.

Au revoir et à bientôt !

Si vous avez des commentaires à nous adresser ou d'autres adresses francophones à nous transmettre, vous pouvez nous écrire à l'adresse électronique suivante : **contact@franco-toronto.ca**

Si vous désirez commander des exemplaires pour vos proches afin de partager avec eux cette extraordinaire expérience, veuillez consulter notre site. Nous offrons des remises intéressantes sur les commandes de dix exemplaires et plus. Veuillez nous contacter pour de plus amples renseignements sur nos prix et sur les frais de livraison pour ces commandes : **contact@franco-toronto.ca**

Consultez régulièrement notre site Internet **www.franco-toronto.ca** pour ne rien manquer des événements culturels et culinaires francophones de Toronto.